FPinME

U.S. FOREIGN POLICY

Back to the Water's Edge

D1615812

Donald M. Snow
Emeritus, University of Alabama

Patrick J. Haney
Miami University

Fifth Edition

ROWMAN & LITTLEFIELD
Lanham • Boulder • New York • London

Executive Editor: Traci Crowell
Assistant Editor: Mary Malley
Marketing Manager: Deborah Hudson
Interior Designer: Ilze Lemesis
Cover Designer: Neil Cotterill

Credits and acknowledgments for material borrowed from other sources, and reproduced with permission, appear on page within the text.

Published by Rowman & Littlefield
A wholly owned subsidiary of The Rowman & Littlefield Publishing Group, Inc.
4501 Forbes Boulevard, Suite 200, Lanham, Maryland 20706
www.rowman.com

Unit A, Whitacre Mews, 26–34 Stannary Street, London SE11 4AB, United Kingdom

Library of Congress Cataloging-in-Publication Data
Names: Snow, Donald M., 1943– author.
Title: U.S. foreign policy : back to the water's edge / Donald M. Snow, Emeritus, University of Alabama Patrick J. Haney, Miami University.
Description: Fifth edition. | Lanham : Rowman & Littlefield, [2018] | Includes index.
Identifiers: LCCN 2017011514 (print) | LCCN 2017021943 (ebook) | ISBN 9781442268180 (electronic) | ISBN 9781442268166 (cloth : alk. paper) | ISBN 9781442268173 (pbk. : alk. paper)
Subjects: LCSH: United States—Foreign relations.
Classification: LCC JZ1480 (ebook) | LCC JZ1480 .S55 2017 (print) | DDC 327.73—dc23
LC record available at https://lccn.loc.gov/2017011514

∞™ The paper used in this publication meets the minimum requirements of American National Standard for Information Sciences—Permanence of Paper for Printed Library Materials, ANSI/NISO Z39.48–1992.

Printed in the United States of America

Brief Contents

Contents

7 Interest Groups and Think Tanks 170

8 The Public and the Media 193

Part III Policy Arenas 215

9 National Security Policy and Problems 216

If Aldous Huxley had not preempted the title with his 1932 classic, one would be tempted to describe the contemporary setting of American politics, including its foreign policy, as part of a "brave new world." The election of Donald J. Trump as president in the 2016 election occurred as this edition of *U.S. Foreign Policy* was being written, and it represented such a potentially significant change event that we felt the need to include some assessment of what the impact of a Trump administration might make for the book's subject matter. It is early in the Trump reign, and it is premature to reach sweeping conclusions about whether the impact of the forty-fifth president will be profound or routine, sweeping or relatively mundane, positive or negative. If the campaign and the transition offer any indications, things will be very different. Citizens—including students—whose interest levels and involvement in foreign policy are peripheral, may find themselves drawn into an unpredictable vortex. Particularly if the new president approaches foreign policy in as unorthodox a manner as he does other aspects of his job, it is incumbent on the citizenry to understand the context that his unorthodoxy represents, and how what he proposes could change things. Providing that context and some hints of the direction and impact of possible change is part of the burden this text tries to undertake.

An event from the transition between the election and inauguration provides an example. Toward the end of the campaign, it was revealed that the Democratic National Committee, including Hillary Clinton campaign chair John Podesta, had been hacked. An investigation by the intelligence agencies of the federal government concluded unanimously that the Russians had conducted the hacking, either through governmental operatives or Russian citizens commissioned by the highest levels of the government. These agencies also concluded that those actions could not have occurred unless they were ordered or approved at the highest levels of the Russian government, namely, Russian president Vladimir Putin. It should be noted, as well, that seeking to be engaged in elections through covert means was a tactic the Soviet Union used in Europe and Asia throughout the Cold War, and that several governments in Europe today have also reported similar tactics being deployed there by Russia to alter the natural dynamics of their national elections.

President-elect Trump disagreed with these conclusions, placing him in a political battle with something called "the intelligence community." Trump initially maintained, citing private sources, that he did not believe the Russians were involved in what the intelligence community viewed as a ham-handed Russian attempt to influence an American presidential election, a position he later softened to stating that hacking had not affected the election outcome. A confrontation was thus created between the new president and the professionals entrusted with monitoring and collecting information on possible threats to American national security.

Who was the public to believe in all this? The new president is a sharply confrontational and divisive political figure, and many people were predisposed to accept or reject his position based on what they thought of Trump. Many, however, were not so sure of how to judge the credence of this intelligence community. Many Americans think that intelligence is conducted by the Central Intelligence Agency (CIA), with some additional electronic snooping by the National Security Agency (NSA). Intelligence reports, however, cited an intelligence community of seventeen agencies. Who are they? Who should we believe—this mysterious congregation or the president of the United States? This is the kind of problem that this modest text hopes to help the reader and student assess. Given the proclivities of the new president, it is probably not the last contentious, confusing episode with which we will have to deal.

This edition is distinguished from its competitors in several ways. The inclusion of materials on the Trump administration, its early policies, and how Trump initiatives fit into the broader pattern of foreign policy in the American experience is certainly a major point of contrast, but there are others. First, the text develops three themes that were included in the last edition but which are, if anything, accentuated in a Trump presidency. One of these is the intermestic nature of foreign affairs: they are partly *inter*national and partly dom*estic*, making it impossible to treat any real matters as exclusively one or the other. To cite one example, the disagreement over U.S.-Russian affairs introduced above cannot fully be understood without looking at the domestic effects of those interactions: one major U.S.-based corporation (ExxonMobil) has major contracts with and investments in Russia to help it produce petroleum from which ExxonMobil stockholders benefit, but increasing Russian prosperity also adds to the ability of Moscow to act as a competitor to the United States.

The second theme is the hyperpartisanship in American politics that has divided Americans politically for more than a decade and was so obvious in the 2016 election. American politics is so deeply divided that it makes completing political tasks difficult in all realms, including foreign policy. The deep, even bitter, fight over building (and paying for) the wall along the Mexican-American border is a vivid example.

The third theme, which goes back to the earliest editions of this book in the 1990s and is reemphasized here, is the old idea that politics ends, or should end, at the water's edge. The basic idea contained in that phrase is that despite domestic differences, Americans should unite "at the water's edge" and present a united front to a hostile world. Extreme partisanship in our political parties and in the body politic, and the intermestic nature of real-world issues, have made attaining this standard more of a hope than an accomplished fact, and the Trump presidency has offered little indication that it will lead the kind of political reconciliation that would make it an actuality.

Second, the text is self-consciously student-centric in several important ways. For one thing, it is more compact than most of its competitors, trying to pack necessary information and concepts into a lean but readable format. Though brief, the chapters include examples of seminal events from the history of American foreign policy, especially since World War II. While not a history book, this text does contain rich historical content used to highlight issues and concepts and to provide the reader with snapshots of some of the truly classic highlights, and lowlights, of America's record in foreign affairs. In addition to trying to engage the student actively, this brevity also allows the book to be sold at a more modest price than most of the competition. Another way it is student-centered is in the approach to the material covered in each chapter. To facilitate an emphasis on the most relevant material, each chapter contains several design features:

- Each chapter begins with a two-part introduction to the contents and message. A "Preview" provides a one-paragraph summary of the chapter's contents, followed by a list of "Key Concepts" found in the chapter. The concepts are listed in the order they appear in the text, and their first definitive mention in the text is in boldface to facilitate recognition.
- In order to help the reader get started with a feeling for the "flavor" of the discussion, each chapter begins with a contemporary example of the material covered.
- Each chapter offers at least two "Intersection" boxes that provide a more detailed look at some idea, event, or concept contained in the chapter. We have made every effort to make these as contemporary as possible.
- The end of each chapter contains two sets of materials designed to reinforce and extend comprehension of the material. Study/Discussion Questions raise matters that should have been learned from the text and can be used to stimulate classroom discussion. The Bibliography contains citations for all works mentioned in the text as well as books and articles that can serve as source material for further exploration or research on the subject.

Third, this text has a specially designed accompanying reader available. *Regional Cases in Foreign Policy*, Second Edition, was written by Donald Snow with the specific intent of providing material and perspectives not contained in the immediate text. The book contains fourteen mini-cases that can accompany classroom discussions or lectures on substantive matters of concern in foreign policy on subjects as diverse as relations with Russia, Israel, or the Islamic State to specific questions like the border fence with Mexico, U.S.-Cuban relations, or the British withdrawal from the European Union (Brexit). Case examples are drawn from all parts of the world. Like the main text, *Regional Cases* is compact enough to minimize the expense to students asked to read it.

Features from the Table of Contents

In terms of general organization, the book content and flow are conventional, presenting the same general topics in one of the several orders of presentation that American foreign policy texts take. Most texts attempt to cover some combination of basic materials: conceptual overview and evolution, political institutions, functional policy areas, and U.S. policy with different regions and states. The first three of those subject areas are covered in this text; regional and state relations are the subject of the *Regional Cases in Foreign Policy* supplemental reader.

The text is divided into four parts that reflect these concerns. Part I, The Context, consists of two chapters. The first, "U.S. Foreign Policy and the Water's Edge," introduces concepts raised as themes earlier and includes a typology of general orientations on foreign policy to facilitate students clarifying their own positions and those of others, including the president. Chapter 2, "Brother, Can You Paradigm?" explores the thematic emphases of U.S. policy since the end of World War II; one of its major conclusions is that the United States has not had a consensual overall organizing principle since the end of the Cold War and that policy would be more coherent if an organizing paradigm could be agreed upon.

Part II, Foreign Policy Processes, is intended to examine in some depth how foreign policy is made in the American process, including both formal requirements and processes and the influence of informal actors and institutions. Chapter 3, "Understanding How It Happens: Decision Making and U.S. Foreign Policy," introduces the topic by surveying some of the leading ways that political scientists have organized thinking about how decisions are made. Chapters 4–8 look sequentially at elements of the process: the president (chapter 4), executive agencies (chapter 5), Congress (chapter 6), and those outside formal government who influence government (interest groups and think tanks in chapter 7 and public opinion and media in chapter 8). This section is distinguished by its detailed examination of those individuals and groups outside the formal process on how foreign policy is made and by its conscious inclusion of how the Trump administration is likely to perform within the framework.

The last two parts move the discussion to the area of substantive policy. Part III, Policy Arenas, consists of three chapters, one each devoted to a major functional policy area. Chapter 9 looks at national security issues, chapter 10 at matters of international economic concern, and chapter 11 reviews the major trans-state issues facing the United States (human rights, including immigration and refugees, and global warming). Part IV, The Future, consists of a single chapter, "Conclusions: Back to the Water's Edge," that summarizes the issues raised in part III and tries to extrapolate them into the future. Once again, the discussions in these last two parts are infused with observations about the early performance and likely direction of the Trump White House on the evolution of these concerns.

Supplements

Test Bank

For each chapter in the text, there is a test bank section that includes multiple choice, true/false, and essay questions. The test bank is available to adopters for download on the text's catalog page at https://rowman.com/ISBN/9781442268166.

Testing Software

This customizable test bank is available as either a Word file or in Respondus. Respondus is a powerful tool for creating and managing exams that can be printed to paper or published directly to the most popular learning management systems. Exams can be created offline or moved from one learning management system to another. Respondus LE is available free and can be used to automate the process of creating print tests. Respondus 4.0, available for purchase or via a school site license, prepares tests to be uploaded to any of the most popular course management systems such as Blackboard. Visit the Respondus Test

Bank Network at http://www.respondus.com/products/testbank/search.php to download the test bank for either Respondus 4.0 or Respondus LE.

Companion Website

Accompanying the text is an open-access companion website designed to engage students with the material and reinforce what they've learned in the classroom. For each chapter, self-quizzes help students master the content and apply that knowledge to real-life situations. Students can access the companion website from their computer or mobile device; it can be found at http://textbooks.row man.com/snow-haney5e.

E-Book

The e-book allows students to access this textbook anytime and anywhere. The e-book for *U.S. Foreign Policy*, Fifth Edition, includes everything that is in the print edition, and features direct links to the companion website where students can access self-quizzes to help test their understanding of the major concepts and terminology in each chapter. The e-book can be purchased at https://rowman. com/ISBN/9781442268166 or at any other e-book retailer.

Acknowledgments

Any book of the breadth of this work is the result of the efforts and insights of more than those of the authors alone, and we would like publicly to acknowledge the assistance of those who made inputs into what appears on these pages. The intellectual lineage of our approach is rooted in two friends and colleagues no longer with us. While the authors were separated by a few years at Indiana University, they share a common link in Professor John Lovell, as bright and supportive a friend and colleague as one would ever find, and an ardent believer in the importance of democracy in American foreign policy. The very first book that laid the path to this text was co-written by Don Snow and the late Eugene Brown, who was Don's office mate and colleague for two years at the U.S. Army War College in Carlisle, Pennsylvania, where their collaboration began and continued until Gene's death in 2002.

Specifically, we would like to thank Traci Crowell, Janice Braunstein, Deborah Hudson, and Mary Malley at Rowman & Littlefield. We'd also like to thank the following reviewers for their useful feedback: Jeannie Grussendorf, Carla Martinez Machain, Philip J. Meeks, Joseph G. Peschek, Jacob Shively, and Jim Zaffiro.

Bibliography

Snow, Donald M. *Regional Cases in U.S. Foreign Policy.* 2nd ed. Lanham, MD: Rowman & Littlefield, 2018.
Snow, Donald M., and Eugene Brown. *Beyond the Water's Edge: An Introduction to U.S. Foreign Policy.* New York: St. Martin's, 1997.

PART I THE CONTEXT

1 U.S. Foreign Policy and the Water's Edge

The Statue of Liberty provides an unmistakable view from the American water's edge.

Preview

American foreign policy, like American politics more generally, is in one of its periodic states of upheaval. The cause, akin to similar periods in the past, lies in basic philosophical and applied differences among Americans about politics and policies. One aspect of this disagreement is about whether foreign policy differences should be confined to internal domestic debates to the extent possible in today's mediated world (the idea that "politics ends at the water's edge") or should be debated more fully and publicly (foreign policy making as an "invitation to struggle"). This basic division within the body politic is manifested in the settings within which policy is honed and is reflected in basic themes that dominate current discussions. It also reflects foreign policy cultural beliefs held by Americans.

Key Concepts

hyperpartisanship	failed states
gridlock	cyber security
intermestic policy	national security state
bipartisanship	foreign policy culture
water's edge	realism
state	idealism
state-centrism	liberalism
diplomacy	conservatism
non-state actors	pragmatism

Americani politics is in one of its periodic states of turmoil. Relations between the political parties and the branches of government (each controlled by a different party in recent years) are fractious and dysfunctional to the point that little new business gets done most of the time. Donald J. Trump's victory in the 2016 election does not seem likely to change these dynamics. The current state of American politics is nothing new, but it certainly does not conform very closely to civics textbook depictions about government and how it works.

The results of this condition are familiar, and their impact on foreign policy is a major theme of this book. One manifestation is **hyperpartisanship**, defined as "a sharply polarized situation in which parties are in sharp disagreement with one another." The result can be considerable vituperation and is not unique to this period. Some level of partisan division is a normal part of politics, but its extreme dimensions have so infested politics that they are now polarized along an ideologically extreme line. The consequences include the collapse of the moderate political center in both parties and disdain for the art of compromise that used to keep the system running. The practical effect is political **gridlock**: a body politic that can agree on virtually nothing and "resolves" its differences by doing hardly anything. Partisanship, including its more extreme variants, and polarization will be used in these pages to discuss this dynamic.

These dynamics extend to the conduct of foreign policy and must be included in discussing American interaction with the world. Political malaise is primarily manifested in the domestic environment, but increasingly foreign policy operates in the **intermestic** realm, because real policies have both INTERnational and domESTIC components. This term was coined in a 1977 *Foreign Affairs* article, and it means almost all foreign policy discussions have some domestic impact and domestic decisions affect how America deals with the world (see also Milner and Tingley). Along with the impact of global mediation on the ability to conduct policy, the intermestic element is a prime part of the foreign policy environment.

These phenomena—extreme partisanship and the intermingling of traditional domestic and international politics—cannot be ignored in any empirical discussion of the past, present, or future directions of American foreign policy. It is not the intention of this volume to decry or salute these trends, but rather to identify them and apply them to the subject matter. Whether these effects are good or bad generally or in specific situations is a separate determination that goes beyond present intents.

Historically, there have been two basic positions on the role of domestic politics on foreign policy. One is that Americans should unite behind their government on foreign policy questions after a thorough internal debate on issues wherein differences are hashed out and reconciled into a united front against foreign opponents. The result should be a **bipartisan** approach and outcome that presents a unified face to the world. This position is most famously associated with Senator Arthur Vandenberg (R-MI), who coined the phrase that "we must set aside partisan politics at the water's edge" in supporting Democratic president Harry S. Truman's advocacy of what became the North Atlantic Treaty Organization (NATO) in 1947. The basic idea, which is the need to unite at the borders (the **"water's edge"**) in matters of national security, is reflected in this book's subtitle, and was the main title of an earlier edition of this book.

The other position, associated with early-twentieth-century political scientist Edward S. Corwin, suggests that disagreement on foreign policy and its vocal expression is simply a part of the intended legacy of the authors of the U.S. Constitution. In Corwin's famous phrase (adopted by Crabb and Holt in an influential 1970s text), the Constitution is an "invitation to struggle for the privilege of directing American foreign policy." That struggle includes the effort both to achieve political power and to exercise it.

Are these positions antithetical? They certainly reflect different perspectives and points of emphasis, but they are not mutually exclusive. The "invitation to struggle" does not preclude reaching accord that can lead to a united stand at the "water's edge." Vandenberg, for instance, argued in 1947 that the country should "unite our official voice at the water's edge" after a "free debate . . . that seeks national security ahead of partisan advantage." That is sometimes easier said than done.

The current environment clearly reflects the dominance of the "struggle" end of the spectrum. Hyperpartisanship in particular dictates that whenever the party that controls the White House proposes any foreign policy action, it will trigger a virtually automatic negative response from the ideological opposition—regardless of the content of the proposal. In the current hyperventilated atmosphere, these responses are often very vitriolic, nasty, and arguably uncivil. One argument that will be explored here is that this intensity of struggle is not only dysfunctional but may be so disabling that it impairs America's ability to defend its interests, to provide world leadership, and to achieve its national interests. The "crises" over Iranian nuclear weapons and the Islamic State (IS) are examples inherited by Trump where overenthusiastic embrace of the invitation to struggle may be hurting America's place in the world by questioning whether this country speaks to the world with a unified voice. Whether a more subdued approach might produce a greater unity at the water's edge and thus a better American foreign policy is a proposition that we will explore here.

Two qualifying points should be made at this point. The first is that neither party has a monopoly on partisan opposition and incivility. Both parties have controlled the executive branch (which normally favors a water's edge approach), and both have been in opposition (which tends to favor the struggle emphasis). The bipartisan accord between Truman and Vandenberg to stand united against the communist threat in the late 1940s was something of an aberration normally associated with times of overwhelming national distress. By the early 1950s, however, that glow had faded, and President Truman and Secretary of State Dean Acheson faced impeachment movements because they were not "tough enough" on Asia. As Casey reminds us, a Republican senator from South Dakota even introduced a bill to abolish the State Department at the time. By contrast, Democratic Senator Henry (Scoop) Jackson introduced what became known as the Jackson-Vanik Amendment in 1973 over strenuous objections from Republican president Richard M. Nixon.

The second point is that hyperpartisanship as a motive to oppose presidents or their policies often fails. The further the policy debate strays from the water's edge of the spectrum, "perceived partisanship on foreign policy can backfire" because, as Casey puts it, "criticism from the sidelines is easier than policymaking in power." Basing his argument on the comparison of the 1950s and today, he concludes, "one might expect to see the punches come thick and fast in the midst of a partisan campaign over foreign policy [to] land far from their intended targets and quite possibly end up hurting those who throw them in the first place." This dynamic can also affect the transition from being a candidate to being president, which President Trump has discovered.

The turmoil of American politics and its effect on foreign policy provides a leitmotif for the discussion that follows. It is organized around the three environments in which policy operates: the international and domestic environments and the intermestic intersection between them. Within the analysis of each environment, two distinctions are made sequentially: the nature or setting in each environment and the themes that arise in analyzing the foreign policy consequences of each in the current context. The chapter concludes by examining foreign policy culture and how different views on cultural distinctions help define different people and groups.

Settings and Themes

Foreign policy has become a much more prominent part of political dialogue than it used to be. Prior to World War II (WWII), most people had little concern for foreign affairs most of the time, because what went on outside the United States had little discernible effect on them. Foreign policy was the virtually exclusive preserve of the State Department, where highly specialized experts produced policies and enforced them outside the public glare. Public coverage of foreign affairs was essentially limited to the media of the time, which meant radio, news magazines, and newspapers. For the most part, coverage of foreign affairs was not a major feature of news concern unless some traumatic events had an unavoidable impact on this country.

Foreign policy concerns flared and became intensely political and partisan in the past. Opposition to the War of 1812, the purchase of Alaska from Russia

("Seward's Folly"), the decision to build the Panama Canal, and rejection of the treaty ending World War I by the Senate are examples. Episodes like this, however, tend to be exceptional, and the norm most of the time was to ignore foreign affairs and to leave them to the Executive.

That has changed dramatically in the current environment. Due to the increasingly intermestic impact of foreign affairs on domestic concerns, the discussion of foreign affairs has increased dramatically. Bayless Manning introduced the term in 1977, as noted, and he referred to the fact that domestic and international politics has been "visibly intermingled" in areas such as trade policy and that this phenomenon "has now become preponderant. The issues of the new international agenda strike instantly into the economic and political interests of domestic constituencies." He argued that this phenomenon was spreading to other areas and concluded, "These new issues are thus simultaneously, profoundly, and inseparably domestic and international."

A large reason is the ubiquitous influence of electronic mediation of events happening worldwide. Global television was the first major source of this spread of access to world events, since augmented by the explosion of social media. With the globalization of outlets such as cell phone pictures of global events on Facebook and Twitter, almost everyone has some access to nearly everything of consequence that happens in the world in real time. The ability to conduct foreign policy in the shadows has disappeared, for better or worse (or both). These changes have an impact on all the settings in which policy must operate and on the themes that dominate each setting.

Although the role of foreign affairs in American politics has expanded, the impact of that extension can be overstated. Americans are more aware of foreign affairs in a general sense than they used to be, but the kind of awareness they have tends to be cursory, the result of a sixty-second network news segment or the expression of an opinion by a news commentator or politician with limited background on the subject. At the same time, it is a truism of American politics that elections are rarely decided on foreign policy issues or differences. Americans are more interested and somewhat more knowledgeable than they were, but the change is not as great as it might seem to be.

The International Environment

By definition and tradition, the international environment is the place where foreign policy takes place. Physically, it refers to every place outside the confines of the United States—the areas "beyond the water's edge," where the United States deals with foreign entities and issues. In traditional terms, a sharp distinction was drawn between this environment and the domestic realm, both in terms of the level of interest people had in international affairs and the role of the United States in dealing with what went on in that realm. Both perceptions and levels of interest have changed.

Setting The international setting is regulated by different rules and entities than is the domestic realm. The major conceptual element in this distinction comes from the principle of sovereignty. Defined as supreme authority over affairs, it is the bedrock principle of international relations, the setting in which foreign policy takes place. This principle applies both to international and domestic affairs, but with diametrically opposite effects that point to why each setting must be dealt with differently.

In domestic affairs, the supreme authority endowed by sovereignty is the basis of domestic order, the source of authority from which governments gain their rightful ability to govern (authority). In the United States, that sovereignty resides with the people, who delegate some of it to government, thus permitting authority to be exercised over those areas where sovereignty has been transferred. Exactly how much authority has been ceded to government (how much sovereignty has been transferred) is a constant source of disagreement. In non-democratic countries, sovereignty may be exercised by an individual or group and may be more or less comprehensive. At any rate, sovereignty is the basis of domestic political order.

The situation in the international realm is quite the opposite. In international affairs, sovereignty resides with the **state**, the physical territory and people living within a particular physical jurisdiction. Within classic international relations as they have evolved since the end of the Thirty Years' War in 1648 (the Peace of Westphalia), sovereignty has resided with the territorial state and has been considered absolute: no entity other than that of the state can exercise jurisdiction over territory claimed by a particular state and accepted by other states. This means effectively that state sovereignty is the overriding principle of international affairs and that the system is **state-centric**: all power and authority reside within the constituent units. Because each state possesses sovereignty, it is the supreme authority in its realm, over which no other state or entity can claim or enforce authority. The practical effect is that within the system of states (sometimes called nation-states), sovereignty produces anarchy (the absence of overriding authority).

This configuration forms the basic parameter within which foreign policy operates. State-centrism creates anarchy, but not necessarily chaos. A major characteristic of states within a state-centered system is that they have national interests, concerns and conditions affecting their sovereign jurisdictions that they consider necessary for their well-being. The most important of these conditions are referred to as *vital*, which means that their non-realization is considered intolerable to the state: protection against hostile states on their borders would be a prime example. Vital interests are contrasted to other, *less-than-vital* (LTV) interests that, if not realized, would be discomforting or inconvenient but could be tolerated.

One way to think about traditional foreign policy is that it deals with how states interact to try to maximize their interests in a state-centric world. States have over time devised a series of rules that govern how their interactions will be conducted in a regularized way. These rules cumulatively are known as **diplomacy**, the formal interactions between the representatives of sovereign states in trying to reconcile their differences. Historically, diplomacy and war have been the most used of so-called instruments of power to realize interests, although there are other means and variations that are introduced and developed in subsequent chapters. Within the American system, sovereign authority to deal with other foreign governments has been given to the executive branch, with congressional oversight and authority over some of the outcomes of presidential interaction with other states. Traditionally, the U.S. State Department has been the institution whose special portfolio features diplomacy.

One can overstate the absolute nature of these principles in the historical sense as well as in the contemporary environment. The principle of state sovereignty dictates that states cannot legitimately interfere with or try to influence what goes on in other states, but that has never been entirely true. States interfere with other states in multiple ways and always have, limited by their physical ability to do so and the importance of that interference. Sovereignty in practice has never been as absolute as it has been in theory. As state boundaries become increasingly porous in terms of things such as electronic information flow and as phenomena such as economic globalization tie public and private entities together across sovereign boundaries, the pretense of absolute sovereignty has been progressively laid bare. States may regulate most of what goes on in their relations with other states, but they do not have the power or ability to regulate everything.

If sovereignty is under some level of assault, so is the diplomacy that has historically been the primary means by which states sought to resolve their differences with one another. The interactions that states had with one another have provided the primary means of conflict resolution among states, but the increasing impact of hyperpartisanship and mediation has threatened to undermine the ability to conduct effective diplomacy, described in intersection 1.1.

Intersection 1.1   Diplomacy 101

Former U.S. secretary of state John Kerry and German chancellor Angela Merkel meet with reporters after a negotiating session.

Diplomacy is generally described as the "profession, activity, or skill of managing international relations, typically by a country's representatives abroad" (*Oxford Dictionary*). The normal method of diplomatic interchanges is negotiation by the accredited representatives of governments over matters of disagreement. Typically, the subject is some conflict of interest between the disputing states over the disposition of something each (or all) values, and the circumstance is one of scarcity, where the disputing parties cannot all simultaneously possess all of the scarce resource they desire. The purpose of diplomacy is to try to reconcile the differences in a way that is acceptable to both or all of them. The key dynamic is compromise by the negotiators to reach outcomes with which all can live.

The key point from which diplomatic negotiations begin is the mutual recognition by the parties that each has conflicting interests that each believes are necessary and legitimate. From this realization flows the process of compromise, since each recognizes that they must find a solution not only with which they can live, but with which the other side can live as well. Both realize there are outcomes that are intolerable for the other (usually outcomes where one side achieves all its goals at the expense of the other) and where, as a result, insisting on maximally desirable outcomes will likely result in a failed negotiation. The "art of diplomacy" is getting each side to compromise enough to create minimal satisfaction from the other side while maximizing one's own outcome. This generally means giving in on some points of contention; the alternative is normally failure of the diplomatic effort.

The dynamics are straightforward. Both sides enter negotiations with their maximum outcomes (realizing all they want, at the expense of the other), knowing these are unachievable if the effort is to succeed and are thus rhetorical starting points. These positions are normally kept secret, because if the public learned of them, they would view compromise as defeat. Each side also has a minimal acceptable deal in mind, but it also keeps that secret from the other party, who will insist on that outcome if he or she knows what it is. The purpose of the diplomatic effort is to find as favorable a ground as possible between the maximum and minimum acceptable outcome. This band of outcomes forms the effective negotiating space for both sides. A successful outcome will fall somewhere between these positions; insistence on more will likely result in failure; acceptance of less will be intolerable for whoever "lost" the negotiation in facing its public. Normally both maximum and minimum remain secret until the negotiation is complete, so that both sides can claim success.

The practice of diplomacy has been under siege for two reasons basic to its success. The first is ideological rigidity. If one side (or both) believes that retaining the purity of its position is more important than reaching agreement, it will not compromise to find a mutually acceptable solution. The second is the increasingly public nature of debating diplomatic situations. When outside parties reveal the positions of their government or the other party, it makes compromise difficult or impossible. Public diplomacy can often represent an oxymoron to hide obstructionism in a hyperpartisan, gridlocked political situation.

The condition of diplomatic efforts and the tatters in which claims to sovereignty exist are emblematic of the ways in which the conduct of foreign policy has changed in recent years. The charges of Russian interference in the 2016 U.S. election are a prime example of sovereignty-eroding change.

Themes The contemporary environment has virtually turned traditional calculations about the conduct of foreign policy on their heads. The world is still composed primarily of sovereign states, but they have been subject to significant challenges in areas such as the rise of failed states that do not really exercise sovereign control of their own territory and the blossoming of **non-state**

actors that pose threats to the traditional order. Both pose problems of where and whether traditional practices such as those associated with sovereign control can be effectively pursued. Neither the state system nor sovereignty are disappearing, but they are increasingly under siege in the most unstable, problematical parts of the world. At the same time, the environment of calm in which traditional foreign policy practices flourish has been upset by the greater publicity about foreign affairs and the rise of a whole new set of actors, often with only a smattering of knowledge on the subject, as very vocal participants in the foreign policy debate.

The rise of new actors is the most dramatic contemporary challenge. It has its roots in the decolonization of European empires during the Cold War, when independence was granted to a number of states unprepared for the burdens of statehood and often aggregated in new sovereign entities that made little sense to those who lived in them. These actors often reject the rules and strictures of the traditional international environment, which was fashioned by the very Europeans who enslaved them and from whose tyranny they escaped. In some cases, these new states have proven incapable of sustenance and have become, in one way or another, **failed states** that are difficult or impossible to interact with in traditional ways. Non-state actors either reject the notion of sovereign statehood altogether or demand radical changes in the pattern or behavior of states in the international environment.

The problem of failed states is that they typically either lack a government altogether or possess a governing group that lacks the support or power to enforce control over state territory. In many of these cases, the power vacuum that is created by state failure virtually invites violent non-state actors to enter the country and establish sway over parts of the territory, a phenomenon the failed state is incapable of preventing or overcoming. Somalia over the past quarter century, for instance, has basically had no central government and has become a haven at times for pirates menacing seaborne traffic off their shore (the *Maersk Alabama* hijacking, which story became a motion picture, is the most famous manifestation) as well as a refuge for terrorist groups that have included Al Qaeda (AQ) and Al-Shabab. The failure of governance in Yemen has made it a chaotic battleground between Shia and Sunni Arabs and the home site for terrorist groups such as Al Qaeda in the Arabian Peninsula (AQAP) and more recently, the Islamic State. As a foreign policy problem, it is not clear with whom the United States (or any other country) can deal on foreign policy issues in these countries.

Non-state actors are the other challenger to the supremacy of states in international relations. They come in two basic varieties. The first are supranational groups, organizations with memberships and goals that transcend state boundaries. Usually, these groups espouse goals that include an assault on the basic structure of the states in which they operate, and they either lack political structures with which states can communicate or refuse to enter into discussions with the states in which they operate (usually because they are viewed as criminals that the states seek to apprehend and punish). Terrorist groups are the most obvious example, with IS being the most obvious challenger of the state system with its advocacy of creating a new state (the caliphate) out of existing states in the Levant, notably Iraq and Syria.

The second category is subnational groups, organizations that operate exclusively within the boundaries of existing states. The most troubling of these groups are engaged in civil wars to gain power within a state at the expense of whatever group has power at any point in time. These movements are most ubiquitous, troubling, and violent in the multinational states (states that include multiple ethnic, religious, linguistic, or other subgroups to which people give primary loyalty) that are common in the developing world. Indeed, the major source of violence and instability in the current world order may be the existence of developing world internal conflicts (DWICs), a problem addressed in more detail in chapter 9. Like supranational groups, subnational groups often eschew traditional forms of interaction, especially with state governments that often try to mediate the conflicts in which they are involved.

Both failed states and non-state actors challenge the basic values and means of operation of the traditional system of sovereign states as the controlling actors in international relations. More explicitly, failed states are generally incapable of normal foreign policy interaction or can only deal with other states in very limited ways. Non-state actors, on the other hand, usually explicitly reject the framework of the traditional order as either causing their problems (poorly drawn state boundaries, a common occurrence in much of the developing world) or as a device to enforce their subjugation.

New actors are the most obvious challengers to the traditional state system, but there are other signs of the decline or complication of traditional foreign policy practice. Three of these stand out for exemplary purposes and form the basis for a general decline in the supremacy and effectiveness of traditional means of conducting foreign policy. The three examples are the rise of nontraditional forms of warfare as dominant methods (asymmetrical warfare), the increasing ubiquity of global electronic information availability, and the rise of **cyber security** as a concern.

A trademark of the traditional, European-based international system was how its members made war. The dominant form of warfare, and the method most in keeping with conflict in a system of sovereign states, was conventional warfare between the armed forces of states. The penultimate expression of this form of violence was the two world wars of the first half of the twentieth century. It was classic interstate warfare, where the units fighting were similar, fought in basic similar ways, and for the same reasons, those of the state. It was generally ended by negotiations between the conflicting parties, sometimes after a formal surrender by the losing side. This form of warfare is referred to as symmetrical warfare.

That genre of violence has virtually disappeared. Modern wars, and especially the DWICs, are generally conducted by non-state actors, and they are fought unconventionally in the sense that they are not conducted within the rules of engagement (ROEs) of traditional warfare or for the purposes of state that motivated traditional wars. They represent a different form, often called asymmetrical war, because the contesting parties fight differently from one another and especially differently from traditional state armed forces. These wars are usually internal, which makes them very personal and furtive, and they rarely end conclusively, through some form of negotiated settlement among the parties.

The impact of these kinds of conflicts on the conduct of foreign policy is direct. If one is a participant in an asymmetrical war, there is no one with whom to try to negotiate an ending. If the conflict is a classic DWIC between internal groups vying for power and neither will come to the table, traditional means of intercession and outside conflict resolution are simply unavailable. The nature of contemporary war makes traditional means of conflict resolution—especially involving diplomatic efforts—impossible to invoke in many situations.

The universality of electronic penetration of what goes on in the world is a second source of change. It is fair to say that virtually no major event (or most minor events) can avoid the scrutiny of one form or another of electronic observation that becomes potentially available for consumption by much of the world's population in something like real time. In some ways, this is a very positive thing. It lets people know of impending or ongoing natural disasters, and it means that human-produced atrocities are extremely difficult to hide from public view and appall. An increasingly transparent world is the bane of the world's thugs, but it also inundates people with more information than they can possibly absorb or understand. Moreover, the impact of electronic engagement is everywhere in everyone's lives through the wide and growing number of platforms by which it enters people's lives. This rate of penetration into individual lives and perceptions of the world around them can only increase, with uncertain consequences. This in turn creates two problems for the conduct of foreign policy.

First, the flood of information makes it much more difficult to make use of the kinds of discreet privacy that have surrounded traditional diplomacy as described in intersection 1.1. The give-and-take dynamics fundamental to reaching agreements are much more difficult when interested, often highly partisan, viewers bombard the media (and thus the participants) with demands outside the realm of possible diplomatic compromise. Second, the flow of information requires interpretation, and there are simply not enough people with expertise to make sense of the explosion of events disseminated on a daily basis. Lacking adequate expertise in turn encourages those who do not truly understand phenomena to become interpreters of dynamics they do not comprehend. This is a particular problem in a hyperpartisan political environment.

The other complicating factor is the rise of cyber security as a limiting influence. Cyberspace, of course, is the medium within which the electronic world operates and is both the conduit among governments, within state apparatuses, and between publics through the media. Space, however, can be penetrated, and operations within it are often difficult both to monitor and to police. The interruption or theft of information that allows governments to function has become a major concern of international actors.

Two sources of difficulty provide obvious examples. One is the sanctity of what are intended to be secure, private, and inviolable communications between governments and between agencies of governments operating in foreign countries. The problem is multidirectional, of course. The U.S. government expends considerable resources attempting to monitor and intercept the cyber-based communications of hostile others (e.g., terrorists), just as those opponents attempt to penetrate American communications. In a potentially more ominous application, cyberspace is also the medium in which a large number of military activities, from satellite reconnaissance to targeted drone air strikes, occur. Apparent Russian hacking and release of communications of the Democratic National Committee in 2016 allegedly to help President Trump's campaign illustrates how ubiquitous this problem has become as a policy concern.

The Domestic Environment

Among the forces that have changed most radically in their influences on the ability to construct and conduct foreign policy, none has become more difficult and vexing than the impact of domestic politics within the United States. The fractiousness that has increasingly gripped the American political system has been extended to a widening political divide on foreign affairs, politicizing areas that historically went unnoticed or remained below the radar of public awareness. At the same time, the often-bitter partisan debate that extends to foreign policy matters greatly complicates the ability of the United States to present a coherent, unified front to the rest of the world.

This condition became particularly obvious and intense during the recently concluded presidency of Barack Obama, and historians will debate the extent to which Obama was the cause or victim of the malaise. The roots of division predate the Obama presidency, reaching back at least to his predecessor George W. Bush and his controversial military actions in Iraq and Afghanistan. These divisions also did not end when Obama sat and listened to the inaugural address of his successor, President Donald J. Trump. The impact of domestic concerns will affect the next president and the country requires looking at the domestic setting and ongoing themes.

Setting The changes in the domestic environment are both more and less fundamental and traumatic than those within the international realm. In the international environment, most of the changes are structural and beyond the direct and unambiguous ability of the United States to rectify: the emergence of terrorists and the rise of asymmetrical warfare, for instance. In the domestic context, most of the changes are more personal, subjective, and nonstructural—mostly involving the way Americans view the people who make policy and the directions they attempt to move that policy. In the international realm, there are real new enemies to confront. In domestic politics, one is drawn to Walt Kelly's observation, voiced by his cartoon character Pogo. The wise little opossum noted, "We have met the enemy, and he is us."

The institutional setting within which domestic politics are conducted, of course, is the constitutional system. Fearful of the accumulation of power in any one source or individual, the framers sought to disperse power among institutions of government. The result was the separation of powers system that allocates different responsibilities to different parts of government, provides that those parts have the ability to monitor and limit the others, sets boundaries between the central and state governments, and attempts to ensure the freedom of individuals in their dealings with government.

The separation of powers concept was intended to apply primarily to the internal workings of the American government. International (effectively European) tyranny had led to the creation of the new country, and there was considerable sentiment to minimize the extent of involvement the United States had with what most Americans considered a corrupt, flawed international system. Anticipating considerable autonomy and isolation from the world—a desire that gradually became less and less tenable—the Founding Fathers placed relatively little emphasis on foreign affairs, and its most extreme form, the conduct of war, in their deliberations. They did, however, embed within the divisions of power between individuals and institutions the "invitation to struggle" over control of foreign policy. The mechanisms for doing so are found largely in the powers and countervailing authorities of the executive and legislative branches, described in chapters 4 and 6.

Before the world wars, the foreign policy mechanisms were of much lesser importance and controversy than they have come to be. For the first century and a half of the nation's existence, a small diplomatic corps operating out of the State Department conducted what relations the United States had with the world, generally with little fanfare or controversy. Occasionally, outside forces pushed the country into relations with the world, as in diplomatic battles over recognition or nonrecognition of the Confederacy during the Civil War, alleged Spanish atrocities and provocations in Cuba, or the country being inexorably drawn into global conflagrations. These events produced occasional controversy— Republican opposition to the Versailles Peace Treaty in 1919, for instance—but not until the Cold War was America drawn into world affairs so thoroughly that it had to make adjustments to its historical institutions and attitudes.

The Cold War was the first long-standing military competition with another power during peacetime. The relationship between the United States and the Soviet Union was a foreign policy interaction, but its most obvious and compelling aspect was an evolving, all-encompassing military confrontation. That relationship's possible consequences included a potentially civilization-ending all-out nuclear war, and it came to dominate foreign policy. Prior to World War II, the United States had spent limited time and resources worrying about military problems on an ongoing, peacetime basis. The Cold War made that practice dangerous and obsolete.

The result was the evolution of the **national security state.** In this construct, originally described by Harold D. Lasswell, matters of national security became the dominant concerns of government, the sine qua non by which other political matters were judged. This perceived necessity was reflected institutionally in adjustments that linger and continue to dominate a quarter-century or more after the Cold War itself has ended. The most notable action was the passage and implementation of the National Security Act of 1947 (as amended in 1949) that, among other things, created the Department of Defense, the National Security Council (with the Secretaries of State and Defense as coequals), an independent air force, and the first peacetime intelligence agency in U.S. history, the Central Intelligence Agency. These institutional adjustments are described in chapter 5.

Themes   If the setting within which foreign policy takes place is largely foundational in the structural aspects of the constitutional system as it has evolved, most of the domestic themes deal with politics, how Americans and their political leaders attempt to use the system for national ends. If the Constitution creates the physical framework that issues the invitation to struggle, political differences within the body politic energize that invitation. In the current context, the result has been the current deadlock of both domestic and foreign policies.

If the problematical dynamics about contemporary American politics are not new, they are different in the ways they have an impact on the conduct of foreign policy. The main factors are what amounts to the democratization of foreign policy debates in the new atmosphere and the intensity and pervasiveness of the assault on the ability of designated decision makers to reach and conclude agreements with other countries, and thus on the traditional contexts within which policy is made.

Mediation is at the heart of foreign policy democratization. In the past, the access that average citizens, and even their political representatives, had to information about the outside world was limited to a relative handful of truly national outlets such as national newspapers, magazines, and television news programs that emanated from the major urban areas of the country. If one, for instance, did not have ready access to something such as the *New York Times* or *Foreign Affairs* magazine (which most people did not), most overseas news, including events that required U.S. foreign policy responses, were simply unknown to most people. Their elected representatives, who generally had little interest or expertise in foreign affairs, felt no particular need to become knowledgeable about things their constituents were not interested in. In that atmosphere, foreign policy largely remained the preserve of the expert community within and outside government.

That situation has changed dramatically with the revolution in information technologies. The access to global events readily available to virtually everyone creates pressure on all politicians to gain enough understanding of foreign affairs that they do not appear ignorant to their constituents. The knowledge that circulates from the public to its representatives and back may be cursory and only minimally informed, but it is at the heart of the democratization of the process.

The superheated, hyperpartisan domestic political atmosphere interacts with this phenomenon. When some event or action requires an official response, there is generally more than one possible option that the president, who is charged with conducting most day-to-day actions, can take. In the current atmosphere where all matters are politicized and each side in the political debate instinctively distrusts and thus opposes the other, the "natural" response whenever anything occurs is to take the opposite side. Democrats assailed George W. Bush for championing unilateral approaches to problems and attacked him for refusing to deal with North Korea in other than a multilateral context. Republicans attacked Barack Obama for being too aggressive toward Libya and not aggressive enough toward the Islamic State. President Trump will face similar criticism.

This condition neither encourages nor promotes traditional foreign policy methods. The traditional foreign policy community is rooted in the diplomatic solution to difficulties, with more strident methods as a backdrop or court of last resort. Diplomacy thrives in a calm atmosphere where processes of give and take outside the public glare can reach accommodations that are impossible within a climate of absolutist, nonnegotiable positions. Traditional foreign policy processes operate most smoothly when diplomats have public and political support for their actions (the "water's edge" end of the spectrum) and where knowledge and expertise has more traction than superheated partisan rhetoric. Foreign policy traditionalists tend to be elitist in their beliefs that foreign policy should only be conducted by the most qualified, knowledgeable representatives—a position that flies in the face of more populist advocacies. All the tensions and difficulties that arise within the international and domestic environments come to a head at the intermestic intersection where they collide.

The Intermestic Intersection

Unlike the international and domestic environments, the intermestic intersection is more a metaphor than a physical place. As explained earlier, the concept refers to the growing interconnection between domestic and foreign policies. The most obvious cases are where an action in one environment directly affects what goes on in the other. In one direction, the domestic exploitation of shale oil and gas in the United States reduces American dependence on Middle Eastern oil and thus has an impact on oil exporters such as Saudi Arabia, on whom the United States no longer relies for its energy needs. In the other direction, fluctuations in the Chinese economy can send shock waves into the American stock market and the value of individual portfolios. Intermestic situations are particularly dramatic and politicized when they are taken in one environment specifically to affect the other. Congressional calls to keep Syrian refugees out of the United States certainly affected the tenuous refugee situation in the Syrian civil war, and open lobbying efforts by foreign leaders such as Israel's Benjamin Netanyahu are intended to have an impact on domestic American politics, including electoral outcomes.

Setting The intermestic intersection has always existed, if not by that name. Governments have always selectively ignored the sovereign entreaty not to interfere in one another's business, sometimes for internal domestic effect, and actions taken to address domestic concerns have always had some overseas impact. What has become different is the pervasiveness of intermestic causes and effects that are the consequences of a globalizing, shrinking world. It used to be that *some* things that governments did crossed into the intersection, but most things did not. In that atmosphere, one could make the reasonable case for dividing domestic from international politics and thus the distinctiveness of the boundary at the water's edge. In the contemporary world, *most* domestic actions have some international repercussions, meaning that the intermestic intersection is a much busier place, and the sharp differentiation between foreign and domestic politics and policy is increasingly artificial.

This phenomenon has a strong impact on the politicization of foreign policy. In earlier, simpler times foreign policy rarely had any direct, discernible impact on the lives of most Americans, and so they were willing to defer to the foreign policy elite centered on the East Coast to conduct it virtually outside the political system. As foreign policy decisions have become increasingly intermestic, however, that distinction is increasingly difficult to make. Trade agreements affect the jobs and livelihoods of American workers, and decisions about U.S. Middle East policy potentially place individual Americans at risk from terrorist attacks. In these circumstances, individuals have developed much more of a vested interest in foreign policy, and that policy arena has entered more fully into the political realm. Foreign policy did not historically matter greatly to most members of the public and their representatives; now it does. This development has been the basis for new themes in the foreign policy arena.

Themes What is special and different about the current environment is the major intrusion of the underlying disruptive influences of domestic political pathology on the process and ability to make foreign policy. The occasional insertion of disagreement into foreign policy concerns is not novel to the present: the political infighting about how to treat the Allies and Axis powers before the United States entered WWII is an example of where domestic lack of consensus threatened to pollute the ability to formulate and execute foreign policy. What is different is the pervasiveness and degree of rancor that is central to this phenomenon.

In the contemporary world, it is not unfair to say that "all politics is global." This construct is, of course, a takeoff on the famous aphorism of the late Speaker of the House of Representatives, Thomas "Tip" O'Neill (D-MA), who declared that "all politics is local." The latter phrase meant roughly that successful political leadership consists of the ability to understand and thus to influence constituents to follow the leadership of their elected representatives. When O'Neill issued this truism, he was referring primarily to the relationship between elected representatives and voters on domestic issues, because most citizens at the local level lacked either an interest or any knowledge about international affairs on which to base opinions. Not much local politics had global roots; now, virtually all politics do.

The absence of a link between foreign policy and constituency politics was, of course, never total. When truly monumental foreign events clearly intruded on the public awareness, the public developed opinions on policy matters, but this generally took time. Support for and then opposition to the Vietnam War, for instance, took several years to build and congeal, influenced both by the lack of discernible progress in the fighting and the growing number of casualties among American conscripts who would have preferred not to be involved.

The ubiquity of the intermestic intersection as a prominent part of the foreign policy environment is largely an artifact of the twenty-first century. The

Internet and widespread ownership and use of computers as information-sharing devices began to appear in the 1990s, but its real impact is a recent phenomenon. It is virtually impossible not to be aware of global events that affect the United States, even if that awareness is limited to a short sound bite or a gruesome photograph. Citizen knowledge has lagged behind this growing exposure, and citizens turn to political figures with whom they agree on other matters but who may also not have great knowledge on foreign affairs. As global politics becomes local, the polluting effect of current domestic politics seeps into the dialogue.

An example may help illustrate the change. The terrorist attacks of 9/11 were, of course, not the first time Al Qaeda attempted to bring down the World Trade Center towers in New York. The first attempt came in 1993, when AQ agents tried to detonate a bomb in a parking garage under the buildings. The attempt failed, the perpetrators were apprehended, and the incident faded from the public consciousness. There were no recriminations against the Clinton administration for showing inadequate diligence in preventing the attempt, and only a few experts inside the counterterrorism community argued that it might be a harbinger for the future. When they were proved correct on 9/11, the public was aroused and demanded a robust response. The two incidents were clearly different in terms of effect and scale, but nearly a decade of media development separated them. Ever since, the public has become much more engaged in foreign policy decisions.

The increasingly intermestic nature of foreign policy and its blending into the internal domestic malaise has arguably made it much more difficult to conduct coherent foreign policy. Certainly, the discretion and privacy in which diplomatic undertakings have traditionally been conducted have been largely stripped away, which is anathema to historic ways of doing foreign policy business. The unity—or at least absence of loud vituperation—at the water's edge has virtually disappeared. One is left to wonder what foreign officials who deal with the United States must think about the resulting cacophony and how much this influence may have a negative impact on the conduct of foreign policy. This question is raised in intersection 1.2 and will recur throughout the text.

Intersection 1.2   Intermestic Diplomacy

Traditional diplomacy as described in intersection 1.1 has two virtues from a negotiating vantage point. First, it allows the parties to discuss matters in the context that what one side says represents some position its government holds and on which the other side can count: diplomatic positions may be negotiable, but they at least derive from some enforceable government position. Second, they allow discussions to proceed without outside "noise" from other sources that can confuse the side that must interpret the authority and believability of what national representatives are saying.

An example may help explain the complications caused by the intrusion of domestically based intermestic influences on diplomacy. On March 9, 2015, a freshman Republican senator from Arkansas, Thomas B. (Tom) Cotton, penned a letter condemning Iran and threatening its leaders with severe consequences if they did not accede to conditions they had already dismissed as unacceptable in their negotiation with Western countries (including the United States) on the issue of nuclear proliferation. Cotton, a former army captain who had been in office for less than two months, persuaded forty-six other GOP senators to cosign the letter, which was then translated and sent to the Iranian government, arguably in violation of existing law. The letter contradicted positions taken by the Obama administration, which roundly condemned it. The Iranian foreign minister also condemned it as denying that governments could enter executive agreements (binding agreements by states not subject to Senate approval through the treaty process), the form the negotiations took.

The point here is not the virtue of either Cotton's or the administration's position. The point is that the Constitution clearly designates the chief executive (or his designated plenipotentiary) as the sole agent who can represent the United States in foreign affairs—a principle shared by essentially all sovereign states as a way to ensure that governments can be certain of the authority of those with whom they negotiate. Cotton's letter effectively said that unless the administration met his demands, the Iranians could not count on the blessing of Congress for the agreement under negotiation. Support for the Cotton position was essentially partisan.

Thinking about Foreign Policy

Changes in the environments in which foreign policy is made are also reflected in both the content and processes by which policy is made. Those changes directly affect the reader of this volume. Both domestic and international changes have caused the visibility of foreign affairs to rise, and the intermestic intersection has seen the heat, if not necessarily the light, of discussions of those events increase as well. In this circumstance, it is more incumbent than ever for citizens with some knowledge to be informed and to try to inform the public debate. By taking a course in foreign affairs, the reader enters a very small portion of the population—less than 10 percent—who have studied the subject even to this extent.

To help the reader develop the skills and perspectives to be an informed citizen, the rest of the chapter proceeds through two concerns that help clarify the problem. The first is the idea of **foreign policy culture**, the distinct ways in which people in different countries view the world and their place in it. The second is an exercise in value clarification, where the reader is asked to consider a series of orientations on foreign policy matters and to determine how the reader places himself or herself on these dimensions. As well as providing a kind of personal inventory, the exercise allows one to categorize the vantage points of people in the process, and to compare them to others or oneself.

Foreign Policy Culture

No two countries have had identical histories or have evolved in exactly the same ways, and the differences in their experiences give states unique ways of viewing the world and their place in it. Each country develops a distinctive worldview that predisposes its members to look in their own special ways at world events and their influences on them. The composite of those experiences and resulting predilections is sometimes referred to as political culture, and in the distinct context of relations with the world, the foreign policy culture. Different factors help shape the cultures of different states. In the American experience, two stand out: the accident of geography and the Anglo-Saxon heritage. Each is described in more detail in *National Security* and has had a distinct impact.

There is an entire approach to the study of international relations, known as geopolitics, devoted to the impact of geography on international relations and the behavior of states. Geopolitics is not the explicit focus of much international relations theorizing today, but its major constituent elements, geographic location and natural resources, continue to influence states and their behavior.

Geographic location, of course, refers to where a country is physically located in the world, including what states are contiguous with or near its boundaries. In this regard, the United States has been uniquely favored. Its core, the contiguous forty-eight states, is bounded on the east and west by broad oceans that effectively make it an island between Europe and Asia. Its borders are shared by two states that have posed no threat to it (the recent debate about the U.S.-Mexican border notwithstanding) and have generally been friendly. Between the last concerted assault on its territory by Great Britain in the War of 1812 and the advent of Soviet nuclear-tipped rockets capable of reaching American soil in 1957, the United States experienced an unprecedented sense of physical safety from foreign invasion. The only American territories that have been under any siege have been remote lands acquired by the country: states such as Alaska and Hawaii and foreign territories such as the Philippines. That fortuitous condition meant that the United States never developed the sense of insecurity and obsession with physical security that is an inherent feature of most European and Asian cultures.

The United States has also been endowed with generous natural resources for most of its existence that have had a benign impact on the American foreign policy culture. Abundant fertile lands have made the United States essentially self-sufficient in the ability to feed itself; the United States has had generally large supplies of both mineral and energy resources, and has thus not had to depend on supplies of these commodities from other, potentially hostile sources. This situation has, of course, become less advantageous in the past half century or so. The United States has exhausted most of its conventionally exploited sources of petroleum energy, which has made it petroleum dependent on unstable parts of the world such as the Middle East until the recent discovery of ways to mine shale oil and gas deposits. The United States lacks some strategic minerals such as titanium that are necessary for modern military uses, and now imports some exotic foodstuffs that do not grow in the American climate. The cumulative result, however, has been a historic culture where Americans could view themselves as essentially independent of what they tended to view as a hostile, corrupt outside world.

The other influence has been America's Anglo-Saxon heritage. Although the United States has become an ethnic melting pot wherein Caucasians of European heritage will cease to be a majority of the population within the next half century or less, the original United States was largely an offshoot of its experience as a

British colony. Most of the original settlers came from an Anglo-Saxon background; this was reflected in the way they viewed the world and the institutions they established as a new, independent state. Two major impacts of that experience are worth noting.

Americans tend to forget or downplay that the United States was born as a British colony on a sparsely populated continent, was largely originally populated by British and other European immigrants, and was the first major state to escape European colonialism. Among the results was to imbue the country with values that arose both from their Anglo-Saxon roots and that formed reactions to the colonial experience. One of these, arising from what American colonists viewed as the oppressive tyranny of the British monarchy, was an insistence on limited, representative government. A major reason for the separation-of-powers system was to assure citizens of the new country that power was atomized so that no individual could accumulate a monopoly of power and impose a new form of tyranny. America was born with an inherent sense of suspicion of power that permeates politics to this day. At the same time, that negative orientation was extended to what early Americans viewed as the corrupt and tainting impact of European politics, creating a suspicion of foreign politics that still endures in attitudes toward foreigners and foreign policy.

The other major impact is ironic in a militarized world where support for the military is one of a handful of political matters on which most Americans agree. Largely thanks to the British practice of posting its army on colonial soil without the explicit assent of the American colonists (who were taxed to pay for these occupiers), the Revolution also produced a negative attitude among Americans of military forces in peacetime. The result for the first century and a half of the American experience was the practice of keeping a very small force under arms during peacetime (augmented by militias and mobilizing in times of military crises), then demobilizing at the end of wars. This practice lasted through World War II, and only in the past seventy years or so has the United States supported a major standing armed force during peacetime. The overwhelming popularity of the all-volunteer force, into which no American is compelled to participate, also reflects this phenomenon.

A Personal Inventory

There is no correct or "American" view of foreign policy. The foreign policy culture influences how Americans feel about foreign matters, but not what conclusions they reach on individual foreign policy issues or regarding basic orientations. Within the normally boisterous political dialogue made more strident in the contemporary environment, a lively level of debate and disagreement is normal and healthy. How individuals (including the reader) feel about the subject is based on basic attitudes and predilections. Admitting that any list of considerations that help form that orientation will be incomplete and subject to challenge, the parameters of those differences can be organized into four categories, each of which has different polar positions. The four categories are basic political worldview, political orientation, approaches to world involvement, and participation preference. We invite the reader to identify and note his or her personal positions on each dimension.

Basic Political Worldview In its broadest terms, this dimension asks people how they look at basic world dynamics and thus how the country should respond to that perception. Basic contributing factors in this orientation include the acceptability of the world as it is, the immutability of world conditions, and whether changing those conditions is possible or worth the effort. The judgments one makes help define how active one is in foreign affairs and the direction and nature of that involvement.

Two basic positions have dominated American debates on this subject. The first is **realism**. Its basic view is that world politics is a geopolitical struggle between sovereign states in an anarchical system where goals are achieved using basic forms of power such as military force or economic coercion. This position, of course, conforms to the principles of the traditional European international system, and as such has been and continues to be the basic worldview of most foreign policy professionals. Realists accept this condition of competition and the exercise of power as natural and that competing in the exercise of power is the only "realistic" way to conduct interactions with the world.

The other position is **idealism**. Most idealists accept the realist description of the world as true, but find the consequences unfortunate and in need of change. Idealists contest the realist view that conflict is a natural or immutable condition and assert that it is both possible and desirable to espouse and advocate different conditions—or ideals—that would make the world a "better" place. This position represents a minority viewpoint within the foreign policy community, which tends to think of the reformist entreaties as being "unrealistic," an aphorism to suggest that idealism is unworldly, dangerous, and naïve. The gulf between the two positions reflects the degree to which people believe that governmental intercession in political affairs at either the domestic or international levels is efficacious or desirable.

Political Orientation How one feels about the nature of the world and what can or should be done about it inevitably derives to some degree from what one feels is the appropriate role of government more generally. At the domestic level, individual orientations reflect assessments of how activist government should be in dealing with societal and individual problems. The traditional dichotomy in this regard has been between **liberalism**, which historically espouses a more expansive view of the role of government, and **conservatism**, which argues for a more restricted role of government and greater autonomy for the private sector. Sandwiched between these two distinctive positions is **pragmatism**, which argues that individual situations should be viewed and assessed on their individual merits. Directionally, they are sometimes referred to as the political left (liberalism), center (pragmatism), and right (conservatism). This set of distinctions is, of course, used to discuss attitudes toward both internal and foreign policy issues and is meaningful at the intermestic intersection.

The designations are imprecise both in substance and in variations among them. The heart of liberalism is a belief in a more activist role of government and the general belief in the efficacy of government solutions to societal problems that liberals believe conservatives will not address and cannot solve. Moreover, a basic tenet of liberalism is tolerance of the views of others; one synonym for liberal as an adjective is tolerant. Social equity, income issues, and taxation are examples of liberal policy areas of emphasis. Liberals diverge on how extensive government activism should be and on its content along a continuum of moderate to radical liberalism.

Conservatism is also not monolithic in content. The heart of conservatism rests on two beliefs. The first is a general suspicion of change, and especially change initiated by government. The core of the word "conservatism" is to "conserve" or preserve. The other tenet is a general belief in minimal government and restrained governmental activism. Conservatives differ in what functions government legitimately performs and the level of its activity in those areas. Most, however, share the mantra of Ronald W. Reagan that the private sector always makes better decisions than does the public sector.

Sandwiched between these extremes is pragmatism. It is not truly a philosophy so much as an approach to solving problems. Pragmatists generally consider themselves non-ideological and moderate in their viewpoints, feeling that reaching compromises of the pure positions of the left and right is most likely to produce government action and that such solutions best serve the public good. The pragmatists are centrist in their orientation, and formerly dominated the moderate wings of both parties. As positions have hardened along party and ideological lines, the moderates have been squeezed out of both electoral parties. The demise of the pragmatists is one of the most obvious, and some would argue deleterious, manifestations of gridlock and hyperpartisanship.

Approaches to World Involvement The third dimension centers on how active the United States should be in world politics. The classic dichotomy has always been between internationalism and isolationism, but the evolving world order since 1945 has altered the contours and practicability of the two positions. Internationalism broadly holds that the United States must inevitably play an active role and that it is morally obligated to do so. This position has been reinforced since the end of the Cold War and the position of the United States as the remaining superpower. Isolationism, the belief that the United States should play a minimalist role and should eschew international involvements as a routine matter, was the basis of foreign policy beyond the effective European-centered international system for most of the first 150 years of the American experience. That orientation has largely disappeared, replaced by neo-isolationism, which seeks a restrained level of American involvement.

The debate surrounding the two positions now manifests itself in specific policy areas. One is the question of military activism: in what situations and how should the United States be willing to use armed force to further its goals? The positions often become muddled. Conservatives, who generally prefer restraint in resorting to government activism, tend to be more expansive about using armed forces in foreign policy situations than do liberals, who generally support

TABLE 1.1   **Personal Political Orientations**

Category	Options
Basic Worldview	Realist, Idealist
Political Orientation	Liberal, Pragmatist, Idealist
Approaches to World Involvement	Internationalist, Isolationist
Participation Preference	Multilateralist, Unilateralist

domestic activism but oppose what they view as the promiscuous application of American force in the world—a debate examined in chapter 9. The basic distinction, however, is between whether the United States should routinely act as a world leader, and in which ways. During the nineteenth and early twentieth centuries, for instance, the United States was isolationist toward Europe but very aggressive in expanding across the continent.

Participation Preference The final dimension refers to how the United States should interact with the world in its foreign policy dealings. The poles in this preference are multilateralism and unilateralism; they refer to whether the United States, as a routine matter of policy, should attempt to enlist the agreement and assistance of other states in trying to achieve its foreign policy goals, or whether the country should be willing to act on its own as a matter of preference or when circumstances dictate. The preference one has reflects both a style of doing business (e.g., building consensus as opposed to disregarding the objections of others) and a general belief in whether the United States should assert its primal power or serve as a more consensual leader. Internationalists are more generally associated with the consensus-building approach, whereas isolationists tend to view cooperation and compromise with others in a less favorable light.

One can array these positions to present different alternatives and to facilitate developing a personal profile, as table 1.1 does. These distinctions can be used in several ways. A personal inventory may help the reader to clarify where he or she stands on foreign policy. If one builds a profile of prominent political figures—elected officials such as President Trump—one can see where that individual stands and how the other individuals' profile is compatible or incompatible with one's own. Applying the framework between individuals such as the president and Congress, one can also see some of the basis of conflict and gridlock in the present environment.

Conclusion

The purpose of this chapter has been to introduce some of the dynamics and issues affecting foreign policy that will help frame discussion in the rest of the book. It begins from an analogy that has recurred in earlier editions of this book, the distinction between a consensual approach that emphasizes the projection of a sense of unity toward the outside world (the "water's edge" position) in contrast to a more domestic politics-driven, conflict-emphasizing image (the "invitation to struggle" analogy). Both are part of the national tradition, and their predominance has ebbed and flowed. In the current hyperpartisan atmosphere, it should be no surprise that the pendulum has swung toward treating foreign, like all other, policy mainly as a struggle between ideological warriors. The question that will recur is whether that situation is good for the country's foreign policy. If it is not, what can or should we do about it?

Foreign policy clearly exists within the multiple environments of its domestic and international sectors and the intermestic intersection that links them. Both environments are beset by controversy and conflict, and the toxicity of the domestic political atmosphere has, at the intersection, infected the conduct of foreign policy. Once again, this situation is not unique to the current period, but is a condition that has recurred throughout American history. It seems particularly blatant today, which partially reflects the enormous enmity among members of the political environment and distortions in its severity because we are living through it.

One effect of the cacophony that marks so much of political intercourse is on the clear articulation of views and orientations toward foreign policy. The distortions of harsh rhetoric make it difficult to assess both your own positions and those of others. The process of applying characteristics of the foreign policy culture to a personal inventory of oneself and others is intended to help bring some clarity to the subject. This is the harsh political environment the Trump administration inherited. How it will deal with and help reshape that environment will be key to its success and a concern of the pages that follow.

Study/Discussion Questions

1. An understanding of how, including how well, American foreign policy works can be partially understood by referring to two conflicting concepts of that process, the "water's edge" and the "invitation to struggle." Describe each of these vantage points. Toward which of these poles has the contemporary debate tended?

2. What are the two basic environments in which American foreign policy operates? What is the intermestic intersection, and how does it affect the making of foreign policy?

3. Discuss the changing nature of the international environment for foreign policy. Include the concepts of sovereignty, state centrism, the rise of non-state actors, and their impacts on traditional notions about the operation of the international environment?

4. How has the domestic environment changed in the recent past? Specifically, what have been the major causes and effects of the rise of extreme partisanship and gridlock on the making and execution of foreign policy? How have they affected the operation of the political process?

5. Discuss how changes in the international and domestic environment have collided at the intermestic intersection and the effects of those collisions on foreign policy making. What does it mean to describe the result as "toxic"?

6. What is the idea of a foreign policy culture? Discuss important elements of the American foreign policy culture and how they give the United States a unique vantage point on how the United States views the world.

7. Describe and discuss the dimensions of the personal inventory for determining one's orientation toward foreign policy. Apply the inventory to yourself and, as best you can, the new president. Where are you most and least in agreement?

Bibliography

Armacost, Michael H. *Bullets, Ballots, and Bargains: American Foreign Policy and Presidential Elections.* New York: Columbia University Press, 2015.

Beasley, Ryan K., Juliet Kaarbo, Jeffrey S. Lantis, and Michael T. Snarr. *Foreign Policy in Comparative Perspective: Domestic and International Influences on State Behavior.* 2nd ed. Washington, DC: CQ, 2012.

Casey, Steven. "When Congress Gets Mad: Foreign Policy Battles in the 1950s and Today." *Foreign Affairs*, January/February 2016, 76–84.

Chase, Harold V., and Craig R. Ducat, eds. *Edward Corwin's The Constitution and What It Means Today.* Princeton, NJ: Princeton University Press, 1978.

Cooper, Andrew F., and Jorge Heine. *The Oxford Handbook of Modern Diplomacy.* Oxford, UK: Oxford University Press, 2015.

Crabb, Cecil V., Jr., and Pat Holt. *Invitation to Struggle.* 4th ed. Washington, DC: CQ, 1992.

Fisher, Louis. *Presidential War Power.* 2nd rev. ed. Lawrence: University Press of Kansas, 2004.

Houghton, David Patrick. *A Citizen's Guide to American Foreign Policy: Tragic Choices and the Limits of Rationality.* New York: Routledge, 2014.

Hunt, Michael H. *Ideology and U.S. Foreign Policy.* New Haven, CT: Yale University Press, 2007.

Kaufman, Joyce. *A Concise History of U.S. Foreign Policy.* 3rd ed. Lanham, MD: Rowman & Littlefield, 2013.

Keohane, Robert, and Joseph S. Nye Jr. *Power and Interdependence.* 4th ed. Longman Classics in Political Science. New York: Longman, 2011.

Kissinger, Henry. *Diplomacy.* Reprint. New York: Simon & Schuster, 1995.

Lasswell, Harold D. *National Security and Individual Freedom.* New York: McGraw-Hill, 1950.

Lott, Trent, and Tom Daschle. *Crisis Point: Why We Must—and How We Can—Overcome Our Broken Politics in Washington and Across America.* London: Bloomsbury Press, 2016.

Lovell, John. "From Defense Policy to National Security: The Tortuous Adjustment for American Military Professionals." *Air University Review* (May–June 1981): 15–20.

Mann, Thomas E., and Norman J. Ornstein. *Even Worse Than It Looks: How the American Constitutional System Collided with the New Politics of Extremism.* New York: Basic, 2013.

Manning, Bayless. "The Congress, the Executive, and Intermestic Affairs: Three Proposals." *Foreign Affairs*, January 1977, 306–24.

Milner, Helen, and Dustin Tingley. *Sailing the Water's Edge: The Domestic Politics of American Foreign Policy*. Princeton, NJ: Princeton University Press, 2015.

Neack, Laura. *The New Foreign Policy: Complex Interactions, Competing Interests*. 3rd ed. Lanham, MD: Rowman & Littlefield, 2013.

O'Neill, Tip, and Gary Hymel. *All Politics Is Local: And Other Rules of the Game*. Avon, MA: Adams, 1995.

Persily, Nathan, ed. *Solutions to Political Polarization in America*. New York: Cambridge University Press, 2015.

Posen, Barry R. *Restraint: A New Foundation for U.S. Grand Strategy*. Cornell Studies in Security Affairs. Ithaca, NY: Cornell University Press, 2014.

Sides, John, and Daniel J. Hopkins, eds. *Political Polarization in American Politics*. London: Bloomsbury Academics, 2015.

Siracusa, Joseph M. *Diplomacy: A Very Short Introduction*. Oxford: Oxford University Press, 2010.

Snow, Donald M. *National Security*. 6th ed. New York: Routledge, 2017.

Snow, Donald M., and Eugene Brown. *Beyond the Water's Edge: An Introduction to U.S. Foreign Policy*. New York: St. Martin's, 1997.

Thurber, James A., and Antoine Yoshinaka, eds. *American Gridlock: The Sources, Character, and Impact of Political Polarization*. New York: Cambridge University Press, 2015.

Zakaria, Fareed. *The Post-American World: Release 2.0*. New York: Norton, 2012.

Zeihan, Peter. *The Next Generation of American Preeminence and the Coming Global Disorder*. New York: Twelve, 2014.

2 Brother, Can You Paradigm? 1945 to the Present

No image symbolizes the change in the American foreign policy problem more than the World Trade Center towers ablaze on September 11, 2001.

Preview

American foreign policy currently lacks an organizing model, or paradigm, around which to organize its foreign policy responses toward the world. This means there is disagreement on what kinds of threats exist, their severity, and what patterned responses the country should make to different challenges. This condition handicaps the ability to reach coherent policy solutions to different problems and simply inflames already existing political animosities at the intermestic intersection. To understand this problem and its dynamics, the chapter first looks at the role of foreign policy and the need for an organizing concept—a paradigm—for viewing and responding to international challenge. It then applies the discussion to the three distinct foreign policy environments of the post–World War II environment. The first is the Cold War, which featured a truly monumental Soviet threat and a consensus on a paradigm with which to deflect that threat. The second and third periods—the post–Cold War era of the 1990s and the post-9/11 era since—have not produced a consensus on either the exact nature of the threat or on paradigmatic responses to conditions. It is not clear when or whether this will change.

Key Concepts

paradigm	rollback
threat	Potemkin village
national interest	fault line
risk	bipolar
strategy	unipolar
policy	multipolar
cold war paradigm	peace dividend
Cuban Missile Crisis	strategic uncertainty
superpower	international terrorism
deterrence	Carter Doctrine
deadliness	existential threats
danger	asymmetrical warfare
containment	

A sizable part of the disarray in contemporary foreign policy arises from differences, often fundamental, on the two most basic questions that face the foreign policy maker. The first question concerns the nature of the environment, and particularly areas of hostility toward the United States that must be addressed for the United States to protect and promote its interests. The second question is what the United States can do to reduce the risks associated with those problems. Put more simply, what is the problem? And what can we do about it? Unfortunately, neither Americans nor their leaders agree on the answers to either concern.

The result is an absence of consistent approaches to world affairs and the American role in managing those affairs. The government is regularly accused of lacking a "strategy" to deal with particular problems as they arise, and that criticism is not without merit. What that condition reflects, however, is a deeper disagreement on an *overall* worldview from which to craft consistent responses that will ameliorate problems that are faced. In other words, the United States lacks a **paradigm** around which to organize policy. This condition both results from and is exacerbated by the general lack of agreement politically across the board in the country. It is a situation inherited by the Trump administration.

The basic function of foreign policy is dealing with **threats** to the country's **national interests.** Every country, including the United States, has interests in the world. These interests are roughly defined as desirable or necessary conditions that enable the country to pursue or protect what it considers important. Traditionally these interests are divided into *vital* and *less-than-vital* (LTV) categories, where the denial of vital interests is considered intolerable and the denial of LTV interests is considered inconveniencing or undesirable but not intolerable. Threats, on the other hand, are actions or statements of intention adversely to affect those interests, in the foreign policy case by other states or non-state actors. How important those threats are, and thus what one may contemplate doing about them, depends on the nature of the interest threatened: a threat against a vital interest will normally cause the consideration of more severe responses than a threat to an LTV.

The problem with interests and threats is that they are subjective, meaning different people view them differently. At the extreme, there is general agreement that the Soviet threat to destroy the United States with nuclear weapons during the Cold War was a very real threat to a vital interest (the survival of the United States) and demanded a determined response, whereas a Honduran threat to stop sending bananas to this country would be regarded as less serious, since there are other sources of the fruit.

Most real-world situations, however, are less unambiguous and thus are matters of disagreement. Most Americans agree that the Islamic State (IS or ISIS) represents a threat to the United States, but not on exactly what that threat is or what exact interests it imperils. The problem arises because not everyone perceives their interests the same way, and different people feel threatened to different degrees by different sources of possible imperilment. Where there is consensus on interests and threats, forming a general or specific national posture about how to deal with them is relatively straightforward. Where there is disagreement—as there is now—a common approach is more difficult if not impossible to achieve.

The subjectivity of interests and threats complicates developing policy and can make political consensus more difficult to achieve. The reason is straightforward. Subjectivity means that different people can perceive different interests, put them in different orders of priority, and thus create a long list whose priorities are the subject of disagreement. Subjectivity also exists in the nature of threats: some people feel threatened or concerned by conditions that do not threaten others. Resolving these differences is at the heart of politics.

The result is **risk.** As Snow has developed the concept elsewhere (see *Thinking about National Security* or *National Security*, Sixth Edition), risk is the gap between perceptions of threat and the ability to counteract the threats one faces. It can be depicted in a heuristic formula: Risk = Threats – Capability ($R = T - C$). Threats consist of all the threatening conditions people perceive, and capability is the ability to counter and negate those threats. Since threats are subjective and expandable, they will exceed capabilities to deal with all of them. Those situations that are left unattended are at risk. Whether risk is tolerable depends on whether an unattended risk is viewed as very important—like a vital interest—by whoever is making the assessment. That judgment, of course, is also a matter of disagreement.

These dynamics create the parameters within which foreign policy can be made. A coherent, consistent, and effective foreign policy (which everyone agrees they want) must try to organize the efforts of the government to deal with the challenges the environment presents. One way to think about the problem of dealing with developing policy in this atmosphere is in terms of the paradigm process, depicted in figure 2.1. The process begins by assessing the nature of the threat that faces the country, and asks several questions. First, what is the nature of the threat? Is it primarily military, economic, or political (the most common categories)? What entity poses the threat? Is it another state, a coalition of states, or a different kind of actor, such as a non-state entity? Is the threat ephemeral in nature, or is it likely to endure over time? In other words, how formidable is the threat?

Second, what is the extent and gravity of the threat? Does it imperil basic security values, such as the existence or integrity of the state or the population, or is it more limited in reach and potential? What interests does it threaten? Are they vital or LTV, and in what ways? If the threat is not countered, what risks will the country have to endure? How tolerable or intolerable are various outcomes in interacting with the threat?

Third, what can be done about the threat? If the threat is important enough that it cannot be allowed to remain an obstacle to realizing the national interests, what actions can be contemplated? Is military force a viable or apparently necessary option? If so, will it work to bring the opponent into compliance with American interests or to remove the opponent from a position where it can continue to threaten interests? What form of military action will be effective? Will the United States have to engage the military instrument of power by itself, or will it be able to enlist the assistance of others? At what price will assistance come? Will the opponent fight in a way that it can be defeated by American forces? What will the cost be of any form of counteraction? Is it acceptable? Is it so important that cost is not a concern?

These are all difficult political questions, the answers to which will differ among individuals and groups responding. To some extent, they will reflect predilections found in the individual inventories in chapter 1. Realists and idealists tend to look at adverse situations through different lenses that suggest different orientations toward threats and their resolution. Liberals tend to be more internationalist in their approaches to problem solving than isolationists, and they also tend to prefer approaching multilateral solutions more favorably than do

Threat Environment $\longrightarrow$ Paradigm $\longrightarrow$ Strategy $\longrightarrow$ Policies

Figure 2.1 Paradigmatic Process

conservatives, who are more likely to either prefer or at least not shy away from unilateral actions.

A unified American view of the world environment seen in these kinds of concerns would make it much easier than a high level of disagreement. As this suggestive list indicates, there are a lot of points on which to disagree, and the more widespread those differences are, the more difficult it is to devise a common vision of the threat that exists and what the United States should do to protect and promote its interests in that environment. The greater the agreement, the easier it is to reach a consensus and to fashion a common national response to it. Conversely, the more disagreement exists, the more difficult is the task. The role of the paradigm is to try to find some common framework within which to confront the threat.

The term "paradigm" is an overused designation in the social sciences. It means, according to the *Oxford Dictionaries*, a "typical example or pattern of something; a model." As it is used here, it refers to an overarching set of ideas that reflect the general orientation that the country has toward its foreign policy interactions with the world, what *Wikipedia* calls "a distinct set of concepts or thought patterns." The paradigm that one chooses includes two basic elements already introduced: a general assessment of the threat environment, notably any overriding threat that may exist; and a general orientation about what must be done to deal effectively with that threat. The latter concern includes an assessment of what actions will be effective in dealing with the threat. To form a paradigm that can be applied to any period, there must be general agreement within the effective political system about these conditions. It is a general statement (or orientation), and its major purpose is to provide guidance for the development of more applied foreign policy strategies and policies.

A **strategy** is a plan of action, a way to achieve foreign policy objectives identified in the paradigm. The root of the term strategy is military, and although it has been appropriated to describe the action plans of other entities such as businesses, its purest meaning is in military terms. Thus, for instance, the major Cold War strategy of the United States was to deter a Soviet attack against the United States using nuclear weapons. To achieve this goal, the United States adopted **policy** (course of action) responses providing large-scale funding for military efforts. This process is discussed in some detail in *Thinking about National Security* and in Drew and Snow, *Making 21st Century Strategy*.

This process and its parts can work in both directions. In developmental terms, the threat produces a need for the paradigm and implementing strategies and policies. A change in the threat environment can render the paradigm irrelevant or in need of modification. The most dramatic example was the end of the Cold War, which invalidated much of the paradigm devised for it. At the same time, the success or failure of implementing policies and strategies can change the calculus: a successful strategy can lessen or obviate the threat; failed policies or strategies can suggest the need for an alteration of the ways of looking at and dealing with the threat. Since the threat environment changes, there may have to be periodic assessments about what does and does not work.

These general descriptions provide a framework within which to examine the evolution of American foreign policy since the end of World War II. The survey does not begin earlier, because prior to the second global conflagration of the last century, American foreign policy was much different than it has been since. The United States was a comparatively minor world player that relished its comparative isolation from world affairs for its first 150 years of existence. After World War II, the United States was thrust onto the center stage of world affairs as a major power, a position it has occupied ever since. Thus, a historical sketch that is particularly applicable to the present can effectively begin with 1945 while recognizing that there are other influences from the more distant American experience.

To organize the discussion, we divide the postwar period into three periods that reflect the chapter's title suggestion. The first is the Cold War between the late 1940s and 1991, when Soviet communism imploded. Among its notable characteristics is that it produced the first truly articulated American approach to world affairs, the **Cold War paradigm**, around which the competition was organized. The second is the post–Cold War period, a respite of sorts between the collapse of the Cold War competition and the emergence of a new overarching threat after the terrorist attacks of September 11, 2001. The third is the post-9/11 period, which extends from the reaction to Al Qaeda's attacks against New York and Washington to the present. A major theme in dealing with both the second and third periods is the absence of a consensual paradigm with which to confront the world. We analyze each using the categories of the paradigm process as an organizing device, partly as a way to order the Trump administration's approach to the problem.

The Cold War World

The Cold War was America's introduction to world leadership, to power politics in which it was a major part, and to central involvement in world politics. Prior to World War II, foreign policy had been a fairly minor and generally noncontroversial part of national political life. This was partly a matter of national predilection that had elevated the policy preference for "splendid isolationism" to a central position, reinforced by the Great Depression of the 1930s, which focused American interests on domestic recovery. The economic downturn was global, but there was little consideration of the depression as an intermestic event. Foreign policy occasionally entered the political fray—as in the Senate's rejection of the Versailles Treaty ending World War I or prewar debates on how to deal with Germany—but these were the exceptions.

The United States could not stand on the postwar sidelines. Virtually all the traditional powers had been badly wounded by the war and were incapable of reasserting leadership ("victors" such as France and Great Britain) or were defeated losers (Germany, Italy, and Japan). The only participants in the war that emerged from the battlefield with significant residual power were the United

States and the Soviet Union. These two countries would have to organize the postwar peace. Since they were wartime allies, it was not clear in 1945 whether they would do so cooperatively or in competition. Increasingly bitter competition prevailed.

The Cold War was not a static, unchanging experience physically or in terms of people's perceptions of it. In the first year or so after the war, it was not entirely clear that the two states would move from friendship to enmity. The United Nations Charter, the document around which the postwar peace was designed, made specific provision either for a continuation of the wartime collaboration or for conflict and rivalry: the operative provisions of the charter for organizing the peace (Chapter VII) were premised on cooperation, but Article 51 also allowed for the formation of alliances by the major states in case a cooperative model of peace was not sustainable.

The principal criterion for the collective security system proposed in the charter was agreement between the two states that there was an order that both could support, and that was the Achilles' heel of the arrangement. Both countries were ideologically evangelical: the American gospel was capitalist economics and political democracy, whereas the Soviets espoused socialist economics and practiced political authoritarianism as a necessary tool to lead to the communist millennium. Not only were these two philosophies strongly held, but both sides sought to spread their gospel at the expense of the other. They could not coexist indefinitely, and neither side could support or promote conditions that led to the success of the other. Historians still argue about whether the outcome had to be as severe as the Cold War was; there is less doubt that some level of rivalry and conflict was inevitable.

The relationship changed. What became the Cold War was joined in the 1940s, as the Soviet Union established communist puppet regimes in the Eastern European states it occupied as an artifact of the wartime alliance, and the United States reinforced Western-style democracy in the states of Western Europe. In 1949, the NATO Treaty that emerged from the Vandenberg-Truman collaboration "at the water's edge" became the first peacetime military alliance in American history, and collective security as envisaged in the UN Charter became the competition's first casualty. The North Korean invasion of South Korea, undertaken with Soviet blessing, symbolized the joining of the competition.

The Cold War was at its height during the 1950s. During this period, there was widespread belief in the mounting horror of the competition. Senator Joseph McCarthy (R-WI) led purges against supposed communists in the State Department and eventually the U.S. Army (which led to his undoing); the pursuit of suspected communists in the entertainment industry led to the destruction of the careers of many performers due to "blacklisting"; and Americans seriously debated whether it was better to surrender to the inevitability of communist victory in the Cold War ("Better Red Than Dead") or to go down in flames in a nuclear holocaust ("Better Dead Than Red"). The country became bitterly divided about internal divisions in ways that are currently familiar.

The turning point of the Cold War was the **Cuban Missile Crisis** of 1962, an event precipitated by active Soviet plans to install offensive nuclear weapons aimed at the United States on the island of Cuba (see Allison, Kennedy, and Thompson for details). As Soviet ships bearing the missiles steamed toward Cuba where the U.S. Navy awaited them, the crisis was the closest the two countries had or would ever come to nuclear war. When the Soviet ships stopped short of a confrontation, the crisis passed, but the experience chastened both sides. Before the crisis, it was assumed that the competition was totally intractable and that the two sides had no common ground between them; after the crisis they both gradually realized a shared interest in avoiding mutual annihilation. Ironically, as this recognition set in and the two sides gradually moved to defuse the confrontational elements of the relationship, the nuclear arsenals that made the prospects of war so apocalyptic continued to grow until both sides had well over 10,000 nuclear warheads aimed at the territory of the other.

Although it was not widely recognized at the time, the missile crisis was the critical watershed in the Cold War. Before the confrontation over "the missiles of October," dangerous confrontations were routine and the assumption of war inevitable. After the crisis, the relationship gradually relaxed, as chess masters, concert pianists, and even hockey teams from one country visited the other. The tenor remained adversarial enough that it would require a largely unanticipated traumatic event to end the Cold War.

Nature of the Threat

The Cold War was a political, economic, and especially a military confrontation between two rival systems that disagreed philosophically and practically on just about everything. Both had theological worldviews they sought to spread and which they believed could only triumph at the expense of the other; it was a zero-sum competition. The political and economic competitions were more transitory: the Soviets promised liberation and freedom but did not practice it, and experience eventually demonstrated that Marxist economics simply could not compete with Western constructs. Both these deficiencies reduced their appeal. The heart of the competition was thus the military confrontation between the two **superpowers**, a term devised largely to indicate their military prowess in the world. Military power, capped by nuclear capabilities, was the centerpiece of the competition. This physical threat remained until the end of the Cold War and formed the basis around which policy and strategy revolved.

This structure of the threat continued throughout the Cold War period, but its dynamics changed. In the years before the missile crisis, much of the relationship was on preparation for a war that many on both sides believed was inevitable. This sentiment was particularly strong in the1950s and included the development of a fatalistic culture symbolized by motion pictures such as *On the Beach* and *Dr. Strangelove*. The missile crisis sobered these calculations, and the focus shifted to **deterrence**, the avoidance of war by convincing the opponent not to start it. Ironically, throughout the period military arsenals (especially nuclear) continued to grow, increasing the **deadliness** of war (making its consequences much more destructive) and simultaneously convincing leaders that it must not occur, thereby decreasing the **danger** of war (the likelihood that it would occur). In the end, it can be argued (as I have in *The Necessary Peace*) that the entire enterprise became ritualistic, an exercise to prevent a war the avoidance of which was the major purpose of the exercise.

The way Americans viewed the nature of the competition partly defined the nature of the threat. At the risk of some simplification, the American perception can be described in four ways. First, the competition was pervasive: the clash between communism and non-communism affected or was based on divisions that permeated the national existence. As long as the competition remained, nothing else was entirely secure or safe. Second, the competition was intractable: the gains of one side came at the expense of the other, and policy areas where cooperation could produce mutually beneficial outcomes were inconceivable. Third, the Cold War was protracted (to borrow a term popularized by Yugoslav critic Milovan Djilas at the time). The competition was going to last for a long time, possibly indefinitely, and only vigilance could keep it from becoming worse.

The fourth perceived characteristic derived from the others and was in many ways most important: the Cold War was endless, with no positive outcome likely or, in the view of many, possible. There were three ways to look at the future and possible conclusions to the competition. One was a peaceful resolution where one side or the other peacefully capitulated. A few savants such as diplomat George F. Kennan and New York senator Daniel Patrick Moynihan predicted the eventual collapse of the Soviet Union, a dynamic discussed in intersection 2.1, but most people believed the Soviet Union was such a powerful and vibrant dictatorship that this could not happen. Successful Soviet subversion of the West seemed more plausible to many observers. Second, the Cold War could turn "hot." The devolution to war between the systems, which many felt was inevitable eventually, likely entailed a nuclear war that neither could win, that could destroy global society, and thus was to be avoided at all costs.

That left the perpetuation of the Cold War as the only acceptable alternative. It was certainly less unacceptable than the fiery Armageddon of a nuclear war or the victory of communism. Since the capitulation of communism seemed a fool's dream that could not occur, keeping the Cold War at least "cool" had to be the object of policy. It was not a pleasing prospect, because the danger of war could never be eliminated altogether while the competition existed—a grisly prospect at best. After the Cuban Missile Crisis, both sides worked to reduce this danger, but it could never be eliminated altogether. Still, maintaining the Cold War seemed preferable to the other plausible outcomes.

The Cold War Paradigm

By the start of the Korean War in 1950, there was virtually universal agreement among Americans about the nature of the threat posed by Soviet-led communism. This growing consensus allowed the United States to rally around a common approach "at the water's edge" in support of the extraordinary step of entering into NATO under bipartisan leadership and in taking on the task of restoring South Korean sovereignty after the invasion. It continued to grow during the 1950s and through the trauma of the Missile Crisis. Only after an apparent misapplication of its tenets in Vietnam were serious questions raised about it. Still, its underlying premises remained intact until—and arguably after—the problem for which this consensus was forged had disappeared.

The heart of the Cold War paradigm arose from a common perception of the overarching Soviet threat. Its core was that the threat was ubiquitous and that it was directed at the most basic vital American interest, self-preservation of American freedom and the maintenance of the American way of life. There was little doubt in the minds of many Americans that the Soviets desired to destroy the United States by imposing "godless communism" on Americans, that such an occurrence was intolerable, and that the most extraordinary steps were both necessary and acceptable to prevent these unacceptable outcomes. British Prime Minister Sir Winston Churchill captured the sobriety in 1947 with his ominous pronouncement that an "iron curtain" had descended upon and divided Europe.

There were dissenters, but they were few and generally consigned to the political fringes. As noted in the last chapter, the original focus of concern was on Europe and the Soviet threat, and some people on the political right argued that it underemphasized Asia and thus led to the "fall" of China to communist rule in 1949. Part of the alarm the threat created led to the suspicion that the omnipresent, virtually omnipotent "international communist conspiracy" had permeated much of American society, resulting in calls to purge major institutions of this befouling influence. When Americans protested the excesses of these purge attempts, they were often branded as subversives by zealous advocates. As American schoolchildren obediently stuck their heads under their school desks during nuclear "duck and cover" drills, the result was a period of xenophobic repressiveness that permeated American society through the 1950s.

The focus of the paradigm, however, was on the external threat posed by the Soviets, and on this dimension, there was virtual consensus among Americans. The Soviet threat to conquer the United States seemed real and its avoidance absolutely necessary. In much of the early Cold War, communism seemed to be on the march at the expense of the United States: the Soviets exploded their first nuclear device in 1949 and kept pace when the United States perfected the first fission-fusion (thermonuclear hydrogen) bomb in 1952. The Soviets beat the Americans into space with the launch of *Sputnik*, a rocket propelling the first satellite into orbit and the harbinger of intercontinental ballistic missiles (ICBMs) with nuclear warheads capable of direct attacks on American soil and against which there was no known defense. In 1959, Soviet Premier Nikita S. Khrushchev banged his shoe on the desk at the United Nations and declared, "We will bury you." He said this referred to the triumph of the Soviet economic system over its American counterpart, but many Americans wondered if he did not have something entirely more ominous in mind.

This set of perceptions allowed a consensus to develop around a common perception of the world, allowing the development and acceptance of the Cold War paradigm. The assessment began with a general agreement among citizens and politicians about the nature, extent, and consequences of the threat if American action did not effectively counter it. The extent of this consensus seems amazing in the contemporary context in which there is little agreement on anything. Its content was also remarkable for a country that had not faced a formidable and committed foe in peacetime and was not used to the idea of national sacrifice that this perception would entail.

The assessment of threat dictated the general content of the American paradigmatic response. Given the nature and designs of the opposition, the American people and their government would have to unite in a common politico-economic and military effort aimed at frustrating and eventually defeating the Soviet opposition. The focus of this effort would have to be the Soviet Union, since it was believed to be the puppet master of the communist conspiracy. The Sino-Soviet split in the latter 1950s added China to the list of communist states that had to be frustrated.

Acceptance and implementation of the implications of this paradigmatic construct occurred with virtually no political opposition. In 1952, Dwight D. Eisenhower, the Republican candidate who had led the military effort in World War II, was elected overwhelmingly both on a pledge to end American military presence in Korea and on the belief that he would be better able to implement the military implications of the paradigm. The Cold War paradigm became the basis of American national security efforts for nearly four decades, virtually without dissent. The fact that it was able to endure and be translated into a strategy and series of policies with hardly any political dissent is testimony to the nature of the circumstances in which it was fashioned.

Cold War Strategy and Policies

The fundamental construct by which the United States implemented the Cold War paradigm was the strategy of **containment**. The principal author of this strategy was a career American diplomat who served in the American embassy in Moscow in the years immediately after World War II, George F. Kennan. He first articulated what became the containment strategy in a 1947 article in the magazine *Foreign Affairs*, "The Sources of Soviet Conduct," under the official authorship of "X" to avoid identifying him to the Soviets and thus causing him to be declared persona non grata and expelled from the USSR.

The heart of containment rested, in essence, on two major premises, one of which formed the basis of the policy and the other of which became prophetic when the strategy succeeded. Acknowledging the considerable challenge that an aggressive communist state posed, Kennan argued that the Soviet threat could nonetheless be blunted by a policy that thwarted the expansion of its domain—the touchstone of the policy of containment.

Kennan's policy became the heart of the Cold War paradigm because it answered both questions that a paradigm should address. It argued that the Soviets indeed posed a fundamental challenge, because their ideology told them that their triumph over capitalism was inevitable and that their system was the wave of the global future. Given this messianic vision, Soviet communism was necessarily expansionist, and Soviet military power posed a threat entirely worthy of opposition if American vital interests at home and elsewhere in the world (notably Europe) were to be protected.

The second part of the paradigm argued that the policy of containment could succeed. Soviet belief in the inevitability of their triumph, fortuitously enough, meant that the communists were obliged neither to rush or force the historically inevitable triumph of their system nor to act in precipitous ways that might jeopardize the inevitable. Thus, a policy that prevented their expansion could be tolerated for the time being, since it appeared to present only a delay of their inevitable success. Kennan also argued that the Soviet system was basically flawed in economic and political terms that would eventually lead to its implosion if it was isolated long enough—a part of the policy that was largely ignored as improbable at the time.

There was some resistance to containment when it was proposed and as it evolved. The heart of that opposition, familiar in the current environment, was that the policy was too passive; the opposition advocated a more proactive stance. In the early 1950s, for instance, some conservative strategists argued for a policy known as **rollback**, the major premise of which was that containment was too passive and that the United States should assist dissidents in communist-occupied areas to overthrow their communist dictators and thus effectively roll back the boundaries of communist domain. Kennan warned that an important characteristic of the Soviet empire was the insecurity of its rulers, who could not accept challenges to their empire and might respond like caged animals, lashing out at such attempts. Confronted with the possible repercussions of coming to the aid of rebels in the Hungarian Revolution of 1956, the advocates of rollback gradually backed off their advocacy.

In the late 1940s, the United States was not well prepared to implement the policy of containment, and it had to develop a series of what were, in historical perspective, revolutionary policies that would have been unthinkable in other periods of peace. At the end of World War II, the United States had characteristically responded largely by demobilizing its armed forces from more than 12 million in 1945 to less than a million in 1946. Institutionally, the prewar maze of jurisdictions within government that had hindered the war effort (e.g., separate independent Departments of the Army and Navy) returned. This pattern was clearly inadequate to deal with a comprehensive national security threat and response. The large and symbolic response was the National Security Act, first passed in 1947 and modified to something like its present configuration in 1949. The act is described in more detail in chapter 5, but its major intents were to unify the national security effort both politically through the creation of the National Security Council (NSC) and militarily by combining the military services within the Department of Defense (DOD), while creating new national security entities such as the CIA and an independent air force. There were some minor complaints (the Department of the Navy, for instance, resisted the loss of its independent ability to lobby Congress for funds once it was folded into the DOD), but the universal acceptance of threat and the need to counter it created virtual unanimity that allowed the paradigm to be accepted and implemented.

One of the most remarkable public indications of support came in the military procurement system. Throughout most of its history, the United States had relied on volunteer forces during peacetime, as it does today. It only engaged in involuntary procurement of armed forces (conscription or a draft) during times of national military emergency, such as the American Civil War (both sides) and the World Wars, disbanding those forces once the emergency was overcome. The country demobilized in 1945, and as a consequence, was caught unprepared when the Korean War broke out. In the wake of that experience, a peacetime draft—a very radical idea given American history—was instituted. The perception of threat was so great and the consensus about countering it was so compelling that the draft was accepted almost universally. Only the preponderance of conscripts serving and dying in the Vietnam War raised enough opposition to lead to its abandonment. The roughly twenty-year period of peacetime conscription is a monument to the perceived potency of the Cold War threat and the consensus behind a largely militarily driven paradigm to counter it. Such a consensus developing behind a return to the draft today is virtually unthinkable, although a few analysts believe it would be desirable to engage the public more fully in proposed military solutions to national problems.

The End of the Cold War

The Cold War came to an official end at the end of 1991, when the Soviet hammer and sickle flag was lowered from the Kremlin and the Russian tricolor replaced it on January 1, 1992. In the end, the kinds of internal contradictions that Kennan proclaimed, rather than the claims of a growing, increasingly omnipotent Soviet threat, proved to be true. The Soviet Union was exposed as essentially a **Potemkin village**, as captured in intersection 2.1.

Intersection 2.1   The Soviet Potemkin Village

A Potemkin village is a false front, a construct deliberately raised to create an inflated image of what it portrays. The genesis of the term was the 1787 attempt by Russian nobleman Grigory Potemkin to deceive the Tsarina Catherine II of the prosperity of the Crimea by erecting false fronts on buildings during her tour of the region to create the false impression of affluence and grandeur. Many historians question the literal truth of the analogy. But false fronts have been called Potemkin villages ever since.

The Soviet false front had political, military, and economic bases. Politically, there was the myth that brutal authoritarian rule had hammered the Soviet population into acceptance of Soviet rule, when in fact it had driven opposition underground. This myth was deflated as dissent grew within the Soviet Union as Eastern European countries revolted against communist rule. Militarily, the omnipotence of the Soviet military machine, largely based on their nuclear arsenal, was deflated by the poor performance of the Soviet armed forces in Afghanistan and their humiliating retreat from that country in 1989. Economically, the regime of Mikhail Gorbachev revealed that Soviet economic performance had been flat since the early 1970s—what was called the "era of stagnation"—and that unless the country entered the global economy, it would fall increasingly behind the rest of the world and become, as some analysts put it, a "frozen banana republic." The Soviets were able to mask these conditions for a long time, but eventually the ruse caught up with them by the end of the 1980s (see Snow, *The Shape of the Future,* for a more detailed description).

In the end, Kennan's admonitions about the internal contradictions of the Soviet system proved correct. His patient strategy of containing the Soviets that was the basis of the Cold War paradigm was effective, and the Soviet Union, along with most of the clone regimes it had imposed elsewhere, simply imploded; by the end of the century, only four communist regimes still existed in the world: in two of them (China and Vietnam), Marxist economics—the core of communist distinction from the West—had been essentially abandoned, leaving only two remaining "true believers," North Korea and Cuba. The West had won the Cold War.

The victory was initially hard for many to accept. A great deal of analysis and preparation had been made based on a vital, muscular Soviet Union, and it was difficult to accept that it had mostly been a Potemkin illusion. Moreover, almost everyone who had looked at the future rejected how the Cold War might end: apocalypse and a perpetual contest seemed the only possible options; the idea that the West would prevail and the Cold War would end with a whimper rather than a bang, which had been dismissed as fuzzy-minded, naïve thought came true. The disbelief was captured well in a 1990 article by political scientist John Mearsheimer, "Why We Will Soon Miss the Cold War."

The end of the Cold War was a difficult concept to accept, although eventually the reality set in. What has been a more difficult adjustment has been to the Cold War paradigm that organized American foreign and national security policy. The whole paradigm had assumed the specific threat of a global communist threat centered, organized, and directed out of a Soviet Union that no longer existed. Without the threat, was the paradigm a viable construct within which to continue to organize the world? That question is still relevant today.

The Post–Cold War World

The collapse of the Soviet Union and its ripple effects throughout the communist bloc and in East-West relations was the first **fault line** of the post–World War II period. The idea of a fault line is that a fundamental change occurs within the dynamics of international interactions because of some change in the structure of the ongoing system. In this particular case, the demise of the Soviet threat and the consequent collapse of communist rule in most of the world represented such a change. The events of September 11, 2001, would reveal a second fault line.

The Cold War international system was profoundly **bipolar**, a condition in which two major states (the U.S. and the USSR) possessed overwhelming power and in which the two powers—or "poles"—were able to aggregate others around them and in which their subsequent competitive interaction was the overriding international dynamic. In this all-encompassing competition, foreign policy effectively became national security policy, with the major criteria for most foreign policy actions measured against their likely impact on the competition and especially the danger that any act might grease the slippery slope toward war. This meant distorting some matters that had little or no inherent communist-anticommunist content but came to be thought of in Cold War terms—the emergence of the developing world and casting its developmental needs in terms of the competition is the most obvious and lasting example.

And then one pole dissolved. When the Russian tricolor rose in Moscow, what was left of the Soviet Union was Russia, a series of former Soviet Republics that had declared and gained independence, and non-communist regimes emerging in Eastern Europe. Communism rapidly dissembled as a rival to the American-led West, leaving only one standing pole. The world was suddenly **unipolar** (containing only one major power) or emerging as a **multipolar** system where there would be several independent sources of power in the world.

Nature of the Threat

The end of the Cold War was breathtaking, exciting, and cautionary. It figuratively took away the breath of most observers and policy makers because it was so unexpected and, for most, inconceivable that little thought had gone into anticipating how it might happen and what the implications would be. It was exciting because it offered the prospect of liberation from the awful prospect of a civilization-ending nuclear war that had been the grimmest prospect of the Cold War. It was cautionary because it was so hard to believe and because so little thought had gone into what would happen next.

One of the most obvious and dramatic effects of the end of the Cold War was to erase the Soviet threat on which the Cold War paradigm had been built. The implementation of this construct had been going on for more than forty years. It was an elaborate model of national security preparations and sacrifices to deter a threat that no longer existed, and it had become the intellectual way of life for many policy makers and civilian and uniformed implementers who suddenly faced an environment that was potentially very different and for which they had spent virtually no time preparing. In this circumstance, the first reactions of many were to deny the fundamental nature of change, to warn that it was reversible (thus requiring continued traditional vigilance), or to soldier on as if things had not really changed. The prospect that somehow something like the threat of the Cold War might return was almost alluring, because it fit into a construct with which those who made and implemented the outgrowths of the paradigm were familiar and comfortable. Thus, one reaction was to warn, fervently but somehow comfortingly, that the "bad old days" of the Cold War threat could return. Those thoughts dominated the immediate aftermath of the Cold War; to some extent, they still do.

Once the reality of the Cold War's end had sunk in, it became clear that there was no equivalent threat in the world or on the horizon, and the result was a transition to a fairly tranquil period in which calculation of the threat receded. In that atmosphere, expenditures on the accoutrement of the competition—notably military spending—came under scrutiny, and advocates waxed rhapsodic over the prospects of a **peace dividend**, savings in reduced defense spending that could be put to other uses.

Threats did not disappear altogether, but they were less compelling and consistent. Instability in Somalia led to an abortive American intervention, the United States sent troops to Haiti to curb instability, and in the second half of the 1990s moved into the Balkans—Bosnia-Herzegovina and later Kosovo. At the same time, it stood by idly during the genocidal rampage in Rwanda. All the triggering events were upsetting, but none clearly imperiled vital American interests, and none posed a threat to the United States even vaguely resembling the Soviet threat. Terrorism began to emerge during the decade and the name Al Qaeda became familiar to terrorism experts but did not permeate the public perception for the balance of the decade. The threat that had formed the touchstone of the Cold War and the response to it were gone. The fact that the threat was not replaced with another compelling substitute, however, meant that there was no compelling reason to work very hard at crafting a replacement.

The Paradigm

The 1990s produced neither a successor paradigm nor a meaningful modification of the Cold War construct. Partly, there was confusion about how the disintegration of operational communism affected the threat: what threat would the successor state of Russia pose? Would the Eastern European countries evolve peacefully or create a new menace in Europe? Would China simply replace the Soviet Union as the new leader of communist threat? To planners and policy makers accustomed to working in a high-threat environment, "worst case planning" seemed the logical, comfortable way to proceed. None of their worst nightmares came to fruition as the millennium wound to an end, but since no other major threats did emerge, their actions were harmless enough. Searching for new monsters may have done little good, but it also did little harm.

In these circumstances, there was little alteration of the basic foreign policy paradigm, although it addressed a problem that no longer existed. Part of the reason was that little thought had gone into crafting an alternative, since the Cold War problem was viewed as perpetual and the paradigm had worked to manage the threat. Planners were caught flat-footed both by the demise of the Cold War and about alternate futures. For most within the policy community, thinking based around the Cold War threat had become such an ingrained part of their political existence that moving "outside the box" to view qualitatively different scenarios and possibly radically different solutions simply went beyond their conceptual comfort zones. The bad days, in one form or another, could always come back, and the Cold War construct had been durable. Why scrap it now?

There was another side to this implicit resistance. The Cold War paradigm had, after all, been implemented through a series of policies and strategies that had formed the basis for the national security state. The strategy of containment had created a worldwide web of commitments and interests for the United States around the containment line (the outward boundary of countries with communist governments) and had created ties with many regimes both for security and other purposes that could not easily be jettisoned with communism in retreat. At the same time, the policy process had restructured that part of government devoted to foreign and national security affairs by adding new functions and structures such as a large intelligence community that could not easily be disassembled. Within the implementing military arena, the United States had constructed a large, highly capable, and expensive military machine and establishment of people dependent upon it, such as workers in defense industries and support facilities around military bases. Each of these provided an inertial drag on change, and especially at the top in terms of paradigmatic questioning.

Strategies and Policies

The 1990s were not a period of great strategic or policy change. Some saw the dissembling of the Cold War threat as a positive step that might allow reductions in spending on the constructs of the national security state. The peace dividend was never realized: there were reductions in areas such as military workforce, but these cuts were by and large replaced by defense spending in other areas such as military modernization. The savings that were the promise of the dividend were largely unrealized; Americans felt relieved of the constant, stressful burden of the Cold War and preferred to look inward rather than outward at foreign policy.

If there was a strategic principle that emerged during this period, it was **strategic uncertainty**, the idea that in an environment where there was no concrete opponent, the real threat came from the unknown, unforeseen, and unforeseeable. In some ways, an uncertain threat was a more difficult opponent than a concrete foe, against which one could plan and implement action: if the Soviets built additional battle tanks (a Soviet proclivity), the answer was to increase one's arsenal of antitank weapons. When the enemy was an unknown quantity, such planning was not possible, and one could only speculate at the challenge that might lie ahead. Worst-case planning suggested that if one could not specify what threat to prepare for, the prudent approach was to prepare for all possible contingencies. Such preparation was speculative and probably inefficient, since it meant preparing for a whole range of possibilities that would never occur, but was, according to critics such as Bacevich and Klare, all those favoring large defense expenditures had to argue for. Like threat perceptions generally, however, the list of potentially imperiling situations was highly expandable and debatable. Disagreement about what threats were likely and dangerous was highly subjective. Different observers could make different assessments of individual possibilities and their implications, largely budgetary.

The absence of serious challenges to the status quo and to the most important American interests leavened the foreign policy debate. The worst fears did not materialize. Most of Eastern Europe made a smooth transition to political democracy and joined the West, and many of the former Soviet republics did the same. The exceptions were in the multinational areas in both places. Multiethnic Yugoslavia was torn apart by its ethnic groups, the Czechs and Slovaks ended their mutual association by splitting Czechoslovakia into two states, and the former states of the Caucasus region and Crimea became restive as the old Soviet Union reconfigured. None of these events threatened the international order or American interests greatly. China decided to join the Western economic system rather than pose a military threat. It was a decade in which it was possible to, in an old phrase, to "sweat the small stuff" in terms of foreign policy activism and activity. As the twenty-first century dawned, that tranquil situation was about to change.

The End of the Post–Cold War World

The second post–Cold War fault line, the terrorist attacks of September 11, 2001, brought to an end the relative foreign policy tranquility of the post–Cold War period. The attacks had their roots in the 1990s and before. Al Qaeda, the terrorist organization that carried out the 9/11 attacks, was an artifact of the end of the Soviet occupation of Afghanistan in 1989, composed mostly of foreign fighters who had been part of the *mujahidin* resistance to the Soviets, and they had carried out a growing number of attacks against American and other targets in the 1990s. The only such attack on American soil had been in 1993, the first attempt to destroy the World Trade Center towers in New York, an effort that failed. Other examples were overseas, such as attacks against the American barracks in Khobar, Saudi Arabia, in 1996; U.S. embassies in Nairobi, Kenya, and Dar es-Salaam, Tanzania, in 1998; and against the USS *Cole* at anchor in Yemen in 2000. They saved their greatest effort for destroying the World Trade Center towers in New York and damaging the Pentagon in Washington (another attack was thwarted by the passengers of a flight over Pennsylvania).

The result was a game changer. After the relatively tranquil period of the 1990s, the United States was suddenly faced with an apparently new and frighteningly deadly new threat in the form of **international terrorism**. Acts of terrorism are ancient, dating back at least to Biblical times, and have often been used for religious purposes (e.g., the Spanish Inquisition). The United States had endured acts of domestic terrorism before—the assassination of President James Garfield, and the attack on the Murrah Federal Building in Oklahoma City in 1995, to cite two instances. A concerted campaign of foreign terrorism against the country represented, however, a fundamentally different threat and created a concern that endures to the present.

The Post-9/11 World

The response to the 9/11 attacks had two major and highly interrelated effects on American foreign policy, creating a change of focus from traditional emphases. The terrorist threat was the first and most obvious source of change, as the

United States responded with the Global War on Terror (GWOT) and declared the eradication of the terrorist problem as its highest national priority. The other, more subtle and yet equally profound, effect was to bring the Middle East, from which most of the terrorist threat emanated, to the center of American foreign policy concern. Both emphases represented new directions for the United States: terrorism had never been more than a peripheral concern, and the Middle East, despite the addiction Americans had to its oil, had been only one of several geographical points of emphasis. Since 2001, terrorism has provided the basis of threat facing the country, and the Middle East and its problems has been the geographic and substantive heart of most foreign policy energies. President Trump largely inherits the world of 2001.

These two emphases are related in two ways, one obvious and the other not so widely acknowledged. The obvious linkage is that the terrorist threat emerges from a segment of the Islamic population concentrated in the Middle East, so that most of the actions the United States can and has undertaken to deal with it are focused on the region. Less advertised, the United States has become increasingly physically present in the region, and this presence may be linked to why so much of Islamic terrorist concentration has been on the United States, an argument raised in intersection 2.2.

Intersection 2.2 — Oil, Terrorism, and the American Role in the Middle East

American forces remain an active part of Middle Eastern politics and American engagement in it.

The Middle East has not historically been an area of great interest to the United States. Before World War II, the United States developed some interest in Middle Eastern oil, but unlike other powers that lacked domestic supplies of oil, its interests were limited. After the war, however, the United States joined the European powers in trying to ensure continuing American access to that resource. Initially, the vehicle for doing so was the "Seven Sisters" Western oil companies; after 1960, the United States and others had to deal more directly with the Arab countries of the Organization of Petroleum Exporting Countries (OPEC).

This source of interest was not critical until the fall of Shah Reza Pahlavi of Iran in 1979. The Shah and the United States had been closely aligned in a marriage of convenience since 1953: the United States provided developmental and military assistance to the Iranians, and in return, the Iranian military guaranteed the secure flow of Persian Gulf oil to the West. When the Shah was overthrown, that arrangement collapsed, and the United States was faced with a hostile Iran that would not protect the oil flow but might even seek to interfere with it. In 1980, President Jimmy Carter declared that guaranteed access to that oil represented a vital American interest (what became known as the **Carter Doctrine**); President Reagan "reflagged" foreign tankers as American to provide U.S. protection, and the result was a permanent American military presence that continues to this day.

The first concrete manifestations of this presence were American material assistance to Iraq in its 1980–1988 war with Iran and its leadership in evicting the Iraqis from Kuwait in Operation Desert Storm (the first Persian Gulf War) in 1990–1991. It continued through American military interventions in Afghanistan in 2001 and Iraq in 2003 as responses to 9/11 and into ongoing American leadership in the attempt to defeat the Islamic State. Particularly in terms of where the United States uses force, the Middle East is now the center of the action.

Oil *may* also provide a link to the terrorist threat that enlivens U.S. Middle East policy today. It is arguable that the reason so much terrorist activity is directed toward the United States is the American presence in the region and American military actions that have taken the lives of many Middle Easterners, including terrorists. This argument is explored in *The Middle East, Oil, and U.S. National Security Policy* and by Klare. It is no more than a hypothesis, but one that we will explore in chapter 9.

The Nature of the Threat

The emergence and evolution of international terrorism represents the first consensual threat to American vital interests since the dissolution of the Soviet threat. It consists both of the direct challenge posed by the various terrorist organizations against American targets abroad but especially at home and the seedbed of that Hydra-headed threat in the Middle East. In addition, the United States has what have been vital interests in secure access to petroleum and in the security of Israel.

All of these threats are different and changing, and each of them is qualitatively distinct from the threat that framed the Cold War. In direct policy terms, the greatest problem is that posed by international terrorism, because it directly threatens the lives of Americans, the most basic vital interest. That threat is, however, different from its Soviet predecessor. As already argued, the Soviet threat was exceedingly deadly (if war came, the results would have been cataclysmic), but that very deadliness made the confrontation less dangerous, as both sides worked assiduously to deter one another and avoid the deadly explosion. Terrorism, on the other hand, is very dangerous, in that the likelihood of attempted terrorist attacks is very high, but the consequences of terrorist actions are far less deadly (at least for now) in the sense that the consequences of terrorist attacks kill far fewer people than a nuclear exchange would. This distinction is important when the Cold War and the contemporary environment are compared as **existential threats**: terrorists do not threaten national existence with their acts;

the prospects of nuclear war do. Although President Trump has questioned the nature of the U.S.-Russian relationship, no one would argue that the terrorist threat is still lively.

The regional threats are not so immediate. Israel faces a potentially existential threat if it were to be attacked by its Islamic neighbors, but its nuclear arsenal and the general quality of its other forces probably make that problem manageable: the Israelis have deterred existence-threatening threats successfully (see Snow, *Regional Cases in Foreign Policy*, Second Edition, chapter 2 for a discussion) and face mostly terrorist prospects such as those periodically arising in Gaza. Thanks in large measure to the exploitation of alternate sources of petroleum (i.e., shale oil and gas), the United States is no longer critically dependent on Persian Gulf oil, raising some questions about the continuing vitality of the Carter Doctrine as a guiding directive to American foreign policy.

The Paradigm

At the heart of the question about how to deal with and manage the terrorist threat is whether the Cold War paradigm that remains implicitly in place is adequate or appropriate to deal with the set of challenges posed by the post-9/11 world. Terrorism does not pose the same existential threat as did the Cold War, meaning what is to be challenged and managed is different qualitatively. Most notably, the level of desperation is not the same: a failure of policy during the Cold War could conceivably have resulted in the end of human civilization as we know it. The terrorist threat may be equally enduring, but the consequences are not so dire. At the same time, the concrete manifestation of the Cold War was a massive, but conceptually familiar, military conflict between the conventional and military forces of two opponents whose frames of reference for that force were fundamentally the same and were an extension of European politics as it had developed over three hundred years. Terrorism is a hybrid military and nonmilitary problem, and its proponents do not use force in the same ways that its opponents do. As a military contest, combating terrorism requires engaging in **asymmetrical warfare**, the situation where the opponents do not fight in the same way.

In these circumstances, the premises and implications of the Cold War paradigm not only do not clearly hold, but are almost entirely irrelevant to the task at hand. The terrorist threat is not an interstate phenomenon, but rather consists of non-state actors (the pretensions of IS to statehood as the caliphate notwithstanding) who neither settle their differences through conventional channels nor represent sovereign entities with which one can interact. Terrorists, for instance, virtually never negotiate, and they are rarely vulnerable to economic actions against them (once again, IS may be a partial exception). Moreover, they are consummate asymmetrical warriors who do not honor conventions of war and against whom traditional military actions are not generally effective. A framework that works against a traditional opponent like the Soviet Union is not obviously appropriate for this kind of opponent.

Despite these obvious conceptual deficiencies, no alternative paradigm has been proposed or adopted to deal with the threat. Why? The answer lies in the intermestic intersection as it applies to terrorism. The hyperpartisan domestic atmosphere has created political gridlock generally, and this domestic inability of various political actors to interact extends to military matters. Instead of collaborating on a new framework that might organize effective policies and strategies, it is politically easier, even less personally dangerous, simply to condemn the other side and to propose actions straight out of the Cold War playbook. Proposing to send ground troops into Syria to destroy the Islamic State presents a prime example. On the international level, fighting the appeal of a sect of a religion that most Americans do not understand is extraordinarily difficult, making it easier simply to condemn different others because they are different. At the same time, the U.S. military has not (possibly because it cannot) devised a military approach that effectively defeats asymmetrical opponents, especially when those opponents have any level of support in the places from which they launch their activities. Terrorism is more than a military problem, and successfully confronting it requires a paradigm that recognizes these unique properties and proposes ways to deal with them that transcend conventional methods. Such approaches have not been proposed and seem unlikely in the current intermestic environment. Both domestic and international environmental influences have poisoned the intersection, and until the toxins are treated, paradigmatic progress is unlikely.

Strategies and Policies

Given the state of gridlock in American politics and the lack of a coherent viable alternative paradigm from the Trump administration around which to organize policy and strategy, it should be no surprise that innovative strategic and policy adaptation that requires concomitant action from both the executive branch and Congress has been essentially a black hole for most of the period since 2001. The early outrage over the attacks forged a temporary consensus behind something like the GWOT, but that quickly dissipated. It was never entirely clear what the "war" part of the analogy meant, and actions taken under its umbrella in Iraq and Afghanistan proved to be less than a resounding success.

The "villain" in this malaise has been the absence of a commonly held vision about how to confront the terrorist threat. It is currently highlighted by the debate over the Islamic State. Advocates such as President Trump during his 2016 campaign supported using massive American military force to crush and destroy IS by applying America's overwhelmingly superior conventional military might to the task. It is a position that flows from the realist, conservative (most conservatives believe that national defense is one of the few legitimate functions of central government), and unilateralist traditions identified in chapter 1. Opposing advocates are more comfortable with positions that reflect a more restrained, even idealistic view of approaching problems, favor a more expansive role of government, and strongly prefer multilateralist approaches to problems. Each sees the other's orientation as wrongheaded, ineffective, and thus doomed to failure. The central point of debate is over the role of conventional armed forces and whether the injection of more-or-less massive infusions of American ground forces into Iraq and possibly Syria would "win" the contest with IS.

The point is not which side, if either, is correct in its position. Rather, it is to highlight two aspects of the current situation. First, the views are sufficiently different that they cannot both be pursued simultaneously in isolation from the other. Second, the only way to achieve reconciliation is to adopt a new framework within which to organize thinking about and reacting to foreign policy crises as they arise or persist. In the absence of a new paradigm, the executive branch pursues its vision to the extent that it can without congressional assent, and Congress advocates its distinct vision and tries to block contrary policies whenever it can. Those who must fashion and implement policy—principally the military with regard to the Middle East and a combination of military and non-military agencies for dealing with terrorism—must try to devise solutions without much "top-down" guidance.

The End of the 9/11 World

Unlike the other periods included in this chapter, the post-9/11 world environment of threats and problems has not ended and shows little indication that it will soon. The shrinking dependence of the United States on Persian Gulf oil may allow the United States to reduce its physical presence on the Middle East, but the absence of an overall framework leaves unanswered what this reduction should look like, how it should be approached, what its goals are, and what the region and American interests should look like during and after the transition. Presently, there is no real agreement that a reduction in presence is desirable, which is the logical preface to answering the other question.

The reason that there is little agreement on American foreign policy in the Middle East is terrorism. While terrorism originates in that region and is aimed at the United States, there will be an understandable predilection to be present and to try to eliminate the phenomenon at the source. Whether this impulse is valid depends both on the nature of the terrorist threat and what can be done about it. An overall framework for guiding regional foreign policy must begin with agreement on both the nature of the terrorist threat and what can be done about it. Currently a consensus does not exist on either concern, and hence there is no terrorist paradigm around which to organize American foreign policy.

Conclusion

The point of this chapter has extended beyond the sheer chronology of the Cold War to the present. Rather, it has been to suggest that the years since World War II have been marked by three different and distinct foreign policy environments, each with its own dynamics and American responses. The central element in the analysis has been whether the United States developed a coherent framework within which to view the threat environment in which it existed—a paradigm—that could provide a satisfactory way to think about and implement responses to major challenges. The key factors in influencing whether such a paradigm was fashioned were the nature of the threat and general agreement on how to manage it. Both are reflections of external conditions and the domestic political climate, and the crucible from which agreement must come is the intermestic intersection between the two sets of influences.

Clearly, the experience has been mixed. In the immediate post–World War II period, there was sufficient agreement about the nature of the threat to produce a bipartisan interlude "at the water's edge." The result was the development of the Cold War paradigm, the implementation of which managed the competition until the demise of the Soviet opponent and the triumph of the policy of containment. During the 1990s, the threat level was low, and the United States grappled to understand the changes that the end of the Cold War implied. It was not a period in which paradigmatic introspection seemed necessary, and the effort to recalibrate a Cold War paradigm robbed of its threat basis was minimal. The events of 9/11 created a new, worthy successor threat to the Cold War. That threat, however, was different from the Cold War, and it has not been clear that the paradigm for one period can accommodate the other. Despite this concern, very little paradigmatic adjustment has occurred or seems likely in the short run. Such a process is arguably needed to return coherence to the American interface with the world.

For progress to be made, both of the primary environments identified in chapter 1 must change, or at least be perceived differently. The international environment is clearly dangerous if not as deadly as before, but consensus about the exact nature of the danger and how to nullify it has not emerged. We will revisit this problem in chapter 9. Domestically, the cacophony of political dysfunction in the country makes it hard to reach accord on virtually anything, and thus makes crafting a truly national, bipartisan organizing framework almost impossible. Domestic concerns form the heart of chapters 3–8.

Perfect agreement on foreign policy matters is, of course, an ideal rarely if ever achieved. Politics literally ending at the water's edge only occurs in the most extreme circumstances—something like the potential catastrophe of World War II. In less traumatic times, such consensus is the exception, and foreign, like domestic, power is more an "invitation to struggle." The pendulum between the two extremes has swung nearly to the "struggle" extreme, and one wonders what may be necessary to cause that pendulum to swing back to some level of equipoise. One victim of this cacophony has been an agreement on a foreign policy framework: Brother, can you paradigm?

Study/Discussion Questions

1. What is a paradigm? What matters should a paradigm address? Frame your answer in terms of national interests, threats, and risk.
2. What is the paradigm process? What are its constituent parts? Define and discuss each. Apply the process to each of the three periods discussed in the text.
3. What are the three distinct periods of post–World War II U.S. foreign

policy? Briefly describe each, with emphasis on the reasons for transition.
4. Discuss the Cold War period and the Cold War paradigm. How did perceptions allow and facilitate development of the paradigm and its accompanying strategy and policies? Briefly describe each. How did the period end? What impact did that ending have on

the paradigm's role in American foreign policy?

5. Describe the post–Cold War period. What was there about its dynamics that inhibited major modifications of the Cold War paradigm?

6. The events of 9/11 ushered in a third post-1945 period in American foreign policy. Describe the dynamics of that change in threat compared to the Cold War. Why has there not been a major paradigmatic shift accompanying this change?

7. What are the two major points of American foreign policy interest in the post-9/11 world? Briefly describe each. How are they related to one another?

Bibliography

Allison, Graham. *Essence of Decision: Explaining the Cuban Missile Crisis.* Boston: Little, Brown, 1971.

Bacevich, Andrew J. *The Limits of Power: The End of American Exceptionalism.* American Empire Project. New York: Henry Holt, 2009.

Combs, Cynthia. *Terrorism in the Twenty-First Century.* 7th ed. New York: Routledge, 2012.

Djilas, Milovan. *The New Class: An Analysis of the Communist System.* San Diego: Harcourt, Brace, Jovanovich, 1957.

Drew, Dennis M., and Donald M. Snow. *Making 21st Century Strategy: An Introduction to Policy and Problems.* Montgomery, AL: Air University Press, 2006.

Gaddis, John Lewis. *The Cold War: A New History.* Reprint. New York: Penguin, 2006.

———. *George F. Kennan: An American Life.* Reprint. New York: Penguin, 2012.

———. *Strategies of Containment: A Critical Appraisal of American National Security Policy During the Cold War.* Rev. and exp. ed. New York: Oxford University Press, 2005.

Hoffman, Bruce. *Inside Terrorism.* 2nd ed. New York: Columbia University Press, 2006.

Kagan, Robert. "The September 12 Paradigm." *Foreign Affairs,* September/October 2008, 25–39.

Kennan, George F. *Memoirs.* Boston: Little, Brown, 1976.

——— (writing as "X"). "The Sources of Soviet Conduct." *Foreign Affairs,* July 1947, 566–82.

Kennedy, Robert F. *The Thirteen Days: A Memoir of the Cuban Missile Crisis.* New York: Norton, 1999. Originally published 1963.

Klare, Michael. "From Scarcity to Abundance: The New Geopolitics of Energy." *Current History* 116, no. 786 (January 2017): 3–9.

———. *Rogue States and Nuclear Outlaws.* New York: Hill and Wang, 1995.

McCants, William. *The ISIS Apocalypse: The History, Strategy, and Doomsday Vision of the Islamic State.* New York: St. Martin's, 2015.

Mearsheimer, John J. "Why We Will Soon Miss the Cold War." *Atlantic Monthly* 266, no. 2 (August 1990): 35–50.

Nye, Joseph S., Jr. *The Paradox of American Power: Why the World's Superpower Can't Go It Alone.* New York: Oxford University Press, 2003.

Rose, Richard, William Mishler, and Neil Munro. *Russia Transformed: Developing Popular Support for a New Regime.* New York: Cambridge University Press, 2006.

Service, Robert. *The End of the Cold War, 1985–1991.* New York: PublicAffairs, 2015.

Snow, Donald M. *The Middle East, Oil, and U.S. National Security Policy: Intractable Conflicts, Impossible Solutions.* Lanham, MD: Rowman & Littlefield, 2016.

————. *National Security.* 6th ed. New York: Routledge, 2017.

————. *The Necessary Peace: Nuclear Weapons and Superpower Relations.* Lexington, MA: Lexington, 1986.

————. *Regional Cases in Foreign Policy.* 2nd ed. Lanham, MD: Rowman & Littlefield, 2017.

————. *The Shape of the Future: The Post–Cold War World.* 2nd ed. Armonk, NY: Sharpe, 1995.

————. *Thinking about National Security: Strategy, Policy, and Issues.* New York: Routledge, 2016.

Stern, Jessica, and J. M. Berger. *ISIS: The State of Terror.* New York: Ecco, 2015.

Thompson, Robert Smith. *The Missiles of October: The Declassified Story of John F. Kennedy and the Cuban Missile Crisis.* New York: Simon & Schuster, 1992.

Trachtenberg, Marc. *The Cold War and After: History, Theory, and the Logic of International Politics.* Princeton Studies in International History and Politics. Princeton, NJ: Princeton University Press, 2012.

Trenin, Dmitri. "Russia Reborn." *Foreign Affairs*, November/December 2009, 64–78.

Understanding How It Happens: Decision Making and U.S. Foreign Policy

3

For 444 days, from November 1979 to January 1981, fifty-two Americans were held hostage in Tehran during the Iranian revolution. In 2016, Iran seized two small U.S. Navy ships, leading to a new crisis.

Preview

This chapter provides an overview of a range of theories and concepts that have been developed to explain the foreign policy decision-making process. Students of foreign policy have sought to explain why and how particular policy decisions are reached, and this effort cuts across several types of explanations and disciplines, with concepts borrowed from political psychology, social psychology, management studies, organizational behavior, economics, and history—to name just a few. This chapter provides a brief overview of some of the key ways that students of the American foreign policy process approach the task of explaining the work of foreign policy decision making.

Key Concepts

standard operating procedures (SOPs)   groupthink

perception   vigilant decision making

political belief systems   bureaucratic politics

operational code   policy types

historical analogies   crisis

cognitive consistency   constructivism

personality

O n January 12, 2016, two small U.S. Navy "riverine" ships, with ten sailors aboard, were seized by the Iranian Revolutionary Guard. The forty-foot-long ships were apparently en route from Kuwait to Bahrain in the Persian Gulf when they were seized for violating Iran's waters. Apparently one ship had mechanical trouble and the other stopped to lend assistance. The crews of both ships were seized: nine men and one woman. Making matters more dramatic, as this happened President Obama was preparing to give the State of the Union address that evening to a joint session of Congress and live television audience. Iran promised to return the sailors quickly and that they would be well treated. The White House tried to downplay the incident, and Secretary of State Kerry worked behind the scenes with his Iranian counterpart to make sure the sailors would be on their way as soon as possible. Indeed, they were released the next morning, after less than twenty-four hours.

Secretary Kerry said this case was "a testament to the critical role that diplomacy plays in keeping our country safe, secure and strong." Others were less generous in their assessment. Senator John McCain (R-AZ) tweeted that Kerry's remarks were "unbelievable," and New Jersey governor Chris Christie (R) retweeted McCain's comment, adding that the case was actually proof that the "administration lives in a fantasy land." Other candidates for the Republican nomination for president sounded similar calls, and when Iran released pictures of the seized sailors—a potential violation of the Geneva Convention on the treatment of detainees, which does not allow using pictures as propaganda—many others were also critical of the administration, including some maritime law experts.

The stakes were high here for two reasons (beyond the importance of the safety of the ten sailors). First, the Obama administration had recently entered into a "nuclear deal" with Iran, which as described in previous chapters was very controversial in the United States, largely but not exclusively on partisan political lines. Surely some hoped to use this incident to add pressure that might kill the deal. And second, the report and then the images of American sailors being seized by Iranian troops brought back painful memories for the United States of the "first" Iran Hostage Crisis in the Carter administration, when the U.S. Embassy in Tehran was overrun during the Iranian Revolution in November 1979 and fifty-two Americans were taken hostage for 444 days. Could this incident have been a second "hostage crisis"? Should it have been used to ramp up pressure on the Iranian regime? Or was it, in fact, a triumph of diplomacy and a signal that relations between the United States and Iran are getting better?

This crisis quickly receded from the public view with little impact. The very fact, however, that an incident such as this elicited such a wide number of choices to top policy makers in the United States underscores how difficult the task is of understanding the foreign policy–making process. What happens when the president of the United States, and the group of advisors the president assembles to give information and advice, actually make decisions? What theories or concepts are available to help one understand this process, to "see" the decision-making process and make sense of it (even though it often happens in secret)?

This case highlights the many different and complex dynamics that are a part of the policy-making process. It matters who the individuals are who are in positions of power, because different people come into their jobs with different beliefs, experiences, and policy preferences. The dynamics set in motion when individuals operate in small groups are also important; sometimes groups fight among themselves, sometimes they work well together, and sometimes they become a mutually reinforcing clique that fails to do their work vigilantly. The role of bureaucratic settings also may exert influence on the process; how the bureaucracy is structured, people's place in the bureaucracy, the influence of **standard operating procedures (SOPs)**, and the games that bureaucrats play when policy equals power and information is the currency that is used—all these too play a role. The role of public opinion and the way the media covers the story can also be important.

The case also underscores that the meaning of all events does not come clearly defined. Individuals imbue events with meaning, constructing the importance of events in world politics in different ways: the subjective side of **perceptions**. While policy makers certainly try to be "rational," there are inherent limits to rationality. With all this in mind, how are we to understand foreign policy decision making?

Some central theoretical approaches to the study of decision making have common reference points, even though the study of foreign policy decision making in general, and American foreign policy making in particular, is laced with work from many disciplines outside political science. Many of these approaches cluster around three different decision-making settings; that is, they explore the dynamics of decision making from the perspectives of individuals, small groups of individuals, or large-scale organizations and bureaucracies. A particular analyst normally tries to build explanations at one of these levels because he or she is persuaded that it is the setting most important for understanding how decisions get made.

There are other approaches that try to get at the dynamics of decision making in other ways; the latter part of the chapter will focus on some of these, including the "policy types" approach and an approach often called "constructivism" or "social constructivism." There is some overlap across all of these theories, but analysts tend to be rooted in one or another of these approaches to explaining American foreign policy decision making.

At the outset, it is useful to recall that the domestic context within which U.S. foreign policy is crafted today and into the future, as noted in chapters 1 and 2, is increasingly intermestic, partisan, and fractured—making the job of crafting foreign policy perhaps harder than ever before. At the same time, the global context that U.S. policy makers work within is increasingly globalized, interconnected, and interdependent—making foreign policy problems perhaps more complex than ever before, and making it extremely difficult to craft solutions. One of the real "tests" for these approaches to the study of the foreign policy process is therefore the extent to which they can capture and explain these dynamics.

Who Makes Decisions and How?

One of the things that distinguish the study of foreign policy (often called "foreign policy analysis") as a subfield is that academics in this area are dedicated to building explanations of foreign policy behavior that mirror the actual dynamics of decision making as much as possible. Much of the study of international relations assumes away these complexities, arguing instead that states act "as if" they were rational actors, and therefore bypass these complicated (and sometimes contradictory) dynamics. While explanations that emerge from foreign policy analysis are perhaps less parsimonious, they are nonetheless sometimes far richer and more realistic.

The study of foreign policy decision making begins with the assumption that policy is made by individuals working in groups, and normally proceeds from the assumption that to understand foreign policy decisions and behaviors the analyst must be able to see situations as the policy makers themselves saw them. Policies, decisions, and behaviors are, in that sense, linked to the nature of the process that is used to reach policy decisions (or to decide *not* to decide). Process *is* policy; change the people, change the process, and the result may be a different policy. Scholars working in this area often think of the "decision" as the unit of analysis in a study, and thus focus on how decision makers define the situations they face.

Beyond this starting point, however, there are many roads. Some scholars have focused their efforts on understanding the psychology and beliefs of individuals as the key to understanding decision making. Others have focused on the dynamics (and often the malfunctions) that emerge when individuals work in small groups. Still others have focused on the role of bureaucracy and bargaining among decision makers as the "essence" of decision. The chapter will briefly review the concepts and dynamics that have been developed at each of these theoretical clusters: individual, small group, and bureaucratic politics.

Individual Explanations

One reason to focus on individuals as the key to understanding the policy-making process arises from the fundamental assumption that individuals matter, individuals make a difference, and individuals are different. Policy decisions depend in some nontrivial way on how the individual sees the world. Different people in the same situation can make different choices. When a person is in a position to actually decide, or to influence the one who does make the decisions, it makes sense to study those people, their role in the process, and how they came to the policy preferences that they hold. Of central importance to those who study the individual decision maker are the concepts of "perception" and "cognition"— how leaders see the world and think about it. From this perspective, it is perhaps less important how you as a student of foreign policy see a situation; what matters is how the policy makers see the situation and how they perceive the world.

Much of the work at this level of analysis has focused on ways to try to study the **political belief systems** of important leaders. A political belief system is a coherently integrated set of images about politics and the political world. Not everyone has a fully developed political belief system, but the presumption is that political leaders are likely to have one. A combination of memories, values, and historical precedents forms belief systems. The belief system is a way of making sense of a complex world. It is a political anchor, as it were, that screens out what is not important and highlights what is important. These screens, meant to be helpful, shape a leader's view of new situations and can perhaps drive policy preferences.

One way that scholars have tried to understand and study belief systems has been to study a leader's **operational code**. A leader's operational code is a set of beliefs about the nature of the political world and about the effective strategies for dealing with that world. By examining a leader's speeches, books, articles, memoirs, and even letters, one can develop an outline of that person's operational code, even "at a distance" (as opposed to having direct access to that person to ask questions of him or her). Then one can try to find links between the leader's beliefs and the policy choices that the person made.

One classic example of this type of analysis was a study of Eisenhower's secretary of state, John Foster Dulles. Dulles was one of the most important players in Ike's foreign policy process during the 1950s. Dulles's operational code about the Soviet Union was so rigid that when the Soviets acted contrary to Dulles's mind-set about them, the information would be discarded rather than incorporated into the operational code. When the Soviets behaved "better" than his operational code believed possible, that information would be rejected. Negative behavior would only underscore the validity of the belief system. Such a closed, rigid mind-set can easily contribute to misperception and policy error. The "belief" that Saddam Hussein had nuclear, chemical, and biological weapons ("weapons of mass destruction") led the Bush administration to invade Iraq in 2002, even though the actual evidence of that arsenal was scant at best (and turned out to be faulty).

A variety of factors influences the way one sees or perceives the world. One of the primary screens through which information of the world must pass to individuals is the memories that policy makers have of the past. Some memories are of things that they experienced; others are lessons they have learned from history. How policy makers see the world is thus conditioned to some extent by what they have seen in the past (or learned from it). New information and experiences get put into place inside this memory, given meaning in that context.

The way that policy makers use history, and in particular utilize **historical analogies**, has received close scrutiny from students of the decision-making process. Analogies are a form of cognitive shortcut, a quick way to make meaning out of something new by referring to something from the past. To say that Situation X is like Situation Y from the past is to employ a historical analogy. Just as students can get these wrong on the SAT or ACT test, however, it turns out that policy makers are often not very good at applying historical precedents. Maybe a lesson to learn from Munich in 1938 (when Great Britain's Neville Chamberlain worked out what he thought was a deal with Hitler, only to find that Hitler would go on to take more of Europe, leading to World War II) is that "appeasement" can be a dangerous strategy; but is it always wrong? Or in another case, just because Korea and Vietnam were both countries divided by an artificially imposed line separating the communist north from the U.S.-allied south, did that mean that the same dynamics were playing out in Vietnam as had played out in Korea, requiring the same kind of policy response? Historical analogies can be great mental shortcuts, but they can also quickly lead one down a path to disaster when the analogy proves to be false or misleading.

In his book *Analogies at War*, Yuen Foong Khong scrutinizes how American policy makers use analogical reasoning in the decision-making process. Khong argues that analogies are devices that policy makers use to help them make decisions, especially in novel situations. Unfortunately, policy makers tend to select analogies that do not quite fit the new situation, which often leads policy astray. The Munich analogy, and also Korea, Khong argues, likely predisposed leaders to view events in Vietnam in a particular way with a particular policy prescription (aggression that required a military response).

One thing that the studies of leaders and political psychology have general agreement about is that human beings are cognitive misers, meaning that they try to find mental shortcuts to reach a decision, and that the techniques used to be miserly can have a profound impact on how one sees the world and responds to it. Several decision-making "pathologies," or failures to be particularly rigorous about decision making, appear to be linked to these shortcuts. One is the way that the effort to attain **"cognitive consistency"** can harm the decision-making process. Cognitive consistency refers to the tendency to process information so as to keep one's views of reality consistent with one's underlying conceptions of reality. Individuals thus often filter out information that does not fit their underlying political belief systems. To the extent that George W. Bush saw the world as divided between "good" and "evil," these categories were also shortcuts that could be used to respond to the behavior of other states more quickly.

The effort to achieve cognitive consistency can be healthy and adaptive. However, when individuals persistently filter out relevant information that does not fit their underlying set of beliefs about politics, the effort has veered off into the area of what is sometimes called "irrational" consistency seeking. This can take one of several forms. One is premature cognitive closure, which means that a decision maker shuts down the process of decision making early, before a rigorous examination of information and preferences is carried out. With such a quick decision, the concern is that it can often lead to disaster. President Eisenhower used to say to his advisors, "Let's not make our mistakes in a hurry."

Foreign policy is an inherently complex issue area, laden with tough choices and difficult trade-offs. The lack of perception of trade-offs is another example of irrational consistency seeking. Here a decision maker fails to consider trade-offs that are invariably a part of political decision making. To see a world without trade-offs is perhaps a sign that a rigorous decision-making process has broken down. U.S.-Cuban policy exemplifies this phenomenon. Decision makers were so wedded to absolute outcomes (the fall of Castro and communism or its retention in pure form) that intermediary solutions that involved trade-offs were perhaps not given full consideration in trying to fashion that policy.

Bolstering, or post-decisional rationalization, is another sign of irrational consistency seeking. The idea here is that after the fact a decision maker creates all the reasons why a decision was made and why it was the right decision to make. Unfortunately, this only happens after a decision is made, not as part of the decision-making process. Thus it is called "bolstering," because the presumption is that a person is trying to bolster his or her sense of having made a good decision (even when the person perhaps did not). A leader might thus be deluded into thinking the policy process was rigorous. The post-invasion rationalizations of the wisdom of invading Iraq may be a good example of bolstering by the Bush administration.

The previous dynamics all dealt with shutting down a thorough decision-making process. Hypervigilance, however, is quite the reverse. Here, time pressure and stress might drive a leader—who wants to make a good and careful decision—to become too open to information, and thus lose the ability to sift it and reach decisions based on it. The capacity for critical reasoning is lost, and a leader might be either frozen in indecision or extremely susceptible to the influence of others. Some have argued that President Carter found himself in this position during the 444-day crisis with Iran, during which Americans from the U.S. Embassy were held hostage.

One thing that is important to note is that the presence of stress is likely to heighten the dangers of these dynamics. Governing is inherently stressful, and foreign policy crises are by definition very stressful events. Crises threaten the country, offer limited time to develop a response, and often emerge by surprise. These situations often include options to use force associated with them as well, and so are literally matters of life and death. Stress, like all the other damaging impacts on purely rational decision making, can result in less-than-optimal outcomes.

If people matter, and people make decisions, then it would follow that different people might behave differently even in the same situations. Following this line of thinking, a great deal of research attention has been paid to **personality** differences among leaders, especially among U.S. presidents. There is a variety of ways that scholars have tried to define and measure "personality" and how it has an impact on decision making. Chapter 4 discusses one way that presidential personality and advisory group structures interact, for example. Here it is worth pondering how leaders' personality characteristics shape the decisions they make.

Foreign policy scholars often focus on an individual's need for control, cognitive complexity, and degree of policy experience as central to framing his or her political personality. As Preston's research shows, for example, Bill Clinton had low needs for control and a high level of cognitive complexity, along with foreign policy inexperience. His preference for less formal decision-making processes and high reliance on expert advisors meant that Clinton often had a less "decisive" style than other presidents, which led him to delegate more. This was evident in the 1993–1994 crisis over North Korea's nuclear program, where Clinton deferred greatly to expert advisors, heavily sought information, and was constantly open to new information and new policy options for dealing with North Korea. The contrast between how Clinton and George W. Bush approached policy making toward North Korea is discussed in the intersection box that follows.

Intersection 3.1 — Beliefs and Policy toward North Korea

The Cold War continues with the Democratic People's Republic of Korea. Troops from the North Korean People's Army march in Pyongyang, a reminder that an unstable peace exists on the Korean Peninsula.

In the early years of the Clinton administration there was grave concern that North Korea, also called the Democratic People's Republic of Korea (DPRK), was trying to develop nuclear weapons. At that time, 1993–1994, the North Korean weapons program was driven by taking spent fuel from nuclear reactors to a breeder plant at Yongbyon, where it was processed into weapons-grade plutonium. Absent good military options for eliminating the North Korean nuclear weapons program and believing that diplomacy was the only possible way to prevent North Korea from becoming a nuclear state, the Clinton administration entered into negotiations with North Korea. While there were a number of contacts between the governments of the United States and North Korea, the most public (but to some extent "unofficial") contact was when former president Jimmy Carter went to North Korea to personally negotiate a deal.

Ultimately an "Agreed Framework" was reached in October 1994. Under the framework, North Korea promised to halt its reprocessing activities and allow inspections by the International Atomic Energy Agency (IAEA). In return, the United States, South Korea, Japan, and others would help provide replacement nuclear reactors (that could not be used to produce weapons-grade fuel); in the meantime, North Korea would get large amounts of fuel oil as a substitute source of energy. While the DPRK was a difficult negotiating partner, key actors in the Clinton administration believed that North Korea's nuclear ambitions could be assuaged through negotiations, including through direct U.S.-DPRK talks.

At the outset of the Bush administration it was clear that a different set of actors held a different set of beliefs. Especially following the attacks of 9/11, when North Korea was listed as part of the "Axis of Evil," it was clear that President Bush, Secretary of Defense

Rumsfeld, Ambassador to the UN John Bolton, and others, believed that a "crime and punishment" approach was more in order than the negotiation strategy of the Clinton years. The early Bush administration refused to meet one-on-one with North Korea, but would only do so through a six-party framework (including North and South Korea, the United States, Russia, China, and Japan). When the administration got tough on North Korea, cutting off fuel oil, North Korea responded by kicking out inspectors and restarting the fuel reprocessing. North Korea tested a small nuclear weapon in 2006, followed by a larger test in 2009. (They would later conduct small test explosions in 2013 and 2016 as well.)

Before jumping to the conclusion that "party" explains the difference in policy approach more than "beliefs," it is worth noting that later in the Bush administration a different set of Republican policy makers began to pursue a more intensive diplomatic approach with North Korea. Secretary of State Rice and her deputy, John Negroponte, approved of the diplomatic missions by longtime Foreign Service officer and then Assistant Secretary of State for East Asian and Pacific Affairs Christopher Hill. At a minimum, the incident demonstrates that different people can look at the same evidence and come away with different conclusions, in part because they have different beliefs that shape what they see.

Small Group Explanations

Very often when the president is faced with a difficult decision, a small team is assembled to help sift through information, generate alternatives, and make suggestions about what policy the president should select. Keeping in mind that the individuals who are members of this small group may well be experiencing some of the personal dynamics mentioned above, when a group of individuals is formed to help make a decision, many would argue that special "small group" dynamics can emerge that impinge on the decision-making process. In those cases where a small group is the "ultimate decision unit," it makes sense to study the group as the locus of decision.

There is a long tradition of research on small-group decision making associated with the concept of **"groupthink**." First generated in the 1960s and 1970s by social psychologist Irving Janis, groupthink refers to "the psychological tendency for individuals within organizations to alter their views or perceptions in ways that allow them to conform with other members of a group with which they all identify." In other words, sometimes it seems that the individuals who are part of a small decision-making group actually set aside their own sense of what needs to be done in order to conform with the group. Rather than "rocking the boat," or advocating personal positions at odds with the group, they "go along to get along"; they place a higher value on being a member of the group than they do on making a vigilant decision. It is important to note that this happens sometimes, not all the time, which is an issue with which research in this area continues to struggle.

Janis came to this study while watching "fiascoes" unfold in American foreign policy: the failed mission at the Bay of Pigs and the Vietnam War, for example. Janis applied his research on small-group dynamics to the U.S. foreign policy process, to see if he could find evidence that the "best and the brightest" had made critical errors because no one wanted to speak up and say what perhaps others also thought.

Janis hypothesized that if groupthink were occurring, the careful observer should be able to detect certain symptoms of concurrence-seeking behavior. He suggested that the group would, for example, overestimate its power and morality, and share illusions of invulnerability, all of which could lead the group to make riskier decisions than any other they as individuals might otherwise select. There should be evidence of "closed-mindedness" by the group, including stereotypes of enemy leaders and also efforts to discount warning signs. If concurrence-seeking behavior were happening, there would also be pressures toward uniformity in the group, including direct pressure on dissenters to "get in line" and be a loyal member of the group. There might even be self-appointed "mind guards"—members who protect the group from adverse information that might shatter their shared complacency about the effectiveness and morality of the decisions.

According to the groupthink hypothesis, if these dynamics occur in a decision-making group, there would likely be severe consequences for the decision-making process. The basic steps of a sound decision-making process would likely be shut off, leading to a short and biased process that fails to thoroughly scrutinize information, examine risks, or develop contingency plans (why plan for contingencies when you know you are right?).

For Janis, the failed invasion at the Bay of Pigs was the "perfect fiasco." The idea behind the April 1961 operation was for a group of 1,400 Cuban exiles to be covertly reinserted into Cuba at the Bay of Pigs, thus triggering the counterrevolution that would drive Fidel Castro from power. What resulted was not just a policy fiasco but also a huge embarrassment for the United States, since American involvement in the plan became apparent. As Janis details, decision makers in this case made several critical mistakes and misjudgments in their assumptions about the operation and in how they handled information. They thought, for example, that no one would find out that the United States was behind the invasion, that Castro's military was too weak to handle this force, and that news of the invasion would spur popular uprisings against Castro. They should have known better.

A great deal of research has followed Janis's lead. Some of the work in this area has explored what sort of situations might trigger groupthink (for example, does a small, cohesive, homogenous group have more of a tendency toward groupthink than a larger, more diverse one?). Other research has explored what the relationship is between decision-making process errors and policy failure or success. While it is rare that groupthink in its full form occurs, there is strong evidence that the emergence of even some of these dynamics can shut down the decision-making process. Conversely, evidence suggests that to the extent a decision-making process is **vigilant**—paying close attention to the tasks that are the essential elements of making a decision—the likelihood of a positive outcome is increased. In general terms, the tasks of decision making include:

• surveying the objectives or goals to be fulfilled;
• canvassing alternative courses of action;
• searching for new information relevant to evaluating the alternatives;

- assimilating that new information;
- examining the benefits, costs, and risks of the preferred alternative; and
- developing, implementing, and monitoring contingency plans.

The groupthink hypothesis is widely used to help understand decision making and is taught in political science, social psychology, organization theory, and even marketing classes and studies of the behavior of juries. Nonetheless, it continues to confound researchers. As mentioned above, it is rare to find groupthink occurring in its full form, and it is very common to find some elements of groupthink present without them resulting in the consequences of groupthink. Yetiv has shown, for example, that several symptoms of groupthink can be seen in the decision-making process that led up to the Persian Gulf War in 1990–1991, and yet that process nonetheless remained relatively vigilant and did not result in a fiasco. Needless to say, why groupthink sometimes happens and sometimes does not continues to occupy foreign policy analysts.

Another way that analysts of U.S. foreign policy have studied these dynamics has focused on the management style of presidents: How do presidents structure and manage the groups they form to help make decisions? Alexander George examines the role of presidential personality and how it interacts with different management strategies for advisors. The "formalistic" model places the president at the top of a hierarchically organized group where jurisdictions are clearly articulated. The "competitive" model places the president on top of a group of advisors who share overlapping responsibilities and who compete for the president's attention. The "collegial" model puts the president at the center of a decision-making team. These are discussed and applied in chapter 4. While small groups do not make all U.S. foreign policy decisions, when they do it makes sense to study the nature of that group and how dynamics within the group may have an impact on the decision-making process and therefore on the choices made in the name of the country.

The Bureaucratic Politics Paradigm

The **bureaucratic politics** paradigm examines the impact of organizational structures on the behavior and choices of political leaders. This scholarly tradition is most associated with the seminal work of Harvard political scientist Graham Allison, who applied different "conceptual lenses" to the record of the Cuban Missile Crisis to show how important bureaucratic and organizational dynamics can be to the foreign policy process. A long tradition of research in this area has followed.

As with work at the individual and small-group level, the bureaucratic politics paradigm begins by setting itself apart from the rational ideal of policy making, noting that there are limits to how close human beings can get to the rational ideal. Allison, who has developed his own typology of bureaucratic interaction based on three "models" (see table 3.1), is still one of the most prominent advocates of this approach.

Allison refers to the rational model as Model 1—the first set of lenses through which one might try to see the foreign policy process. In this model the presumption is that foreign policy is the product of rational actions and choices.

TABLE 3.1 What Does "Policy" Mean?	
Allison's Model	**See "Policy" As**
1. Rational	A *rational act* or choice
2. Organizational Process	The *output* of preestablished routines and procedures
3. Bureaucratic Politics	The *outcome* of bargaining games among bureaucratic actors

Foreign policy is arrived at through an exhaustive information search, followed by a rigorous process of assigning the outcomes that are likely to follow from different policies and then weighing the benefits of those outcomes. The action chosen will be the one that corresponds with the policy most likely to lead to the most preferred outcome. As with the use of the rational model in previous forms of explanation, this model often takes on a prescriptive function, suggesting that it is the ideal for which policy makers should aim when they make decisions.

Allison calls Model 2 the organizational process model. This model sees foreign policy as perhaps nothing more than the "outputs" of large organizations functioning according to standardized patterns of behavior. Policy making, in this view, is driven by standard operating procedures (SOPs), divided responsibilities and jurisdictions, and coordination procedures that are established long before a particular foreign policy choice emerges. The search for information in this model is seen as nonexhaustive and problem driven; the effort is to get enough information to be able to make a policy choice and move on. SOPs drive the information search and also the way that participants see the information and evaluate alternatives. Organizational goals can be equated with "the national interest" in this model. This model focuses on the way an organization processes information, which can have an impact on the way it perceives, evaluates, and acts on information and a situation.

The bureaucratic politics model, Model 3, sees government behavior as the outcome of bargaining games where power is shared. It sees policy as the outcome of a political process that includes compromise, coalitions, competition, and even confusion among government officials who see different faces of a situation. This model emphasizes "players in position" who promote parochial interests and the way that "where you stand depends on where you sit"; that is, where one stands on an issue will be rooted in where one sits around the cabinet table. In this view, the foreign policy–making process is driven by a limited information search, hidden motives, and "pulling and hauling" among participants who are vying to "win" the policy game. It sees the outcomes of this infighting and political maneuvering as important to explaining foreign policy decisions. In this sense, the bureaucratic politics model sees foreign policy as nothing more than the outcome of these bargaining games among participants. It is not necessarily rational or irrational; rather, it reflects the interests of who won the policy game. Intersection 3.2 shows a dramatic example of how elements other than the purely "rational" must be examined in order to understand a policy-making process.

Intersection 3.2	**Wiretapping, Beliefs, and the Domestic Politics of Foreign Policy**

The U.S. government undertook a number of steps to try to make the homeland more secure following the terrorist attacks of 9/11, including military action in Afghanistan against Al Qaeda and the Taliban. Some measures were taken inside the United States and included bold new measures to monitor communications to try to uncover terrorist plots. Part of the reason for this step was that many of the 9/11 hijackers had lived in the United States for years, had traveled frequently, and had regular contact with sponsors abroad. The Bush administration therefore set about trying to unearth any similar future plots by, among other means, developing new ways to monitor telephone, e-mail, and web traffic by the National Security Agency—including traffic inside the United States by U.S. citizens. Depending on one's stance toward these measures (only some of which are known to this day), these programs came to be called the "Terrorist Surveillance Program" (TSP), "Electronic Eavesdropping," or "Illegal Wiretapping" since the program ran afoul of the law in the eyes of many. (Will Smith's 1998 movie, *Enemy of the State*, might come to mind.) This provides another classic example of how foreign policy and domestic politics run right into one another.

One of the things that made the Bush program so controversial—once word of the program was leaked to the press and the public—was that Congress had created an avenue for seeking "wiretaps" of American citizens for national security purposes in 1978, following the Watergate scandal. The Foreign Intelligence Surveillance Act (FISA) recognized the need to monitor the communications of some Americans who might be working with foreign agents to undermine national security, and established a process for acquiring warrants for wiretaps from a special court that came to be called the FISA court. In its history, the FISA court hardly ever turned down a warrant request, and did not do so immediately after 9/11 either. However, something about what the Bush administration was doing by 2003 and 2004 started to worry the court, and warrants started to be rejected as illegal, a source of concern in the administration.

Bush and his top advisors decided to circumvent the FISA court, arguing that he had all the authority he needed to run this program based on the Constitution's grant of executive authority to the president, the president's role as commander in chief, and the congressional authorization to use military force that was passed after 9/11. Rather than run the program through the FISA court, Bush decided to have the Office of Legal Counsel inside the Justice Department, and the attorney general, sign off that the program was "legal."

As personnel in these offices changed over time, new actors came to view the program differently and were concerned about its legality. These concerns came to a dramatic crescendo, as detailed in Eric Lichtblau's book, *Bush's Law*, in March 2004, when it was time for the Justice Department to once again certify that the program was legal. The deputy attorney general, James Comey (who came to public prominence during the 2016 presidential campaign as the head of the FBI and who was fired in May 2017) had come to believe that it was not; Attorney General Ashcroft had come to agree with him. Just then, Ashcroft took ill and was rushed to the hospital with a dire case of pancreatitis. In his absence, Comey served as the acting attorney general until Ashcroft was well enough to return to work.

Comey, who would later testify before Congress about these events (and would become the FBI director in the Obama administration), met with Bush's top aides on March 10, 2004, the day before the program had to be recertified. He told them that he would not recertify the program. That night Comey got a call advising him that White House Chief of Staff Andrew Card and White House Counsel Alberto Gonzales were on their way to the hospital to see the very ill John Ashcroft, apparently to try to convince him to sign off on the program since Comey would not. A key foreign and national security policy decision was about to play out in a hospital room!

Comey rushed to the hospital to be there with Ashcroft when the others arrived. They came carrying an envelope—the documents they wanted Ashcroft to sign. The very ill Ashcroft lifted his head and in a moment of great clarity rattled off his concerns about the program, making it clear that he agreed with Comey. He then concluded by saying it did not matter what he thought anyway because, "I'm not the attorney general." He pointed at Comey and said, "There is the attorney general."

The scene ended, but not the drama. Comey was summoned to a meeting at the White House the next day. Fearing that the White House would push ahead anyway, Comey and many others (apparently including the FBI director and several top Justice Department officials) were ready to resign en masse. (Such an event would have been reminiscent of the "Saturday Night Massacre" during Watergate, when the attorney general, his deputy, and the special prosecutor investigating President Nixon were all fired.) Comey met privately with President Bush, and Bush agreed that the program should be brought into compliance with the Justice Department's concerns. The "crisis" was over; the program would be altered somewhat, and thus ended a dramatic example of how complex, political, *and personal*, foreign and national security policy decision making can get. The "rational" model of decision making could never account for this kind of pulling and hauling—the importance of different leaders' beliefs and the way they "see" different sides of the same issue.

In order to show the utility of thinking about the foreign policy process from these different perspectives, Allison—joined by coauthor Philip Zelikow for a new edition of the book recently—applies the models to the October 1962 Cuban Missile Crisis. The crisis was precipitated by intelligence information that the Soviet Union was building missile launchers in Cuba that would allow Soviet offensive ballistic nuclear missiles to be placed in Cuba. President John F. Kennedy assembled a team of advisors, which came to be called the ExComm (short for "Executive Committee of the National Security Council"), to help him decide how to respond to the crisis. For two weeks, the world teetered at the brink of nuclear war.

The rational model does an excellent job of showing how the choice of a naval quarantine, or "blockade," of Cuba was the only real—and rational—option under the circumstances. Given that Kennedy and his advisors wanted to prevent the Soviet missiles from being put in place, and did not want open war with the Soviets to break out, the choice of the quarantine was the only option that held out the hope of meeting those goals. Using military force to "remove" the missile sites would have ended the missile threat, but would quite likely have led to war with the

Soviets. Diplomacy through the United Nations would allow the Soviets to put the missiles in place while diplomatic processes went on. The quarantine prevented the missiles from arriving in Cuba while allowing time for diplomacy to proceed.

However, the story is not quite that simple. The organizational process model helps make sense of the politics of running the quarantine, showing how the actual tactics of the blockade were dictated by existing routines (SOPs) that the U.S. Navy had previously developed. Knowing that one day it might have to blockade a location, the navy had developed rules for how to do it. In this instance, however, the navy's rules clashed with JFK's goals. The navy wanted to be far away from Cuba, so its ships could not get shot at from the island. Kennedy wanted the navy close to Cuba to buy time for Soviet leader Nikita Khrushchev to decide to stop the ships en route to Cuba. If they ran the blockade line, war could result. Kennedy wanted the blockade line moved closer to the island. This led to a famous exchange between Secretary of Defense Robert McNamara and Chief of Naval Operations George Anderson, where the two loudly squared off over the rules of the blockade. The meeting ended with Admiral Anderson literally throwing the navy regulations at the secretary as a way to answer his intrusive questions. While not very rational, it is the kind of thing one would expect to see when SOPs and routines drive behavior.

The bureaucratic politics model, when applied to the historical record, shows that even the choice of the blockade was not as rational as it might seem. The model shows that in fact the option of the blockade was chosen as a result of bargaining games in which the president's brother, Attorney General Robert F. Kennedy, figured prominently. A political struggle in which a winning coalition was built led to the blockade option, in which proponents of the blockade tried to plant warnings in the mind of the president, including the fear that war could come about by accident—trying to warn him off the military option that some argued would be manageable and successful.

Merging Models 2 and 3 together as a single approach to studying decision making forms what is often called the "bureaucratic politics paradigm"; it is one of the most used (and often criticized) approaches to studying American foreign policy. The approach holds many interesting insights, including a way to understand the policy process as one where leaders come to situations with "preferences" already formed. Policy making is perhaps less about discovering preferences than it is about trying to convince others about one's preexisting preferences. That was certainly true of many in the George W. Bush administration, who had argued for military force to remove Saddam Hussein from power since the George H. W. Bush administration. It may not always be the case, but the bureaucratic politics paradigm can be very useful in helping us make sense of the often very political nature of the foreign policy process.

Other Approaches

While perhaps the bulk of the work on the study of foreign policy decision making focuses on one level or the other, there are some other approaches to studying the foreign policy process that try to cut across those specific clusters. One is a type of approach that emphasizes how the decision-making process varies depending on "policy type"; another emerges from a school of thought called "constructivism," or "social constructivism." Both of these perspectives on the policy process merit some individual consideration.

Policy Types

One interesting perspective on the policy process is the idea that foreign policy is really an umbrella term, and that to understand who actually makes foreign policy decisions, one needs to break up that umbrella term into its subparts. Drawing on the work of Ripley and Franklin, the suggestion is that there are really three **policy types**, each with different patterns of access and power to the foreign policy–making process.

First, **"crisis"** policy deals with emergency threats to national interests or values. Emergencies often come as a surprise; typically, they offer limited response time, entail threats to the national interest, and usually include options to the use of force. These are the kinds of situations that people often have in mind when they use the term *foreign policy*. North Korea's invasion of South Korea in 1950 created a "crisis" for the United States; Iraq's invasion of Kuwait in 1990 did as well; so did the 9/11 terrorist attacks.

The political dynamics that drive crisis policy making tend to be dominated by the president and the small group of advisors around the Oval Office. Indeed, since crises often come with great stress and high threat levels associated with them, psychological and social psychological dynamics of crisis can be of heightened importance during these situations. Congress tends not to be especially engaged in crisis policy making, and often watches with the rest of the public (and the world) as presidents and their advisors decide how to respond during crises. The choice of going to war in Iraq in 2003, for example, was made by President Bush and a small number of key government policy makers around him. Congress voted on a war authorization, and public opinion was an issue, but the locus of decision making was the president and his war cabinet, with Congress playing a legitimating but not decision-making role.

Second, "strategic" policy lays out the basic stance of the United States toward another country or a particular problem. Containment, for example, as discussed in the previous chapter, was the basic strategy for dealing with the Soviet Union during the Cold War. Free trade is a basic foreign economic policy for promoting U.S. interests in a global trading system.

Strategic policy is normally formulated inside the executive branch, but usually deep in the bureaucracy rather than at the top (presidential) levels. Before grand strategies become public, interest groups and concerned members of Congress have an opportunity to lobby for certain positions they hold. The public usually learns about these policies once the president announces them. Containment, for example, was developed largely in the State Department and then approved by President Truman. The Reagan Doctrine, which announced that the United States would not view communist regimes around the world as permanent but instead would take steps to undermine those governments, especially in Central America, was a strategic policy mostly developed inside the State and Defense departments and the Central Intelligence Agency, and then approved by the president. The

Trans-Pacific Partnership (TPP) trade agreement between the United States and a slate of countries that ring the Pacific Ocean was worked out between the U.S. Trade Representative and the governments of other countries in 2015 following several years of negotiations. Ultimately the TPP found itself a victim of the 2016 election cycle and appears to have been scuttled by the new Trump administration.

Third, "structural defense" policy focuses on the defense budget, or the policies and programs that deal with defense spending and military bases. These policies usually focus on, for example, buying new aircraft for the air force and navy, or deciding what military bases to consolidate or close down. With the defense budget taking up as much as one-fifth of the total federal budget, this is an area of enormous concern and importance.

Structural defense policy usually starts in the executive branch, but is largely crafted in Congress, whose members tend to have their fingers closely on the pulses of their constituents, where monies authorized in support of particular policies will be expended. The Defense Department bureaucracy, interest groups, and defense contractors have much weight in this process as well. Congress regularly votes to spend more money on defense than the president or the secretary of defense asks for; they see defense spending to some extent as jobs programs for their districts and states.

One of the important contributions of this perspective on the policy process is that it helps orient the analyst with respect to what and who is likely to matter in foreign policy making. If one wants to understand who was involved in the decision to use U.S. air power in Libya in 2011 (a crisis situation), for example, this perspective points toward the president and the group of advisors around him as the central set of decision makers to study in order to understand the policy process in that case. If one wants to better understand the decision to build the F-35 fighter jet (which has variations used by the air force, navy, and marine corps), however, this perspective points the analyst toward Congress, congressional staffs, DOD staffers, and defense contractors. It allows for a more nuanced approach to understanding the politics of foreign policy making than perhaps some of the single approaches discussed above can provide.

Constructivism

There is a variety of approaches to the study of foreign policy that are motivated by what is sometimes called a "critical," or "reflectivist," approach. The idea is that while classic foreign policy studies might do well to explain why a particular policy was selected, they do not dig beneath this surface in order to unearth the "how possible" questions, as Roxanne Doty puts it. This set of approaches has come to be called "**constructivism**" or "social constructivism" because of this focus on the structures of power and meaning that identify some actors as "threats" and others not, some actions as acceptable and others not. In other words, the focus is on how actors use power and position to "construct" meaning out of a world where such meaning is not always obvious on the surface. Policy makers define their own world in terms they understand, and constructivism tries to understand how that process happens.

The social world is very different from the natural world, as Houghton notes. Everyone agrees that standing in the way of a tornado is a bad idea, but not all agree that, for example, Iran and North Korea pose a vital threat to the United States requiring a military response. Lightning exists in the natural world as a threat; defining someone as a threat, however, is a social activity. Constructivism highlights the ways that learning emerges from the interaction, and even socialization, of policy makers. As argued in chapter 1, people disagree on things like threats. The question is why.

Trying to understand how that meaning is constructed requires the analyst to study not a single layer but actually multiple layers of analysis at the same time, and to unearth how they interact with one another. The close examination of language and the symbolic meaning of the words that leaders choose is common in constructivist approaches. Some would even argue that politics is all about picking the labels that are attached to things. Constructivism thus focuses primary attention on how policy makers create and construct realities.

An example of studies of the Cuban Missile Crisis can help show how constructivism differs from traditional levels of analysis. As discussed above, Graham Allison's classic study of the missile crisis examined the way that organizational factors (such as standard operating procedures) and bureaucratic politics (the "pulling and hauling" among JFK's advisors) helped shape U.S. policy in the crisis, including the selection of the quarantine option and the way that the U.S. Navy ran the blockade. Jutta Weldes, however, in a classic constructivist study of the same episode, is far less interested in option selection than she is in understanding why there was a missile "crisis" at all. Weldes wants to know why U.S. decision makers saw the missiles as an intolerable threat, one that the United States had an obligation to remove. Her study, and others like it, in some sense begins well before the option selection stage of decision making, believing that the real politics lies in the construction of the situation.

Constructivism wants to know where "ideas" come from in the first place, and how they are put into action. The close study of what words (which are symbols of meaning) are used to convince others of a position is often called the study of "discourse," and is common in constructivist approaches. The study of "identity" is also central to constructivist approaches, since identity plays such a critical role in seeing and responding to the world. As Houghton notes, the fact that Great Britain and France have nuclear arsenals does not greatly worry U.S. policy makers—or Americans in general; a very small stockpile of weapons held by North Korea, or Iran's potential to build nuclear weapons, concerns them very much. The United States tends to identify itself as friendly with these European "allies," but identifies North Korea and Iran as "enemies." Why? How did that happen? Those are the kinds of questions pursued by a constructivist approach to the study of U.S. foreign policy.

A final example may be helpful. A common theme of American foreign policy over the years has been the "promotion of democracy." Various interventions have had democracy promotion as their aim, ranging from the support of the Contras in Nicaragua to overthrow the leftist Sandinista government in the 1980s, to the invasion of Panama to overthrow Manuel Noriega in 1989, to justifications given for the invasion of Iraq in 2003. William Robinson steps behind the record in his book *Promoting Polyarchy*. Robinson begins with a constructivist tone, noting that different people can mean different things by the term *democracy*. So what does the U.S. government mean when it promotes democracy, especially when it does so via the use of force?

Robinson argues that in case after case, U.S. intervention has been aimed at implementing a distinct form of democracy that he calls "polyarchy," or a type of democracy where a small group of elites actually rules while mass participation is relegated to only one form of political participation: elections. The meaning of democracy as constructed by the United States, in his view, is a limited form of democracy that focuses on procedural forms and institutions (elections) more than on meaningful and deep public participation. Robinson calls polyarchy a form of "low intensity democracy," one that is conducive to the political and economic interests of U.S. elites. Obviously a critic, he sees democracy promotion as a façade that enables a narrow slice of elites to have power both in the United States and around the world.

Conclusion

Analysts of U.S. foreign policy spend a considerable amount of time studying "process." How is foreign policy actually made? Why was a particular course of action taken, rather than a different one? How was it that policy makers came to see a problem in a particular way, and to respond to it in the way that they did? Who decides, and how? This chapter has reviewed some of the main concepts, theories, and approaches to studying the foreign policy process.

Political scientists and political psychologists have identified a variety of factors at the individual level that can affect decision making. Personality, beliefs, the drive to maintain cognitive consistency, the way cognitive filters can lead to misperception, and the use of historical analogies all shape how policy makers do their work. The stress that comes from operating under crisis conditions can heighten these dynamics and threaten to shut down the decision-making process, leading to poor decisions and bad outcomes.

A variety of small-group and bureaucratic dynamics can also shape policy making. Often foreign policy is made by individuals working in small groups and by actors who are rooted in the bureaucracy. Understanding how these factors can shape foreign policy decisions is a long-standing concern of students of U.S. foreign and national security policy. The impact of increased political polarization, however, is less well understood; it is reasonable to hypothesize that these conditions will make the policy process even more complex and make vigilant decision making an even harder goal to attain. Trying to cope with foreign policy problems in a complex, interdependent, globalized world only makes the tasks of decision making harder.

Several approaches have been developed that try to go beyond studying one level at a time. The "policy type" approach is rooted in the idea that different types of foreign policy are driven by different dynamics and have different patterns of access and power. Constructivism is a set of approaches that starts from the presumption that politics and political choice exist in a social world, and thus are constructed and perpetuated by leaders. Rather than focusing on the "why" questions that dominate so much of the field, constructivists are interested in answering the "how possible" questions; how a situation even came to be defined the way that policy makers saw it, since that construction then drives the policy-making process.

As is evident from this discussion, there is a broad range of potential approaches that try to understand how U.S. leaders make foreign policy—and there are others not covered here. Many of these approaches are complementary and can build on one another; some of them are quite distinct from each other. All, though, are inspired to some extent by the classic perspective from Snyder et al., that people make foreign policy decisions, and so to understand the roots of policy means understanding how these people do their work.

It is premature to be able to predict much about how the Trump administration will approach a variety of foreign policy issues based on the personal and cognitive variables discussed here—and given that many of the members of his policy team have little government service in their backgrounds we do not know as much about their policy predispositions as we normally would know. On the other hand, the way that Donald Trump uses Twitter may provide us with a nearly instantaneous window into his cognitive processes!

The chapters that follow examine various structural aspects and influences on how decisions are made in the foreign policy realm. We begin with the governmental structures by which policy is made and then examine those areas where people who are not officially part of the process—societal forces—attempt to influence and shape foreign policy. While the approaches discussed in this chapter deal mostly with explaining governmental leaders and their role in decision making, understanding these approaches can be helpful in understanding how decisions are made more generally.

Study/Discussion Questions

1. What cognitive dynamics can impinge on foreign policy decision making? How might these be heightened during a crisis?
2. What is groupthink? How can the president try to avoid it?
3. If humans, especially under stress, cannot be fully rational, can they at least be more vigilant than not? What barriers to rationality exist in the foreign policy–making process?
4. We often think of the president as a "decider," but less often as a "manager." How have presidents tried to manage their advisors to help make foreign policy decisions?
5. What is the bureaucratic politics paradigm? How does it help us see the "essence of decision"?
6. How does the "type" of policy affect the pattern of who is involved in decision making and how they are involved?
7. What is constructivism, and what does it help us understand about the foreign policy process that other approaches likely miss?

8. How can theories of decision making, such as those discussed in this chapter, incorporate domestic politics into their explanations? How does the increasingly complex global environment within which U.S. leaders must make decisions shape the foreign policy process?

Bibliography

Allison, Graham T., and Philip Zelikow. *Essence of Decision: Explaining the Cuban Missile Crisis.* 2nd ed. New York: Pearson Longman, 1999.

Barber, James David. *The Presidential Character: Predicting Performance in the White House.* 4th ed. Upper Saddle River, NJ: Prentice Hall, 2008.

Burke, John P., and Fred I. Greenstein. *How Presidents Test Reality: Decisions on Vietnam, 1954 and 1965.* New York: Russell Sage Foundation, 1991.

Checkel, Jeffrey T. "Constructivism and Foreign Policy." In *Foreign Policy: Theories, Actors, Cases,* edited by Steve Smith. New York: Oxford University Press, 2008.

Cohn, Carol. "Sex and Death in the Rational World of Defense Intellectuals." *Signs* 4 (1987): 687–718.

De Rivera, Joseph H. *The Psychological Dimension of Foreign Policy.* Columbus, OH: Merrill, 1968.

Doty, Roxanne Lynn. "Foreign Policy as Social Construction: A Post-Positivist Analysis of U.S. Counterinsurgency Policy in the Philippines." *International Studies Quarterly* 37 (1993): 297–320.

Enloe, Cynthia. *Bananas, Beaches, and Bases: Making Feminist Sense of International Politics.* Berkeley: University of California Press, 2000.

Garrison, Jean A. *Games Advisors Play: Foreign Policy in the Nixon and Carter Administrations.* College Station: Texas A&M Press, 1999.

George, Alexander L. "The 'Operational Code': A Neglected Approach to the Study of Political Leaders and Decision Making." *International Studies Quarterly* 13 (1969): 190–222.

———. *Presidential Decisionmaking in Foreign Policy: The Effective Use of Information and Advice.* Boulder, CO: Westview, 1980.

Goldgeier, James M. "Foreign Policy Decision Making." In *The International Studies Encyclopedia,* edited by Robert A. Denemark. Hoboken, NJ: Wiley, 2010.

Goodwin, Doris Kearns. *Lyndon Johnson and the American Dream.* New York: St. Martin's, 1991.

Haney, Patrick J. "Soccer Fields and Submarines in Cuba: The Politics of Problem Definition." *Naval War College Review* 50, no. 4 (Autumn 1997): 67–84.

Herek, Gregory M., Irving L. Janis, and Paul Huth. "Decision Making During International Crisis." *Journal of Conflict Resolution* 31 (1987): 203–226.

Hermann, Charles F., ed. *International Crises.* New York: Free Press, 1972.

Hermann, Margaret G., and Charles F. Hermann. "Who Makes Foreign Policy Decisions and How? An Empirical Inquiry." *International Studies Quarterly* 33 (1989): 361–87.

Holsti, Ole R. "Crisis Decision Making." In *Behavior, Society, and Nuclear War,* edited by Philip E. Tetlock, Charles Tilly, Robert Jervis, Jo L. Husbands, and Paul C. Stern. New York: Oxford University Press, 1989.

———. "The Operational Code Approach to the Study of Political Leaders: John Foster Dulles' Philosophical and Instrumental Beliefs." *Canadian Journal of Political Science* 3 (1970): 123–57.

Houghton, David Patrick. "Reinvigorating the Study of Foreign Policy Decision Making: Toward a Constructivist Approach." *Foreign Policy Analysis* 3 (2007): 24–45.

Janis, Irving L. *Groupthink: Psychological Studies of Policy Decisions and Fiascoes.* 2nd ed. New York: Cengage, 1982.

Jervis, Robert. *Perception and Misperception in International Politics.* Cambridge, MA: Harvard University Press, 1976.

Khong, Yuen Foong. *Analogies at War.* Princeton, NJ: Princeton University Press, 1992.

Kinzer, Stephen. *The Brothers: John Foster Dulles, Allen Dulles, and Their Secret World War.* New York: Times Books, 2013.

Larson, Deborah Welch. *Origins of Containment: A Psychological Explanation.* Princeton, NJ: Princeton University Press, 1985.

Lichtblau, Eric. *Bush's Law: The Remaking of American Justice.* New York: Pantheon, 2008.

March, James G., and Johan P. Olsen. *Rediscovering Institutions: The Organizational Basis of Politics.* New York: Free Press, 1989.

McCalla, Robert B. *Uncertain Perceptions: U.S. Cold War Crisis Decision Making.* Ann Arbor: University of Michigan Press, 1992.

Mintz, Alex, and Karl DeRouen Jr. *Understanding Foreign Policy Decision Making.* New York: Cambridge University Press, 2010.

Mintz, Alex, and Carly Wayne. *The Polythink Syndrome: U.S. Foreign Policy Decisions on 9/11, Afghanistan, Iraq, Iran, Syria, and ISIS.* Stanford, CA: Stanford University Press, 2016.

Mitchell, David. *Making Foreign Policy: Presidential Management of the Decision-Making Process.* Burlington, VT: Ashgate, 2005.

Preston, Thomas. *The President and His Inner Circle: Leadership Style and the Advisory Process in Foreign Affairs.* New York: Columbia University Press, 2001.

Ripley, Randall B., and Grace Franklin. *Congress, the Bureaucracy, and Public Policy.* 5th ed. Pacific Grove, CA: Brooks/Cole, 1991.

Robinson, William I. *Promoting Polyarchy: Globalization, U.S. Intervention, and Hegemony.* New York: Cambridge University Press, 1996.

Rosati, Jerel A. *The Carter Administration's Quest for Global Community: Beliefs and Their Impact on Behavior.* Columbia: University of South Carolina Press, 1991.

Rosati, Jerel A., and Colleen E. Miller. "Political Psychology, Cognition, and Foreign Policy Analysis." In *The International Studies Encyclopedia*, edited by Robert A. Denemark. Hoboken, NJ: Wiley, 2010.

Rothkopf, David. *National Insecurity: American Leadership in an Age of Fear.* New York: PublicAffairs, 2014.

Schafer, Mark, and Scott Crichlow. *Groupthink Versus High-Quality Decision Making in International Relations.* New York: Columbia University Press, 2010.

Sigal, Leon V. *Disarming Strangers: Nuclear Diplomacy with North Korea.* Princeton, NJ: Princeton University Press, 1988.

Snyder, Richard C., H. W. Bruck, Burton Sapin, Valerie Hudson, Derek H. Chollet, and James M. Goldgeier. *Foreign Policy Decision Making (Revisited).* New York: Palgrave Macmillan, 2002.

Sprout, Harold, and Margaret Sprout. *The Ecological Perspective on Human Affairs.* Princeton, NJ: Princeton University Press, 1965.

Sylvan, Donald, and James Voss. *Problem Representation in Foreign Policy Decision-Making.* New York: Cambridge University Press, 1998.

't Hart, Paul. *Groupthink in Government: A Study of Small Groups and Policy Failure.* Baltimore: Johns Hopkins University Press, 1990.

't Hart, Paul, Eric K. Stern, and Bengt Sundelis, eds. *Beyond Groupthink: Political Group Dynamics and Foreign Policy-Making.* Ann Arbor: University of Michigan Press, 1997.

Walker, Stephen G., and Mark Schafer. "Operational Code Theory: Beliefs and Foreign Policy Decisions." In *The International Studies Encyclopedia*, edited by Robert A. Denemark. Hoboken, NJ: Wiley, 2010.

Weldes, Jutta. *Constructing National Interests: The United States and the Cuban Missile Crisis.* Minneapolis: University of Minnesota Press, 1999.

Yetiv, Steve A. *Explaining Foreign Policy: U.S. Decision-Making in the Gulf Wars.* 2nd ed. Baltimore: Johns Hopkins University Press, 2011.

Zegart, Amy B. *Spying Blind: The CIA, the FBI, and the Origins of 9/11.* Princeton, NJ: Princeton University Press, 2007.

4 The President

Donald J. Trump takes the oath of office as the forty-fifth president of the United States in January 2017.

Preview

The president of the United States is the most visible symbol of the United States in the making of foreign policy. The bases of presidential power are both constitutional and political, and are mostly balanced by limiting powers either held by Congress or arising from the political process. The chapter begins by analyzing the bases of presidential power, including those powers and limitations placed on the president by the Constitution, and the discussion then moves to politically based sources of presidential advantage and limitation in the foreign policy area. Following these institutional impacts, the chapter examines the human side of the presidential role, examining specifically presidential personality and preferred decision-making styles as influences that help explain how different presidents approach the foreign policy aspect of their job differently and have different experiences and outcomes on foreign policy matters.

Key Concepts

codetermination	limits of policy possibility
head of government	cognitive style
head of state	sense of efficacy and confidence
Commander in Chief	orientation toward political conflict
treaty negotiator	competitive model
plenipotentiary	formalistic model
executive agreements	collegial model
presidential singularity	

The recently concluded presidential campaign of 2016, despite any other characteristics one attributes to it, showed markedly two things about American politics and foreign policy as a component of those politics. First, it showed the primary components of politics: the influence of individuals and their personalities and of political institutions in action. Much of the campaign centered on an examination of people, their personalities, their partisan positions, and assessments about their personalities and thus their temperament and preparation for office. The depictions that opponents made of one another from the party primaries through the general election were often stark, raw, and unkind.

At the same time, they all occurred within and about the political framework within which politics, and foreign policy, are made. Republicans, for instance, often accused departing President Obama as a chief executive who regularly overextended and abused his constitutional prerogatives and promised to return government to a more sensible position within the constitutional system. Democrats accused Republicans of attempting to retract government by unwisely manipulating constitutional powers should they gain office.

The second thing the campaign demonstrated was the distinction between normal partisanship and the super-partisanship that has come to mark so much of American politics. The questions were often not so much about what policies a given candidate would pursue (although that debate was present) as it was about ancillary matters (e.g., who would get to nominate new justices for the Supreme Court). If one did not know better, one would have suspected that the opposition was composed of aliens intent on destroying the system. This tenor meant that whoever triumphed, the political atmosphere would be polluted to the point that whoever won would face a fiercely super-partisan opposition. It is within these parameters that a discussion of the executive in the foreign policy process must begin.

Based on a concept known as **codetermination**, the power to make foreign policy is divided between the executive and legislative branches of government. The principle is that each body determines its views on foreign issues, and by interactions between them, they codetermine what policy will be. In broad terms, it is a straightforward process; in practice, it is much less tidy.

By granting separate powers and authorities (described separately in this chapter and chapter 6) to the two branches, the result has been Corwin's invitation to struggle, wherein individuals and groups in each branch seek to create and influence perceptions, interests, and policies. There are differences on most issues, so the interactions are often spirited and difficult to resolve. In the gridlocked, super-partisan contemporary environment, the result is often policy paralysis. Since so many issues collide at the intermestic intersection, that paralysis is increasing for both the United States and the foreign actors with which it interacts.

Levels of animosity and paralysis reached a zenith during the Obama presidency, largely along partisan lines. A great deal of the often bitter disagreements centered on the Middle East, where Democrats and Republicans clashed on multiple fronts, from how to deal with Israel to what to do about the Islamic State as a threat. There was very little disagreement on basic interests and objectives: contributing to greater American security and interests in the world. The disagreements, which have carried over after the election, were about virtually everything dealing with how to reach those objectives.

Will these trends continue now that a new president has taken the oath of office? Will the new administration be successful in reducing the roughest edges on the invitation to struggle, or will harsh and often bitter super-partisanship continue to prevail? The answers to those questions begin by examining the constitutional and political roles of the chief executive.

Presidents have varied considerably in how they approach foreign policy and how effective they are in its pursuit. To understand the presidential role in foreign policy and how that role differs among different holders of the office, the rest of the chapter will proceed along two dimensions. The first dimension is presidential powers in the foreign policy area, divided into formal, constitutional powers and limitations and more informal, political sources of presidential authority and limits on presidential behavior. The second dimension will be the human side of the equation, dealing specifically with how individual presidential characteristics such as presidential personality and preferred decision-making styles affect how different presidents conduct foreign policy.

Presidential Powers and Constraints

The underlying purpose of the U.S. Constitution is to divide political power and authority among the various branches of government, the so-called separation of powers, and this principle applies to the area of foreign policy as well as it does to other areas of governance. Both the executive and legislative branches are given independent sources of authority (the judicial branch, by constitutional provision and tradition, basically limits its role to refereeing differences between the branches), and the result is a system based on codetermination in making and executing power.

In contemporary times, the presidency has been the more prominent actor in most foreign policy matters, creating the impression of presidential preeminence. That impression is certainly constitutionally false. The framers of the Constitution envisaged a much simpler, less prominent role for foreign affairs and did not elaborate formal powers extensively, but they clearly intended that the legislative and executive branches would both be vital, active participants in the process. Times, however, change. The sheer volume and complexity of foreign affairs in the modern world make it virtually impossible for Congress to oversee all foreign policy matters to the extent the framers would have preferred.

Over time, the pendulum of presidential or congressional primacy has swung back and forth. When foreign affairs were less frequent and less urgent, as they were during the first century and a half or so of the American republic, Congress was more assertive, sometimes even dominant, as in the Senate's refusal to ratify the Versailles Treaty ending World War I. The Cold War and the events surrounding international terrorism swung the center of activity firmly toward the executive branch. Whether a new president will be able to overcome the polarization of government and bring some codetermination remains to be seen.

These trends certainly mean that the president is not a free agent who can carry on whatever foreign policy he or she may favor. Indeed, the presidency operates within a web of authority and limitations on that authority. To understand the opportunities and constraints that exist, the discussion moves sequentially in three steps. First, it will describe and briefly analyze the constitutional powers of and limits on the president. Second, it will move from the formal nexus to the political advantages that the president, as the highest elected politician in the country, has in the foreign policy area. Third, it will conclude with some of the major limitations on presidential authority and autonomy in this area of public policy.

Formal Powers of the President

The framers did not view foreign policy as a major part of the political life of the country, so they were reasonably sparse in their enumeration of presidential authorities. The Constitution itself describes six specific, and to some extent overlapping, powers and responsibilities for the president. By virtue of office, the president is (1) chief executive (**head of government**), (2) chief (head) of state; and (3) commander in chief of the armed forces of the United States. The president's enumerated powers cover (4) treaty negotiations, (5) nomination and appointment of key personnel, and (6) recognition of foreign regimes. Nearly all of these are balanced by sources of congressional limitation to provide codetermination.

Chief Executive (Head of Government) Article II, Section 1, of the Constitution makes the president the country's chief executive. In this role, the president exercises the rights and privileges associated with the executive branch of the government, including supervision and control over the resources of the federal bureaucracy, virtually all of which is part of the executive branch. At the same time, this role makes the president the head of the government, which means he or she is the highest elected politician in the country (the only nationally elected politician) and thus the partisan head of one of the two operational political bodies (the executive and the legislative).

The chief executive/head of government role creates two distinct but important aspects of the presidency in foreign policy. As chief executive, the president is the ultimate reporting channel for all the millions of individuals who work within the various executive agencies of the government. In the foreign policy area, this means that the State and Defense departments report to the president, as do the various parts of the intelligence community (the Central Intelligence Agency and the various intelligence agencies attached to the Defense Department, for instance) and the entire Homeland Security complex of agencies. The president does not directly supervise each of these efforts personally in detail (to the occasional embarrassment of the presidency), but it does mean that the federal bureaucracy works for the president and is expected—within some limits—to carry out presidential preferences and demands. It also means that the majority of federal expertise resides in these agencies and is available to the president in the making and execution of whatever foreign policy the president as chief elected politician chooses to pursue.

By virtue of being the chief executive, the president is also the country's major political leader—a partisan politician pursuing a partisan agenda who just happens to occupy the country's most powerful single position. The chief executive defines federal actions within congressional mandates, so the president is thus a partisan political figure who is not above partisan disagreements. This aspect of the presidential role—the president as head politician—stands in stark contrast to the office's second role.

Chief (Head) of State The president is the recognized face of the United States to foreign governments and the world at large. As such, the position extends beyond the partisan role as the chief politician to being the active symbol of the American government and the rallying point of the American people. In addition to being the partisan politician president, in other words, the president is also the current embodiment of the presidency (the constitutionally provided office of president).

This role is particularly prominent in the foreign policy area, although it is an implied role in strictly constitutional terms and reflects international law and practice as well. The president is the sole American official who can initiate and carry on interactions with foreign governments. Part of the reason for this comes from international law and practice connected to the principle of sovereignty. This concept traditionally assigns the sovereign authority of the state to its highest symbolic ruler; at the time the practice took hold in Europe in the seventeenth century, the sovereign was typically a monarch, and the practice has extended in modern times to elected chief executives.

The **head of state** function is, in important ways, the symbolic or ceremonial role of the president. Under its guise, presidents meet with and host the heads of government and state of other countries. As the embodiment of the state in much the same way as the flag or national anthem, the presidency (and its occupant) is treated with extraordinary deference, in ways that apparently exceed presidential grants of authority in the Constitution itself. As head of state, the president is the recognizable leader whom everyone knows. The president has his or her own personal airplane and helicopter (Air Force One and Marine One), a personal armored limousine transported to wherever the president goes, and a personal anthem, "Hail to the Chief." No other political figure is accorded any of these perquisites.

The American system's combination of the roles of head of government and head of state is the source of some confusion and friction within the American political system (see intersection 4.1). Many countries assign the roles of head of government and head of state to different institutions and individuals, thereby separating the roles and personages of the head of government and head of state. In the United Kingdom, for instance, the prime minister is the head of government, whereas the monarch is the head of state. This dichotomy allows Britons to engage in active, even acrimonious debate about the political leader of the country (the prime minister) and that person's policies, without simultaneously engaging in actions that may undercut the country, symbolized by Queen Elizabeth II for the past sixty-five years.

Intersection 4.1	The President, the Presidency, Polarization, and Iran

The Iranians remain a vocal and often emotional adversary for the United States.

One implication of the principle of sovereignty is that the countries of the world look to a single individual within each of the states with which they interact as the authority who represents the policies of those countries and has the authority to conduct national business. In the United States, the president—as chief executive and symbol of the presidency—fulfills that role.

The fact that the president is both head of government and of state sometimes complicates international dealings, particularly in a hyperpartisan environment. When foreign governments deal with the United States, the presumption is that the president's position on items under discussion is the official position of the country. This has never been entirely the case on controversial matters, and current levels of hyperpartisanship virtually guarantee opposition to the president's position on virtually any matter; this division may have the effect of weakening the authority of the head of the U.S. government with other countries.

The multilateral negotiations between Iran and leading Western states (spearheaded by the United States) to prevent that country from obtaining nuclear weapons is an example. The so-called P+1 countries (the five permanent members of the UN Security Council and Germany) conducted the Western side of the negotiations with the government of Iran—the only people under international law and practice who could legitimately carry on and conclude the agreements. Ultimately, they reached an accord that took force in January 2016.

Defenders of the water's edge preference had little to cheer about; partisan rhetoric in the United States attacked the bargain, informed the Iranians they would oppose its implementation unless their other (largely unacceptable) conditions were met, and even vowed to rescind the agreement if their candidate won the 2016 presidential election. In that atmosphere, who would relish negotiating with the United States in the future?

Commander in Chief Article II, Section 2, of the Constitution makes the president "**Commander in Chief** of the Army and Navy of the United States, and of the Militia of the several States, when called into the actual Service of the United States." That language is straightforward enough, but it does not include a definitive statement about what the commander in chief is authorized to do with those forces it authorizes the president to command. Article I of the Constitution reserves the right to declare war to Congress (discussed in chapter 6), and the framers almost certainly presumed that the actual employment of armed forces would occur only after some positive authorization from Congress. In practice, that has not been the case, and the result has been ambivalence and controversy over the extent of the power of the president as commander in chief.

In fact, the formal war-making power of the presidency has been used very sparingly during the country's existence. Formal declarations of war have preceded only five American military actions (the War of 1812, Mexican-American War, Spanish-American War, and the two world wars), whereas American military forces have been employed in warlike situations hundreds of other times, the exact number depending on how one defines an act of war. These other employments of force have sometimes been authorized by some kind of informal congressional resolution (the Vietnam War, Persian Gulf War of 1990, and the American invasion of Iraq, or instance), but sometimes they have been preceded by no formal action of Congress at all (the initial deployment of American forces in Afghanistan or American action in Libya, for instance). Over time, there have been congressional attempts to limit the commander in chief's ability to employ force without prior congressional authorization (the War Powers Act of 1973 is an example), but none have been particularly effective and have been challenged by the executive branch as unnecessarily prohibitive of the country's need to be able to respond to national emergencies.

Treaty Negotiator The authority as **treaty negotiator**—to commit the country to legally binding international commitments—is found in Article II, Section 2 of the Constitution and is a major source of presidential power. The head of state role makes the president the only internationally recognized representative of the U.S. government, and thus the president (or his or her officially designated representatives, known as **plenipotentiaries**) is the only official of the government authorized to negotiate legally binding agreements for the government. This grant of power is, however, tempered by dividing the authority between the president and the Senate in the stipulation that the president "shall have Power, by and with the Advice and Consent of the Senate, to make Treaties, provided two-thirds of the Senators present concur."

The framers presumed that all binding agreements between the United States would be conducted through the formal treaty process. Like war fighting, this proved not to be the case. Presidents have employed force without prior authorization for a variety of reasons, but the eclipse of the sole utilization of the treaty process can be traced to two factors, one quite specific and concrete, and the other more general.

The specific instance was the refusal of the U.S. Senate to ratify the peace treaty ending World War I. This refusal was the result of complex interactions and feuds between President Wilson and the Senate, but meant that the United States did not participate in the League of Nations, the major edifice by which it helped create the peace. This display of senatorial obstinacy led to reexamination of the possibility of alternatives to formal senatorial approval of foreign policy commitments.

The momentum to find an alternative was reinforced by the increasing volume of international interactions between the United States and other countries creating legal obligations on the United States government. The framers did not anticipate this eventuality, given their beliefs in the relative unimportance and infrequency of international events. In the more contemporary world, however, the United States has been increasingly involved in multiple negotiations with many countries, the result of which is to create international obligations for the United States in a volume that the Senate could not possibly process. If the Senate tried to deal with all these obligations, it would have time to do absolutely nothing else, and still would almost certainly not get the job done.

The result was the practice of employing **executive agreements** as an alternative to treaties. These documents are identical to treaties in the legal obligations they create for the United States, but they do not require the approval of the Senate. Originally, the use of this tool was limited to routine matters that did not require the active assent of the Senate because of their noncontroversial nature, but they have increased in volume to the point that now the ratio of executive agreements to treaties is over twenty to one, and inevitably, some of these agreements are on matters that contain some controversy. The Iran nonproliferation accord is an executive agreement.

Since executive agreements are not mentioned in the Constitution, there is no formal limitation on when such agreements should be used rather than employing the full treaty approval process. Limits have, however, evolved. For one thing, most international agreements (treaties or executive agreements) are non-self-executing, which means their implementation requires some further governmental action (usually the expenditure of funds) to put them fully into effect. Thus a president who negotiates an executive agreement the Senate opposes may well find that he lacks the resources to implement its provisions. Possibly of even greater importance in contemporary international relations, executive agreements can be rescinded by subsequent presidents without congressional acquiescence. The logic, quite simply, is that since the Senate did not approve them in the first place, then the Senate has no veto over canceling them. In the wake of the 2016 election, President Trump suggested that he might rescind a number of executive agreements negotiated by his predecessor, including both the Iran nuclear agreement and American participation in the Paris Agreement (see chapter 11).

Nominator of Key Personnel Article II, Section 2, also authorizes the president to nominate "Ambassadors, Other Public Ministers and Counsels" to federal positions, subject to the same advice and consent process assigned to treaties. This means that the president can nominate foreign policy officials who share his or her views to conduct foreign policy, although those views must not be so offensive that more than a third of the Senate rejects them.

This process becomes controversial in two instances of presidential nominations. In some cases, candidates may be so obnoxious or objectionable on personal or ideological grounds that they are rejected. In 1989, for instance, George H. W. Bush nominated ex-Senator John Tower of Texas as his secretary of defense. Tower had been a particularly unpopular chair of the Senate Armed Services Committee (which held the hearings on his nomination), and was reputed to be a heavy drinker and womanizer, traits hardly suited to someone who would be entrusted with some of the country's most closely guarded secrets. Thus the Senate committee rejected his nomination, and Bush was forced to replace him with a more acceptable, less controversial candidate, Richard Cheney. Occasionally as well, the appointment process is used for political patronage, such as appointing large political contributors to ambassadorships. President Reagan, for instance, nominated a St. Louis businessman, Theodore Maino, as his ambassador to Botswana. Asked his credentials for the job in Senate Foreign Relations Committee confirmation hearings, Maino replied he was qualified by virtue of a "commitment to public service, having a lifetime association with the Boy Scouts of America." Maino was confirmed.

The appointment power also contains one of the few exceptions to codetermination. Although the president must have senatorial power to appoint high-level officials, he is not limited when he chooses to dismiss those officials. Since presidential appointees serve at the pleasure of the chief executive, they are subject to removal if their service becomes displeasing, and the Senate has no formal recourse to prevent a president firing people it has approved.

Recognizer of Foreign Governments This derived constitutional grant comes from Article II, Section 3, of the Constitution, which declares that the president "shall receive Ambassadors and other public Ministers" from foreign governments. This grant has been interpreted to extend to enabling presidents either to commence or terminate relations with other countries by appointing or refusing to appoint personnel to other countries or by accepting or rejecting foreign emissaries.

Sometimes this power can have dramatic effect. From 1949, when the Chinese communists prevailed in the Chinese civil war, until 1972, the United States had no relations with the People's Republic of China (PRC), maintaining that the legal government of all China was the Nationalist Chinese government located on Taiwan (where they fled after losing the war in 1949). President Nixon, however, felt strongly that this diplomatic anomaly was not in the best foreign policy interests of the country and began a process to open relations between the U.S. government and the mainland Chinese. This process commenced unofficially with the visit of an American table tennis team to China (so-called Ping-Pong diplomacy) and reached official status in 1972 when Nixon visited the PRC. President Carter completed the process by extending full recognition to China in 1979. None of these actions required formal congressional assent.

Informal (Political) Powers of the Presidency

An assortment of informal sources of presidential power augments the formal, constitutional powers of the president. Three of these will be described for illustrative purposes: presidential singularity, the role of public opinion and media access, and the president's position as a world leader.

Presidential Singularity One of the greatest presidential advantages over his colleagues and rivals in Congress is **singularity**: there is one president as opposed to 535 members of Congress. The members of Congress are generally much more faceless and less well known than the president outside their individual states or districts (although electronic media are making it easier for some to become recognizable, at least on select matters). Moreover, the president of the United States is unique in that the incumbent is the only American politician who can claim a national constituency, since he or she is elected by the entire American electorate rather than some narrower group of Americans. On policy matters, the president is the only politician who can claim to have a national mandate to act by virtue of his status as the country's leading politician (head of government).

When combined with his symbolic role as head of state, this makes the president of the United States by far the most prominent political figure in the country. In important national moments such as crises, the American people look instinctively to the president for leadership and guidance, whether the occasion is a foreign policy disaster like 9/11 or a domestic emergency like Hurricane Katrina or the BP oil spill of 2010. If presidents act appropriately in these moments, the fact that they, rather than their more numerous counterparts in the legislative branch, can take action gives them a distinct leadership advantage.

Public Opinion and Media Access Presidential singularity also makes the president the prime national object of public and media scrutiny. The American people, by and large, are more interested in the activities and thoughts of the president than they are of any other politician; what the president does or says is news in a way that is not true for anyone else. It is not, for instance, a coincidence that major news-gathering organizations all have reporters assigned full-time to covering the president (the White House press corps). President Trump, with his penchant for tweeting, has raised the centrality of the president's access to the population to new levels.

Public opinion and interest and media access are, of course, related. The fact that the public wants to know what the president is doing drives much media attention, and media coverage creates public awareness and interest. Presidents use this dynamic relationship to try to rally support for their positions. Their access to the White House press corps, for instance, means they can call formal or informal press conferences simply by announcing their intent to or, more informally, by simply wandering down to the press room in the White House and sitting down for a conversation with journalists. Often these sessions are "off the record" (not for attribution), and electronic or print sources will often quote "unnamed White House sources" who are in fact the president speaking off the record.

In an age of extreme partisanship and polarity, media access has had a flip side. The proliferation of media outlets such as websites and cable television has meant that presidents are scrutinized in more detail than ever before, and this observation is often conducted by people who lack the objectivity of traditional journalists and who have strong political agendas that they layer upon their analysis of presidential activities.

International Diplomacy and World Leadership Most presidents either enter office with or develop an affinity for foreign policy. Partly, foreign affairs are more glamorous than domestic politics, particularly when the president is acting in his or her ceremonial role as head of state. President George H. W. Bush admitted this attraction during a 1990 domestic budget summit, saying, "When you get a problem with the complexities that the Middle East has now . . . I enjoy putting the coalition together and . . . seeing this aggression does not succeed. I can't say I just rejoice every time I go up and talk to (former congressman) Danny Rostenkowski . . . about what he's going to do on taxes." Foreign policy issues, in other words, have an inherent glamour not possessed by many domestic issues.

Some of this glamour has eroded, for several reasons, in recent years. First, the tradition of bipartisanship in foreign affairs (the "water's edge") used to make overt criticism of foreign policy largely off limits. This principle has eroded in a more partisan political environment. Second, the public by and large does not understand foreign affairs and thus has traditionally given the chief executive more deference due to the expertise of the presidency. This restraint has also been eroded by exploding media coverage of international events (often by reporters of dubious expertise) that makes everyone believe that he or she is an expert. Third, foreign policy has traditionally been abstract to average Americans, and its impacts have not clearly and obviously had a personal effect on individual Americans. The increasingly intermestic impact of foreign affairs has limited this advantage as well. Finally, the president's role as world leader does afford opportunities for the office holder to travel overseas and be presented as a symbol of the American people (reviewing troops in foreign capitals during state visits, for instance) that puts the president in a favorable light. Increasingly, however, presidential visits and the like are made to multilateral affairs where organized opposition to the proceedings may diminish the positive impact or where other leaders share the limelight.

Presidential Constraints

The constitutional and political advantages of the president do not establish the chief executive as such an overarching figure as to be a "free agent" in making foreign policy. In addition to political advantages, there are constraints on the president's capabilities and actions. Five are worth noting as examples.

Presidents do not propose or implement their policy preferences starting from a tabula rasa (blank slate). Rather, they take office within a context of previous history, and thus one of the constraints they face is a network of past programs and policies. When the new president comes from the same party (and possibly even administration) as his or her predecessor, he or she may support most of the existing policies and not find the existing reality too constraining. When the new president is a member of the opposite party, the existing policy network may represent a major obstacle. This is especially true in policy areas where the two parties are divided fundamentally along ideological, partisan lines and in which the new president campaigned actively based on repudiating and reversing existing policies.

This situation is particularly pregnant in times of extreme partisanship and polarization. When President Obama entered office, his first foreign policy goal was to end the long Iraq War started under his Republican predecessor. In 2016, GOP presidential candidates like Trump were equally intent on changing U.S.-Iran relations. Both were difficult tasks.

This leads to the second, related constraint, the **limits of policy possibility**. New presidents, and especially outsiders to the White House, typically enter office with a more expansive view of what they can accomplish (and especially what they can change) than is indeed possible. To some degree, this problem arises from the network of policies and programs already in place, but is augmented by the realization that there had to have been considerable support for those policies to have been implemented and kept in place that must be overcome. In the current partisan environment, almost any attack on a previous administration's policies will be resisted along party and ideological lines if a new administration comes from the other party.

The limits are especially vivid in domestic politics. The heated debate over the Affordable Care Act is an example. They also exist over foreign policy matters. In some cases, the limits of possibility may be even more extreme, because policies may be formalized in binding agreements (treaties or executive agreements) between the United States and foreign governments that are difficult to abridge or rescind without considerable diplomatic activity and the possibility of negative impacts on U.S. relations with the country or countries involved. "Tearing up" the arms control agreement with Iran, which Republican presidential candidates such as Donald Trump proposed, is a case in point. That executive agreement not only entailed obligations between the U.S. and Iranian governments, but also obligations to other members of the P+1 group.

A third constraint on the president is bureaucratic responsiveness. While it is true that the entire federal bureaucracy assigned to the executive branch technically works for and is controlled by the chief executive, the actual degree to which the constituent agencies and members of that bureaucracy relate to and enthusiastically support the policies of the occupant of the Oval Office will vary considerably. When any president enters office, it cannot be taken for granted that all its members supported the particular candidate who won or embrace the policy initiatives the new president may favor, and it is indeed part of the limits on policy possibility that particular dissonance within the bureaucracy can make a president less successful than he or she might otherwise be.

Presidents come to understand this problem and try to deal with it. When George W. Bush created the Department of Homeland Security or DHS (discussed in chapter 5), part of that act required shuffling relevant agencies from their traditional places in the federal hierarchy to the new department, a prospect that was not entirely welcomed. Realizing that some agencies would resent their reassignment and that their employees might react by trying to undercut the president's mission, Bush responded with an initiative to remove civil service protection from all employees, leaving all members of the DHS as political appointees who could be dismissed at will by the White House. This proposal was universally opposed within the federal bureaucracy for its potential precedential value and particularly by those whose job security would have been endangered, and Bush was forced to back down to get the new agency approved at all.

Presidents attempt to ensure the responsiveness of their bureaucracies through the political appointment process. Within the executive branch, several thousand of the top-level jobs are political appointments, people specifically chosen by the administration for positions at the secretarial or sub-secretarial levels. In addition to serving as a political reward, these appointees are named because of their devotion to the president's agenda, and it is their job to ensure that presidential wishes are carried out within their agencies. Such officials, however, serve entirely at the pleasure of the president, and as already pointed out, can be removed at presidential whim. The clear majority of officials in these agencies, however, are career professionals, people with considerable expertise in their fields who are protected from removal from office by civil service protection that is intended to ensure that they cannot be forced into actions they view as unconscionable. Keeping political appointees "in line" is always easier than with career officials.

The fourth constraint is presidential time and time management. The array of national and international problems that confronts any is are clearly excessive to the abilities of any chief executive to perform them all, meaning that much presidential leadership is an exercise in time management. Presidents can tilt their activity levels toward domestic or foreign policy emphases partially dependent on individual preferences, but they are also constrained by the amount of time they allot to their offices various aspects of their responsibilities. Often, presidential attention must be given to crises, and these often have foreign policy content, since national security may be involved. Try as the individual might, the president's time may be dictated by events, not personal preferences.

Fifth, there is the matter of the extreme partisanship that is a central feature of the contemporary environment. Knowing that anything a president may propose will become part of the polarized wrangle among Washington partisans adds a further dimension to the constraints on presidential activity. This problem is especially acute in the transition between administrations, as suggested in intersection 4.2.

Intersection 4.2 — The Revolving Door: Forming a New Administration as Opportunity and Constraint

Whenever a presidential election results in a new chief executive, as it did in 2016, there is a change in the cast of political appointees who assist the president in the conduct of his or her administration. This process and its outcomes provide both opportunities and constraints on the presidential ability to conduct foreign policy.

The domestic situation a newly elected president faces has two major physical dimensions that are affected by the hyperpartisanship of many people in the policy process. The first dimension is the new president's party affiliation: does he or she come from the same party as the outgoing incumbent? If it is the same party, many officials will likely share the new occupant's philosophies, will want to stay on, and will be welcome. The effect will be to minimize the number of people who will have to be recruited, vetted, and put through the confirmation process. If the new president comes from the other party, partisan consideration will likely result in a "house cleaning," since incumbents will likely be ideologically unacceptable to the new regime. Each party has a virtually mutually exclusive stable of potential appointees (discussed in chapter 7), making the process lengthier and more arduous.

How onerous this process is depends to a large degree on the second dimension: which party controls Congress, and especially the Senate, which has jurisdiction over officials requiring confirmation. If the Senate is controlled by the new president's party, appointing and confirming new officials is relatively simpler than if the opposition party is in the majority. In the former case, most of the obstruction will amount to legislative chicanery (e.g., use of the filibuster). If the opposition party controls the Senate, it will control the approval process and can seriously impede the filling of administration positions.

The process is particularly vivid when the two dimensions are combined in matrix form:

		Congress	
		Same Party	Other Party
President	Same Party		
	Other Party		

In this example, same party as the president refers to a continuation of the party from the preceding president. The same party as Congress means that Congress (especially the Senate) is controlled by the same party as the new president.

The matrix represents four outcomes that maximize the opportunities or constraints on the new president. If both are of the same party, opportunities are maximized: the president can appoint like-minded officials and have the reasonable expectation that they will be confirmed. If the out party's candidate is elected president and has a Senate controlled by his or her party, there will be opportunities constrained by the need to construct a whole new team. If different parties control the White House and the Senate, polarization is likely to produce a contentious atmosphere emphasizing constraints. Comprehending these distinctions can help in understanding the transition period since the 2016 election.

The Human Side: Presidential Personality and Decision Style

Formal and informal opportunities and constraints frame how individual presidents conduct foreign policy. Knowing these, however, is not enough to understand the differences in how and why different presidents conduct the foreign policies that they do. Presidents are not only "political actors"; they are also human beings. Trying to understand the role of presidents without also comprehending their human dimensions is a sterile, unfulfilling enterprise resulting in only a partial picture of what the president does in foreign policy. To capture this dimension requires considering two aspects of the human element: presidential personality and the preferred decision-making style of different presidents. They are related in the sense that personality will influence preferred ways of organizing decision making in ways that are comfortable and effective for the individual president.

Typologies of Presidential Personality and Management Style

To organize the discussion, the analysis will borrow from two frameworks devised by prominent political scientists. The typology for dealing with presidential personality is borrowed from Professor Alexander George of Stanford from his seminal 1980 work, *Presidential Decisionmaking in Foreign Policy*. For dealing with different management style preferences, the analysis leans on distinctions made by Richard T. Johnson in his 1974 classic, *Managing the White House*.

Presidential Personality The taxonomy for differentiating presidential styles around personality is based on three selected personality traits that are directly relevant to understanding how individual presidents approach foreign policy tasks. For this purpose, the three traits that George argues accentuate this understanding are **cognitive style**, **sense of efficacy and confidence**, and **orientation**

toward political conflict. The first two of these traits are clearly related to one another, whereas the third is less closely correlated with the first two.

A president's cognitive style refers to how presidents process information, how they define personal needs for information, and how individuals acquire the information that they want. The key influences on these traits include the level of interest a president has in policy material generally, detailed foreign policy information in particular, and how much information the president feels comfortable dealing with.

Some presidents have been information minimalists. Ronald Reagan was a prime example: he seldom read serious material, displayed minimal intellectual curiosity about the details of policy issues he was deciding, and had a limited attention span for receiving oral briefings on material (his favored method of receiving information). In fact, his aides made a point of keeping information sessions with him brief because he tended to nod off during long presentations. George W. Bush shared this cognitive style. Donald Trump does not seem to search out policy details as well.

Other presidents are more information maximalists. John Kennedy immersed himself in the intricacies and details of policy issues, as did Nixon, Carter, and Clinton. All were voracious readers with remarkable memories who felt comfortable with the nuances of policy, which they took great pride in having mastered. To Carter, this attention to detail included micromanaging some concerns; for instance, he personally scheduled time on the White House tennis court.

Cognitive style also is manifested in how presidents like to receive information. Some presidents (Nixon in particular) preferred receiving information in written form, whereas others (both Bushes, for instance) preferred oral briefings and discussions with senior aides and subject experts. This preference in turn relates to the level of detail a president wants, since written materials generally provide much more detail than oral presentations.

The second key personality trait is a president's sense of efficacy and confidence. This refers to what a president feels he understands and is good at doing and, conversely, those areas where he or she feels less confident and qualified. Efficacy is essentially a measure of how comfortable a president feels both about making decisions in this area of policy, and also how good the incumbent is at convincing others of the merits of those positions and decisions.

There are really two elements at work here. The first is the degree of mastery of foreign policy issues. Some presidents, by background and experience, enter office with more knowledge than others: Obama and Clinton, for instance, studied international relations as undergraduate students, and George H. W. Bush had considerable foreign policy experience before entering office (as ambassador to the United Nations, head of the liaison office in Beijing prior to full recognition of China in 1979, and as director of the CIA). Other presidents, like George W. Bush, Reagan, and Trump, enter office with virtually no prior experience or obvious interest in foreign affairs. What may be crucial is the degree to which a president understands his or her own strengths and weaknesses. Reagan recognized his limits as a thinker and hands-on manager and delegated authority to those who did. George W. Bush generally did the same, but occasionally overstepped his expertise, as in his famous initial assessment that Vladimir Putin as a reasonable individual with whom he could "work."

The imprint that a president makes is also related to his or her ability to communicate foreign policy ideas and themes. Reagan, for instance, was the "great communicator," and could galvanize and convert audiences with soaring rhetoric usually based on extrapolations of his own ideas, an apparent trait of Trump. His 1987 entreaty to Gorbachev at the Berlin Wall ("Mr. Gorbachev, tear down this wall") stands as a monument to this capability. Presidents who combine great interpersonal and rhetorical skills like Clinton excel in dealing with supporters and opponents alike in convincing them to support ideas. At the other end of the spectrum, Richard Nixon, one of the most reclusive of all presidents, was at his best when dealing with difficult issues in the privacy of the Oval Office, but was chronically uncomfortable in interpersonal settings and had almost no knack for small talk. Standing atop the Great Wall of China in 1972 with China's Deng Xiaoping, the only thing Nixon could think to say was, "This sure is a great wall."

The third key personality variable is a president's orientation toward political conflict. Differences in political ideas and solutions (political conflict) are, of course, an integral part of the political process, but people differ greatly in how they react to and handle personally situations of conflict. Some presidents, Franklin Roosevelt being the most prominent example, positively flourished in situations where ideas were being argued and felt that the free-for-all of open, candid interchange produced the best policy results. FDR always felt in control of these kinds of situations. At the other extreme, an introverted person like Nixon felt so uncomfortable in situations of disagreement (especially with his own ideas) that he shunned interpersonal settings where even his chief advisors disagreed with one another or with him. Because he experienced considerable familial conflict as a child, Clinton also developed a reputation as an interpersonal conflict avoider.

Decision-Making Models   The three personality traits help predispose different presidents in how they organize the foreign policy apparatus. As Johnson points out, each president's personality leads the individual, implicitly or explicitly, toward one of three general models of management decision-making style.

The three models can be viewed on a continuum, with one model emphasizing greatest interaction and creativity on one end and greater order and formality on the other end. These extremes reflect a preference for greater effectiveness (emphasis on thorough consideration of all alternatives and choice of best alternatives) of efficiency (reaching decisions in the most orderly, timely manner). Between these two extremes is a model that tries to achieve a compromise. At the disorderly, effectiveness-oriented end of the spectrum, as suggested in figure 4.1, is the **competitive model**, while the **formalistic model** stands at the other extreme. In between is the **collegial model**.

The management style of the competitive model stresses the free and open expression of diverse advice and analysis within the executive branch. Individuals,

Competitive Model	Collegial Model	Formalistic Model
(Effectiveness)	(Compromise)	(Efficiency)

Figure 4.1 Decision Model Continuum

departments, and agencies are encouraged openly to compete with one another to influence the president's decisions. This decision style both tolerates and encourages disagreement on policy issues between agencies and their leaders. Presidents who employ this style want as many options as possible to reach them before any decisions are made rather than having policy discord resolved at lower bureaucratic levels. This model is untidy and lacks efficiency as a basic value, since the percolation of ideas is a more time-consuming process than a more hierarchical approach produces. It also requires great flexibility and a high sense of self-confidence in the president and his or her ability to ride herd on a purposely disorderly process.

The second extreme style is the formalistic model. In important ways, its values are the obverse of the competitive model. The formalistic model, as the name implies, places greatest emphasis on an orderly decision-making process with structured and predictable procedures for making decisions through well-established, hierarchical lines of reporting. Decision options are winnowed upward through the decision process so that a limited number of options reach the president's desk, and implementation of decisions is delegated downward through this same system. The effect—and intent—is to isolate the president from many of the details of policy making while allowing the incumbent to maintain maximum control over the system.

The third option is the collegial model. The purpose of this model is to retain the advantages of the two extreme models while eliminating their disadvantages. As such, it is essentially a compromise between the two extremes where a balance between effectiveness and efficiency is attempted. As an approach, it is not unlike American pragmatism within the ideological orientations discussed in chapter 1, where the end product is valued more than strict adherence to the process that produces it.

Presidents who employ the collegial model attempt to assemble a team of key advisors, aides, and cabinet officers with generally compatible but not identical views on policy but who can act as a team. The key notions are an adherence to the concept of "team" and "compatible." Within this approach, there is ideally a fairly free and open interchange of ideas between major advisors on policy alternatives, but with the agency heads thinking of themselves more as members of the presidential team than as advocates of their particular agencies. When decisions are reached, however, the members of the team are then expected to fall in line behind the decision and to embrace it. In the process, the competitive model's emphasis on thorough consideration of policy alternatives is accomplished by open discussions, and the emphasis on team loyalty adds some of the discipline and order associated with the formalistic model.

Patterns of Presidential Decision Style

Not all presidents have had identical (or even similar) personalities. Personal characteristics and circumstances surrounding their incumbencies have caused different presidents to have to choose different ways to run foreign policy. Thus, different presidents since World War II have chosen different basic decision-making models.

Table 4.1 categorizes the thirteen presidents who have occupied the office during or since World War II by the basic decision model they utilized. Examining the pattern helps understand better how different administrations have acted and may help organize thinking about future alternatives.

Several characteristics about the models and the different presidents who adopted them stand out. The first and most obvious is that the three models have not been equally popular. Almost half the presidents since 1945 have chosen the formalistic model, no president has chosen the competitive model in over forty years, and the collegial model has been chosen more often in recent years.

There are three other apparent commonalities among those choosing the various models. They are somewhat related to one another, particularly in the context of comparing those who have chosen the formalistic and collegial models that are the currently competing means of organization of administration styles. The second characteristic is that the presidents who have chosen the formalistic model were about a decade older (average age of sixty when they entered office) than those who chose the collegial model (average of fifty). Third, the formalistic

TABLE 4.1   **Presidential Decision Styles by Decision-Making Model**

Competitive Model

Franklin D. Roosevelt (1933–1945)
Lyndon B. Johnson (1963–1969)   Total: 2

Formalistic Model

Harry S. Truman (1945–1953)
Dwight D. Eisenhower (1953–1961)
Richard M. Nixon (1969–1974)
Gerald R. Ford (1974–1977)
Ronald W. Reagan (1981–1989)
George W. Bush (2001–2009)   Total: 6

Collegial Model

John F. Kennedy (1961–1963)
James E. Carter (1977–1981)
George H. W. Bush (1989–1993)
William J. Clinton (1993–2001)
Barack H. Obama (2009–2017)   Total: 5

model has been more associated with Republican than Democratic leaders. The only Democrat who adopted the formalistic model was Harry Truman at the end of World War II, and all the adherents to the collegial model except George H. W. Bush have been Democrats. Finally, there is an apparent connection to the Cold War as well. All of the Cold War presidents except Kennedy and Carter chose the formalistic model, whereas the only post–Cold War president who did not choose the collegial model was George W. Bush.

Whether these apparent relationships are meaningful or spurious cannot, of course, be established scientifically because of the small numbers of people involved, but there does seem to be some interconnection. The gravity of managing the Cold War, for instance, may have led to the election of leaders stressing experience (age) that is related to choice of the greater predictability of the formalistic model (John Kennedy, the youngest man elected president at age forty-three during the height of the Cold War, is the glaring exception). At the same time, the more fluid, less structured international system since the end of the Cold War has produced generally younger presidents for whom the greater flexibility of the collegial model may have appeal (George W. Bush is the obvious exception). A discussion of how different presidents have employed the various models may shed some additional light on these distinctions.

The Competitive Model

This has been the least utilized decision style by presidents, and no president has attempted to employ it in almost a half century. The reasons are probably multiple, but they relate to the fact that this is by far the most demanding decision system for the president to manage, placing the incumbent squarely in the middle of policy disagreements (on purpose) and maximizing the extent and depth of presidential involvement in the decision process. It thus requires an incumbent with an extraordinarily positive self-sense (arguably ego) and belief that he or she can surmount and make order of the chaos inherent in its operation. Only two presidents have tried; arguably only one has succeeded.

Why would a president choose this particular style? At the most obvious level and congruent with points already made, it ensures that the maximum number of opinions and options reach the president, rather than being compromised or condensed effectively into footnotes at lower levels of the political process. The result is to maximize personal presidential control over what goes on in the foreign policy area. The outcomes of policy disputes by presidents who use this model bear the authentic presidential imprint.

The competitive model is a consummate politician's model. Exposing, debating, and choosing among the largest set of options requires a nimble mind and the political skills to reconcile opposing views and to reach decisions that even those with contrary views can be brought around to support. The political leader who lacks considerable interpersonal persuasive skills will feel intensely uncomfortable in the kinds of debate forums the model encourages and will likely be drowned in the stridency and even acrimony of the competing advocacy of positions. Because the president will be virtually inundated by information and opinions when employing this model, the danger is informational overload that either paralyzes the ability to decide or consumes so much time that other priorities are neglected. It is probably no surprise that, as the demands of the contemporary presidency have proliferated in recent times, contemporary occupants of the White House have rejected this model.

As noted, only Franklin Roosevelt and Lyndon Johnson have employed this model. They were different men and they adopted the method for different reasons. Because it suited his personality, FDR was successful in employing it, as his success in managing the largest military coalition in world history while ending the Great Depression attests. LBJ, with a more brittle personality, was less successful.

The presidency of Franklin Roosevelt was the prototype of the competitive model. It fit his personality and personal style very well. Cognitively, FDR had an almost insatiable appetite for immersion in and command of policy detail that allowed him to operate in the intensely competitive policy environment he had created. He also preferred to sift through options in direct, face-to-face encounters with opposing agency heads, thereby sharpening his own sense of policies. Because he had a commanding personality and brimmed over with personal self-confidence, he felt that he was capable of managing the untidy, sometimes acrimonious, and fractious consequences of this model of operation. His style frustrated those around him (particularly agency heads who were bypassed when the president went to lower-level officials who possessed information or expertise he wanted), and in the hands of a less skilled politician, the result could have been political chaos. FDR was, however, the consummate politician of his day and arguably in the history of the presidency.

Lyndon Johnson tried, but in the end could not make the system succeed and eventually abandoned it. The primary reason was that LBJ, who was considered the premier legislative politician of his day, possessed neither the personal sense of expertise and efficacy to impose his views on the advisors he inherited from the Kennedy administration nor the enormous skill of FDR, his personal role model and the principal reason he attempted to adopt the model. In the end, LBJ was simply not FDR.

Johnson's style contrasted sharply with Roosevelt's. Prior to his service as Kennedy's vice president, his efforts and reputation were based on his skill as the leading congressional figure on domestic policy. As a result, he had spent little time on foreign affairs and lacked confidence in debating or arbitrating foreign policy disputes. He had to rely on the advice of holdovers from the JFK administration who held him in some intellectual disdain as a "country rube" amid the Ivy League "Camelot" that had surrounded the fallen Kennedy. Johnson had a legendary ability to "jawbone" members of Congress into accepting his positions (which he largely succeeded in doing in pushing through the Great Society entitlement and civil rights programs after Kennedy's death), but this skill did not extend to of a foreign policy management system built in the FDR style. Over time, his lack of oratorical skills decreased his ability to explain his positions on Vietnam effectively to the public, and his fragile sense of self-efficacy was further overwhelmed by mounting criticism (antiwar protesters chanting "LBJ, LBJ, how many kids did you kill today?" outside the White House gates, for instance).

Gradually, Johnson withdrew from the public. By the election year of 1968, his only major public appearances were on military bases where criticism could be controlled, and he eventually dropped out of the race for reelection. LBJ's lack of expertise on foreign policy matters also helped undermine the effective operation of that model.

It is difficult to imagine future presidents trying to institute the competitive model. Contemporary politics simply do not produce figures with the political strength and personal confidence of the aristocratic Roosevelt. The LBJ experience with the model demonstrated what happens when a politician with a more fragile personal sense of efficacy and personal assertiveness tries to employ this model. Given the sheer volume of presidential activity in both foreign and domestic politics, it is hard to imagine how any new incumbent could carve out the time to employ the competitive model effectively.

The Formalistic Model

Since the end of World War II, more presidents have employed the formalistic model than either of the other two models. This model was especially popular during the Cold War, and has been particularly attractive to older, Republican presidents. Why has this been the case?

The tie-in to the Cold War may be related to the kind of environment created by the global competition with communism. The Cold War spawned the mentality of the national security states and a sense of grim determination and steadfastness in the face of a visible and menacing enemy. The purpose of the Cold War exercise was explicitly conservative in the true meaning of the term: to preserve Western democracies in the face of the communist onslaught. It was further conservative in that the stakes were very high and the consequences of making a strategic error potentially catastrophic. Going with tried and true, conservative solutions seemed more prudent than more innovative, change-oriented approaches. Thus, investing the country's leadership in older, more conservative, and presumably calmer heads had an appeal not so necessarily attractive in a more fluid environment in which adaptation to change was the major value. Virtually all the presidents who adopted the formalistic model fit the mold that would flow from that kind of assessment.

The formalistic model is designed to promote order, structure, and discipline in decision making, all valued characteristics in a highly threatening, militarized environment. Its strong emphasis is on highly structured procedures and hierarchical lines of reporting that promote a well-defined set of procedures for considering and winnowing options for decision up the organizational ladder and for implementation once decisions are reached. Open conflict among agencies with different perspectives is discouraged, and an orderly process is preferred. This set of preferences led to the development of what is now known as the interagency process (discussed in chapter 5) by the Eisenhower administration. When it operates effectively, the formalistic model produces maximum efficiency in decision making, but not necessarily the most thorough, effective consideration of all possible outcomes. This trade-off, however, was reasonable in a Cold

War atmosphere where the options seemed narrow and "out of the box" thinking could prove calamitous.

Analysts agree that for the formalistic approach to work well, at least one of three conditions must be present. The first is a firm, hands-on management style at the top to achieve policy coherence. Normally this leadership must come personally from the president. If the president chooses not to assume this role, the second condition is to delegate the leadership role to a strong national security advisor or set of advisors—effective delegation of authority. The third condition is a commonly held worldview among all the major foreign policy actors that allows them to function together on common goals and policies. One or another of these principles applied in each of the cases of adherents of the formalistic model.

Of the six presidents who have adopted the formalistic model, five were Republicans. The single Democrat to employ the model was Harry Truman, whose reasons for doing so were basically idiosyncratic. The five Republicans, on the other hand, adopted the formalistic model for one of two basically contradictory reasons: either to maintain maximum personal control of the foreign policy process, or to allow for the orderly delegation of power to trusted subordinates in situations where the president lacked either the expertise or interest (or both) for heavy personal involvement.

The two Republican presidents who used the formalistic model to impose personal control over the process were Dwight D. Eisenhower and Richard M. Nixon. They operated the formalistic system differently and for different reasons, but their obvious connection was that Nixon served as Eisenhower's vice president and thus had eight years' experience operating in this kind of environment.

The formalistic model was a natural form of organization for someone with Eisenhower's background in the military. Ike had gained considerable experience commanding and coordinating the politico-military effort to overthrow Hitler in Europe, and he believed that the lessons he had learned in the process made him uncommonly well informed on international affairs and thus provided him the necessary expertise to navigate foreign policy. Moreover, his long and distinguished military career provided him with considerable experience in managing hierarchical decision-making structures, hallmarks of both military organizations and the formalistic model. Eisenhower had a sufficient sense of self-efficacy and confidence that he did not personally feel the need to take the public lead in foreign policy initiatives, a role he assigned to his colorful secretary of state, John Foster Dulles, but there was never any question whether Eisenhower was in firm charge and control of foreign policy.

Richard Nixon's reclusive personality caused him to choose the formalistic model. Nixon had a very firm command of international relations and felt himself eminently qualified to command and control the country's foreign policy. Nixon's personality caused him to shun interpersonal contact except with a small circle of advisors, and the formalistic model provided him with a shield to protect him against unwanted outside intrusion. The formalistic model thus put a cocoon around Nixon, allowing him to isolate himself in the White House surrounded only by trusted and self-reinforcing advisors like Henry Kissinger. Information flowed up the system to Nixon in controlled channels, and he could funnel his decisions downward through the bureaucracy for implementation. Moreover, Nixon's personality was deeply conspiratorial, and he distrusted many of the foreign policy mechanisms of the government, including the State Department, with whom he had a long-standing feud that dated back to his participation in investigations of the State Department's alleged infiltration by communists in the late 1940s and early 1950s. Using the formalistic model to insulate himself from outside influences, Nixon was able to control foreign policy while largely ignoring the State Department—at least until he dispatched Kissinger to the Secretary of State's job in 1973.

If Nixon used the formalistic model to provide himself the cover to control foreign policy, the other Republicans have used it to avoid heavy direct involvement in the making of foreign policy. Gerald Ford, Ronald Reagan, and George W. Bush all came to the presidency without demonstrated expertise or special interest in foreign policy, and each chose to employ the formalistic model to insulate him from foreign policy by delegating maximum authority to trusted advisors.

Ford's reasons are unique, reflecting the entirely idiosyncratic nature of his tenure in office. President Ford has the distinction of being the only chief executive who was never elected to any national office by the American people. The former House minority leader became vice president in 1973 when Nixon's elected second in command, Spiro T. Agnew, resigned his office amid controversy (accusation of participation in corruption while he was governor of Maryland); Ford was confirmed as vice president by the Senate. He became president according to the constitutional rule of succession when Nixon resigned the presidency in 1974. Thus, Ford became the only wholly unelected president and the only chief executive who could not lay claim to being the only politician chosen by the American people and having a mandate from them.

A personally unassuming, modest person, Ford understood the limitations both of his mandate and of his inexperience in foreign policy, and he left the formalistic model that he inherited from Nixon basically in place, relying heavily on Kissinger and the State Department to take the lead in foreign policy. The choice was probably a wise one, as a foreign policy gaffe during his 1976 election bid in which he declared communist Poland to be a free and independent state helped undermine his campaign and led to the election of President Carter.

The lure of the formalistic model to Reagan and Bush had similar roots in their lack of foreign policy expertise, but it also added a further element of disinterest and information minimalism that represented a conscious choice on each of their parts not to achieve command of the intricacies of foreign policy. Reagan had a notoriously short attention span in receiving information, and when he met with foreign leaders, his aides equipped him with three-by-five-inch note cards to guide him through policy discussions. Although he excelled at the ceremonial aspects of the presidency and had some very firm general ideas (such as his aversion to nuclear weapons), he lacked the perseverance to engage in detailed supervision of policy processes. This latter characteristic gave considerable leeway to subordinates operating under general guidance from the Oval Office and led to the most embarrassing foreign policy episode of the Reagan years, the Iran-Contra scandal, in which administration officials engaged in illegal and unwise policy acts in the name of the president. Bush largely followed this practice, adopting a "hands off" approach to foreign policy concerns not closely associated with his "war on terror."

The Democrat who adopted the formalistic model, Harry Truman, did so for different reasons. Truman became president in April 1945 on the death of FDR, two weeks before the war in Europe officially ended. Truman was not a foreign policy expert, but in his brief tenure as vice president (a job to which he was first elected in 1944), he had gained confidence in his abilities, which he applied to the struggle in the 1940s that produced the strategy of containment. Regarding foreign policy making, however, Truman was mainly motivated by a deep concern for what he considered the dignity of the office of the White House (the presidency). He felt that the highly disorderly competitive atmosphere of the FDR years diminished that dignity and did not fit his own less flamboyant style. As a result, he found the higher degree of order associated with the formalistic model attractive.

The Collegial Model

The collegial and formalistic models are, in some important ways, alternatives to one another. Adherence to the formalistic model dominated the Cold War era but, other than George W. Bush, more recent presidents have chosen the collegial model. Those who have chosen this model have also been younger and more Democratic than their formalistic counterparts. One can only speculate why.

The Cold War or its absence is one obvious source of difference. The collegial model has been favored since the end of the Cold War, and one reason may be differences in the foreign policy environment of the Cold War and post–Cold War periods. The Cold War was a tense and potentially explosive and apocalyptic period, whereas the post–Cold War period began more tranquilly, only to be jolted by the shocking yet amorphous emergence of terrorism as the major national threat. In this setting, a decision process that provides a freer rein to different ideas rather than a more highly disciplined approach to information and idea management may be more appropriate, and presidential aspirants who appear to possess more rigid views may seem less attractive than in the more structured, high-conflict times like the Cold War.

The heart of the collegial model is a foreign policy team of key aides, advisors, and cabinet officers with varying perspectives on policy matters but who can act as an effective team of equals, which the term "collegial" describes. It is a team approach, the major purpose of which is to encourage diversity of outlook among policy alternatives through group problem solving among equals. This notion of equality is supposed to foster a collegial, cooperative environment rather than serve as a venue for bureaucratic infighting, and members are encouraged to identify with the foreign policy team above the interests of their particular agencies. The system works best when the president, as the first among equals, has a coherent worldview around which to structure discussions.

For the collegial model to work well, one of two conditions must be met. One is a commanding president who articulates a clear vision from which participants in the collegial deliberation of policy specifics can take their bearing and direction. The second is an essential commonality of outlook among the principal actors. When one or the other of these principles has been in place, the collegial model has operated effectively; where they are not present, the model falters.

Five presidents have chosen this model. Two (Kennedy and Carter) came from the Cold War era. These two had different experiences with the model's operation. In the case of JFK, the model evolved from a foreign policy disaster at the beginning of his short tenure; in the case of Carter, he ultimately was less successful because neither condition was fully met.

John Kennedy, at age forty-three, was the youngest man elected president of the United States, and he arrived in office amid considerable controversy. His youth contrasted greatly with the age and stature of Eisenhower, whom he succeeded; the fact that he was the first Catholic to hold the office created fears in some parts of the population; and his defeat of Richard Nixon was razor close, decided in a few controversial precincts in Chicago. Moreover, he brought with him a group of advisors from the academic setting of his native Massachusetts.

Kennedy stumbled out of the blocks, authorizing the disastrously unsuccessful Bay of Pigs invasion of Cuba in 1961, a decision urged upon him by holdovers from Eisenhower's formalistic system. In the wake of that experience, JFK brought together a more congenial group of advisors whom he fashioned into an effective team in time to meet the Cuban Missile Crisis.

Kennedy came from one of the most established and popular political families in the country, and he had the instincts and serene self-confidence of a professional politician. He possessed an unquenchable cognitive appetite for information and immersed himself in the intricacies of policy. He was also a voracious reader and writer, whose book *Profiles in Courage* won him the Pulitzer Prize in literature in 1957. Kennedy's management style also featured a strong personal involvement in the details of policy making, a characteristic shared by other presidents employing the collegial model. By the time of his assassination in November 1963, JFK had devised an effective collegial style of foreign policy management that probably would have served him well in a second administration.

James Earl (Jimmy) Carter was the second president to attempt to implement the collegial model, and he was ultimately less successful in doing so. Carter was not as gifted an orator as Kennedy, but they did share some characteristics. Carter was also a voracious reader who sought to compensate for his personal inexperience in foreign affairs by immersing himself in books, documents, and reports on foreign affairs, and he engaged himself in the details of policy decisions. He was also comfortable in the give-and-take of policy debates and did not shy away from political conflict (a trait he has retained in his highly public post-presidency). As he has demonstrated in his very active post-presidential career, he has a high degree of confidence in his command of complex policy issues.

What undermined Carter's practice of the collegial model was that he could not meet either of the conditions for success. While Carter had a prodigious knowledge of the details of policy, he did not project a strong personal philosophy or paradigm beyond his personal belief that foreign policy should be grounded in American advocacy of human rights, a theme that never achieved traction within the volatile atmosphere of the Cold War. At the same time, the Carter foreign policy team was fractious, marked particularly by the clash between his hawkish national security advisor, Zbigniew Brzezinski, and his more dovish secretary of state, Cyrus Vance. The result was that foreign policy never achieved the coherence or unity that is a hallmark of successful collegial presidents.

The first post–Cold War president to attempt the collegial model was George H. W. Bush, whose term in office oversaw the end of the Cold War. Like Kennedy, Bush came from a patrician New England political family, and had both a long history of political service and a high sense of his personal expertise in the area based on his experience in Beijing, at the UN, as director of the CIA, and as vice president under Reagan for eight years. He also possessed excellent interpersonal skills and was especially effective in one-on-one debates over policy. Unlike Kennedy, he was not a particularly polished public figure (his most famous gaffe was being caught during one of his presidential debates with Clinton, looking at his watch as if he were bored and wanted the debate over), and he preferred to receive most of his information through verbal briefings.

Bush was ultimately partially successful in operating the collegial model. The heart of his success came from his assemblage of a foreign policy staff that was notably congenial and worked well together. Virtually the entire group was "alumni" of the Ford presidency and shared a commonality of outlook that some critics said bordered on "groupthink." The Achilles' heel for his presidency, however, was the lack of a strategic vision by the president himself, particularly in the light of fundamental changes in the international environment accompanying the end of the Cold War. By his own admission, Bush always had a problem with what he called the "vision thing."

The next president to employ the collegial model was Bill Clinton. Clinton, quite consciously, had a style very close to his political hero, JFK, whom he admired and sought to emulate. Like JFK, Clinton was an avid reader who considered himself a "quick study" on complex issues and possessed a remarkable memory that made him an extremely effective orator and debater on complex, extemporaneous subjects. He also possessed an exceptional sense of personal efficacy that manifested itself in great personal skills and a supreme confidence in his ability to "jawbone" political friends and foes alike into agreement on his positions. Unlike Kennedy, however, the "man from Hope (Arkansas)" came from a difficult personal childhood and avoided personal and political conflict whenever possible.

Clinton evolved his collegial approach over time. Clinton was an overwhelming personality who clearly enjoyed and demanded the spotlight, and he initially surrounded himself with a team of advisors who lacked conceptual or personal flair, which meant Clinton himself could dominate policy proceedings. Like Bush before him, however, he entered office without a clear initial vision about how to manage the post–Cold War world, and his administration foundered conceptually until it hit upon dual emphases on globalization and peacekeeping as tethers for his foreign policy.

Barack H. Obama also adopted his own version of the collegial model. He came to office with a high sense of efficacy and comfort with the model. He was an undergraduate international relations major, and his experience as a law professor made running the national security enterprise as a graduate seminar a natural fit. In the early days of his administration, the fallout of the recession of 2008 dominated his attention and limited the amount of time he could devote to foreign affairs. His central role in assassinating Osama bin Laden in 2011 and the dual Syrian-IS crisis beginning in 2012 combined with domestic gridlock to shift his emphasis to foreign affairs in his second term.

Like many progressives, Obama was a liberal internationalist, preferring multilateral diplomatic over military solutions to problems. To this end, he appointed strong, like-minded secretaries of state (Hillary Clinton and John Kerry) and was assisted by Vice President Joe Biden, a veteran of the Senate Foreign Relations Committee who shared his predilections. By contrast, he went through four secretaries of defense (Robert Gates, Leon Panetta, Chuck Hagel, and Ashton Carter), an indication of his lower priority on defense.

The distinction of the presidents who have adopted the collegial approach is their common overall personality, and particularly their sense of self-efficacy and interest in the foreign affairs area. The president in the collegial model is not unlike a professor guiding a graduate seminar by the Socratic method; his effectiveness is likely to reflect his personal ability to project his own interpretation of events and dynamics while simultaneously encouraging and incorporating the views of others. When presidents have a vision to share and a group of advisors with whom the individual can work constructively, the collegial model seems to work at its best.

There is one other characteristic of the presidents who have employed the collegial model worth mentioning. Because they had distinctly high levels of interest in and knowledge of foreign affairs when they entered office, they have been extraordinarily active in the field after they left office. Jimmy Carter rivals Richard Nixon in his production of books and articles on foreign policy topics, and has been an active monitor of foreign elections and other events internationally. George H. W. Bush has joined Bill Clinton in spearheading relief efforts for the 2006 tsunami in Asia and in response to the 2010 Haiti earthquake, and Clinton's foundation has been very active in promoting the solution to a variety of international problem areas. The only surviving practitioner of the formalistic model, George W. Bush, has demonstrated no equivalent penchant for continuing activity, and neither did most of the other presidents who followed the model. The post-presidency of Obama remains to be seen, but is unlikely to be passive.

The Trump Model

Capturing the personality and likely administrative pattern of the forty-fifth president is difficult. Donald Trump is simply different from past presidents. First, he is not a traditional politician. He had never previously run for public office and has no record as a public official. He ran a highly unorthodox, populist campaign, in which he offered only the most general descriptions of what he would do in office. "Make America Great Again" was his mantra; what that meant was unclear.

Trump does not have a politician's personality. Although it is somewhat oversimplifying, the Myers-Briggs Personality scale offers some intuitive hints at Trump the person. In Myers-Briggs terms, he is probably an ENTJ. People with that profile tend to be highly competitive, drawn to leadership and challenge situations, and believe they understand and can simplify complex problems. They tend to be intuitive and feel little need to consult evidence to "know" things. They are also commanding presences who disdain knowledge and information they lack and tend to be impatient and unsympathetic to opposing views. They also tend to be natural public speakers who detest inefficiency and tend to act impulsively. The profile is said to suit corporate and military leaders well—people who thrive in hierarchical, command structures.

Trump has not been in office long enough to measure him definitively, but the ENTJ profile fits his campaign and early performance as president-elect and president. His handling of the Russian hacking controversy provides an example. He disagreed with the consensual conclusions of the intelligence community about the Russian government's complicity in the hacking, simply asserting that "no one knows for sure" who authorized and performed the hacking. On environmental matters, he stated that "I am a really smart guy" who could decide on these questions better than the so-called experts. During the campaign, he asserted that he understood the problem of defeating ISIS better than the generals (a position he backed away from as he surrounded himself with generals in his administration). His cabinet choices feature a heavy concentration on corporate executives and retired military officers, an indication of symbiosis.

These characteristics suggest how Trump may fit into the categories of presidents developed here. On personality variables, Trump appears to be a cognitive minimalist, content with only a general grasp of issues. He believes that he is capable of dealing with foreign policy despite a minimal background or experience in the field. His campaign clearly demonstrated that he is not averse to disagreeing with others.

No administrative arrangement perfectly fits any presidency, but it seems likely that Trump will adopt a formalistic approach to the foreign policy effort. This model has a commitment to order and efficiency deriving from its top-down, hierarchical organization. Trump clearly likes to be in control of situations, and being able to funnel orders downward maximizes his ability to do so. He is much more likely to follow this model to maximize personal control (like Eisenhower and Nixon) than to insulate himself from foreign policy in which he has little interest (like Reagan and George W. Bush).

Conclusion

The president is the most visible political figure in American foreign policy. The president is chief executive (head of government) and ceremonial leader of the American people (head of state). These constitutionally mandated positions place the American president in the unique position of being the only politician with international status as the head of the American state and as the only individual who can negotiate with and enter into agreements with foreign governments.

He has additional powers (e.g., commander in chief, appointment of officials) that also have constitutional bases, and in addition, there are political advantages and constraints on the ability of the president to carry out his constitutional role.

The preeminence of the president has been circumscribed in the contemporary political environment. The transparency of international affairs has meant that the legislative branch of government has more opportunity to watchdog foreign policy interactions, even if the preponderance of expertise on foreign affairs is possessed by the executive branch. This advantage, however, is lessened both by the rise in political partisanship within the political system and increased media coverage of international events. Increased partisanship means anything the president does receives intense scrutiny and likely criticism along partisan party lines; foreign affairs are not exempt from this phenomenon. Indeed, it is an arguable consequence of extreme polarization that any action by the president in either domestic or foreign policy will be opposed simply because the president proposes it. Increased electronic media coverage means that the public is aware, at some cursory level, of events in the world that hitherto had escaped them. Foreign policy no longer plays out in the shadows.

How effective presidents are in conducting foreign policy is also the result of who they are. What the individual president does in office is clearly the result of differences in factors such as knowledge and confidence in that knowledge and how the individual deals with political controversy and conflict. The particular configuration of a president's personality characteristics, in turn, helps form the management style that different presidents adopt, and the president's ultimate performance is also inevitably affected by the international political environment and how well the president's personality and management style meshes with the environment that he or she faces.

Study/Discussion Questions

1. Describe the toxic political environment in which the Obama administration had to make foreign policy. Will this likely continue or moderate in the Trump administration?

2. What is codetermination? What does it mean in terms of the constitutional allocation of powers between the president and the Congress in foreign policy?

3. What are the constitutional powers of the president in foreign policy? Describe each, with special emphasis on the roles of head of state and head of government. How has practice expanded some of these powers?

4. What informal (or political) powers does the president have in addition to the formal powers specified or implied in the Constitution? Describe each. How are these affected by political limits or constraints on presidential powers?

5. What are the three dimensions of presidential personality discussed in the text as they relate to foreign policy? How does each affect how a given president approaches foreign policy?

6. What are the three management models for dealing with foreign policy discussed in the text? Describe

each and the presidents who have adopted the different models.

7. Apply the personality types and management styles to the conduct of foreign policy by different presidents, using the management models as an organizing device. Are different personal and environmental characteristics attached to different models?

8. What personality traits and managerial preferences does the new president appear to have? How are these likely to help explain foreign policy approaches for the rest of his term?

Bibliography

Barilleaux, Ryan J. *The President as World Leader*. New York: St. Martin's, 1991.

Brose, Christian. "The Making of George W. Obama." *Foreign Policy*, January/February 2009, 52–55.

Brzezinski, Zbigniew. "From Hope to Audacity." *Foreign Affairs*, January/February 2010, 16–29.

Campbell, Kurt M., and Jordan Tama. *Difficult Transitions: Foreign Policy Troubles at the Outset of Presidential Power*. Washington, DC: Brookings, 2008.

Corwin, Edward S. *The President's Control of Foreign Policy*. Princeton, NJ: Princeton University Press, 1917.

Falkowski, Lawrence S. *Presidents, Secretaries of State, and Crises in U.S. Foreign Relations: A Model and Predictive Analysis*. Boulder, CO: Westview, 1978.

Frum, David. "Think Again: Bush's Legacy." *Foreign Policy*, September/October 2008, 32–38.

Gaddis, John Lewis. *Strategies of Containment: A Critical Appraisal of American National Security Policy during the Cold War*. Rev. and exp. ed. New York: Oxford University Press, 2005.

George, Alexander L. *Presidential Decisionmaking in Foreign Policy: The Effective Use of Information and Advice*. Boulder, CO: Westview, 1980.

Hamilton, Lee H., and Jordan Tama. *A Critical Tension: The Foreign Policy Roles of the President and Congress*. Wilson Forum. Washington, DC: Woodrow Wilson Center Press, 2008.

Johnson, Richard T. *Managing the White House*. New York: Harper and Row, 1974.

Kagan, Robert. "The September 12 Paradigm." *Foreign Affairs*, September/October 2008, 25–39.

Mead, Walter Russell. "The Carter Syndrome." *Foreign Policy*, January/February 2010, 58–64.

Mosher, Frederick W., David Clinton, and Daniel G. Lang. *Presidential Transitions and Foreign Affairs*. Baton Rouge: Louisiana State University Press, 1985.

Neustadt, Richard E. *Presidential Power and the Modern Presidents: The Politics of Leadership from Roosevelt to Reagan*. New York: Free Press, 1990.

Reagan, Ronald W. *An American Life*. New York: Simon & Schuster, 1990.

The Role of 5
Executive Agencies

The Pentagon, home of the U.S. Department of Defense, is the physically largest office building in the world and the home of the largest American cabinet-level agency.

Preview

While the executive and legislative branches codetermine what foreign policy decisions are made, most actual implementation of policy falls to relevant federal agencies, which are part of the executive branch. These agencies are also the repository of much government knowledge and analysis about foreign policy matters. They are, however, part of the political process, disagreeing and competing with one another and with elements within the legislative branch. This chapter will introduce these sources of influence and competition and survey the roles of the major executive branch agencies that form the so-called interagency process: the National Security Council (NSC) and its subsidiary bodies; the State Department; the Department of Defense; the intelligence community; the Department of Homeland Security; and the various economic agencies involved in foreign affairs.

Key Concepts ▓▓▓▓▓▓▓▓▓▓▓▓▓▓▓▓▓▓▓▓▓▓▓▓▓▓▓▓▓

terrorism

interagency process

National Security Council

National Security Act

Principals Committee

Deputies Committee

Interagency Policy Committees

State Department

Foreign Service Officers (FSOs)

Department of Defense

civilian control of the military
  intelligence community

Central Intelligence Agency (CIA)

Director of Central Intelligence
  (DCI)

Director of National Intelligence
  (DNI)

Department of Homeland Security
  (DHS)

homeland security

Federal Emergency Management
  Agency (FEMA)

intermestic agencies

economic agencies

National Economic Council (NEC)

United States Trade Representative
  (USTR)

errorism is, and has been since 9/11, the primary focus of American foreign and national security policy, a distinction it is unlikely to relinquish anytime soon. It is a foreign policy concern because almost all terrorism emanates from outside the United States (in the international environment). And it is a national security problem both because it affects the safety and security of Americans and because at least part of the "solution" to the terrorist problem includes the use of traditional national security tools, notably military force.

Terrorism and its eradication or control is a particularly vexing problem for at least three reasons that can be expressed as questions. The first question is, "what is terrorism?" The answer includes how one defines the term and thus the phenomenon. There is a reasonable consensus on the definition of terrorism, detailed in chapter 9, but much less understanding or agreement about the dynamics and motivations that impel terrorists to do what they do. Who, for instance, can explain why two people assaulted and killed fourteen people in the facility at which the husband worked in San Bernardino, California, in February 2016? Terrorism is simply too alien a phenomenon for most Americans to fully comprehend.

This leads to the second question, which is, "what should be done about terrorism?" The first reflexive response is to destroy it. But how? Terrorism has been an episodic part of the international environment for at least two millennia, and nobody has succeeded in destroying it yet. Is the task impossible to accomplish? If not, what can be done? Can individual terrorists and their organizations be throttled and somehow decimated? Does doing so somehow solve the problem? If not, what can be done? Or is containing the problem at a low level the best we can do? Nobody really knows.

The complicated, poorly understood nature of terrorism leads to the third question: "who should do whatever we decide to try to do about the problem?"

Clearly, the problem exists in the public sector, meaning government has a leading role. But what part of government should do so? As a foreign/national security problem, the major responsibility falls within the executive, but which parts should deal with this complex set of problems? None fall neatly or entirely within the jurisdiction of any single agency. It is to deal with precisely this kind of difficulty that the executive branch (overseen and funded by Congress) has evolved the interagency process to coordinate efforts that do not neatly fall to any one of its parts. Terrorism is the most current and pressing example of this approach to problem solving, but it is by no means the only one.

The **interagency process** is the mechanism by which complex matters are considered and acted upon. It is composed of a group of diverse agencies, including core actors such as the State Department (core in the sense that foreign policy is its central, or core, responsibility) and more peripheral actors such as the Agriculture Department, whose interest is confined largely to matters of international commerce in American agricultural products. The agencies also vary enormously in size: the State Department, according to 2009 government sources, employs about 36,500 professional personnel, whereas the Department of Defense employs nearly 700,000 civilian employees, in addition to the 1.34 million American men and women on active duty and nearly a million reserves.

This chapter focuses on the core interagency actors: the most prominent executive branch departments and agencies in the general area of foreign policy. Much of the coordination of these agencies has, since the system began to be formalized by President Eisenhower, been focused in the **National Security Council** (NSC) system, the other name for the interagency process, and that complex of interactions is the starting point for the discussion. The chapter then turns to the primary agencies and departments that form the NSC system: the State Department, Department of Defense, intelligence community, Department of Homeland Security (DHS), and the economic agencies that promote overseas American economic interests.

The Interagency Process

The interagency process is an artifact of the **National Security Act of 1947**. That landmark piece of legislation was, as indicated in chapter 2, a major part of the American political response to the growing Cold War confrontation. Its effect was to create the framework within which to fashion the national security state that was the foreign policy vehicle for conducting the Cold War policy of containment. To achieve those ends, the act did several notable things, the most central of which was to create the National Security Council as the primary coordinating device within the executive branch for dealing with foreign and national security matters, and a more extensive series of supportive institutions has evolved to assist the NSC in doing its work. Additionally, the National Security Act created an independent Department of Defense, U.S. Air Force, and the Central Intelligence Agency (CIA), all of which are discussed in this chapter.

The structure of the contemporary NSC system began to develop during the presidency of Eisenhower, and it reflected both his military sense of hierarchy and structure and his preference for a formalistic model for dealing with foreign policy. Subsequent presidents have made greater or lesser use of the interagency process, but by the end of the Cold War, the shape of the organization was basically in place and has survived mostly intact to the present.

The core interagency process consists of four hierarchically ordered institutions, each composed of appropriate representatives from the major core foreign policy agencies within the executive branch. At the apex is the NSC itself. Directly below the NSC is the **Principals Committee**, and a step below it is the **Deputies Committee**. At the bottom of the process are a series of **Interagency Policy Committees**. These four bodies make up the foreign policy decision process within the White House.

The National Security Council (NSC)

The NSC sits atop the interagency process. Unlike the other constituent bodies in the process, the NSC was directly mandated by the National Security Act and thus has statutory standing (meaning it cannot be disbanded without congressional permission). The other bodies within the process were all created by executive order and thus could be repealed without direct congressional approval or disapproval, although no president has formally proposed to do so. The National Security Act both specifies the core composition of the NSC (those members who must be included in its deliberations) and the function of the NSC, which is to assist the president in integrating all aspects of foreign and national security policy.

Membership in the NSC varies depending on the preferences and needs of individual presidents. The National Security Act of 1947, as amended in 1949, specified certain parts of the membership. By statute, the council has four members: the president, the vice president, the secretary of state, and the secretary of defense. The chair of the Joint Chiefs of Staff (CJCS) and the Director of National Intelligence (DNI) are permanent members as the chief advisors to the president on military and intelligence matters. It sometimes includes the secretary of the treasury, the attorney general, the secretary of homeland security, and the representative of the United States to the United Nations as full-time members, as well as the assistant for national security affairs (national security advisor or NSA). The president may invite any other officials to attend depending on the matters being discussed at a particular meeting. This pattern varies somewhat between presidents, and the Trump administration created controversy by adding a political advisor to the list.

The NSC operates strictly as an advisory body to help inform the president on foreign policy issues. By tradition, no votes are taken in the NSC, for fear that the outcomes might constrict the president's perceived options. Rather, the tenor of NSC meetings is to provide an exchange of views from the perspectives of the president's closest advisors to help the president reach ultimate decisions.

The dynamics of NSC meetings vary considerably from president to president, and both their composition and style of operation reflect the president's personality and management style. Presidents who opt for the formalistic model use the NSC differently from those who prefer the collegial model. George W. Bush, for instance, assembled a very like-minded team of advisors prone to very little internal disagreement among themselves and with the chief executive. Collegial presidents, on the other hand, are more likely to choose NSC teams of compatible but not identical views and to use the NSC as a more free-flowing forum wherein differences are aired and eventually reconciled. President Trump will develop his own distinctive style as well.

To aid the NSC in formulating policy options, reaching decisions among the options, and implementing and monitoring those decisions, a hierarchy of three subgroups has evolved. Most mirror the composition of the NSC itself, with top aides to designated NSC officials as the participants. These mechanisms are the Principals Committee, the Deputies Committee, and the Interagency Policy Committees (formerly the Policy Coordinating Committees).

Principals Committee (PC)

This group is the NSC when the president is not in attendance at what would be the NSC if the president were there. It serves several purposes. First, it can meet when the president is unavailable for one reason or another. Second, it can conduct business when the president is personally uninterested in a topic or when the president's input is not needed. Third and arguably most important, the president can use it to allow the freest possible exchange of views when his or her mere presence might stifle the frank exchange of views. The most famous example was in 1962, when President Kennedy used the Executive Committee (ExComm) of the NSC so that the participants would not be intimidated by his presence and fail to consider all options during the Cuban Missile Crisis.

Deputies Committee (DC)

Composed of the chief assistants (or deputies) of the members of the PC, the DC is arguably the major working group among those assisting the NSC. The deputy national security advisor convenes and chairs this group, which has core members from the state, defense, treasury, energy, and homeland security departments, as well as others depending on the agenda. The functions of the DC include reviewing and monitoring the entire interagency process, analyzing and preparing issues for the NSC and PC, overseeing implementation of decisions reached by the NSC, periodic reviews or major foreign policy initiatives, and day-to-day crisis management.

Interagency Policy Committees (IPCs)

At the base of the process are the IPCs. Their principal duties include providing forums for monitoring policies set at or being considered at higher levels, laying out background for consideration by the DC, PC, or NSC before decisions are reached, and guaranteeing that policies are implemented as intended by the NSC. This group of committees is the most fluid part of the NSC process and is the level most likely to be altered by a new administration.

The Executive Agencies

The broad purpose of the interagency process is to compile, reconcile, and reach decisions on foreign policy matters, but most of the detailed, day-to-day work is done by the various executive branch agencies represented in that process. These agencies possess the vast majority of officials and expertise in their areas. The staff of the NSA within the White House numbers in the hundreds. Personnel in the various agencies who help formulate and execute policy number in the hundreds of thousands. They provide the expert resource base that is an important part of the informational advantage of the president over other parts of government. These agencies have different perspectives and mandates, and they often have very conflicting opinions about appropriate policy in any given matter, which is part of the reason an interagency process is necessary to determine U.S. policy.

This section describes and analyzes the principal agencies that advise the president on foreign affairs matters. It begins with the State Department, which has historically been at the center of foreign policy making and which, at least until World War II, was virtually the synonym for the foreign policy enterprise. The advent of the Cold War widened the concerns of foreign policy enormously, notably to incorporate a much more prominent role for national security and the national security state. The National Security Act of 1947 created both a Department of Defense and a Central Intelligence Agency to respond to a new and more overtly threatening international environment. The attacks of 9/11 elevated the idea of homeland security, always an implicit part of the charge of the DOD, to greater centrality and resulted in the creation and evolution of the Department of Homeland Security. Finally, the boundaries between foreign and domestic policy have become blurred, and this has made some agencies with primary domestic responsibilities part-time foreign policy participants, so this section concludes with these "intermestic agencies."

The State Department

The most venerable agency in the foreign policy process is the **State Department**. It was the first federal agency authorized under the Constitution in 1789 (its original name was the Department of Foreign Affairs; it was changed to the Department of State later that same year). Its first secretary was Thomas Jefferson, and five other early presidents first served in that capacity. It was the lead agency in America's interactions with the world at least until World War II, when the increasing militarization of the international environment led to its partial eclipse by other agencies, notably the Defense Department.

It is one of Washington's most predictable rituals for an incoming president to proclaim that he will look to the State Department to play the lead role in foreign policy, and the position of secretary of state is among the most coveted positions within any administration, attracting some of what become the most prominent members of any new administration: Colin Powell within the first George W. Bush administration and Hillary Clinton in the Obama administration were exemplary of the prestige that still surrounds the secretary's position. Secretary Tillerson's status is evolving.

The State Department is physically located at the opposite end of Washington's mall from the Capitol in an area known as Foggy Bottom. The area gets its name originally from its proximity to the Potomac River and the resulting fog from that stream, but the epithet is also a less charitable way of describing the quality of thinking that allegedly goes on within its walls. Some presidents have thought it too unresponsive to presidential preferences (President Carter thought it was too conservative; Presidents Nixon and Reagan thought it too liberal) and not aggressive enough to lead in interagency battles (John Kennedy dismissed the State Department bureaucracy as "a bowl of Jell-O"). Most colorfully, Franklin Roosevelt once disparaged the speed and responsiveness of the agency, saying, "Dealing with the State Department is like watching an elephant become pregnant; everything is done on a very high level, there's a lot of commotion, and it takes twenty-two months for anything to happen."

The State Department remains at the center of American foreign policy. It is the only organization within the U.S. government whose mission is entirely devoted to foreign affairs, both in terms of the scope and emphasis of its area of responsibility and in its role as the interface between the American government and other world governments. It accomplishes this mission despite having one of the smallest bureaucracies of any major executive agency.

Organization The Founding Fathers would not recognize the agency they created in 1789. Thomas Jefferson presided over a "bureaucracy" consisting of five clerks, one translator, two messengers, and two overseas diplomatic missions. By contrast, the bulk of its U.S.-based employees are housed in a ponderous eight-story building on Washington's C Street that sprawls across twelve acres of Foggy Bottom near the Lincoln Memorial. Despite its growth, however, it is indeed one of the smallest cabinet-level agencies, with a budget and personnel size absolutely dwarfed by foreign policy competitor agencies such as the Department of Defense.

At the head of the State Department is its secretary. As already noted, it is one of the most coveted positions within the federal bureaucracy, and when a new administration comes to office (or a vacancy occurs for some other reason), there are always multiple high-profile contenders for the job and great speculation about who will fill it. The inevitable debate that surrounds the appointment occurs both in Washington and in foreign capitals, where the stature and policy position of the new secretary is viewed as an important indication of the likely direction of U.S. foreign policy.

Different presidents appoint different kinds of secretaries, at least partly based on the management style that they employ in the foreign policy area. One dimension of differentiation is whether secretaries are viewed as strong or weak actors in the foreign policy process. Presidents who want to dominate the foreign policy personally tend to appoint less visible and less forceful secretaries, who are generally categorized as weak. Examples include Nixon's 1969 appointment of William P. Rogers, a New York lawyer with little international experience, or Clinton's appointment of the knowledgeable but nonassertive Warren Christopher to the post. At the other extreme, presidents who want to avoid heavy involvement tend to appoint strong secretaries who can dominate the foreign policy area and leave the president free for other parts of the job. Gerald Ford's retention of Henry Kissinger, Reagan's choice of George Shultz, and George W. Bush's appointment of Colin Powell are notable examples.

A second dimension differentiating secretaries is whether they consider themselves as primarily advocates of State Department positions or as White House team players. This distinction has particular symbolic importance within Foggy Bottom itself, where the department's highly qualified professionals often feel their advice is underappreciated and underutilized. When a forceful advocate of the department is appointed, their morale is lifted measurably. The appointment of Clinton, and her early and repeated praise for the department, for instance, was greatly appreciated by department professionals who felt somewhat ignored by Secretary Condoleezza Rice, whose loyalties were much more closely tied to the White House. At the same time, some secretaries view themselves as such strong and qualified people as to be virtually above advice from the department, thereby harming morale. Secretaries stressing a team approach, of course, are more generally associated with the collegial style of management, whereas either very strong and independent or weak individuals are more closely connected with formalistic presidents.

Secretaries of State thus mirror and give strong indications about the way presidents want to organize foreign policy. Regardless of who the secretary is, however, a professionally expert and organized bureaucracy supports the incumbent to help formulate, execute, and coordinate America's face toward the outside world. Below the secretary are two deputy secretaries, as well as reporting officials such as the administrator of the Agency for International Development (USAID) and the U.S. permanent representative to the United Nations (USUN). Most of the department's detailed expertise, however, resides within the functional bureaus and agencies.

At the operational level, the department is divided into six functional areas, each headed by an undersecretary. The heart of departmental expertise falls within the jurisdiction of the undersecretary for political affairs, listed as the department's "third-ranking official and its senior career diplomat." The undersecretary is assisted by a series of assistant secretaries for the various geographical regions and offices under his or her jurisdiction, including African Affairs, European and Eurasian Affairs, East Asian and Pacific Affairs, Near Eastern Affairs, South and Central Asian Affairs, and Western Hemisphere Affairs.

In addition to those activities reporting to the undersecretary of political affairs, substantive expertise is also housed within operations reporting to undersecretaries for economics, energy and agricultural affairs, arms control and international security (ACIS) affairs, and democracy and global affairs. Historically, the ACIS function, which includes the bureau of Politico-Military Affairs (PM), has acted as a mirror and watchdog of the activities of the Department of Defense, which has a corresponding office to serve the same function vis-à-vis State. The complex of democracy and global affairs initiatives encompasses a kind of grab bag of functions, some arising from changes apparent in the post– Cold War world. Included in its charge are democracy, human rights, and labor;

oceans and international environmental and scientific affairs; population, refugees, and migration; and the office to monitor and combat trafficking in persons.

The core of expertise within the State Department comes from its highly select core of career professionals in the Foreign Service. **Foreign Service Officers (FSOs)** make up merely 6,000 of the employees of the State Department (former secretary of defense Robert Gates was fond of saying, as a sign of misplaced priorities, that there are more members of U.S. military bands than there are members of the Foreign Service). They are a highly select group, chosen based on a highly competitive written and oral testing procedure, passage of rigorous background checks necessary for security clearance, matching of career preference with departmental needs, and the availability of open positions within the Foreign Service. In any given year, thousands of individuals who meet the general qualifications for the service take the Foreign Service written examination, but by the time the results are filtered through the process, only a few hundred or fewer are selected for the pool of qualified candidates. Many of those people must wait extended periods before a slot becomes available for which they are qualified. Successful applicants are typically very highly educated, generally with some graduate degree(s) and/or practical working experience in the areas for which they are applying.

Foreign Policy Role   The primacy of the State Department has been in general decline since the end of World War II. Much day-to-day American business with the world remains firmly within the grasp of the department. The embassies and their ambassadors are still part of the State Department, Americans overseas rely on offices under the jurisdiction of the State Department for assistance and advice, and the granting or withholding of passports and visas are State Department functions. These kinds of functions once largely defined foreign affairs and ensured the dominance of State in the foreign policy decision process. But times have changed.

The role of the embassy is exemplary. Historically, the system of American embassies in foreign countries was the heart of foreign policy conduct. Particularly before telephonic and other electronic means of communication, these missions were nearly autonomous; it could take days or even weeks or months for messages to be conveyed between the embassy in some faraway country and Washington. For many practical purposes, the embassies were independent actors in a hostile world environment, and the ambassadors served as the chief advisors to the U.S. government on matters concerning the countries to which they were accredited.

That role has largely disappeared. With the flow of electronic media coverage of events and information from intelligence sources only nominally related to the embassies, they are no longer the major source of U.S. government knowledge of what is happening in most countries. There is the apocryphal story during the Bush administration of Secretary of State Powell calling the ambassador in a country undergoing upheaval and asking him the details of some disturbance that was occurring. The ambassador was apparently unaware of the incident and asked Powell if he was sure of what he was asking about. Powell apparently retorted that he knew it was happening, because he was watching it live on CNN in his office. This also means that the ambassador no longer makes major decisions. Rather, decisions are made in Washington and relayed to the ambassador, who passes them along to the host government.

The erosion of State Department centrality and power in decision making can be attributed to other interconnected factors, three of which can be mentioned here. First, the content of foreign policy has changed dramatically. Foreign policy used to be largely about diplomacy, which is the core competence and preferred tool of the State Department, but the increasingly military content of American interaction with the rest of the world has eclipsed the diplomatic role and effectively moved influence into other agencies.

Second, this expansion of and change in the foreign policy agenda have spawned rivals to the State Department. The most obvious rival has, of course, been the Department of Defense, the existence of which can be thought of, in one sense, as the admission that the problem of foreign policy has been broadened beyond the expertise of the FSOs at the core of the department. Indeed, the need for something like an interagency process is testimony that foreign policy is now more than the activities of the State Department.

Third, this broadened menu of problems and assortment of actors has provided a challenge to the perception that the State Department is even the most competent agency with which to entrust important problems or particularly adept at reasserting its own primacy. An example from the Bush administration illustrates this dilemma particularly well. In the run-up to the American invasion of Iraq in 2003, the White House designated the Defense Department as the lead planning agency (see intersection 5.2), and Secretary of Defense Donald Rumsfeld interpreted this mandate to allow him essentially to exclude the State Department (which basically opposed the idea of the war) from pre-invasion planning. At one point, for instance, the State Department delivered to the Defense Department its analysis of the problems they believed would be encountered if the invasion occurred—projections that proved to be almost completely prescient. When the Pentagon received the report, it was sent to a midlevel office in the Defense bureaucracy, where it was effectively buried and its contents ignored.

Department of Defense

Across the Potomac from Washington in Virginia sits the five-sided building that houses the **Department of Defense**. Its headquarters, newly remodeled at a cost of $4.5 billion in 2011, is known as the Pentagon because its five-sided shape was designed for the parcel of land on which it was originally supposed to have been built, a design retained when its location was moved to its current space, which does not require the design. To some outsiders, it joins the highly secretive National Security Agency in being called the "puzzle palace" (a term Reagan used for it); to many of those who work in it, it is known simply as "the Building."

Physically, the DOD's most notable characteristic is its size. The Pentagon itself is claimed to be the largest office building in the world (the amount of space it provides was a major reason for keeping the original design even after its location changed). Size is also measured by the number of people who work in the Pentagon and at other DOD entities around the world. The Department of Defense is the largest employer in the federal government. In addition to the roughly 700,000 civilian employees already mentioned, there are currently more than 1.3 million Americans on active duty in the armed forces and nearly a million additional military reservists. There are more than 200,000 civilian contractors doing business with the DOD in a variety of roles, from building military equipment to foodservice to semi-military roles.

The size of these commitments has varied across time. Before the Cold War ended, the active-duty forces of the United States stood at around 2.15 million. During the 1990s, the armed forces were "downsized" to about 1.3 million on active duty. Because of the all-volunteer status of the military itself, an increasing number of defense matters have shifted to civilian contractors, a practice under some scrutiny when these individuals are used in combat zones.

The DOD also is one of the major claimants to monetary resources. Within the federal structure of budgetary categories by function, DOD and service on the national debt compete as the second-largest category of budgetary commitments after expenditures on entitlement programs (Social Security, Medicare, and Medicaid, for instance). Before the entitlement programs were expanded in the early 1960s, expenditures on defense were the largest federal expense, accounting for about half of federal spending in the mid-1950s. Current annual appropriations are in the $500–$600 billion range and account for a little more than one-fifth of the budget.

The budgetary claim of the DOD is important for a number of reasons. One is its size relative to spending by the rest of the world. In 2003, the United States achieved the distinction of spending more on defense *than the rest of the countries of the world combined*. While that distinction has not been consistently maintained since, the United States annually spends at or just below half of what the world spends on defense. Supporters argue that these levels are necessary to keep the country safe from hostile forces in the world; critics see it as excessive and as a negative symbol of America's supposedly peaceful role in the world. President Trump has vowed to increase defense spending.

The defense budget is symbolically important for at least two other reasons. The first reason represents a paradox of sorts about defense spending arising from two contrary domestic political forces. The defense budget is the largest so-called controllable (also called discretionary) element in the federal budget. This designation arises from a budget distinction between *uncontrollable* and *controllable* budget items. An uncontrollable element is a government expenditure authorized by law that is automatically spent unless there is specific legislation that rescinds that expenditure. Almost all entitlement spending is of this nature: the amount of money the United States spends on Medicare/Medicaid, for instance, is automatic unless intervening legislation during any Congress changes it. Controllable spending, on the other hand, refers to expenditures that must be appropriated on an annual basis or the function they support does not receive funding. Within the federal budget, the vast majority (upward of 75–80 percent) is uncontrollable; of the controllable elements, defense accounts for the largest amounts, upward of two-thirds of all the controllable expenditures of the government. From that vantage point alone, defense spending would seem to be the most vulnerable part of the federal budget at times of budgetary scarcity and budget cutting.

This distinction is not inconsequential. When Congress and the White House failed to agree on budget reductions in 2011, the result was to trigger so-called sequestration. This action requires automatic budget cuts from federal coffers. These cuts were exclusively from controllable elements of the budget concentration in the DOD budget, which is why defense bears one-half of the reductions imposed. The sequester took effect in 2013 and remains in force, despite vows by Trump and others to rescind it.

Political legerdemain in the process further complicates the situation. One major way to make it appear that defense spending was not too high during the George W. Bush administration was to move spending elements "off budget." In the case of the war efforts in Iraq and Afghanistan, most of the costs did not come out of the regular defense budget but instead were funded by so-called special appropriations. This provision, which has historically been used to deal with natural and other disasters, allows the government to provide funds in the event of disastrous occurrences requiring timely reaction outside the regular budget—but with the expectation that these expenditures will be made up in subsequent budget cycles. Virtually the entire war efforts were funded that way at estimated costs well over $1 trillion. No subsequent budgetary provision has been made to repay them. They are thus elements in the federal debt technically unrelated to the budget process.

Another important aspect of the defense budget is its domestic impact. The defense department is a major source of patronage-based appropriations to individual states and congressional districts, far exceeding the amounts of what some would characterize as "pork barrel" funding. It is a simple matter of fact that members of Congress battle monumentally to try to ensure that, for instance, defense contracts to build aircraft or naval vessels are allocated to their states or districts, and the impact of opening or closing military bases and other installations in particular locales can have a major economic impact on individual communities. This impact is particularly acute for "large ticket" projects such as ships and aircraft that require considerable funding over a long period.

Organization The basic operating principle underlying the entire defense establishment is **civilian control of the military**. This principle goes back to the American Revolution and even before, arising from the fear that an uncontrolled military might pose a threat to the freedom of the civilian population. Since the American colonies were heavily influenced by the British experience, this early concern was associated with the British reaction to the Cromwellian period, and was expressed in the Continental Congress during the Revolution itself. An exasperated General Washington once opined that he could understand why the Congress opposed an army during peacetime, but he could not understand why they opposed it during wartime. After the American Revolution ended, the regular army essentially disbanded.

The result of this early history is the tradition that civilian authorities should control the armed forces. Within the structure of the defense establishment, this means that all military authorities have civilian counterparts to whom they report and whose permission is necessary for the military to carry out crucial tasks. There is little if any disagreement in principle within the DOD on this arrangement, but it does cause some friction between career military officers with considerable experience in their areas of responsibility and politically appointed civilian overseers who sometimes get their jobs for reasons other than their expertise. One manifestation is that the Secretary of Defense (SECDEF) must be a civilian, or a military officer who has been retired for at least seven years, which is why a special exception had to be granted for SECDEF James Mattis, a Marine general who retired in 2013 (see intersection 5.1).

Intersection 5.1 General/SECDEF Mattis

General James Mattis became the Secretary of Defense under President Trump in January 2017. A retired Marine, his appointment required a special exception from Congress, since the National Security Act of 1947 (amended) requires that a retired military officer be retired for seven years before achieving eligibility to be SECDEF.

The idea that civilians should control the military has a long history in the United States. When the National Security Act of 1947 formally consolidated the military into the Department of Defense, this relationship was formalized in Section 10 (a) of the law regarding the secretary. It states specifically that "a person may not be appointed as Secretary of Defense within seven years after relief from active duty as a commissioned officer of a regular component of an armed force."

Prior to the appointment of General Mattis, there had only been one exception to this rule. In 1950, General George C. Marshall, at the time still a serving officer, was permitted to become SECDEF, a testament to his exceptional service in matters such as the creation and administration of the so-called Marshall Plan of reconstructive monetary relief to Europe after World War II. In the interim between Marshall's tenure and the appointment of Mattis, no retired military officer has been proposed as a SECDEF out of deference to the principle of civilian control of the military.

The appointment of General Mattis required a specific waiver of the prohibition on a seven-year waiting period before he could be considered. Mattis's record was so overwhelmingly favorable that the Marine won overwhelming bipartisan support, and his appointment was confirmed in the Senate by a vote of ninety-eight to one on January 20, 2017, Inauguration Day. He was one of two Trump appointees confirmed on that day, joining retired Marine General John Kelly, the new secretary of Homeland Security.

Any depiction of an organization as vast and complex as the DOD requires some potentially distorting simplification. For present purposes, the organization can be thought of in four parts. At the pinnacle is the secretary of defense, who reports directly to the president and is responsible for the overall operation of the department. At the second layer, the secretary is assisted by a civilian-dominated series of subcabinet-level functions cutting across the military services and comprising the Office of the Secretary of Defense (OSD). The third part is the military services themselves, each with their separate bureaucracies and sets of interests. Finally, there is the Joint Chiefs of Staff, which has the role of coordinating the military activities of the services and reporting to the president.

The Secretary of Defense (or SECDEF) is the chief advisor to the president on defense matters, a role designated by the National Security Act. (By contrast, the chair of the Joint Chiefs of Staff is by statute the chief military advisor to the president.) The SECDEF advises the president on matters such as the advisability of using force in a particular situation and what kinds of personnel and equipment the military needs to perform its duties. The SECDEF is responsible for implementing policies mandated by the commander in chief and Congress, as well as managing the internal affairs of the department. The degree to which the SECDEF is a major player in foreign policy formulation varies considerably from secretary to secretary and depending on presidential preference. William Cohen within the Clinton administration was not an overt major contributor to overall foreign policy, for instance, whereas George W. Bush's first SECDEF, Donald Rumsfeld, was a major architect of the war in Iraq and of other foreign policy matters. Secretary Gates kept a low but influential policy profile as part of the Obama team's early approach to foreign policy, as did Ashton Carter. Mattis's role will evolve.

The Office of the Secretary of Defense is the principal civilian bureaucracy within the structure of the DOD. It is specifically organized to provide direct assistance and advice to the SECDEF on all matters of policy that affect the department and its mission as a whole (in other words, functions that cut across service lines) and to ensure that directives and policy decisions from the SEDEF are indeed implemented within the various services. The OSD often acts as the principal instrument for ensuring civilian control of the military departments, despite the fact that each service department is headed by a civilian secretary. The exact organization and personnel of DOD vary from administration to administration.

The third layer of the DOD is the service departments. Each military service has its own department that represents and administers the interests and programs of the individual service. At the top of each bureaucracy is a civilian service secretary (the secretaries of the army, air force, and navy), and this official is assisted by the highest-ranking military official in each department (the chiefs of staff of the army and air force and the chief of naval operations, whose jurisdiction includes both the navy and marines). Each service chief is responsible for the internal operation of the individual service departments and acts as the service's representative on the Joint Chiefs of Staff.

The service departments stand in juxtaposition to one another and to the civilian OSD. In terms of missions, forces, and the like, there is considerable overlap between the services that each jealously seeks to protect. It has been argued, for instance, that the U.S. military has four air forces (the regular air force, naval and marine air assets, and army unarmed airplanes and armed helicopters), at least three armies (the regular army, the marines—which are administratively part of the navy—and the air force, which has independent personnel to guard air force bases), as well as four sets of special forces (army, navy, marines, and air force), all with somewhat different missions, each of which the principal service attempts to protect.

The result is an organization of the Department of Defense that appears chaotic and inefficient from the outside; reformers regularly raise criticisms of many of the overlaps and redundancies. It used to be worse. Before the National Security Act of 1947, the various service departments were entirely independent (for instance, each lobbied Congress independently for funding), and bringing them together under one roof was a major purpose of the National Security Act.

The Joint Chiefs of Staff (JCS) is the fourth layer of organization within the DOD structure. The JCS consists of the chiefs of staff of the services (army, navy/marines, and air force), from whose ranks the administrative head and chief military advisor to the president, the chair of the Joint Chiefs of Staff (CJCS), is chosen. The original reason for creating the body was to overcome service rivalries and to facilitate interservice cooperation by creating a small staff of officers drawn from the services to facilitate interchange and coordination. For most of its early existence, however, the loyalty and reward system of the services favored actions demonstrating loyalty to the services and not to joint action, meaning service on the JCS (becoming what was known as a "purple suiter," the alleged color one gets if the colors of the various service uniforms are mixed together) was an absolute hindrance to an officer's career and such service was to be avoided if possible.

In 1986, Congress passed the Goldwater-Nichols Defense Reorganization Act in part to strengthen the CJCS and the Joint Staff. The large purpose was to promote and require "jointness" in military affairs: the services acting together rather than in isolation or even competition in military operations. The impetus for this requirement was the negative experience of the United States in military operations intended to free the Iranian hostages in 1980 (the so-called Desert One mission that ended in disaster) and in Grenada in 1983. Among other things, the act required that all officers achieving flag rank (general or admiral) must have experience on the Joint Staff, thereby elevating service there to a career-making, rather than career-breaking, assignment and creating more interservice requirements for the services.

Foreign Policy Role   The role of the defense establishment in the making and implementation of American foreign policy has changed markedly across time and with changing circumstance. Before World War II, there was no formal institution like the Department of Defense around which to organize military views on foreign policy, and such efforts were generally carried out by the individual services and their supporting institutions such as retired veterans' groups. After World War II, this situation greatly changed, as the Cold War confrontation elevated military concerns to a central place in the making and execution of foreign policy. As noted, the National Security Act enshrined this growing importance by making the secretary of defense a coequal partner to the secretary of state in the NSC, and this expanded role has endured.

The American military establishment was originally not well suited to an expanded role in foreign policy. The tradition of suspicion of a standing military had historically dictated a small and highly apolitical military officer corps that neither sought nor received access to policy-making councils. The World War II experience of leaders such as Eisenhower, who served as both the military and political leader of the wartime coalition in Europe, began the process by which the American military has become a more sophisticated and influential part of the foreign policy scene.

Increasing sophistication within the officer corps has made it a more sensitive and critical force within the foreign policy process. The historic role of the military has been that of policy implementer, carrying out orders from civilian authorities that they had very little influence in formulating in the first place. The role of the military as advisor in the traditional setting was simply to assess how difficult a mission might be and what the requirements were to carry it out, and then to go about that implementation. Because the international environment has become so much more varied and the geopolitical aspects of threatening situations so complex and intertwined, however, a more sophisticated military establishment has had to arise that can go beyond implementing policies to advising responsibly about what policies are prudent and attainable.

The Intelligence Community

No other aspect of foreign policy within the U.S. government has been subject to as much critical analysis as the intelligence function. The so-called **intelligence community**, the accumulation of all the various agencies within the federal government that collect and analyze information with foreign and national security implications, has been under close scrutiny since the end of the Cold War, when scandals and revelations raised questions about the competency and skill of American intelligence efforts (the failure to know in advance about the Indian and Pakistani nuclear test plans in 1998 is a good example); this criticism was amplified by the inability of the **Central Intelligence Agency (CIA)** and other intelligence agencies to anticipate the 9/11 attacks, a failure that has led to a basic effort to reform the entire undertaking.

The intelligence function is a relatively new phenomenon in the American political experience. Prior to creating the CIA as part of the National Security Act of 1947, the country had never possessed a formal civilian intelligence agency during peacetime. The CIA was built essentially from scratch, using only the wartime Office of Strategic Services (OSS) as a model and source of employees. The whole effort gathered steam during the Cold War, and in important and ultimately controversial ways came at least partly to mirror its opponent, the Soviet KGB. Since the end of the Cold War, efforts have been under way, with varying success, to adapt the intelligence community to the contemporary environment.

An intelligence organization potentially plays all or part of four roles. The first and most basic is information gathering, collecting so-called raw data about the activities of people, organizations, and countries in which the United States may have an interest. This is the most basic and noncontroversial activity in the intelligence business, although some disagreements emerge about certain clandestine means of learning about events (e.g., placing operatives inside foreign organizations or bribing officials to provide information). The second role is information analysis, providing interpretations of what that information means and what its implications might be. This function is slightly more controversial, because raw information is usually susceptible to numerous interpretations, and which one the analyst chooses may reflect personal views of the subject and policy preferences as well as the "facts." On the other hand, the failure to provide some ordering of raw data may lead to confusion and the ability to greatly distort information by some "consumers" (people who use intelligence to help them make decisions). Some critics, for instance, argued that failures of analysis facilitated how some officials in the Bush administration misused raw information about Iraqi weapons of mass destruction (WMD) to "cook the books" and make the case for invading Iraq.

The third potential role is in policy recommendation. It involves the collectors of information going a step beyond gathering and analysis to advocating policies based on that intelligence. The danger of expanding intelligence to this function is that it might cause the gatherers and analysts to selectively choose information ("cherry picking") that supports particular policy courses, thereby tainting the objectivity of the information provided. For this reason, the intelligence official who is the major statutory advisor to the president (originally the **Director of Central Intelligence** or **DCI**, now the **Director of National Intelligence** or **DNI**) does not have this function as part of his or her role.

The fourth and final role is that of policy implementer, what is also known as operations. This function involves carrying out covert or clandestine activities against foreign entities to influence what they do in their relations with the United States. This role is controversial, partly because it is a direct mirror of activities such as those associated with the old KGB that the United States has generally condemned, and because it often involves law-breaking in the jurisdictions in which it is carried out.

Some argue that it is not an intelligence function at all, and that if it is to be a part of the American effort in the world, it should occur outside of intelligence agencies, as is the case in Great Britain. Supporters of the function argue that clandestine, including illegal, activities are necessary in an anarchical, lawless world, and that since covert actions routinely employ covertly collected intelligence, the intelligence umbrella is the proper organizational location for operations. Regardless of its formal location within the federal bureaucracy, however, operations perform an often crucial foreign policy role. The killing of Osama bin

Laden in May 2011 is a dramatic example, where the CIA was largely responsible for developing the information and plan that the U.S. Navy SEALs executed in Pakistan. Within the CIA, the major operating directorates are the Directorate of Intelligence (DI), which performs the first two tasks, and the Directorate of Operations (DO), which performs the fourth task.

The United States has now possessed a peacetime intelligence community for nearly two-thirds of a century, but it remains an unsettled, controversial part of the government. A major aspect of the disagreement that surrounds the intelligence community is organizational, and is captured in the reform process that was a major feature of intelligence concern during the 2000s. At the same time, there is also disagreement about the foreign policy role of the intelligence community, particularly in the realm of interagency dealing with the problem of international religious terrorism.

Organization The traditional organization of America's intelligence efforts began with the National Security Act's creation of the CIA in 1947. As the intelligence effort matured, the CIA became the centerpiece and public face of American intelligence, although the effort was in fact much more diverse and complex than that. The DCI was seen as the focal point of the intelligence community and as the chief advisor to the president on intelligence matters, in much the same way that the CJCS is the chief military advisor to the president.

This public image of orderliness has never conformed to fact. One aspect of disorder is the fact that the CIA is only one of the intelligence agencies of the government. Although it is the most public, it is not even the largest, employing only about 15 percent of those in the intelligence service of the country. Additional intelligence assets are found in various other sectors of the government, but especially in the Department of Defense. DOD houses institutions such as the super-secret National Security Agency (NSA), the Defense Intelligence Agency (DIA), and the intelligence units of each of the major uniformed services. These agencies possess the great bulk of the intelligence assets of the U.S. government (exact accounting is impossible, because they have "black"—or secret—budgets). The activities of these agencies are nominally coordinated by the DCI, but this supervision is imperfect, since the secretary of defense is the reporting channel and administrative head of the DOD intelligence units. For these reasons, the SECDEF has normally been the greatest opponent of reform efforts aimed at centralizing intelligence functions.

The other traditional organization problem surrounds the roles of the DCI. In Washington-speak, the DCI has traditionally been "dual hatted." What this curious phrase means is that the DCI has traditionally been simultaneously the administrative head of the CIA (one hat) *and* the head of the intelligence community, the aggregation of the various intelligence units throughout government (the second hat). Wearing this second hat, the DCI is supposed to coordinate the activities of all agencies, including the parsing of roles and missions among the various agencies. Since those agencies include the CIA, the two hats leave the DCI with a built-in conflict of interest. In addition, the DCI wears a third "hat" as chief intelligence source for the president, a further drain on his or her energies.

This organization sufficed during the Cold War, dealing as it did with an essentially monolithic, if very difficult, opponent. As the Cold War dissolved and more diffuse and diverse sources of opposition to American interests emerged, the intelligence community was forced to adapt, and it was not altogether successful in doing so. Prior to 1991, for instance, the CIA had placed great emphasis on analysts and agents with Russian and Eastern European language skills, but had placed very little emphasis on language competencies such as Arabic or Chinese. It has thus had to scramble, with only partial success, to achieve the kinds of competencies necessary to deal with the contemporary environment and its challenges.

The failure to produce actionable and timely intelligence to prevent the 9/11 disasters brought the entire intelligence community, and the CIA as its most visible symbol, to the forefront. An examination of the disaster revealed that there had been significant intelligence failures in the process. The presidentially appointed 9/11 Commission was commissioned to recommend reforms of the process. The commission found two major faults in the existing system. First, it discovered an intelligence system built for a different operational environment than it now faced. Rather than facing what it called a "few very dangerous adversaries" (the Soviet Union and its allies), the commission identified a "number of less visible challenges" (such as Al Qaeda). Second, the commission argued that the intelligence community was so dispersed in terms of allocating authority that it was ill-equipped to meet these new challenges.

The commission made several recommendations that have only been partially implemented. Two stand out. First, it recommended establishing a National Counterterrorism Center (NCTC) with personnel drawn from various agencies to create a central focus on terrorism and to coordinate joint planning and operations among agencies dealing with terrorism. To ensure that the NCTC had sufficient authority to do its job, the commission recommended it be placed within the White House and headed by a director appointed directly by the president at the level of deputy secretary, thereby giving the incumbent coequal status to the Deputies Committee of the NSC. Further, it recommended that the director be subject to congressional approval and subject to providing testimony to Congress, both of which would raise the public visibility of the director and the NCTC. Although most of its work is conducted outside the public view, NCTC has evolved as a central element in the national anti-terrorism effort.

The other recommendation was the establishment of the DNI as the chief intelligence figure for the United States, above the DCI. Part of the rationale was to remove one of the DCI's hats and thus the built-in conflict of interest; the DNI would become chair of the intelligence community. The reorganization also called for having the DCI and various intelligence units housed in other administrative departments placed under the DNI (for instance, the undersecretary of defense for intelligence). To further aid the DNI, formerly black budgets were to be made public, and intelligence budget aspects formerly housed principally in the DOD were to be transferred to the control of the DNI.

This latter transfer of power out of traditional departments to the DNI created a bureaucratic firestorm led by SECDEF Rumsfeld, who was entirely opposed to both the control and budgetary implications for the DOD of the DNI as it was recommended. President Bush sided with those who opposed fundamental change, creating the position of DNI but not giving the position or its incumbent the important authorities necessary to enact change. Like the role of the NCTC, the DNI's position evolved under the Obama presidency, because Obama was more sympathetic to the reform than the Bush White House was. The DNI has become the central figure in the intelligence community, and the DNI has basically replaced the DCI as the major face and voice of the intelligence effort.

Foreign Policy Role Exactly how important reform and a more efficient and orderly intelligence process are to foreign policy depends on the role one envisages for the intelligence community in the contemporary environment. When the competition was largely framed in the politico-military confrontation between the United States and the Soviet Union, a system of loose coordination of the military and political aspects of the competition worked passably well, but that structure of opposition no longer exists, as the 9/11 Commission advocated, and so the emphasis on a new and more diverse world environment has required a different policy approach and role as well.

Geographically, the old structure clearly no longer matched the problems with which the intelligence community is forced to deal. That environment has changed in two important ways. On one hand, the emphasis has moved geographically from a European-centered contest (the Cold War confrontation across the Iron Curtain) to a much more fluid emphasis on Third World conflicts, especially centering on the Islamic Middle East. On the other hand, the structure of threats the United States faces is not as clearly defined as it once was. The kind of advice that came from the Cold War structure is neither well suited nor particularly expert when dealing with the kinds of quasi- and semi-military threats from nontraditional sources associated with the developing world and with international religious terrorism. What exactly must the intelligence community contribute to this new structure and content of threat?

Much of the current content of foreign policy for which the intelligence community has relevant expertise and authority is focused on the foreign aspects of the terrorism threat to the United States. Part of that threat is operational, dealing violently with opponents such as Al Qaeda and IS in ways that sometimes mimic military operations (drone attacks against Al Qaeda targets in Yemen controlled and directed by the CIA is an example), but part of it is a cooperative effort with other parts of the government that also have areas of responsibility for dealing with the terrorism problem and counterpart agencies in other countries. The exact nature of interaction and policy contribution of the intelligence community in what is generally described under the rubric of homeland security is still a matter of some development and contention, to which the discussion now turns.

Department of Homeland Security

The major institutional response to 9/11 was the creation of the **Department of Homeland Security (DHS)**. Unlike the more traditional foreign policy agencies, the role and mission of DHS is more explicitly intermestic and diverse than the roles and missions of agencies such as the Department of State. In concept, **homeland security** is more akin to and arguably a major component of national security, one of the major purposes of which (some would argue *the* major purpose) is protecting the country from harm—in other words, homeland security. The two efforts are mostly differentiated by the forces against which each protects the United States: conventional military threats (DOD) or unconventional threats such as terrorism (DHS). These distinctions are easier to make in the abstract than in practice because of the semi-military nature of terrorism and counterterrorism. The comparison is further clouded by the diverse nature of additional duties assigned to DHS, such as border protection, immigration, and emergency management.

The movement to create DHS cascaded rapidly through the political process during 2002 after the 9/11 attacks and as a direct response to the personal insecurity most Americans felt—that the government was institutionally unprepared for that tragedy and what might follow. The bill to create DHS was introduced in both houses of Congress on May 2, 2002, and finally passed and signed by President Bush on November 25, 2002; the DHS formally came into existence on January 24, 2003. Former Pennsylvania governor Tom Ridge, who had served as director of the Office of Homeland Security, was named the first secretary, followed in 2005 by former federal judge Michael Chertoff. Two secretaries served under Obama (Janet Napolitano and Jeh Johnson). President Trump appointed retired marine general John Kelly to the job.

Controversy has plagued the new department since it was formed. It was not, in a sense, a new agency at all, but rather the shuffling and cobbling together of a diverse and sometimes reluctant group of existing agencies from other parts of the federal bureaucracy. The only truly new unit within DHS was the Transportation Safety Agency (TSA). The agency was hastily formed as a quick and visible response to the terrorist threat, and some of its most important problems have arisen from how quickly it was put together and from the combination of agencies that were and were not included under its umbrella. At the same time, this diversity resulted in its association with problems that arose within the operation of some of its assembled units. The most famous was the response by the **Federal Emergency Management Agency (FEMA)** to the Hurricane Katrina disaster in New Orleans in 2005 and more recent involvement in the illegal immigrant problem along the Mexican border (the Border Patrol is also a part of DHS). All have significant political causes and consequences.

Organization The new department was organized into four functional directorates reflecting its organizational rationale: informational analysis and infrastructure protection; science and technology; border and transportation security; and emergency preparedness and response. Appropriate agencies lifted from other government departments are assigned to one or another of these directorates: FEMA as the heart of emergency management and preparation, for instance. In addition, the Homeland Security Act created some anomalous responsibilities, such as monitoring drug trafficking to determine possible connections between that trafficking and terrorism and to coordinate responses.

Organizational problems have beset the DHS since its inception, three of which are worth noting. The first and most serious problem was which agencies would and would not be included within DHS. The second has been the organizational model for DHS. The federal government had one previous experience with creating a new agency out of existing agencies (the Department of Energy or DOE), which was less than a great success, but which foreshadowed difficulties for DHS. The third is funding, a problem that has largely been the result of the difficulty of removing existing agencies from their former homes and moving them to DHS.

The DHS brought together twenty-two existing federal agencies with more than 170,000 employees under the new umbrella. Appropriated from departments and agencies throughout the government, this diverse set of employees had different loyalties, ways of doing things, and cultural perspectives on problems and their solutions, and they all were more or less enthusiastically included in the DHS. The agency thus faced a formidable task in trying to integrate all these groups into a coherent team under the new anti-terrorism mandate. Despite all the bureaucratic shuffling that occurred, however, significant candidates escaped inclusion for largely political reasons.

The list of those succeeding in avoiding inclusion started at the very pinnacle of the anti-terrorism effort. The three agencies with the core responsibility for protecting the country against terrorism (the "golden triangle") were the CIA, the Federal Bureau of Investigation (FBI), and the Immigration and Naturalization Service (INS, rechristened as the now familiar Immigration and Customs Enforcement or ICE). The connection is intuitive. The CIA has responsibility for foreign intelligence, including identifying foreign terrorists and monitoring their attempts to enter the United States, INS/ICE monitors and filters individuals—including terrorists—attempting to cross the border into the United States, and the FBI is assigned primary policing duties against terrorists on American soil. These functions are closely interrelated and seem to require maximum coordination and cooperation, making their inclusion within the new DHS appear natural. It did not, however, happen.

Of the three key actors, only INS/ICE ended up as part of DHS. The FBI is one of the gemstones of the Department of Justice, did not want to move, and represents an asset that the attorney general (who administers the department) would relinquish only very reluctantly. The CIA is an independent agency not part of any cabinet department, guards its independence, and had enough political clout to stay out. Only INS/ICE, an agency with a spotty past that no other agency truly wanted, was included in the new structure. Both the CIA and FBI argued that their organizational missions included anti-terrorism but also included other major obligations unrelated to the DHS charter (for instance, the FBI's responsibility for organized crime, clearly not a part of DHS responsibility). The more basic reason, however, is that neither agency wanted to be included in DHS, and the historical agencies of which they were part had enough political clout to avoid their transfer to the new DHS.

Intersection 5.2   DHS and the Fight against Terror

The express reason for forming DHS was as the government's premier response to the terrorist challenge. The DHS has played an increasingly large role in the overall federal effort as it has matured as an agency and internally reconciled many of the cultural and operational difficulties among its constituent parts. Because the terrorist problem is so multifaceted and occurs as a domestic and international (thus intermestic) problem, its dominance as the "lead agency" in the terrorism effort has never been clearly established.

The golden triangle of agencies already identified illustrates why not. The terrorism effort is conducted in three separate environments, each of which has different core agencies and supporting institutions, only a fraction of which are part of DHS. In the international environment, the effort centers on identifying and monitoring terrorists (intelligence functions under CIA), attacking and killing terrorists (a DOD function much of the time), and negotiating international efforts against terrorists (a diplomatic effort under State). Essentially none of the international activities are under the purview of DHS.

The second venue is at the border. The primary role here is to monitor who enters and leaves the country, which *is* largely the province of the ICE and the border patrol, both parts of DHS. To accomplish this task, however, requires cooperation with other, non-DHS agencies: notifications on suspected terrorists attempting to enter from the CIA and efforts to monitor and apprehend suspected terrorists, which is largely a federal law enforcement priority (FBI), and local law enforcement agencies. The third venue is the domestic environment. The major thrust here is to monitor the activities of suspected potential terrorists, identify emerging domestic sources, and apprehend suspects planning or trying to commit terrorist acts before they occur. Virtually all these activities are carried out by federal law enforcement agencies outside DHS.

The golden triangle principle illustrates why DHS is not central to all this. A different agency dominates each venue: foreign intelligence by CIA, the domestic environment by the FBI, and the domestic intersection at the border by DHS. If all these agencies were part of DHS and controlled by its secretary, that person could mandate and organize a maximally coordinated effort. That organizational framework does not exist, and thus DHS is only one part of solving the problem for which it was created.

These key exclusions arguably reduce the effectiveness of cooperative efforts of golden triangle agencies, since they all report to different cabinet-level officials rather than a single secretary who can mandate their cooperation as a first priority. All three are represented in forums such as the NCTC, but they remain administratively independent of one another.

Not all relevant agencies were able to avoid the DHS net. Among the twenty-two agencies included were the U.S. Coast Guard, the Customs Service (although some of its functions, notably revenue collection, remain within the Treasury Department), the Secret Service, the Federal Protective Service, the

INS (technically split into two successor parts, a Bureau of Border Security and a Bureau of Citizenship and Immigration Services, of which ICE is the more public symbol), FEMA, the Transportation Safety Administration (TSA), and the FBI's National Infrastructure Protection Center.

The second organizational problem has been the proper organizational model for DHS. Part of the difficulty is the diverse set of mandates the various parts of the agency have, some of which are almost entirely separate from one another (e.g., FEMA's natural disaster relief mandate as contrasted with airport security for the TSA). More fundamental, however, is the issue of how to put together a new federal agency from existing components.

The federal precedent for doing so was the Department of Energy (DOE). Like DHS, DOE was a response to a foreign policy crisis, the oil shocks of 1973 and 1977 in the oil-rich Middle East. As a response, the Carter administration shuffled existing agencies in the federal government to create DOE in 1977. This reshuffling also created problems of congressional oversight, although less severe than those for DHS (functions folded into DOE reported to seventeen congressional committees; DHS functions reported to eighty-eight committees). The DOE remains less than a model of bureaucratic efficiency, and DHS has followed hard on its tracks.

The third problem has been funding for DHS and homeland security more generally. The original problem was that DHS was created "on the cheap," with the Bush administration arguing in 2002 that it would require no additional federal spending, since its operation would be funded by transferring budget resources to the new agency from the traditional departments of agencies moved into DHS. The agencies from which functions were transferred resisted this movement of funds, and with the sympathetic assistance of congressional oversight committees, were largely successful. The result was that DHS efforts were initially underfunded, but accompanied by the myth that this underfunding was proper given the hoped-for contribution of other agencies to the cause.

There have been two negative legacies of the funding problem. The first is the perception that large-scale funding is unnecessary, despite the very visible profile of the anti-terrorism mission. Thus, as recently as 2014, the budget of DHS was about $55 billion, a small part of the federal budget. The other negative legacy is that DHS funds are not well spent. The FEMA response to Katrina is cited as an example of waste in the budget, and there have also been accusations that much DHS money has had a pork barrel impact. In one locale, for instance, federal funds purchased more hazmat (hazardous materials) suits than there were police officers and firefighters to wear them.

Foreign Policy Role The role and mission of DHS is classically intermestic, combining foreign policy and domestic priorities in a world where many issues are increasingly intermestic. So many of the agencies brought under the DHS umbrella had roles in addition to those that logically flowed from homeland protection from terrorist attack that refinement of the mission has been difficult. This problem, of course, was the basis on which the FBI and CIA avoided inclusion successfully, but not all those who tried that ploy succeeded. FEMA, for instance, has as an integral part of its responsibility responding to natural disasters that have no relationship to terrorism other than the destruction and suffering that either can create. But it was included because no one had the clout to keep it out.

Within the foreign policy realm, the obvious DHS role is its position as part of the interagency effort to combat terrorism, which is the principal rationale for its existence and the inclusion of its secretary on the NSC. That role, however, is largely domestic, and specifically related to intercepting potential terrorists seeking to enter the United States surreptitiously, a role in which the coast guard and border patrol have major parts. In addition, the DHS has a major role in mitigating the impact of terrorist attacks that do occur, mainly through its capabilities in emergency management.

The other roles of the DHS intermix with and may serve to dilute the accomplishment of its central mission. In recent years, for instance, the thrust of border protection has moved from guarding against terrorist penetration to assisting in efforts to stem illegal immigration, mostly across the Mexican-American border. This latter effort includes participation in joint endeavors to interfere with the illicit drug trade, and while these efforts do not negate a retained emphasis on protection against terrorist penetration, they certainly do act as a competitor for departmental time and resources. While there is some overlap in these responsibilities (e.g., presumably some potential terrorists attempt to enter the United States surreptitiously across the Mexican border) and they all fall broadly under the category of homeland protection, they may nonetheless represent a diversion of attention away from the primary mission.

Intermestic Agencies Few contemporary public policy areas have no intermestic facet; one of the reasons it is difficult to enforce a separation between the two traditional realms is that virtually all foreign policy matters have some international content and almost all foreign policy concerns have domestic barriers and impacts. The figurative water's edge is not a wall (if it ever was); it is an intermestic mixing bowl.

This phenomenon is reflected institutionally within the U.S. government. The discussion to this point has centered on the core foreign policy agencies: governmental institutions and agencies whose major responsibility is foreign policy and that have a stake and participate in virtually all foreign policy matters. The growing intermestic impact, however, means that agencies more closely identified with domestic priorities are also foreign policy actors some of the time— hence their designation as **intermestic agencies**.

The most obvious examples are in the economic realm. Widespread concern over economic issues first rose in prominence in the 1980s and 1990s surrounding globalization, a concept discussed in more detail in chapter 10. The growing belief that the international economy was becoming increasingly intertwined led, among other things, to the development of international agencies promoting trade arrangements such as the Asia-Pacific Economic Cooperation (APEC) and a series of international trade agreements such as the North American Free Trade Agreement (NAFTA). The negative impact of some of these mechanisms on the domestic economy (especially American jobs) became a major intermestic issue in the 2016 presidential election.

Organizations with an overtly economic agenda are not the only executive branch agencies with concerns in the international arena. Some of the others have a primarily economic focus, but others do not. For present purposes, these "part-timers" can be divided into economic and noneconomic categories.

The Economic Agencies Economic issues, and particularly the asserted dilatory effects of free trade agreements on American jobs, was a foreign policy concern during both the 2016 primary and general election campaigns, and coming to grips with this problem will be an important concern for the new administration. How economic policies affect the livelihoods of American voters has always been a prominent election issue. Historically, it has been considered a primarily domestic issue; the emergence of economic globalization in the 1990s has transformed economic policy into an intermestic issue.

The first contemporary American administration to fully embrace and promote international economic matters as a centerpiece of foreign policy was Bill Clinton's, and many of the institutions and emphases in the current environment came into being during his tenure in the 1990s. The Bush administration of the early 2000s was not so attuned to these concerns and even briefly flirted with the idea of dismantling some of the Clinton emphases before their attention was diverted to international religious terrorism after 9/11. The Obama administration revived and sought to build upon the Clinton initiative, although the more pressing need to deal with the crisis of the domestic economy restrained their efforts. Given his business background, Trump is likely to be very personally involved in international economic—and especially trade—policy.

The role of the **economic agencies** is a bellwether of where different presidents place economic considerations within the hierarchy of their foreign policy priorities. For the Clinton administration, that role was especially important as the vehicle for spreading American ideals to the world, or widening the "circle of market democracies," as he put it. The chief instrument for promoting globalization and democratization was the promotion of free trade as a principle and as the cornerstone for economic organizations such as NAFTA and APEC, both of which came under fire in 2016. George W. Bush shared Clinton's belief in free trade, but placed greater emphasis on the military instrument of power to promote American policy.

The economic agencies are unlike the other entities discussed in this chapter. They are not organized into a single department such as State or Defense, and they do not all have a signature role or mission, such as intelligence collection within the intelligence community. Rather, the function of promoting the economic aspects of foreign policy falls to a number of agencies inside and independent of other cabinet-level departments and brought together under the banner of the NSC.

The only economic agency representative with full membership (if unstated in the National Security Act) on the NSC is the secretary of the treasury, whose portfolio includes the promotion of foreign policy, but he or she is more correctly thought of as the chief advisor to the president on domestic economic concerns that become intermestic, rather than with a primary international economic focus. The other economic agencies involved in the process are NSC part-timers who become involved when an issue affects their interests or expertise.

In terms of foreign policy impact, two economic agencies have stood out as particularly interesting. The first is the **National Economic Council (NEC)**, of which the assistant to the president for economic affairs is the administrative head. The NEC was created in January 1993 by the executive order of President Clinton, fulfilling a campaign promise to place greater emphasis on economic growth and prosperity. It also had the symbolic intent and effect of raising the importance of economic policy to a plane close to the military thrust of the NSC. The name National Economic Council and acronym NEC were chosen purposely to mirror the NSC designations, and Clinton tended to treat them as virtually coequal, if independent, entities. The chief difference between the NSC and NEC, however, is that the former was created as the result of an act of Congress, which means it can only be disbanded by legislative action, whereas the president can disband the NEC by simple executive order such as one that created it.

The importance of the NEC depends to a large degree on the president's personal involvement with it. Clinton was personally very interested in economic aspects of foreign policy, saw the NEC as the prime motor of that interest, felt entirely at home dealing with the details of economic policy, and thus placed himself at the center of the NEC, often chairing NEC meetings personally. Bush, by contrast, was not personally heavily invested in the NEC or in economic policy in particular; he became more comfortable dealing with traditional national security concerns such as the war on terrorism and the military involvement in Iraq. Obama shared much of Clinton's interest in economics and thus elevated the economic agencies within, rather than parallel to, the more general national security process. He personally chaired the NEC.

The other position is that of the **United States Trade Representative (USTR)**. This position and the support for it came into being in 1962 with the express purpose of promoting American trade in the world. The position was formalized by the Trade Act of 1974 and clarified by the Trade Agreement Act of 1988. Originally housed in Washington alone, it has gradually expanded its operations so that the more than 200 professionals who form its core staff are located in the national capital as well as in Geneva, Switzerland (location of the headquarters of the World Trade Organization), and Brussels, Belgium (headquarters of the European Community). The USTR also has an office in Beijing, China.

Organizationally, the office of the USTR is part of the executive office of the president, rather than being housed in any cabinet-level agency. Its basic roles as they evolved from the 1990s to the present include coordination of U.S. participation in various multilateral trade negotiations, the promotion of American trade, and assistance to other agencies in trade-related matters.

The Noneconomic Agencies In addition to the core agencies, the intermestic content of foreign policy draws other agencies into the process. What distinguishes the agencies from others is that international economic concerns only represent a part of their responsibility. The U.S. Department of Agriculture, for instance, becomes intermestic in its mandate to promote the sale of American agricultural products overseas and to regulate the flow of foreign foodstuffs into the country. The Commerce Department has trade promotion as a major part of its efforts in support of the American private sector, and the Treasury Department advises the White House on international financial issues. At a step removed, cabinet-level agencies such as Health and Human Services are occasional actors when things such as foreign-originating diseases threaten the United States. At some level, nearly all agencies get into the action at one time or another.

Conclusion

The executive branch of the government houses a large and diverse set of agencies that have as their sole or partial mandated purpose assisting in the formulation and execution of foreign policy. Since 1947, the centerpiece has been the National Security Council (NSC) system created by the National Security Act of 1947. The NSC system has gradually expanded and transformed itself into what is now commonly known in Washington as the interagency process, an evolving and constantly changing set of actors and institutions that responds to the preferences of different presidents and changes in the international environment toward which foreign policy is directed.

Within the structure of the executive agencies that assist the president, the National Security Act elevated the role of national security to near coequality with that of traditional diplomatic activity by naming the State and Defense departments as the major statutory partners of the president and vice president as the core members of the NSC. As time and circumstances have changed, other actors have been added to the process and the roles and configurations of various actors have changed. The addition of the DHS to represent the response to the emergence of international religious terrorism represents the kind of organizational innovation that has occurred, and efforts to change the pattern of relationships within the intelligence community demonstrate how attempts are made to alter the existing way that some functions are performed. The growing level of intermestic issues and concerns also adds to the need for adaptation.

The juxtaposition of impressive and seemingly permanent edifices such as the Foggy Bottom headquarters of the State Department and the Pentagon across the Potomac River from it creates a semblance of permanence and immutability that is probably misleading to some extent. There will always be a State Department to represent the United States as its diplomatic face and to advocate the use of diplomacy in solving the country's foreign policy problems, and there will also always be a military establishment that can try to impose some solutions to the country's challenges by force. That does not, however, mean that the configuration at any point is immutable, and those with the greatest influence today may exercise less influence at some time in the future.

Study/Discussion Questions

1. How does the effort to deal with international religious terrorism provide a vantage point for seeing the complexity of the interactions of various governmental entities active in the foreign policy process? How is this complexity reflected in the evolution of the interagency process?
2. What is the National Security Council (NSC)? Describe its formation, role, and changing membership across time.
3. What is the interagency process? Describe this system, using the structure of the NSC committees as prime examples of the process in action.
4. What are the principal executive agencies that assist the president in the formulation and execution of foreign policy? Which of these do you consider to be the core actors? Why?
5. Describe each of the following in terms of history, organization, and foreign policy role: Department of State, Department of Defense, intelligence community, Department of Homeland Security, intermestic agencies.
6. How have the comparative roles of the State and Defense departments changed over time? Why have they changed?
7. Why has the intelligence community been a controversial part of the interagency process? What attempts at reform have been attempted? Why have they not entirely succeeded?
8. Discuss the Department of Homeland Security. What problems have been associated with its formation and subsequent operation?
9. What are the principal intermestic agencies active in foreign policy? Briefly describe each. How does their changing role reflect presidential preferences in foreign policy?

Bibliography

Berkowitz, Peter, ed. *The Future of American Intelligence.* Palo Alto, CA: Stanford University Press, 2006.
Betts, Richard K. "Fixing Intelligence." *Foreign Affairs* 81, no. 1 (January/February 2002): 43–59.
Boren, David L., and Edward J. Perkins, eds. *Who Speaks for America? Why Democracy Matters in Foreign Policy.* Ithaca, NY: Cornell University Press, 1998.
Clarke, Richard. *Against All Enemies: Inside America's War on Terror.* New York: Free Press, 2004.
Destler, I. M. *The National Economic Council: A Work in Progress.* Washington, DC: Institute for International Economics, 1996.
Destler, I. M., and Anthony Lake. *Our Own Worst Enemy: The Unmaking of American Foreign Policy.* Rev. ed. New York: Touchstone, 2014.
Flynn, Stephen. *America the Vulnerable: How Our Government Is Failing to Protect Us from Terrorism.* New York: HarperPerennial, 2005.
Friedman, Benjamin. "Think Again: Homeland Security." *Foreign Policy,* July/August 2005, 22–29.

Halperin, Morton. *Bureaucratic Politics and Foreign Policy.* Washington, DC: Brookings, 1974.

Hilsman, Roger. *The Politics of Policy Making in Defense and Foreign Affairs: Conceptual Models and Bureaucratic Politics.* 3rd ed. Englewood Cliffs, NJ: Prentice Hall, 1993.

Hillyard, Michael J. "Organizing for Homeland Security." *Parameters* 32, no. 1 (Spring 2002): 75–85.

Inderfurth, Karl E., and Loch K. Johnson. *Decisions of the Highest Order: Perspectives on the National Security Council.* Pacific Grove, CA: Brooks/Cole, 1988.

————, eds. *Fateful Decisions: Inside the National Security Council.* New York: Oxford University Press, 2004.

Kettl, Donald L. *System Under Stress: Homeland Security and American Politics.* 3rd ed. Washington, DC: CQ, 2014.

Lowenthal, Mark M. *Intelligence: From Secrets to Policy.* 6th ed. Washington, DC: CQ, 2015.

Maxwell, Bruce, ed. *Homeland Security: A Documentary History.* Washington, DC: CQ, 2004.

9/11 Commission. *The 9/11 Commission Report: Final Report of the National Commission on Terrorist Attacks on the United States.* Authorized ed. New York: Norton, 2004.

Richelson, Jeffrey T. *The U.S. Intelligence Community.* 7th ed. Boulder, CO: Westview, 2015.

Rothkopf, David. *National Insecurity: American Leadership in a World of Fear.* New York: PublicAffairs, 2014.

Sauter, Mark D., and James Carafano. *Homeland Security: A Complete Guide to Understanding, Preventing, and Surviving Terrorism.* New York: McGraw-Hill, 2005.

Snow, Donald M. *National Security.* 6th ed. New York: Routledge, 2017.

Trubowitz, Peter. *Defining the National Interest: Conflict and Change in American Foreign Policy.* Chicago: University of Chicago Press, 1998.

White, Jonathan. *Terrorism and Homeland Security.* 9th ed. New York: Wadsworth/Cengage, 2016.

Congress and Foreign Policy 6

The Constitution gives significant foreign policy powers to Congress.

Preview

Congress was the "first branch" of government, as the framers spelled out the powers of the legislative branch in Article 1 of the Constitution. Over time, however, Congress has come to take more of a backseat to the president when it comes to foreign policy—especially when it comes to war powers. Congress and the president both have significant foreign policy powers, which can lead to gridlock when the branches disagree. Since the 1960s and 1970s—following Vietnam, the civil rights movement, and Watergate—a partisan divide has opened in the area of foreign policy that can also lead to policy stalemate. This chapter examines the foreign policy powers of Congress and its advantages and disadvantages relative to the rest of the government. It explores the ebbs and flows of congressional activism that have evolved even as presidential power has steadily increased in the foreign policy domain.

Key Concepts

treaty ratification

polarization

substantive legislation

procedural legislation

power of the purse

confirmation power

congressional oversight

U.S. v. Curtiss-Wright Export Corporation

Youngstown Sheet & Tube v. Sawyer

Tonkin Gulf Resolution

War Powers Act (WPA)

crisis policy

strategic policy

structural defense policy

invitation to struggle

They say presidential elections are a race for the "middle," as candidates vie for the votes of the large swath of voters who are moderate. The 2016 election sure put that idea to the test! Over time as the parties and now perhaps the public too have become more polarized, elections can lead to significant shifts in policy. Foreign policy perhaps used to be more "stable" against these tides, but no longer. Donald Trump promised to build a wall on the southern border with Mexico, to aggressively pursue the deportation of immigrants here without work authorization (starting first with criminals), to tear up and renegotiate the North American Free Trade Agreement, to more closely align the United States with Putin's Russia, to scrutinize the value of NATO and our alliances with Japan and South Korea, to halt the opening to Cuba, and to withdraw from the Paris Agreement to confront climate change and from the new Trans-Pacific Partnership—which was to be the centerpiece not just of American economic activity in the Pacific and Asia but also of our security infrastructure with a resurgent China and a dangerous North Korea. Time will tell, and will also tell us when and how Congress, with Republicans in charge of the House and the Senate, will decide to get in on these policy shifts. Many of these policies were crafted over the years with significant congressional input, and a **treaty ratification** process; and some (such as the wall) will need funding by Congress (assuming Mexico does not pay for the wall)—so it is hard to believe they would sit supine while the president runs in the open field on such a broad range of issues.

Even though the attention of the public and the media tends to focus on the president when it comes to foreign policy, the American Constitution's framers clearly intended that Congress would equally share power and responsibility with the executive in all areas, including foreign policy. Throughout American history the extent of coequality has ebbed and flowed, and most observers agree that the country is currently in a period of presidential dominance. The Constitution has been called an "invitation to struggle" because it contains foreign policy powers for both Congress and the president. Conflict between the branches is no accident; indeed, it is at the heart of the American political system.

The United States is one of the few democracies to adopt a system where separate institutions share power, and this has distinct effects on how the American system makes foreign policy. Under this system, the powers of government are constitutionally distributed among the three branches of the federal government. Originally conceived as a means of warding off the tyranny that could result if any one leader or group of leaders consolidated the coercive capabilities available to modern governments, a system of separate institutions sharing power has two principal consequences for U.S. foreign policy making today.

First, it creates a legislature with an extraordinary amount of independent policy-making authority. It is the powers of Congress, after all, that Article I discusses—and in considerably more detail than the executive branch's powers introduced in Article II. Second, having distinct branches of government that share power also means that authority is fragmented, which can—and often does—produce policy gridlock. Gridlock is especially likely to occur when partisan divisions intensify the institutional rivalry inherent in our system of governing. Today's partisan and polarized political environment has made gridlock a nearly constant part of the contemporary environment.

Congress is constitutionally empowered to wield significant foreign policy power, but it has not always done so. American history has witnessed repeated oscillations between periods of executive and congressional dominance of the policy process. As a broad generalization, from the 1930s to the 1970s Congress tended to defer to presidential leadership in dealing with the crises of the Great Depression, World War II, and the first half of the Cold War. During the first quarter-century of the Cold War, Congress was usually content to follow the foreign policy course set by the president in the belief that the country could not afford to appear divided and irresolute in the face of a protracted global crisis.

By the time of the civil rights movement, the public's turn against the Vietnam War, and then the constitutional crisis of Watergate, this dynamic started to change and Congress began to reassert itself. Senator J. William Fulbright (D-AR) captured the mood in 1974, calling the presidency "a dangerously powerful office." "Whatever may be said against Congress . . . It poses no threat to the liberties of the American people" (quoted in Brown 1985). One of the legacies of this period was the desire to limit the president's war-making authority, a subject examined later in this chapter. Some of the issues raised in the 1970s are eerily similar to today's concerns surrounding American policy in Afghanistan, Iraq, Libya, and Syria.

In addition to the diminished luster of the presidency were other developments that combined to produce a much more assertive Congress. These developments included a large infusion of young representatives and senators in the mid-1970s, the weakening of party discipline, the erosion of the seniority system, the proliferation and expanded authority of subcommittees, and the growth in congressional staff. All these changes culminated in the reality the United States confronted in the 1990s when the Cold War collapsed: a Congress unwilling to submit meekly to the president's lead in defining U.S. foreign policy. Although patriotic responses to 9/11 produced a greater deference toward presidential authority, congressional assertiveness would return, especially in the context of the continuing U.S. involvement in Afghanistan and Iraq and debates about Syria and Libya.

Congress: Organizing Mechanisms and Structures

Although there is a tendency to speak of Congress in the singular, it is a bicameral body. It consists of a House of Representatives, comprising 435 members who represent roughly comparably sized districts and who serve two-year terms, and a Senate, consisting of two senators from each of the fifty states who serve six-year terms (staggered so that roughly one-third of the Senate seats are contested in each two-year election cycle). Because of their size, as well as the wave of internal democratization that swept Congress in the mid-1970s, both chambers are highly decentralized bodies with many committees and subcommittees—which offer both leadership opportunities and veto points. While the fragmentation of congressional authority expands the opportunities for individual legislators to affect foreign policy and opens the body to a wide spectrum of opinion, it also creates obstacles to forging legislative coalitions. These dynamics have been on full display as divisions in the House Republican Party essentially drove Speaker John Boehner (R-OH) from Congress in 2015, and posed at least as much challenge to Speaker Ryan (R-WI) as they did to President Obama in 2016.

Despite their caricature as corrupt and out of touch, most members of Congress are intelligent, hardworking, honest, and well informed of the views of their constituents. The very diversity of those constituent views, however, can make legislative agreement elusive. Unsurprisingly, a representative from Pittsburgh will be more likely to seek protectionist relief for the country's (and his or her district's) troubled steel industry, whereas a representative from rural Iowa will argue against trade protectionism, in part because his or her district depends heavily on export markets for its agricultural products. The constant turbulence of competing outlooks is the essence of legislative life, and it is also one of the real challenges we must confront; constituent interests and the reelection interests of individual members of Congress do not necessarily add up to "the national interest."

Political parties can be thought of as an organizing mechanism in Congress to impose a measure of order and coherence on the behavior of members of the institution. The majority in each chamber chooses its leader and an array of lieutenants to oversee the flow of legislation and attempt to unite party members behind major bills. The minority does the same. Although the discipline of political parties has eroded over the years, each party has actually become much more ideologically homogeneous. Thirty years ago, both parties were divided between their own liberal and more conservative wings, and there were "moderates" in both parties. Today, the Democratic Party is more consistently the home of political liberals while the Republicans are overwhelmingly conservative; rarely is there any meeting in the middle. This **polarization** in the parties has increased dramatically over the last thirty years, spurred in part by more moderate members being beaten in their party's primary election by more ideologically extreme challengers. While more ideologically "pure," it has not made the parties on the Hill more compliant (as we discussed in the start of this chapter).

Another organizing mechanism in the House and Senate is the system of committees, organized by subject matter, that ordinarily determine the fate of legislative proposals in their domain. About ten thousand bills and resolutions are submitted to each Congress (a "congress" lasts two years; the 115th Congress was seated in January 2017). Of these, less than 5 percent clear all the legislative hurdles to become law. The committee system makes Congress's workload possible. By dividing the vast number of proposals among its standing committees (twenty in both chambers, plus special "joint" and "select" committees), members are able to give bills closer attention and to develop a degree of policy expertise that comes with specialization. Since the early 1970s, the proliferating number of subcommittees increasingly handles the work once performed by full committees (there are on average between three and six subcommittees in each committee). This development was necessitated by the growing complexity of policy proposals and the demand of junior members to expand the policy-making opportunities available to them within Congress. Today, about 90 percent of legislative hearings occur before subcommittees. Similarly, subcommittees, by developing expertise on the proposals before them, very nearly hold life-and-death power over bills. An unfavorable vote in a subcommittee makes it unlikely that the bill will even be considered by the full committee, let alone by the full House or Senate.

In the Senate, the most important foreign policy committees are Foreign Relations, Armed Services, Appropriations, and the Select Committee on Intelligence. Given the Senate's special prerogatives in approving presidential appointments and ratifying treaties, its Foreign Relations Committee has long been among the most august in Congress. It has had many powerful chairs since the 1970s, leaders who sometimes work well with presidents and who sometimes work against them. Under the leadership of Jesse Helms (R-NC) between 1995 and 2001, the Foreign Relations Committee certainly became a thorn in President Clinton's side. Joseph Biden (D-DE) chaired the committee intermittently during the George W. Bush administration and oversaw an active committee. Bob Corker (R-TN) was new to the role in 2015, and opposed several of President Obama's foreign policy positions, especially on dealing with Russia, Ukraine, and nuclear weapons testing.

The committee structure in the House mirrors that of the Senate. The House's most prominent foreign policy committees are Foreign Affairs, Armed Services, Appropriations, and the Permanent Select Committee on Intelligence. In 2004 both the House and the Senate constructed Homeland Security committees that would help legislate in this area and oversee the Homeland Security Department.

In addition to congressional committees, congressional caucuses are another set of organizations on the Hill that are important for foreign policy. Caucuses are organizations that help draw attention to issues of interest to members, and can provide a forum both to learn more about the issues and to be a vehicle for legislative germination. Many caucuses are bipartisan, providing a means for members of the two parties to work together on issues of common interest; some are exclusive to one party or the other. Some examples of foreign policy–relevant congressional caucuses include the Iran Human Rights and Democracy Caucus, the Friends of Ireland Caucus, and the U.S.-Japan Caucus.

The congressional committee and caucus systems are more than just organizing devices. One of the challenges for Congress as an institution and for its members in the area of foreign policy is to be able to "compete" with the president when they have far less expertise and information than does the executive. Committees and caucuses are central ways for members of Congress to gain information on foreign policy issues and thus help them position themselves to be foreign policy players.

Congressional Foreign Policy Powers

The Founding Fathers were determined to prevent too much power from being concentrated in the hands of the executive, and so they bestowed generous grants of constitutional authority on Congress—including in the foreign policy domain. The constitutional foreign policy powers of Congress include: (1) legislation, (2) appropriations, (3) confirmations, (4) oversight, (5) war, and (6) treaties. All six of these formal powers are either specifically enumerated in the Constitution or are direct derivatives of explicit constitutional grants.

Legislative Power

Legislative power is the capacity to create legal authority that allows, requires, or forbids certain actions. The person or agency that possesses the lawmaking power is thus a matter of fundamental importance in the political system. The Founding Fathers settled this crucial issue in the very first section of the first article of the Constitution, which reads in its entirety: "All legislative Powers herein granted shall be vested in a Congress of the United States, which shall consist of a Senate and House of Representatives." Although ordinary legislative enactments are subject to presidential veto, vetoes can be overridden by two-thirds of the House and Senate, thus giving Congress the last word on defining what is and what is not legal.

In the field of international affairs, Congress uses its lawmaking power to shape policy in a variety of ways that tend to fall into one of two categories: substantive or procedural legislation. **Substantive legislation** directly defines the content of U.S. policy toward a particular issue, actor, or country beyond the United States. For example, the 1996 Cuban Liberty and Democratic Solidarity Act, sometimes called the "Helms-Burton Act" after its sponsors (North Carolina Republican senator Jesse Helms and Indiana Republican representative Dan Burton), made the embargo of Cuba the law of the land. While the embargo has been around in one form or another since the end of the Eisenhower administration, it had existed solely by presidential order until the Helms-Burton Act. Concerned that President Clinton might try to normalize relations with Cuba, and spurred by the 1995 shooting down of two airplanes piloted by a Cuban exile group by the Cuban Air Force (killing four), Congress seized the reins of Cuba policy (or tried to, at least) with this act.

Another classic example is the 1986 South Africa sanctions bill. The white minority had ruled South Africa since its independence in 1910. That rule became especially odious in 1948, when the right-wing National Party instituted the policy of apartheid, or racial separation. The nation's black majority was systematically oppressed through forced segregation, inferior education and jobs, and the denial of basic liberties. By the 1980s, South Africa's 25 million blacks increasingly challenged a system that denied them any political voice.

The Reagan administration's "constructive engagement" policy assumed that through quiet diplomacy the United States could encourage the South African regime to dismantle apartheid, but by the summer of 1986 Congress moved through a tough bipartisan sanctions bill. President Reagan vetoed the bill, pitting him not only against congressional Democrats but also against some of the leading Republicans in Congress. Congress overrode Reagan's veto, and the stringent U.S. economic sanctions proved to be instrumental in the decision of South African president F. W. de Klerk to begin dismantling apartheid in 1990, leading ultimately to the election of Nelson Mandela and the process of long-term democratization.

Another form of congressional lawmaking is **procedural legislation**. Procedural legislation can take many forms, but in general it attempts to play a role in foreign policy by laying out the procedures that the executive must follow, including crafting reporting requirements, or creating or changing executive branch agencies. The idea is to alter policy indirectly by changing the flow of political life that creates policy, rather than creating new policy directly. Some examples will help clarify. In terms of agency creation or reform, the 2002 construction of the Department of Homeland Security and the 2004 intelligence community reformulation that created the Director of National Intelligence and the National Counterterrorism Center (NCTC) are two of the most recent examples of Congress using procedural legislation in foreign affairs. The aim of Congress was to address the performance failures of 9/11 by altering the way the intelligence community worked and to create more synergies across the elements of the government that pertain to securing the homeland.

The 1986 Goldwater-Nichols Act, or the Department of Defense Reorganization Act, is a classic example of procedural legislation. Not talked about much today, it was hugely controversial when passed. Frustrated by the lack of coordination across military branches that seemed to be hindering operations, Congress tried to force more "jointness" on the armed forces by centralizing operational control in the hands of the chairman of the Joint Chiefs of Staff (JCS) and also the commanders in the different regions of the globe—the CINCs, or commanders in chief (later renamed Regional Combatant Commanders). The act also created the position of the vice chairman of the JCS, whose key mission is to find ways for the separate services to work together, perhaps in joint training or even joint acquisitions. In terms of reporting requirements, the War Powers Act of 1973 is a classic example of Congress trying to alter executive behavior by changing the rules by which the president has to play. We discuss the War Powers Act later in this chapter.

Appropriations Power

The Constitution is crystal clear on the **power of the purse**: Article I, Section 9, states, "No money shall be drawn from the Treasury, but in Consequences of Appropriations made by Law." Because the lawmaking power belongs to Congress, it follows that the all-important power to determine "appropriations made by Law" is also a congressional prerogative. If policy is what gets funded, then the power to decide what gets funded is a very great power indeed. The power to resolve perennial issues such as the size and composition of the defense budget and the U.S. contribution to the UN budget indicates the kind of policy influence Congress has through its control of the nation's purse strings.

Congressional decisions about spending can lead to funding a program or to the prohibition on the use of funds. The decision to end funding is uniquely a congressional function and an extremely political one. In the 1980s, for example, Congress banned the expenditure of funds to support military or paramilitary operations by the Nicaraguan Contras, who were carrying out a guerrilla war against the leftist Sandinista government—a favorite of the Reagan administration but not of the U.S. public or the Democrat-controlled Congress. Ultimately the Reagan administration tried to find a way around this law, called the Boland Amendment, to continue funding the Contras, which led to the "Contra" side of the Iran-Contra scandal.

Congress used its spending power to pull the financial plug on the Vietnam War in 1973 and 1974. On the one hand, this was a momentous decision—cutting off funds for military operations when there were still forces in the theater of operations. On the other hand, however, the American public had already turned against the war; indeed, the decision came as late as three years after the tide had turned against the war. It is worth considering the different dynamics of the Vietnam case compared to the case of the war in Iraq: many assumed the Democrats in Congress, having seized control in the 2006 midterm elections, would cut off funding for the Iraq War, given its (and George W. Bush's) increasing unpopularity. Congress never did cut off those funds, however. Perhaps there are different political dynamics that surround the presence of U.S. troops in the field today than in the previous era.

Confirmation Power

Unlike the lawmaking and budgetary powers, only the Senate exercises **confirmation power**. The Constitution stipulates that the president "shall appoint ambassadors, other public ministers and consuls . . . and all other officers of the United States" subject to "the advice and consent of the Senate." Thus, foreign policy makers, such as the secretary of state, the secretary of defense, and many of their associates, must win Senate approval before they can take up their duties. Confirmation applies to about 1,200 or so executive branch positions; the need for confirmation ensures that the Senate has some voice in these appointments and can block appointees of which it disapproves—a way for the separate branches to "share" power. The confirmation process itself also gives a vehicle to the Senate to influence the policy process. Confirmation hearings are by their very nature highly public forums that can serve as a way to air substantive policy disagreements between senators and the White House, and perhaps as a way to alter the president's positions on important issues.

Presidential nominees normally win Senate approval; indeed, failure to confirm the president's choice for a position is regarded as a major setback for the White House. Rather than risk the embarrassment of Senate rejection, presidents sometimes choose to withdraw or not nominate their more problematic choices. In the area of foreign and national security policy, presidents can also decide to avoid a confirmation fight by putting a potentially controversial nominee on the National Security Council staff instead—now about 400 positions are not subject to Senate confirmation because they sit entirely within the executive office of the president.

From time to time, a confirmation fight will break out (such as what we saw in 2016 with President Obama's nominee to the Supreme Court, Merrick Garland, for whom the Republicans in the Senate refused to even hold a hearing, thus delivering a seat to the new President Trump). After several controversial foreign policy nominations to begin his presidency in 2001, another emerged in 2005 when President George W. Bush nominated John Bolton—a harsh critic of the United Nations—to serve as the ambassador at the UN at the start of Bush's second term. Ultimately President Bush used a maneuver called a "recess appointment" to put Bolton in place, essentially bypassing the Senate while it was not in session when Bush could not overcome a filibuster to Bolton led by a Republican Senator, George Voinovich from Ohio. (In 2014 the Supreme Court took up the constitutionality of recess appointments, seeking to limit them somewhat, although they are already rarely used—but when they are, such as in the Bolton case, they are controversial.) Rejections happen too. In foreign affairs, one of the most striking was the defeat of former senator John Tower (R-TX) for the position of secretary of defense in 1989. A twenty-four-year Senate veteran and former chair of the Armed Services Committee, Tower was well versed in the substance of defense policy but his nomination ran into political and personal complications. After Tower's defeat, President Bush nominated former congressman Dick Cheney (R-WY), who of course would later be elected vice president with a different President Bush.

President Obama ended his two terms with an interesting foreign policy confirmation issue: how to get an ambassador to the U.S. Embassy in Cuba, which reopened in July 2015 after more than fifty years (starting in 1977 the United States had an "interests section" inside the Swiss Embassy in Havana, as the Cubans did in the Swiss Embassy in Washington, D.C.). President Obama dispatched a chargé d'affaires, the number two person at an embassy (career diplomat Jeffrey DeLaurentis), but Senators Ted Cruz (R-TX) and Marco Rubio (R-FL)—both Cuban Americans—blocked the appointment of an ambassador as part of their opposition to Obama's Cuba policy. The confirmation power, then, gives the Senate real leverage in the foreign policy process, should it decide to use it.

Oversight Power

Although not specifically enumerated in the Constitution, the legislative branch's power to review how new laws are implemented and to examine the actual effects of new policies follows logically from the constitutional grant of lawmaking authority. In the course of exercising its oversight prerogatives and responsibilities, Congress engages in ongoing studies, hearings, and investigations. Those activities, in turn, require a substantial amount of time and effort from executive branch officials, who are called on to prepare reports and to provide testimony to congressional committees engaged in oversight activities.

It is useful to distinguish routine **congressional oversight** from the more dramatic investigations that sometimes occur. A good example of routine foreign policy oversight is congressional monitoring of CIA activities. Until its burst of institutional assertiveness in the mid-1970s, Congress had little awareness of U.S. intelligence and covert operations and lacked a systematic means of acquiring information about them. In 1975, however, the Senate established a select committee to investigate allegations of CIA involvement in covert activities including destabilizing the leftist regime of Chilean president Salvador Allende and orchestrating a secret war in Cambodia. Chaired by Senator Frank Church (D-ID), the committee uncovered evidence of covert operations about which Congress had virtually no previous knowledge. Determined to make its oversight of intelligence activities more routine, Congress established new intelligence committees in both houses and adopted legislation that required the president to both authorize any covert operations and report those operations to the House and Senate Intelligence Committees—examples of reporting requirements that are a hallmark of procedural legislation. The purpose of the legislation was to strengthen democratic accountability over secret CIA operations, and by requiring both presidential approval and congressional notification, the two elected branches of government would be more firmly in control of and responsible for covert operations.

Most of the time, of course, the activities of the intelligence committees remain in the shadows, outside the glare of the public spotlight. These committees returned to the fore after the attacks of 9/11 because part of the blame for the traumatic events was laid at the CIA's door, and a series of high-profile hearings followed. Senate Intelligence Committee Chair Bob Graham (D-FL) and Vice Chair Richard Shelby (R-AL) led demands for a full accounting of the intelligence community's failures leading up to 9/11 and to try to forge a plan to make sure such an attack never happens again. Among the reforms that emerged from the committee in 2002 was the creation of a cabinet-level intelligence position superior to the Director of Central Intelligence, which came to be known as the Director of National Intelligence.

The congressional hearings on the Iran-Contra scandal were a particularly dramatic example of congressional oversight (and a media spectacle). "Iran-Contra" comprised two separate, but joined, misadventures. The "Iran" half arose from a series of illegal arms sales to the Iranian regime that had overthrown the Shah and that had held the American embassy staff in Tehran hostage for more than a year beginning in 1979. President Reagan, over the objections of most of his advisors, authorized the sale of missiles to the Tehran regime in 1985 in the hopes that the Iranians would help free American hostages in Lebanon and that doing so would lead to better U.S.-Iranian relations. The arms were sold at a profit; proceeds from the missile sales were used to finance the "Contra" half of the scandal—clandestine support for an American-sponsored rebellion in Nicaragua by a group known as the Contras, who sought to overthrow the country's Marxist Sandinista regime—activities, as we mention above, in direct violation of a congressional ban on such assistance. When these secret activities were revealed in 1986, a scandal ensued and investigations followed in the summer of 1987.

A more recent set of hearings occurred following the attack on the U.S. Consulate in Benghazi, Libya, on September 11, 2012, which led to the death of Ambassador Chris Stevens and three other officials. In the confusion that followed, the statements from the Obama administration were less than clear about what had happened, whether it was a terrorist attack—"what they knew and when they knew it"—leading many in Congress to conclude that the administration was hiding something. Several congressional committees investigated, and ultimately a "Select Committee on Benghazi" was assembled to pursue these questions in 2014–2015, culminating in the eleven-hour testimony of then secretary of state Hillary Clinton—the leading 2016 Democratic candidate for president.

War Power

Article I, Section 8, of the Constitution established that "the congress shall have Power . . . to declare War." Records of the Constitutional Convention show broad agreement that the executive should not be enabled to commit the country to war on its own independent authority. While bestowing on the president the role of commander in chief of the armed forces and acknowledging the inherent authority to use force to repel sudden attacks, the Constitution's framers were nonetheless clear in their insistence that the decision to initiate war must come from Congress.

The practice of the past two centuries, however, has borne little resemblance to the framers' carefully constructed design. As the United States rose to global leadership and as technological change created the requirement for rapid response to international crises, the actual power to initiate and carry out wars tilted decidedly toward the White House. Of the more than two hundred instances in which U.S. armed forces have been used abroad, only five followed formal declarations of war—the last being World War II. By the middle of the twentieth century, some authorities believed that the whole concept of declaring war was obsolete. So too, some argued, was the constitutional concept of joint war making by the president and Congress. Instead, broad congressional authorizations have become the norm since Vietnam's Tonkin Gulf Resolution, a blank check to wage war in Southeast Asia. The wars in the Persian Gulf, Afghanistan, and Iraq all followed such authorizations.

The trauma of the protracted, failed, and undeclared war in Vietnam stimulated Congress to set out to recapture its atrophied war powers. The resulting and controversial War Powers Resolution of 1973 (discussed later in the chapter) represented a historic effort by Congress to restore the interbranch balance to something more closely approximating the codetermination originally envisioned in the Constitution.

Treaty Power

Article II, Section 2, of the Constitution states that presidents may make treaties with foreign governments "by and with the Advice and Consent of the Senate . . . provided two thirds of the Senators present concur." As with the confirmation power, the congressional treaty power is assigned to the Senate alone.

The Constitution creates the need for an extraordinary majority to ratify treaties. Simple majorities are difficult enough to attain in fractious legislative assemblies; getting two-thirds of the Senate's members to agree on anything presents a formidable challenge. Why would the Founding Fathers have designed a process that makes treaties so difficult to attain? Deeply isolationist and profoundly suspicious of the monarchies then ruling Europe, the framers of the Constitution deliberately made it quite difficult for leaders to enter into formal "entanglements" with foreign governments. George Washington's famous farewell address that warned against the pernicious lure of "permanent alliances" faithfully mirrored the American outlook of the day.

As with confirmations, presidents do not always get the treaties they want. This difficulty was illustrated classically after World War I when President Woodrow Wilson was unable to secure Senate ratification of the Treaty of Versailles. American membership in the newly created League of Nations was one of the treaty's chief provisions, but the Senate refused to accept it. The fact that the United States did not join the league seriously weakened it, leaving it not up to the task of confronting armed aggression by the fascist regimes of Germany, Italy, and Japan that would follow and lead to WWII.

Wilson was not the only president to fail to get a treaty ratified, but in general, contemporary presidents try to ensure congressional involvement in the treaty-making process in hopes of improving the chances that the negotiated document will be ratified. Sometimes, however, even this strategy is not enough. For example, despite his efforts President Carter was unable to get the second Strategic Arms Limitation Talks (SALT II) Treaty ratified in the 1970s—thanks in part to the Soviet invasion of Afghanistan in 1979 that led (among other things) to Carter withdrawing the treaty from Senate consideration. President Clinton failed to get the Comprehensive Test Ban Treaty—which would ban all nuclear explosions for testing—ratified. The United States nevertheless continues to act under the treaty limits, and has not tested a weapon since 1992. Only North Korea dramatically violates this international norm by testing nuclear weapons, as it did for a fifth time in September 2016.

Before concluding this section on congressional foreign policy powers, it is important to remember the way that Congress and the presidency interact over these checked powers. As the chapter on the presidency discussed, the executive has many advantages in each of these areas, often able to act first, leaving Congress in a reactive position. The treaty power is a nice example of this tug-and-pull. The Senate certainly looks to be in a powerful position when it comes to treaties, and it is. However, it is also true that the percentage of all international agreements that the United States enters into that take the form of treaties has rapidly and dramatically decreased. Presidents increasingly use "executive agreements" as the preferred form of international agreements, rather than treaties. Unlike treaties, the Senate has no real authority over executive agreements and even had to pass a law—the Case-Zablocki Act of 1972—to try to curb their use by the president and to require that the president (through the secretary of state) inform the Senate when executive agreements are made. In recent decades executive agreements have come to be used far more often than are treaties, now making up nearly 95 percent of all international agreements.

Even though the foreign policy powers of Congress play out in an interactive context relative to the president, this section should dispel the myth that the Founding Fathers intended Congress to play second fiddle to the president in charting the nation's international course. Its impressive array of constitutional powers—to pass laws, fund programs, confirm executive appointments, oversee executive conduct, declare war, and ratify treaties—gives Congress a strong base of formal authority to be a coequal partner in the foreign policy–making process. Interaction between the branches is also a political matter, not just a constitutional one, and it is to this arena of foreign policy–making power that the discussion now turns.

Congressional Activism in Foreign Policy

Just as the president has political advantages and constraints on his conduct of foreign policy, so too does Congress. The large effect of presidential advantage is to encourage the chief executive to exercise more latitude in making policy with less congressional restraint and criticism. We have seen congressional willingness to assert its authority in foreign affairs ebb and flow. The most recent congressional challenge to a major presidential foreign policy initiative was probably over authorization of the use of force in the Persian Gulf War of 1991, although some Democrats certainly objected to the Bush 2007 "surge" policy in Iraq, and some Republicans objected to Obama's limited use of force in Libya and to his drawdown of forces in Iraq in 2011. Here we examine the sources of congressional activism and restraint—with a particular eye on the use of war powers from the Vietnam period to today.

Sources of Activism

The congressional activism that marked the period beginning with the reaction to the Vietnam conflict and continued through the 1990s resulted from several different factors. First, we should note the expanded role of the United States in world affairs. Prior to World War II, the United States and individual Americans could maintain, and plausibly believe, that their role in foreign affairs was very limited: What happened in the world did not much affect them, and what the United States did in the world had little impact on international affairs. In that setting, most members of Congress stood back and left the bulk of foreign relations to the executive branch, and notably the State Department, with the tacit approval of constituents who felt similarly unaffected.

The Cold War and the post–Cold War world changed all that. As already noted, the United States emerged from World War II as one of the world's two remaining major powers, and the foreign affairs of the Cold War dealt with the potentially life-and-death struggle between Soviet communism and American democracy. In that light, what the United States did in the world directly affected, at least potentially, every American, and members of Congress could no longer afford to be uninformed bystanders to the foreign policy process without incurring the wrath of at least some of their constituents. A post–Cold War world in which the United States is the sole remaining superpower and in which

American interests are virtually universal only magnifies the importance of how the United States deals with the world. The ongoing struggle to fashion effective policies to deal with global terrorism provides a classic example of this importance. These dynamics push Congress and its members toward activism in foreign affairs.

Second, and related, are the increasing domestic implications of foreign affairs. Before World War II it was often said that "politics stops at the water's edge," suggesting that the realm of partisan politics should remain tethered to domestic concerns and that when conflicts with other countries emerged, Americans should band together against external opponents. This position was easy enough to sustain when there were relatively few domestic consequences of foreign policy actions, but that is clearly no longer the case. In the language and argument used in this text, foreign policy has become intermestic and increasingly politicized.

Traditionally, Congress has been much more closely attuned to domestic concerns, because domestic decisions most strongly affect congressional constituencies in the United States. Now, however, when significant foreign policy issues have an effect on a member's constituents, Congress must pay more attention to foreign affairs, and foreign policy has become part of the political struggle for power in America as well.

Third, congressional activism has been spurred by high-profile foreign policy mistakes and misadventures by the president. As the domestic stakes of foreign policy have risen, so too has the willingness of Congress to rise up against the president over policy disagreements and failures and to take corrective action. The Vietnam War is the textbook example of this dynamic, but not the only one. The Vietnam conflict spawned the War Powers Resolution to put limits on the president's ability to deploy troops, but it was not alone as a military action that brought the wisdom of the executive into doubt (rightly or wrongly). In 1975, for instance, American lives were wasted in the *Mayaguez* incident, where U.S. Marines attempted to seize a pirated U.S. commercial vessel that had actually already been released, resulting in the loss of American lives. In 1980, the ill-fated Desert One rescue of the American hostages in Tehran, Iran, resulted in no American hostages being released and nine rescuers dying in the Iranian desert. The loss of life at the consulate at Benghazi, Libya, is a more recent case of the loss of life abroad that led many to raise questions about the policy wisdom involved.

Some of this congressional activism is about classic political "point scoring," but some of it also has led to significant reforms that have led to better foreign policy execution. Congress's reaction to the failure of Desert One included the Cohen-Nunn Act in 1986 that sparked the development and integration of the Special Forces, which at the time were small and lacked coordination across the services. Cohen-Nunn created prominent civilian and military leadership positions in the Special Forces, and began the movement toward the well-developed and coordinated kind of Special Forces that could be seen on display in the operation that killed Osama bin Laden, for example. The Pentagon opposed this legislation, and it probably would not have been enacted were it not for the executive branch's poor performance. It is generally agreed that this act—another example of procedural foreign policy legislation—has had far-reaching positive impact on military performance.

Fourth, a variety of internal changes in Congress over the past forty years has stimulated congressional activism in foreign affairs. The seniority system, for instance, has greatly eroded, sapping power from the political parties that manipulated seniority to their advantage. At the same time, the traditional power and deference accorded to committee chairs has also eroded; members no longer feel as obligated to take the lead from chairs or ranking members on committees. Influxes of new members in the 1970s, the 1990s, and in recent elections have resulted in a different kind of Congress, one both more independent, less able to be led (witness the departure of Speaker Boehner and the difficulties of Speaker Ryan to control even the Republican side of the House), and often less predictable for several reasons. For one thing, the members are, in general, younger than they used to be, better educated, and less patient to wait for power. Their willingness to form independent judgments—including those in opposition to executive positions—is further enhanced by the growth in congressional staffs. Most members of Congress, for instance, have a nominal expert on foreign policy on their personal staffs; if they do not, they can turn to staff experts on the committees to which they are assigned. The traditional view of quiet, orderly "back benchers" (relatively junior members) deferring to their senior colleagues has given way to a much more disorderly Congress. The rise in activism by the Tea Party is particularly symptomatic of this change.

Fifth, the modern media—especially the explosion of television news programming and the ubiquitous presence of the Internet—have greatly changed the policy context for both citizens and policy makers. Round-the-clock news available on TV, computer, and smartphone provides an exposure to world events for everyone that was quite impossible to receive as little as fifteen years ago. The result is that people, at least within the informed public (see chapter 8), are more aware of what is going on in the world than before, and this fact affects members of Congress.

Prior to the telecommunications revolution, it was possible and even reasonable for most members of Congress to be somewhat ignorant of most foreign affairs since most of a member's constituents were also ignorant of these matters. At the same time, it was difficult for members to communicate directly with the "folks at home" most of the time. Modern technology has changed that. Local news people can interview senators or representatives live in interactive forums and in real time as foreign crises or events unfold. If a member of Congress is uninformed on an issue or at odds with his or her constituents, there is no way to hide that fact other than ducking interviews, which may send a message in and of itself. The result may not be to force all members of Congress to be experts on foreign affairs, but it does mean they must *appear* to have a working understanding of foreign policy issues to avoid embarrassment. Having to develop opinions rather than simply accepting the views of the leadership inevitably increases the diversity of the opinions that will reach the floors of the two chambers.

Another dynamic facilitated by these technological changes has been the emergence of "candidate-centered campaigns," where the story of the person running in a congressional election trumps the story of the party. While the candidates who win election caucus with the party, their loyalty to the party can be reduced because of their often-national reputations or their allegiance to a "sub-party," such as the Freedom Caucus in the House that challenged fellow Republican Speaker Boehner so often and creates challenges for Speaker Ryan more than they did for President Obama, a Democrat. These (sort of) free agents can be quite active, including in the area of foreign policy.

Constraints on Activism

The tendency toward activism, of course, is by no means unrestrained. Although Congress may from time to time assert itself in foreign policy matters, it also remains constrained from doing so for a variety of reasons.

First, while we note above that the norm of not confronting the president on foreign affairs has eroded, it is not totally dead. The need to present a united front still tugs at some members, and some observers (and some presidents) argue that congressional activity undermines our foreign policy. Politics *must* end at the water's edge, some say. Without clearly accepted presidential leadership, it is argued, other governments will be confused as to who is speaking for the United States and what the country's policy is. Whereas the executive branch is headed by a single chief executive and thus can speak with one voice, the decentralized Congress sometimes threatens to act like "535 secretaries of state," the critics say. It is confusing enough for leaders around the world to gauge American resolve during an election season when presidential challengers pillory the current office holder; it is more complicated still when elected members of Congress express many different views.

The assertion that congressional disagreement with the executive should be muted or suppressed most often occurs, and is probably most convincing, during times of national crisis. During normal times, the attempts to stifle congressional dissent can be criticized as an infringement on free speech, on legitimate congressional prerogative, and on necessary political discourse. These distinctions become more blurred when policy is controversial or the country is in the throes of crisis.

The period after 9/11 illustrates the tensions and pressures involved when national crises intrude on the political process. In the immediate wake of the tragedy, the patriotic outpouring and the need to unite against a common foe overwhelmed dissent, including questioning how the government had performed in anticipating the event and why it had failed to prevent or vitiate its occurrence. As time passed public concerns began to be expressed in Congress, but even then, questions of loyalty and the need for a common front remained a major part of the debate. There was a real absence of critical dissent and debate before the U.S. invasion of Iraq. There is no permanent resolution to this debate, but this notion constrains foreign policy activism in Congress, and the debate over how this "should" work will continue to be a part of our ongoing experiment in self-government.

Another thing that constrains congressional activism is the relative lack of foreign policy expertise on the Hill. Few members of Congress are true foreign policy experts, and the ones who might be are exceptions to the rule. Even the chair of the Senate Foreign Relations Committee, Bob Corker (R-TN), had little foreign policy experience before assuming this role. His background was in business, construction, and real estate, and he was the mayor of Chattanooga before he came to the Senate in 2007. By 2015 he chaired the most powerful foreign policy post on the Hill.

Because of the general lack of expertise, the argument goes, members of Congress are likely to be outmatched by the vast expertise that exists in the executive branch. Some would go even further and argue that a policy shaped by Congress is bound to be amateurish by comparison. It is indeed a fact of legislative life that members of Congress must deal with the whole spectrum of policy issues confronting the country. In any given legislative session, members will have to make more or less informed voting choices on issues ranging from farm price support subsidies to Alaskan wildlife preservation to school voucher programs to health care and the problems of urban decay. For most members, the pressures to be reasonably adept generalists make it difficult, if not impossible, to attain the depth of knowledge they need to become true foreign affairs specialists. The presence of congressional staffs and the Congressional Research Service, and the ease with which one can get foreign policy news today, ameliorate this dynamic somewhat, but they do not eliminate it.

It does not follow, however, that Congress is inherently incapable of acting wisely on foreign affairs. Not all presidents arrived at the White House as foreign policy experts—indeed they rarely do. Presidents, no less than legislators, are faced with similar demands to be more or less conversant with the whole spectrum of policy issues facing the country, no matter how much they might wish to focus on foreign affairs. Yet no one argues that, as a consequence, the president is unable to handle the foreign affairs aspects of the job.

Although it may be true that the number of foreign policy experts available to the executive far exceeds the human resources available to Congress, this does not mean that Congress is disabled from taking part in the foreign policy debate in a knowledgeable, responsible manner. It is worth noting that the move to reduce congressional staffs following the 2010 elections has had the unintended consequence of weakening Congress relative to the president in the area of foreign policy.

Third, there are structural aspects of foreign affairs that make it hard for Congress to act. As two large deliberative bodies, the strength of Congress is its ability to debate and expose areas of public policy to a thorough analysis and vetting. Congress, at its best, is a magnificent deliberative body where issues of policy are brought to the public eye and resolved in the public interest. This process is often ponderous and time consuming, and Congress is rarely accused of being overly efficient in its operations. The virtues of Congress, however, can often become impediments in the area of foreign policy in several ways.

One is the sheer volume of foreign policy interactions. If Congress were to review and approve every legally binding interaction with other governments negotiated by the United States, it would simply drown in the responsibility. A second problem is the need for speed and flexibility in decision making that accompanies some foreign policy items, especially fast-breaking crises or opportunities. Often foreign policy events unfold rapidly and certainly in a manner that does not permit the kind of full debate and consideration at which Congress excels. What role should Congress play in these situations? In practice, the role is often limited to brief consultation with the leadership of Congress as events unfold, and the adequacy and timing of those consultations are almost always a matter of some controversy, usually along partisan lines. These disputes are most frequent when the use of force may be one of the policy options, a circumstance that intrudes directly on the debate over war powers.

A final problem is the need for secrecy. It is not uncommon for some of the information surrounding particular foreign policy events to be "classified." Although members of Congress automatically receive access to classified information by virtue of office, the executive branch inevitably voices concern about who should be given access to the country's highest secrets. More people who know a secret, after all, means more people who could leak it (either on purpose or by accident). This problem, it should be added, is not unique to Congress. It is a matter of fact that most of the "leaking" of privileged information occurs within the executive branch itself, in the actions of disaffected agencies or individuals who have been rejected in favor of other policy options.

A fourth dynamic that constrains congressional activism is the general orientation of the branch toward domestic issues and constituent service. Senators and representatives are elected from specific states and districts; their primary charge is to represent those areas from which they are elected, and the major concerns of most of their constituents, most of the time, are on domestic policies that affect them directly. The emergence of intermestic policies and globalization has eroded this historic trend, but the general orientation remains. However, it is worth pointing out that a member of Congress with the viewpoint that protecting the interests of constituents is his or her first priority will naturally look at foreign policy concerns first from the vantage point of domestic impact, where the partisan nature of the political process is most obvious. In areas such as foreign economic and trade policy, immigration, or environmental issues, for instance, we would expect partisanship to emerge and indeed we have witnessed that in recent years—with gusto!

Congressional Activism in Action: The Battle over War Powers

The most dramatic instances of the power clash between Congress and the White House happen over war powers—often even while American troops are in combat. In situations where troop deployments are proposed, the president almost invariably seeks maximum discretion in his role as commander in chief and in the name of national unity. Congress normally responds with an appeal to its constitutional war-making authority—triggering a debate over the appropriate balance of power assigned to the branches.

War powers clashes between the two ends of Pennsylvania Avenue have become increasingly frequent since the Vietnam War. Until nearly the end of the U.S. involvement in Vietnam (which was ultimately mandated by Congress), members of Congress felt that it had been excluded from the important decisions that had defined the American commitment to the conflict. The time was ripe for a congressional reassertion of power, with the foreign policy consensus broken by the war and support for the executive shaken by the Watergate scandal.

The conflict in Vietnam, discussed earlier, set in motion the dynamics that tend to stimulate congressional activism in at least three ways. First, when members of Congress perceive that their constituencies are directly and adversely affected by foreign or national security matters, Congress becomes active and will oppose the executive, as it did in this case. A second dynamic involves executive overreach: the so-called imperial presidency, wherein the Nixon administration essentially considered itself so well qualified in the foreign policy arena that it did not need—and thus did not solicit—congressional advice. In other words, the emperor knew best; if the president does it, it must be right (and legal). Third, Congress came to believe that the executive was mishandling foreign affairs. In this case, the length of time it took to extricate the country from Vietnam, as well as from other arguably illegal activities such as the Cambodian incursion of 1970 (when American troops violated Cambodian sovereignty in pursuit of the North Vietnamese), only added fuel to the fire.

The result of these factors was a concerted effort by Congress to rein in the executive's discretion in using force. The War Powers Resolution was the final product of a long-brewing debate among constitutional scholars and policy makers in the two elected branches over the question, "Whose power is the war power?" To understand why it was necessary to pass legislation to clarify this most fundamental issue, and why that controversial legislation was politically viable at that time, we must examine four factors: inherent constitutional ambiguity, a long-term trend toward executive dominance on matters of war and peace, the bitter legacy of Vietnam, and the shifting political balance of power between a Democratic-controlled Congress and the Republican administration of Richard Nixon.

Constitutional Ambiguity Concerning War Powers

The Constitution's framers wanted to ensure that the new republic they were creating would be free of what they regarded as the ultimate vice of the European monarchies of the day: the easy resort to war by an unaccountable and unresponsive executive. This preference was especially pronounced in matters involving war and peace.

Records of the Constitutional Convention's debates reflect surprisingly little discussion on allocating the power to commit the country to war. This reflects a broad, though not universal, consensus among the convention's delegates that the executive must not have unilateral power to take the country into war. This consensus was mirrored in the Constitution's working draft, which gave Congress sole power to "make war." As James Madison's notes make clear, the slight change to "declare war" was intended to give presidents the ability to respond to sudden, unexpected attacks. This change was most definitely not intended to alter the Founding Fathers' determination to assign to the legislative branch the supreme power of determining if and when the country should initiate hostilities against another country. The desire was for checks and balances, for separate institutions to share power, but the ultimate power to declare war clearly resided with Congress.

In light of this, why would there be any constitutional ambiguity with regard to war powers? First, the Constitution named the president as commander in chief of the armed forces in order to establish the important principle of civilian supremacy over the country's armed forces. However, the role itself contains the seeds of ambiguity. Ambitious presidents eager to maximize their powers have advanced expansive interpretations of what it means to be commander in chief.

Another source of constitutional ambiguity is the later disagreement among the men who wrote the Constitution over the meaning of what they had written. By 1793, James Madison and Alexander Hamilton, both prominent delegates at Philadelphia, were promoting opposite interpretations of the Constitution's war powers provisions. Hamilton argued that the war power was an inherently executive function, subject to a few legislative checks but not thereby denied to U.S. presidents. In contrast, Madison insisted that the Constitution had clearly made the war power a legislative power, leaving the execution of legislative decisions to the president in his capacity as commander in chief. The result of this debate is what former Supreme Court justice Robert Jackson once spoke of as "a zone of twilight" that lay between the powers of the Congress and the president on matters of war and peace. Presidents and legislators have found themselves in that "twilight zone" for the past two centuries. Intersection 6.1 discusses some of the key court cases that have addressed the distribution of power in foreign affairs between the White House and the Capitol.

Intersection 6.1   The Courts and War Powers

Drones, or unpiloted aerial vehicles (UAVs), have become weapons of choice for counterterrorism strikes.

The political struggle over war powers has from time to time included the U.S. Supreme Court. The courts normally avoid foreign policy cases, either because they are not yet "ripe" for decision or because the courts see them as political—as opposed to legal—questions. Several times the courts have weighed in, though their efforts have certainly not ended the debate about the proper distribution of foreign policy and war powers among the branches.

In the landmark case **U.S. v. Curtiss-Wright Export Corporation**

(1936), the Supreme Court (by an eight-to-one vote) gave a big victory to those who argue that the president ought to be dominant in the area of foreign policy. At issue was a ban on arms sales to Bolivia and Paraguay that Curtiss-Wright violated; they argued that the ban was unconstitutional because it emanated from a broad delegation of power from Congress to the president. Here Congress passed a joint resolution that handed to President Franklin D. Roosevelt the right to decide when and where to apply bans on arms sales. The court disagreed, however, finding that the president is the sole guardian of foreign policy power by nature of the office. In a concurring opinion, Justice George Sutherland even argued that the president is the "sole organ" of American foreign policy

In a subsequent case, however, the court took a more balanced approach to institutional cooperation in foreign policy. In **Youngstown Sheet & Tube v. Sawyer** (1952), at issue was President Harry Truman's order to the secretary of commerce (Charles W. Sawyer) during a steel mill strike to seize the steel mills and keep them operating. The war in Korea necessitated such an extraordinary emergency exercise of presidential power, the Truman administration argued. The court disagreed, however, with a six-to-three majority finding no support for Truman's assertion of emergency powers (when war had not even been declared).

In his famous concurring opinion, Justice Robert H. Jackson argued that there are three zones of presidential power relative to Congress. The first zone is when the president acts "pursuant to the express or implied authorization of Congress." Here the president enjoys the greatest amount of power—its zenith. A second, and opposite, zone is when the president acts contrary to the "express or implied will of Congress." Here presidential power is at its nadir. The middle zone is perhaps the most interesting area, the zone where the president acts but Congress remains silent. Congress has not said the president may act, nor has it said that the president may not. The "zone of twilight" is an area of "concurrent authority," and the area from which much of the foreign policy and war powers debate emanates.

The Supreme Court mostly dodged other war powers cases through the 1960s and 1970s, which is perhaps hard to believe given that the Vietnam War raged through this period. Time has mostly leaned away from the "zone of twilight" viewpoint, with an eight-to-one majority of the court ruling in *Dames & Moore v. Regan* (1981) in a way that cut against Justice Jackson's "twilight zone" rubric. In that case, most of the court argued that really there are only two cases: ones where Congress objects, and everything else. Thus by the mid-1980s the balance seemed to be tilting back in favor of a strong president in the area of foreign policy, both in terms of Reagan's assertive actions and also the Supreme Court's rulings.

The war on terrorism would bring another set of interesting cases that speak to the balance of power between the branches, especially focusing on the power of the president to detain and try people captured by U.S. forces and held at the U.S. military installation at Guantanamo Bay, Cuba. In a key rebuke of executive preeminence, a five-to-three majority of the court overturned the plan to try enemy combatants at Guantanamo in *Hamdan v. Rumsfeld* (2006). In another loss for the president, the same court later struck down parts of the process that President Bush then developed with Congress in the Military Commissions Act. The court was standing up for its own prerogatives as much as it was for Congress's, since there had been an effort to limit court oversight of the executive in the War on Terror and in these cases.

As the effort against terrorists in the Obama administration shifted toward the use of drone strikes, in 2011 an American citizen and alleged leader of Al Qaeda in Yemen, Anwar al-Awlaki, along with two other Americans, was killed in a drone strike without any charges having been brought or a trial having been held. A lawsuit against the administration argued that this was an unconstitutional action, but a federal court dismissed the suit and an appeals court upheld that dismissal—shifting power back to the president.

These cases together speak to the political nature of the question of the proper distribution of power among the branches in the area of foreign policy and war powers. Politics in this domain is partisan, institutional, political, and personal—leading to an even more vociferous form of politics. This trend has intensified in recent years as the parties have become more polarized, contributing to an increasingly coarse politics in foreign policy.

Executive Dominance on Matters of War and Peace

U.S. armed forces have been deployed abroad more than two hundred times since the founding of the Republic, as we noted before, but only five times with a formal declaration of war. Although some conflicts, such as Operation Desert Storm in 1991 and the invasion of Iraq in 2003, were authorized by congressional action short of formal declarations of war, the fact remains that the overwhelming majority of these foreign conflicts was undertaken by presidents whose interpretation of their prerogatives as commander in chief included putting forces into harm's way without a prior formal authorization by Congress.

A long list of precedents of presidential supremacy had buttressed those presidents' broad view of their powers. For example, President Truman dispatched U.S. troops to Korea in the summer of 1950, leading the country into a major conflict that lasted for three years, with neither a declaration of war nor any congressional approval of his actions. He believed that he was empowered to undertake such a step on his own authority, a position buttressed by a State Department memorandum prepared within days of the troop dispatch that asserted that a president's power as commander in chief is virtually unlimited and the president can order troops into combat without congressional authorization owing to his inherent foreign affairs powers. By the late 1960s and early 1970s, a mounting record of presidentially initiated hostilities persuaded a growing number of legislators of the need to restore the balance between the two elected branches to a level that more closely approximated the framers' intentions.

Vietnam's Legacy

Reaction to the American experience in Vietnam pushed Congress over the edge into an activist role aimed at curbing the president's ability to use armed force. Some of the reaction was the result of self-examination. Before American ground troops were committed to combat, Congress granted the president broad latitude to use force in Vietnam, a grant later regretted. This permission came in August 1964 as the **Tonkin Gulf Resolution**. Passed after only token debate, the measure was unanimously endorsed by the House of Representatives and met with only two dissenting votes in the Senate.

In its haste to demonstrate a unified U.S. front to the Vietnamese communists, Congress enacted a resolution in support of the president. The exceedingly sweeping language gave the president the power "to take all necessary measures to repel any armed attack against the forces of the United States and to prevent further aggression." Within a week of passing the Tonkin Gulf Resolution, the Johnson administration's Justice Department argued that it was the "functional equivalent" of a declaration of war.

Years later, as the national consensus that spawned the Tonkin Gulf Resolution dissolved in a monsoon of failure in Southeast Asia, members of Congress would look back bitterly on their fateful votes of August 1964. By the early 1970s, with the magnitude of the Vietnam disaster clear for all to see, and as questions emerged about the factual circumstances that prompted the 1964 resolution in the first place, even the most passive lawmakers knew that something had to be done. Never again, they vowed, should the Congress so promiscuously hand over its constitutional prerogatives to the president. Their determination to reclaim legislative war-making powers was strengthened in 1971 when Congress repealed the Gulf of Tonkin Resolution, only to have the Nixon administration claim an inherent executive right to prosecute the Vietnam War, with or without explicit congressional authorization.

It was in this context that Congress used its spending power to shut down American involvement in the war. Starting in 1970, Congress prohibited the use of funds for military operations in Cambodia. In 1973 and 1974 it ended the use of funds for operations in Vietnam itself, as well as in Laos and Cambodia, unless the administration came to Congress to secure a new specific authorization for military force. The next step was to prevent future presidents from waging secret and endless wars.

The War Powers Act

Congress was determined to construct a piece of procedural legislation that would help prevent future wars that drag on forever (Vietnam) as well as secret wars about which Congress is not informed (Cambodia). The resulting **War Powers Act (WPA)** was passed in 1973 over the veto of President Nixon; every president since has opposed the WPA to some degree, seeing it as an unconstitutional infringement on the powers of the presidency. Compliance with the requirements of the act has been, at best, imperfect—leading many to see the WPA as a failure; some point to some hidden successes of the act, however.

The WPA has three key provisions that specify when the president must *consult* with Congress, when he must *report* to Congress, and when he must *terminate* hostilities and withdraw U.S. armed forces. Much of the WPA is relatively noncontroversial, but the components that deal with introducing forces into hostilities are quite contentious.

The first WPA requirement is that the president consult with Congress before committing armed forces "into hostilities or into situations where imminent involvement in hostilities is clearly indicated by the circumstances."

Although the section's intent is clear, translating that intention into executive conduct presents several problems. It is not entirely clear what presidents would have to do to satisfy the requirement to "consult with Congress." Do they need to acquire congressional approval before acting? The WPA does not seem to go quite that far, but it does suggest a good bit more than mere presidential notification of impending moves. If the precise meaning of consultation is not entirely clear, neither is the precise identity of with whom the president must consult. The WPA does not stipulate who and how many members of Congress must be consulted to fulfill the spirit of the act. Finally, as the resolution's language concedes, the president must consult with Congress "in every possible instance," implying that in some instances prior consultations are exempted as impractical. For example, at the time of the *Mayaguez* incident in 1975, four key congressional leaders were in Greece, four others were in China, and others were scattered in their states and districts. With whom did President Ford have to consult in that case?

The resolution's second key provision obligates the president to report to Congress within forty-eight hours anytime U.S. armed forces are dispatched (1) "into hostilities or into situations where imminent involvement in hostilities is clearly indicated by the circumstances"; (2) into foreign territory while "equipped for combat"; or (3) "in numbers which substantially enlarge United States Armed Forces equipped for combat already located in a foreign nation." Between these two provisions, the WPA should serve to prevent future wars from being kept secret from Congress and help protect Congress's constitutional powers in a new era of undeclared wars.

The third and final key provision of the WPA deals with the termination of hostilities and the withdrawal of forces. The drafters of the War Powers Act were determined to prevent prolonged conflicts such as Vietnam in the future, so they rewrote the ground rules so that any protracted hostilities involving U.S. forces would require explicit legislative approval. Congress, it was said, would share the controls of using force—not just the crash landings.

The WPA spells out two means for achieving this congressional codetermination. First, once the president has reported to Congress that U.S. forces are being introduced into hostilities or into circumstances indicating imminent hostilities, the so-called sixty-day clock begins. Thus, the president will be without legal authority to continue conducting hostilities unless Congress acts within sixty days to (1) declare war; (2) adopt a specific authorization (such as the Gulf of Tonkin Resolution or the resolution that preceded the invasion of Iraq); or (3) extend the president's war-making authority beyond sixty days. Here is the really controversial part: Under the WPA, if the Congress takes no action at all following the president's report, the president is legally bound to terminate hostilities sixty days after that initial report to Congress. (An additional thirty days are authorized if needed for the safe withdrawal of troops, for a total of no more than ninety days maximum, unless Congress specifically provides otherwise.)

The War Powers Act includes another congressional tool for terminating hostilities, although the constitutionality of this mechanism would seem to have been found lacking by the U.S. Supreme Court. This second mechanism included in the WPA provides that Congress can order a cessation of U.S. involvement in hostilities at any point simply by adopting what is called a "concurrent resolution." The crucial point here is that a concurrent resolution is one that is adopted by simple majorities of the House and Senate, and thus does not require the president's signature to take effect and is not subject to presidential veto. In light of a 1983 Supreme Court ruling (*INS v. Chadha*) that struck down so-called legislative vetoes, this particular mechanism would appear to be unconstitutional if it were invoked.

Presidents since 1973 have opposed the WPA on the political grounds that it unwisely restricts presidential prerogative in dealing with foreign adversaries and on veiled grounds of constitutionality (the legislative veto). No one has tested the WPA in court. Most argue that Congress has not because it fears the resolution would be ruled unconstitutional, and presidents have not because the mere threat of a test allows them to elude or sidestep its requirements. Auerswald and Cowhey, however, show that there is some evidence that since the passage of the WPA presidents have tended to use force for shorter durations and have been perhaps more sensitive to Congress's concerns about the uses of force than had previously been the case. The use of force in Somalia and the first Persian Gulf War, for example, both had significant "negotiated" elements to them, even though the WPA itself was not invoked. In Intersection 6.2 we discuss the politics of the WPA in recent cases in Libya and Syria.

Intersection 6.2   Intervention in Libya and Syria

In February 2011, uprisings in Libya thrust that North African Arab state onto the list of "Arab Spring" countries as Muammar Gaddafi's forces unleashed brutal attacks not just on rebels but also on civilians around the country. In March, the United Nations Security Council authorized member states to take all steps necessary to protect civilian populations, including a "no-fly zone," and NATO began to enforce the no-fly zone and to launch strikes against government forces in "Operation Odyssey Dawn." U.S. involvement in the NATO attacks was comprised mostly of missile strikes from drone aircraft. Nonetheless, controversy stirred about whether the Obama administration was thus using force in ways that violated the War Powers Act. Obama did not pursue congressional "approval" of the Libyan intervention, even though this operation arguably moved troops into hostilities. Congressional Republicans, who have been largely critical of the WPA since the 1980s, embraced it here as a way to attack President Obama politically for exceeding his authority to use force. The top legal advisor for the State Department, Harold Koh—a fierce critic of executive overreaching on war powers in his academic career—argued that U.S. involvement in the operation fell short of "hostilities" as contemplated in the WPA. In fall 2011 the Gaddafi regime collapsed, leaving a largely failed state in its place.

So is Congress starting to get serious again about restraining the president's use of force? Interestingly, many Democrats who objected to George W. Bush's use of war powers in Iraq and Afghanistan found the Libyan intervention acceptable; and perhaps curiously, many of those same Republicans criticized President Obama for not using *more* force in the battle against ISIS in Syria and against the Assad regime there. In fact, in that case, President Obama was about to ask Congress for an authorization to use force, but fearing it would fail and not convinced that American forces could alter the war's course without a large infusion of ground troops (which had its own drawbacks), Obama did not seek the vote. Too much force? Not enough? While these two cases are not identical, they nevertheless remind us of how partisan and political questions about the use of force are now. As if to underscore this point, in April 2017 President Trump ordered a military strike with fifty-nine cruise missiles against an air base in Syria from which a sarin gas attack had been launched against the Syrian people. Most of the Republicans who objected that President Obama did not have the authority to launch such a strike (following a larger chemical weapons attack), nor thought such an attack would be wise, praised President Trump for his decisive action. James Madison and Alexander Hamilton could probably not have even imagined a foreign policy setting like the one we now see as "normal."

As a practical matter, compliance with the WPA occurs when it is easy and convenient to do so, and it is ignored or violated (for instance, reporting after the fact or informing rather than consulting) when it is not. A frequent presidential reaction is to ask for a congressional resolution supporting military action in advance of hostilities, as was done in 1990–1991 before the Persian Gulf War and again in 2001 after 9/11 and in 2002 in anticipation of hostilities with Iraq. Presidents generally have dodged the sixty-day clock by reporting to congressional leadership "consistent with but not *pursuant* to" the requirements of the War Powers Act. Critics of the WPA see this record of reporting as indicative of the act's failures. Some, however, have argued that the WPA has nonetheless accomplished the spirit of what it set out to do—to stimulate more partnership between the branches in the area of war powers—if not in the exact form specified in the War Powers Act.

Congressional Powers and Policy Types

One thing that this chapter should make clear is that not all "foreign policy" is alike; indeed, there are different kinds of foreign policy, and Congress tends to play a different role (vis-à-vis the president, for example) in these different policy types. As Ripley and Franklin discuss in *Congress, the Bureaucracy and Public Policy* (and as introduced in chapter 3 of this book) one type of foreign policy that exists—and perhaps the type that most Americans think of when they think of foreign policy—is "crisis policy." **Crisis policy** deals with emergencies and threats to the country. Crises often are a surprise, and they usually include at least the potential for the use of force. These are the kinds of situations in which people tend to rally to the president. The 9/11 attacks were a crisis. Crisis policy making tends to be dominated by the president and a small group of advisors who presidents draw on to help make decisions. There is not much congressional activism in this area, since all the dynamics accrue to the advantage of the president. The battle over war powers tends to play out in this context.

Another type of foreign policy is **strategic policy**, which lays out the basic stance of the United States toward another country (U.S. policy toward Cuba, for example) or toward a particular issue or problem (for example, terrorism or climate change). Foreign policy strategy tends to be developed by the executive branch, often through the type of interagency process discussed earlier. Nonetheless, Congress and its members can get access to strategic policy by finding out that a strategy review is under way and making their preferences known, sometimes by holding hearings on the topic.

In 2016 the Obama administration undertook a review of U.S. nuclear policy, with an eye toward perhaps stating that the United States would not use nuclear weapons first in a crisis—which would make a major departure from traditional nuclear policy dating to the end of World War II. It was no secret that the review was under way, and many members of Congress got engaged to try to coax the process along in one way or another, as did many other current and former defense officials and foreign leaders. By late September 2016, President Obama appeared to decide to not take on a "no first use" policy, reserving the threat that the United States would use these weapons first and thus hopefully deter other states from doing things that might provoke such an attack.

Some dramatic examples of Congress taking the reins of strategic policy were discussed previously, such as the South Africa sanctions bill and the Helms-Burton Act that codified the U.S. embargo of Cuba. While these cases are the exception, not the rule, and Congress is far more likely to legislate procedurally (as in Cohen-Nunn) and substantively (as with Helms-Burton), the opportunities to set the course of the ship of state certainly exist.

Another interesting example of procedural legislation in the strategic policy domain has to do with treaties in the area of free trade. Sometimes called "Fast Track," Trade Promotion Authority (also discussed in chapter 10) was first constructed in the 1970s to try to make it easier for presidents to negotiate and pass trade agreements. When a president works within Fast Track, which has been authorized several times, most recently in 2015 in the Obama administration, foreign trade treaties come under a rule that allows no changes to the treaty—making it easier for the president to be able to negotiate, in theory, because there is less concern that Congress will change the terms of the agreement. Such agreements also require only a majority in the Senate, rather than the supermajority specified in the Constitution. However, they also must pass a majority vote in the House of Representatives. The North American Free Trade Act, NAFTA, was passed under these rules, for example, and the controversial Trans-Pacific Partnership was created under Fast Track as well.

The third type of foreign policy is called **structural defense policy**, which focuses on the policies and programs that deal with the defense budget and military bases, such as buying new aircraft. Congress tends to actually include more things in the defense budget than the president or even the Pentagon wants, for example, because those projects mean jobs in congressional districts.

If many members of Congress see more defense spending as a good thing, less defense spending is often seen as a bad thing, killing jobs in members' districts. When it comes to closing military bases in the United States—the warning sirens really sound. Starting in the 1990s, as the Cold War ended, Congress even constructed a special process for determining base closings, a process that attempted to protect individual members so that their constituents would not blame them for being ineffective if they lost a military base. The Defense Base Realignment and Closure process (BRAC) was established and when utilized would require the Pentagon to issue a study and make recommendations for base closings and consolidations that would be submitted to the BRAC Commission. The members of the commission are appointed by the president but confirmed by the Senate. The commission is meant to be independent and nonpartisan. The commission issues recommendations to Congress about base closings and realignment. Congress then must vote up or down, whole hog or none, on the entire list; no changes or substitutions allowed. Congress is central to the defense budget process; they can't dodge it even when they want to.

Conclusion

As the combined discussions in chapters 4–6 have sought to convey, our constitutional system purposely overlapped political powers among the separate branches of the federal government and created what has famously been called an **invitation to struggle** between them. The Constitution carefully sought to create a coequality of power between the Congress and the president, although, as noted, opinions differed about the exact nature of that balance at the time—and the relationship on foreign policy powers has been evolving since. In order to understand the foreign policy powers of these two branches, it is necessary to see the powers of each body in interactive form.

The political struggle for preeminence is one where the executive has formidable advantages over the less-focused legislative branch. For instance, no single member of Congress is the clear focus of national attention in the foreign policy area the way the president is. While Congress can pass legislation, the president can veto it, which can be overridden, but only with a supermajority of both Houses—a steep standard. The Senate must ratify treaties, but presidents have increasingly eluded this power by using executive agreements. Similarly, the Senate must ratify many presidential appointments, but the president can dodge this power in foreign affairs by appointing controversial figures to work on the National Security Council staff. And while Congress has the power to declare war, the commander in chief has sent troops to use force abroad absent such a declaration dozens of times since the end of World War II, and more than twenty times since the passage of the War Powers Act. Table 6.1 summarizes the powers that each branch retains in foreign policy.

At the same time, it is also true that Congress has a useful monitoring and oversight role, even when it is generally acquiescing to presidential leadership. Individual members of Congress have become increasingly active in the foreign

TABLE 6.1	Sharing Foreign Policy Power	
Congressional Powers	**Presidential Powers**	**Presidential Advantage**
Pass legislation and override vetoes	Veto legislation	Difficult for Congress to harness the votes to override veto
Spending power	—	—
Senate confirmation power	Nominate and appoint	Can appoint controversial nominees to National Security Council (staff)
Oversight power	—	Stymie oversight by classifying information and operations
Declare war	Commander in chief	Take initiative to send troops abroad
Senate treaty ratification	Make treaties	Use executive agreements
—	Receive foreign ambassadors	Broad powers to recognize states and governments

policy arena since Vietnam, with much of that activity driven both by policy interest and by partisanship. Congress has become more politically polarized in recent decades, and it tends to be more assertive in the midst of controversial presidential action—although these days there is never a guarantee of smooth sailing for foreign policy either at home or abroad.

Times of crisis tend to galvanize the relationship: crises such as 9/11 tend to cement support around the executive (the rally around the flag effect), but controversial executive actions (for example, Vietnam) may turn such events into points of contention wherein Congress asserts itself once again. Congress has real power over the defense budget, and even during periods of acquiescence Congress is at the center of the budgetary process.

A period of unified government began in January 2017, with Republicans in charge of both Congress and the White House. The agenda will be large and in many cases the two branches will agree completely: cutting regulations, repealing Obamacare, and advancing President Trump's nominations. Other areas will inevitably lead to conflict—even inside the family. Many leading Republicans on the Hill disagree with Trump's view of Putin's Russia, and the defense budgeting process can lead to disagreements, to name only two. In the transition process Donald Trump and his surrogates suggested an expansive view of presidential power, claiming that the president cannot have a conflict of interest, by definition, and that President Trump could use his pardon power to pardon anyone in his administration who violates the law. So while the spirit of unified government is in the air now, institutional priorities will likely lead to conflicts down Pennsylvania Avenue.

Study/Discussion Questions

1. What are the main foreign policy powers of Congress?
2. How are Congress's powers often at a disadvantage relative to the president?
3. How is Congress constrained from being a major foreign policy player, especially when it comes to war powers?
4. Congressional activism in the foreign policy domain has been on the rise since Vietnam; why?

5. Why are war powers such a complicated question, when the Constitution spells out the powers of each branch?
6. What is the War Powers Act? Has it been a success or a failure?
7. What are "policy types," and how do they help us understand foreign policy power?

Bibliography

Auerswald, David P., and Peter F. Cowhey. "Ballotbox Diplomacy: The War Powers Resolution and the Use of Force." *International Studies Quarterly* 41 (1997): 505–28.

Blechman, Barry M. *The Politics of National Security: Congress and U.S. Defense Policy.* New York: Oxford University Press, 1990.

Brown, Eugene. J. *William Fulbright: Advice and Dissent.* Iowa City: University of Iowa Press, 1985.

Brown, Sherrod. *Congress from the Inside.* Kent, OH: Kent State University Press, 2000.

Campbell, Colin C., Nicole C. Rae, and John F. Stack Jr., eds. *Congress and the Politics of Foreign Policy.* Upper Saddle River, NJ: Prentice Hall, 2003.

Carter, Ralph G., and James M. Scott. *Choosing to Lead: Understanding Congressional Foreign Policy Entrepreneurs.* Durham, NC: Duke University Press, 2009.

Crabb, Cecil V. M. *Invitation to Struggle: Congress, the President, and Foreign Policy.* 4th ed. Washington, DC: CQ, 2004.

Fisher, Louis. *The Constitution and 9/11: Recurring Threats to America's Freedom.* Lawrence: University Press of Kansas, 2008.

———. *Constitutional Abdication on War and Spending.* College Station: Texas A&M University Press, 2000.

Frank, Thomas M., and Edward Weisband. *Foreign Policy by Congress.* New York: Oxford University Press, 1979.

Hersman, Rebecca K. C. *Friends and Foes: How Congress and the President Really Make Foreign Policy.* Washington, DC: Brookings, 2000.

Hinckley, Barbara. *Less Than Meets the Eye: Foreign Policy Making and the Myth of the Assertive Congress.* Chicago: University of Chicago Press, 1994.

Howell, William G., and Jon C. Pevehouse. "When Congress Stops Wars." *Foreign Affairs,* September/October 2007, 1–7.

Johnson, Robert David. *Congress and the Cold War.* New York: Cambridge University Press, 2005.

Kelley, Donald R. *Divided Power: The Presidency, Congress, and the Formation of American Foreign Policy.* Little Rock: University of Arkansas Press, 2005.

Koh, Harold H. *The National Security Constitution.* New Haven, CT: Yale University Press, 1990.

Kriner, Douglas L. *After the Rubicon: Congress, Presidents, and the Politics of Waging War.* Chicago: University of Chicago Press, 2010.

Lindsay, James M. *Congress and the Politics of U.S. Foreign Policy.* Baltimore: Johns Hopkins University Press, 1994.

Mann, Thomas E., and Norman J. Ornstein. *The Broken Branch: How Congress Is Failing America and How to Get It Back on Track.* New York: Oxford University Press, 2008.

———. *Even Worse Than It Looks: How the American Constitutional System Collided with the New Politics of Extremism.* New York: Basic, 2013.

Moss, Kenneth B. *Undeclared War and the Future of U.S. Foreign Policy.* Baltimore: Johns Hopkins University Press, 2008.

Ripley, Randall B., and Grace A. Franklin. *Congress, the Bureaucracy and Public Policy.* Pacific Grove, CA: Brooks/Cole, 1987.

Sanger, David E., and William J. Broad. "Obama Unlikely to Drop Option of First Strike." *New York Times*, September 6, 2016, A1.

Wilson, George C. *This War Really Matters: Inside the Fight for Defense Dollars.* Washington, DC: CQ, 1999.

7 Interest Groups and Think Tanks

Secretary of State John Kerry speaks at the convention of the American Israel Public Affairs Committee, March 3, 2014.

Preview

Interest groups and think tanks exist outside the formal structures of government and try to influence the foreign policy of the United States. Interest groups are formal organizations with members who share a common interest who try to pool their resources to promote policies that are in line with their common interest. The primary way that interest groups try to do this is through lobbying Congress and the president. Many interest groups also have political action committees (PACs) that raise and donate money to candidates for office. The number and complexity of these groups have dramatically expanded since the 1970s. Think tanks have traditionally been organizations that pursue knowledge in a scholarly way and try to bring that knowledge to bear on the world of policy making. In recent years, however, many new think tanks have emerged that are not bound by the norms of disinterested social science. Indeed, the think tank world has become far more ideological and partisan as these groups vie for influence using some of the same techniques as interest groups. In practical terms the dividing line between what is an interest group and what is a think tank is starting to become quite blurry.

Key Concepts

American Israel Public Affairs
   Committee (AIPAC)
J Street
revolving door
Council on Foreign Relations (CFR)
iron triangle
subgovernment
lobbying
political action committee (PAC)

military-industrial complex
think tank
Brookings Institution
interest group
ethnic interest groups
Cuban American National
   Foundation (CANF)
Heritage Foundation
Heritage Action

Since the end of the Cold War there has been an explosion of foreign policy lobbying in Washington, D.C., including lobbying by ethnic interest groups. When people think about ethnic lobbying, they often point to the **American Israel Public Affairs Committee**, or **AIPAC**, as the model for other groups and one of the most powerful interest groups in D.C. AIPAC was founded in 1951 to promote a close relationship between the United States and Israel, in part because many Jewish Americans (and others) were concerned that U.S. policy in the Middle East at that time was tilted toward the Arab states in the region.

While AIPAC has broad bipartisan support in Washington, it also has critics (including Jewish Americans) who see AIPAC as tied too closely to policy preferences of the Likud, or conservative, party in Israel. In 2008 a new group was formed called **J Street** (the name is metaphorical; there is no actual "J Street" in Washington), to counter AIPAC's power and to press for continued U.S. involvement in the Middle East peace process toward the goal of a peaceful and enduring settlement including the states of Israel and Palestine. Practically overnight J Street emerged as a significant policy player. Some of this success came about because the views of Jewish Americans (and Americans generally) toward the peace process and a two-state solution evolved enough in recent years that there was an opening for a different type of policy advocacy than that of AIPAC. But part of it emerged because of the efforts of the Obama presidential campaign and administration—which embraced the group—to try to change the dynamics of the lobbying universe around U.S. policy toward the peace process.

J Street tried to capitalize on the changing views of Jewish Americans toward the Middle East, making the case that AIPAC was out of step. For instance, a July 2009 survey found that 60 percent of American Jews opposed further Israeli settlements in the occupied territories, and they supported the proposition that the United States should be actively engaged in the peace process even if that entailed "publicly stating its disagreements with both the Israelis and the Arabs" by large margins.

Despite high hopes that the Obama administration would be able to move the peace process forward, there was little progress. In part this illustrates how difficult it is to craft foreign policy today. The forces of globalization unleashed by the end of the Cold War have made the world more complex in a variety of ways, making it far harder for the United States to control events than it was during the Cold War. And extreme partisanship at home has made foreign policy proposals far more "political" than was the case in the past. Domestic political changes in Israel have also moved that government away from a peace process. The rapid emergence of J Street, and the help it got from the White House, suggested to many that a new environment for the peace process might exist, as well as the increasing role of interest groups (and think tanks) in the policy-making process, but in 2017 prospects for peace in the Middle East look bleak, to say the least, and J Street seems far less significant that it did before.

So far in the discussion of how U.S. foreign policy is made, primary attention has been focused on the governmental actors who are involved in the policy process, but not everyone who is involved—or wants to be involved—in foreign policy development gets a paycheck from the government. In addition to the elected and appointed officials who comprise the federal government, there is a large, diverse, and increasingly complex set of individuals and groups who exist outside the formal realm of government but who nonetheless seek to influence the ship of state. Most of these people and groups can be found in the Washington, D.C., area, and whether their offices are actually inside or outside the Interstate 495 beltway that rings the District of Columbia, they are (or aspire to be) "inside the beltway" operators who try to influence foreign policy.

Historically, most of these actors have tried to stay out of the public spotlight, lobbying members of Congress or of the executive branch informally at cocktail parties, fund raisers, and at charity and sporting events. This "invisible government," as it is sometimes called, provides a **revolving door** for individuals to move in and out of government and the organizations that seek to influence government over time. When the Obama administration arrived as the Bush team left, the ritual shuffling of insiders and outsiders also followed—as is happening again in 2017.

One of the results of this constant shuffling is an added opaqueness to the public's understanding of what really transpires in government, particularly in the area of foreign policy. In this realm, the general lack of public attention to and awareness of foreign policy matters has meant that not only do most people not understand how foreign policy is made, but those who try to influence and make foreign policy do so with relatively little public scrutiny. Foreign policy is perhaps the last preserve of elite groups and individuals with special expertise; these elites are often only too happy to protect the myth that foreign policy is too complicated, too important, or both, for most Americans to be involved in it.

This dynamic is what ensures that individuals and small elite groups can have an impact on foreign policy that is greatly out of proportion with their relative numerical size. There are about 320 million people in the United States, but one of the most powerful and respected foreign policy organizations in the United States has about 4,300 members: the **Council on Foreign Relations (CFR)**. Perhaps the granddaddy of all foreign policy organizations, the CFR was founded in 1921; it has its headquarters on Park Avenue in New York City and offices in Washington, D.C., just two blocks from the White House. The CFR has a large professional staff and publishes the influential *Foreign Affairs* magazine. In the area of national defense, the highly technical and usually classified nature of defense issues has meant that organizations and companies hire scores of retired military officers to try to influence decisions in the exact same areas where those people previously worked, forming the so-called **iron triangle** involving defense contractors, the Pentagon, and legislators (see the intersection box that follows).

The conventional roles of those who seek to influence the government have also bred orthodox ways of categorizing and looking at what those people do. As discussed in this chapter, some of these roles are changing as the post–Cold War and post-9/11 environment evolves. Another important point is that the nature and types of these groups are also changing because of the changing political, electoral, and even legal environment in which these groups operate. So before going any further, it is necessary to start with some basic definitions and distinctions.

Intersection 7.1   Ike's Farewell Address

President Dwight D. Eisenhower, in his farewell address in January 1961, warned of the power of the "Military-Industrial Complex."

President Dwight D. Eisenhower, as he prepared to leave office in January 1961, gave a farewell address to the nation that included one of the most famous warnings a president has ever given. Noting that the rise of a large standing military in peacetime and a permanent arms industry was a necessity of waging the Cold War against the Soviet Union, Eisenhower warned that these forces could have serious consequences for the country. "In the councils of government, we must guard against the acquisition of unwarranted influence, whether sought or unsought, by the military-industrial complex. The potential for the disastrous rise of misplaced power exists and will persist." Ike went on to issue a second, less noted, warning as well, that policy in an increasingly technological age could become captured by a "scientific-technological elite."

Scholars still debate the meaning of Ike's warnings; clearly he wanted to call closer attention to the power of the three clusters of actors in the "iron triangle": the Pentagon, defense contractors, and congressional appropriators. In this area, Ike warned, what might at first look like "foreign" policy is really very much "domestic" policy—what this book calls "intermestic" policy.

The imagery of an "iron" arrangement that locks these three actors into agreement about the need for more defense spending and locks out other actors might not be entirely accurate. In an empirical sense, some have argued that a better way to think about the role of interest groups and think tanks in the policy process is with a term called **subgovernments**. The idea behind this concept is that while a substantial area of mutual interest exists in the agencies, Congress, and lobbying world, and these actors work together regularly on these issues, the relationship can be less "iron" than the iron triangle suggests. Other domestic actors can get into the policy-making mix, and there is not always a perfect concert of interests. Whether in the form of an iron triangle, a subgovernment, or some other formulation, the bottom line is that the process of making foreign policy is very domestic. Former speaker of the house Thomas P. "Tip" O'Neill famously said, "All politics is local." This is certainly true of foreign policy—increasingly so, and interest groups and think tanks are on the front lines of this intermestic policy process.

Interest Groups

The first and historically most powerful influence from outside government have been "interest groups," organizations that represent a group of people or institutions with common interests that they want to see promoted or protected. These organizations have traditionally served as key gatekeepers between the mass public and the formal structures of the government itself, funneling the public's preferences and positions toward public policy. Interest groups gather information about policies their followers want and then represent those preferences to the Congress and the executive branch through a variety of means. The ways that these groups try to promote their interests to the government can be through **lobbying** (trying to convince members of Congress or their staffs or executive agency officials to support their position), education (such as writing articles for newspapers or testifying before Congress), and electoral pressure (trying to convince officials that they will suffer electoral defeat if they defy the will of the group, or by offering electoral support if they support the position of the group). In this sense, interest groups are also classic "linkage" mechanisms that connect the people to the government.

The function performed by interest groups is provided for in the First Amendment to the Constitution, which guarantees the right to "petition the

Government for a redress of grievances," and finds its modern expression in the idea of pluralism, the notion that multiple competing interests should be able to compete freely for influence in our governmental system.

Largely because these groups seek to exert pressure on the government, their work has always come under some public suspicion and continues to do so—although interest groups are important, legal, and long-standing members of the American political system. While those who make their careers as lobbyists for pressure groups see their efforts as "Washington representation" for interests that are dispersed across the country, the public—and sometimes aspiring officeholders—can view these groups in a less favorable light. A variety of types of legislation requiring groups and individuals who lobby the government to register and to disclose many of their activities reflects the suspicion that many have about these groups (although the rigor with which these regulations are enforced remains a matter of some debate). As discussed below, much of the impetus for campaign finance reform is also aimed at reining in the influence of these pressure groups. Public suspicion of interest groups and their activities also parallels the American people's suspicion of government. The term "Washington insider" has become a pejorative phrase in some circles, encompassing all professional Washington politicians, and is often a phrase used as a rallying cry by candidates who run for office against incumbents, whom they seek to defile by using the term.

The aura of favoritism and elitism that surrounds many of the traditional methods of influence—images of fancy fund raisers, contributions to campaign funds or to a candidate's favorite charity, or lavish vacations and golf outings under the guise of a "seminar"—offends public sensibilities in an ethics-conscious era, and these images are made more offensive during a time of economic difficulty for many Americans. Nonetheless, many of the top contributors to political candidates over the last twenty years are big companies, banks, and key defense industry players, such as Lockheed Martin, General Electric, Boeing, Northrop Grumman, General Dynamics, Honeywell, and Raytheon. Whether this pattern of giving is connected to the size or resilience of the U.S. defense budget (which makes up about 40 percent of all military spending in the world today) is something citizens will have to decide for themselves.

Another source of suspicion about interest groups concerns the resources that they have at their disposal, resources that some see as leading these groups to have disproportionate power. Many interest groups have **political action committees**, or **PACs**. The primary purpose of the PACs is to raise money and give it to candidates for office in the form of campaign contributions. The donation strategy of a PAC is obviously linked to the pressure strategy of the group; campaign funds can be directed to officials who have supported a group's interests in the past, or used to try to target an official for defeat if that official has not been supportive in the past. Over the last thirty years, a variety of attempts have been made to limit the amount of this kind of money in political campaigns. Like water finding the lowest point, however, money seems to always find a way around these restrictions, making the world of money and politics one of the most complex and fast-changing arenas around.

The foreign policy–making process, and the defense budget process in particular, is not immune to these kinds of activities and suspicions. One of the first and most widely publicized critiques of the possible nefarious relationship between interest groups, money, and the policy-making process was made by President Dwight D. Eisenhower in his 1961 farewell address (see intersection 7.1), which warned of the potential power of the **"military-industrial complex"** and the potentially erosive and corrupting influence it could have on the American system.

The military-industrial complex is only one example, although an important one, of a common concept in the U.S. political system: the "iron triangle" (see figure 7.1). Iron triangles are formed when agencies of government in a given policy area find common cause with the congressional committee overseeing that policy area and with interest groups or PACs that promote policy in that area. This mutually supportive and reinforcing relationship, where there is very little disagreement among the parties and where other voices are shut out of the policy process, is what makes the triangle an iron one. The iron triangle, as it relates to the military-industrial complex, consists of the defense industry, which has big contracts from the Pentagon, the DOD, which works closely with these contractors over time, and the armed services and defense appropriations committees in the House and Senate that oversee these expenditures for various weapons systems. Remember, too, as mentioned previously, that there is often a revolving door in the middle of an iron triangle, where the lobbyist for a defense contractor recently worked on the Hill, or where a military officer near retirement who is monitoring a project takes a position with the defense contractor that he or she was just monitoring, as examples of the common movement across roles that happens in Washington, D.C.

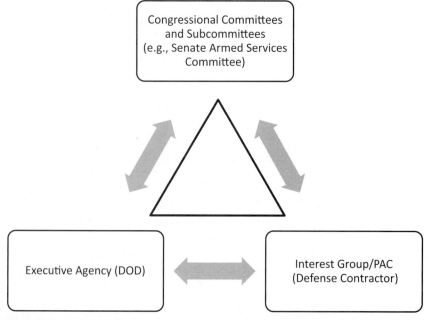

Figure 7.1 The Iron Triangle

There is nothing necessarily illegal, unnatural, or even wrong about these relationships; nor are they limited to the defense area. The air force, for example, wants the best possible military aircraft and shares with defense manufacturers the desire to produce such aircraft. At the same time, all three sides of the triangle share expertise and common interests in military aircraft. (A member of Congress with no personal or constituency interests in military procurement is unlikely to seek out a seat on committees that deal with these issues.) The relationship develops into a problem when it becomes incestuous and when interests become entrenched and vested. The revolving-door phenomenon is one of the main roots of vested interests. Indeed, you can see the arrows in figure 7.1 not just as indications of mutual interest and power, but also as a map of personnel movement across and among the actors. Abuses have spawned a variety of laws and guidelines intended to regulate these movements back and forth between government and industry. The Clinton administration, for example, made staff members sign a pledge that they would not go to work for a private enterprise with which they were dealing as part of the administration for at least a year after leaving government to avoid the appearance of impropriety. The Obama administration set out to ban registered lobbyists from sitting on government advisory boards and panels, and an executive order would bar a registered lobbyist for two years from taking an appointed position in the administration in an area where that person had previously lobbied; progress, perhaps, but even these efforts had loopholes.

A relatively new type of outside influence is exemplified by **think tanks**. In their traditional form, think tanks are relatively scholarly, research-based organizations that offer expert advice to various governmental organs. Sometimes these organizations act as scholarly outlets, providing academic analyses of different problems. Much of the prestige associated with individual think tanks derives from their reputations for scholarly integrity and impartiality. At the same time, however, many of them engage in the same activities usually associated with interest groups. They are certainly, and increasingly, a part of the revolving-door phenomenon. If interest groups serve as a kind of gatekeeper between the mass public and the government, then in a way think tanks serve a similar function between the world of expert advice and government. And in an era of hyperpartisanship, and the growing number and types of think tanks, the dividing line between what is a think tank and an interest group is quickly eroding. Today there is a range of think tanks situated around every side of just about every issue, offering "expert" support for practically any policy initiative, including the arena of foreign policy. The information revolution has contributed to this dynamic as well; these organizations have taken to the web to post their "research" and to reach out to the public and policy makers. Some call them "advocacy tanks" now, in that they push for solutions they already hold dear rather than truly promote disinterested research into how to solve policy problems.

Sources of Change

A variety of dynamics is helping to drive change in the roles and influence of interest groups, PACs, and hybrid organizations that blur the lines between these ideal forms. Note that these factors reflect changes that, in most cases, have already been described in earlier chapters. Almost all of the factors reflect the information explosion directly or indirectly, and the era of polarization and gridlock.

The first factor is the convergence of foreign and domestic issues. The old distinctions between a foreign and a domestic issue have largely disappeared into the realm of intermestic policies, especially in the globalized world. Although that confluence affects the way the government itself is organized, it also influences how the public views what government does. Foreign policy had already become increasingly political and partisan, certainly since the Vietnam era. The end of the Cold War made foreign policy more of a domestic issue as well, and it seemed "safer" to debate these issues now that the Soviet bear was gone from the scene. The expansion of foreign trade, especially in the form of the North American Free Trade Agreement (NAFTA) and the emergence of the World Trade Organization (WTO), opened the American economy to global forces in new ways. The 9/11 attacks brought foreign and national security policy up close and personal to Americans and attacks around the world by ISIS help fuel a political environment of fear.

Public awareness and access is made easier by the increased transparency of international events. The global information revolution is at the heart of the public's greater access to foreign affairs at a time when those events are more immediate to them. Moreover, through global television outlets available on cable and satellite, the initial information on breaking international affairs available to the public is often nearly identical to the information available to decision makers. The president and his advisors, as well as members of the public, see the same reportage on CNN, Fox News, and MSNBC (to name a few). Humanitarian and natural disasters seem closer to home thanks to cable and satellite television and the Internet. Policy makers must worry about the "news cycle," and know that the policy process happens in the context of great public scrutiny. The leaks from Edward Snowden and WikiLeaks further contributed to this environment, before the 2016 election and during it. And remember that this news environment is now a global news environment, not just a national one.

Third is the rise of so-called electronic experts, or those people who have acknowledged expertise and whom all the networks use to provide legitimacy to the interpretation of currently breaking events. These individuals, first seen during the 1990–1991 Persian Gulf War, are especially important in the defense and foreign policy arena, because much of that material is relatively technical and the public is unfamiliar with it. As a result, these experts augment the expertise of the news organizations and help better inform (or perhaps confuse) the public. In the Persian Gulf War, all the networks featured both military and political experts drawn from outside their regular staffs. They explained everything from the logistics of ground attack to the operation of precision-guided munitions. The same has certainly been true of the wars in Afghanistan and Iraq, about Al Qaeda and ISIS, and the civil war in Syria—to name but a few.

These experts are usually unpaid and tend to come from the military, think tanks, and academia. Many are retired military officers (mostly colonels and generals or the equivalent) who have experience, knowledge, and contacts within the Pentagon that give them superior information than that available to regular reporters, whom the military distrusts in most cases. Many work at Washington-based think tanks such as the CFR, the Center for Strategic and International Studies (CSIS), the American Enterprise Institute (AEI), and the **Brookings Institution**—which also gives further public exposure to these organizations. Finally, experts found in academia, particularly international relations experts from around New York and Washington, frequently appear in the media. The use of these experts can become controversial, as it did in 2008, when the news networks do not disclose to their viewers that the experts were not disinterested observers but in some cases had contracts with the very government organizations about whom they were commenting, which could slant their view and interpretation of events.

The final source of change is growing public disaffection with the competency of the political leadership, a phenomenon enhanced by the level of media scrutiny under which officials exist. Running against Washington and its insiders first became a prominent strategy in Jimmy Carter's successful run for the White House. It was a theme in Ronald Reagan's first campaign and became virtually an art form in the H. Ross Perot campaign of 1992. Dissatisfaction with how the system works extends beyond presidential elections to races for the House and Senate as well—although while people do still tend to love their member of Congress, they increasingly despise the rest of them! Public approval of Congress sits at between 15 and 20 percent these days, even while 95 percent or more of incumbents are reelected. The emergence of the Tea Party and the rise of Donald Trump can certainly be tied, in part, to an increasing distaste with "politics as usual" and people looking for "change." Part of this dissatisfaction is undoubtedly fueled by the greater access to information that is a legacy of the electronic revolution, and the echo chamber that is created by TV and the Internet.

The discussion that follows provides the basis for examining how interest groups and think tanks operate outside of the government's formal structure and some of the forces that are changing how they operate. The emphasis of the discussion is on how these groups relate specifically to foreign and national security matters.

Interest Group Tactics

An **interest group** can be defined as any organized group of people who share common interests distinct from those of others and who attempt to influence public policy in the direction of that interest. As such, interest groups begin with a shared common interest, whether it is maintenance of a strong national defense, the preservation of the environment, or the end of the Cuban embargo. They come together into some formal organization of like-minded individuals to form a group, and that group seeks to represent their common interest to the political system and to influence public policy in the direction of their interest.

Interest groups do not just appear out of nowhere. Many people have interests in common but do not organize to influence policy; political scientists call this the "collective action problem." To overcome the collective action problem, someone has to want a group to form around an existing common interest much more than most people who share the common interest—so much more that they are willing to go to the trouble (and often cost) of forming a formal organization. These individuals are sometimes called "political entrepreneurs" because like the entrepreneurs of capitalism who invest their own time and resources to gain an economic profit, these political entrepreneurs are willing to invest in order to get a type of political profit: the policy they want.

Theoretically, the ability to form interest groups and to compete in the political arena is an option available to all Americans, but most do not organize. Numerous studies have shown that the upper strata of society—the wealthiest and most highly educated—are overrepresented in interest-group activity. In one sense this stands to reason; interest-group activities, like almost everything else, cost money. Hence, those who possess monetary resources will have more access to the system they seek to influence. Similarly, educational attainment and levels of political activity are positively correlated. Related to this, some interests are much better funded to do their work than are others; big business and defense contracts, for example, tend to have access to far greater resources to promote their interests than do many human rights groups.

Interest groups use a variety of tactics to pursue their work that generally fall into three categories: lobbying, education, and pressure. Interest groups are most closely associated with lobbying—a term that goes back to the 1870s. Although the Constitution's First Amendment provides for the right of petition, it prohibits the presentation of petitions on the floors of the House and Senate. As a result, those seeking to influence legislation were forced to make their case outside the chambers, especially in the lobbies of the Capitol; hence the term *lobbying*.

The purpose of lobbying, like all interest-group activity, is to persuade those with the ability to make decisions—in Congress or the executive branch—that their interests should be reflected in public policy. Lobbying connotes the personal representations of positions to individual members of Congress or executive branch agents in the effort to convince them of the virtue of their positions.

The cornerstones of federal lobbying are the Washington-based offices of the various interest groups and lobbyists. Many of these offices are clustered around K Street leading "K Street" to be a common name for the world of interest groups. The watchdog group Center for Responsive Politics reports on its website (www.opensecrets.org) that there are more than nine thousand registered lobbyists today in the United States who focus on the federal government, spending a little less than $1 billion to do their work. These lobbying firms do work for interest groups as well as companies and even foreign countries. The interesting thing about those numbers is that they are down considerably from 2008, when more than 14,000 lobbyists spent more than $3 billion on their efforts in D.C. This is not because there is less lobbying going on today; quite the contrary, in fact. What it does show, though, is the way the public mood (and Obama rules) turned against lobbyists, and so during his administration organizations and individuals tried not to be called that if they could help it.

Today most lobbyists are professionals, usually people with considerable government service within a particular policy area who have developed expertise and extensive contacts that they are willing to share with clients for a price. Professional lobbyists typically work for several clients rather than one. Many of these individuals are lawyers who have developed expertise in specific areas of the law, such as food and drug laws; hence they are attractive representatives for clients such as the pharmaceutical industry. In the foreign policy area, Henry Kissinger Associates, founded by the former secretary of state and national security advisor, is probably the most famous and powerful example of a professional lobbying organization. It is no longer uncommon for former secretaries of state to start a lobby group or a "consulting" firm; Condoleezza Rice began a firm after she left government, along with her former colleague Stephen Hadley (who served as President George W. Bush's national security advisor during his second term).

While most interest groups contract with a lobby firm to do their lobbying, another type of lobbyist is the staff lobbyist who works full-time for the Washington office of a company or organization that seeks to influence the policy process. The aerospace industries and their typically large Washington operations represent an example in the defense area.

The purpose of all lobbying efforts is to gain access to decision makers and to persuade them of the efficacy of the interest the lobbyist represents. Highly successful lobbyists become so invaluable to people within the process that they virtually become a part of it: for instance, having such great knowledge of a policy area that they are consulted on crafting the language for a piece of legislation.

Another key way that interest groups seek to influence policy is with education, by providing expert information in an issue area that can be used to educate and persuade both those in power and the public at large of the desirability of their positions. Some educational efforts are aimed at the public, often in the form of TV and magazine advertising campaigns, to try to persuade them of a point of view. Another educational effort may be to provide speakers to college campuses or communication groups, or to make speakers available for newspaper and television interviews and to write op-ed articles for local newspapers. At the same time, groups often provide news releases in the hope to have them printed in local papers.

More commonly, educational efforts are directed toward members of Congress and their staffs. Interest groups collect and make available information about their particular policy area, which, although self-interested, may provide a useful supplement to the members' ability to gain information through their staffs. This information may come in the form of position papers, fact books, reference services to which a member has access, or even expert testimony to congressional committees and subcommittees. Often this information is also available to interest-group members and even the public through the Internet. They also place ads in magazines that professional politicians read; just as ABC places ads in *People* magazine to get you to watch a TV show, for example, if you picked up a copy of *Congressional Quarterly Weekly Reports* or the *National Journal* you would see ads for Boeing, fighter jets, and tanks.

Members and their staffs greatly appreciate this form of activity, if provided honestly rather than as obviously biased propaganda. Despite the expansion of staffs described in chapter 6, Congress is still at a disadvantage in its competition for information with the executive branch. An interest group that provides honest, valuable information thus extends Congress's capabilities. When interest groups present conflicting information or interpretations on an issue, the contrast helps the member develop a comparative assessment of the various positions.

A good example of an interest group that uses educational programs as a primary tool is the Arms Control Association (ACA). The ACA publishes its own journal, *Arms Control Today*, which it distributes to libraries and interested citizens. The association features a speakers' bureau for places such as college campuses, and its leading staff members are regularly available for interviews. Congressional members also receive the journal, and the ACA provides both expert witnesses for testimony before congressional committees and a resource for information on weapons levels, characteristics, and the like. As a further means of outreach, *Arms Control Today* frequently publishes articles and speeches by sympathetic members of Congress.

Interest groups also seek to influence policy by exerting political pressure on government officials, a form of influence peddling that represents the most negative and controversial side of interest-group activities. Pressure activities comprise actions designed not so much to persuade officials of the virtue of the group's position as to convince the officials of the negative consequences of opposing the interest or the positive benefits of support. In the past thirty years or so, the negative side of pressure has come to be associated with the emergence of the political action committees introduced earlier. The basic purpose and tactic of PACs is to influence elections by collecting money and using it to support candidates sympathetic to their causes and to oppose their opponents. Sometimes the PACs accomplish this by making direct contributions to campaigns. Limits on the amount that can be given to any candidate by an organization necessitate a second tactic, which is for the PACs to encourage members of the group to contribute as well, and the group then "bundles" those checks and presents them to candidates. Following a controversial U.S. Supreme Court decision in 2009 (referred to by the shorthand *Citizens United*), groups, unions, and corporations can spend unlimited amounts of money on political campaigns, including campaigns to elect or to defeat candidates, so long as their efforts are not coordinated with the campaign of the candidate whom they seek to assist. Other groups have also emerged (sometimes called Super PACs) that do not even have to disclose the donors behind the large sums of money used to wage electoral warfare.

The world of money in political campaigns has changed dramatically in the last few years, with a range of new "independent expenditure" groups that spend money on campaigns. These groups tend to be organized under various parts of the Internal Revenue Service tax code, such as "527" groups (for example, the notorious Swiftboat Veterans for Truth that targeted John Kerry in the 2004 presidential campaign) and "501(c)(4)" groups (nonprofit, income-tax exempt organizations such as Crossroads GPS formed by Karl Rove in 2010, which spent more than $70 million in the 2012 presidential election cycle). Altogether these groups and others spent well over $1 billion in the 2016 election cycle. The activities of the PACs and other expenditure groups are more closely associated with domestic than foreign and defense issues, but it is certainly the case that corporate PACs that seek to influence the size and direction of defense procurement are very large and influential; the defense industry is particularly active in this regard. Defense industry PACs alone spent nearly $30 million in 2016.

The enormity of the stakes involved inevitably leads to abuses and even bribery, or the offer and acceptance of illegal funds by some official from an interest group. Instances of bribery are rather infrequent, but when they do occur, they are spectacular. One large-scale bribery case involved banking magnate Charles Keating and his defrauding of the federal government in the savings and loan scandal of the mid-1980s. The corruption touched five U.S. senators, who became known as the Keating Five (Alan Cranston of California, John Glenn of Ohio, Dennis DeConcini of Arizona, John McCain of Arizona, and Donald Riegle of Michigan).

In the foreign and defense area, one of the most famous cases involved a foreign lobbyist, Tong Sun Park of the Republic of Korea. Park, a flashy, well-liked figure, induced support for his government through lavish social occasions for governmental officials, including gifts for congressional members and their spouses during the 1970s and 1980s. The gifts ultimately got him in trouble because they exceeded allowable limits. One person who was forced to resign his position because of this scandal was Ronald Reagan's first national security advisor, Richard V. Allen, who had accepted two watches from Park.

Types of Interest Groups

Many kinds of interest groups exist in the country, with most concentrating on influencing the domestic agenda. However, the reader should recognize that the blurring of domestic and foreign policy means that international events affect almost all interests some of the time. Some groups have interests that span the spectrum of policy areas, including, but not specifically emphasizing, foreign policy. These general interest groups, such as the American Federation of Labor and Congress of Industrial Organizations (AFL-CIO), take an interest in foreign or defense policy when it may directly affect their constituents. The AFL-CIO is sensitive to any foreign policies that may favor lower-paid foreign workers over American workers who belong to unions—and so trade policy is something that draws the careful attention of the AFL-CIO. Groups such as this can have thousands and even tens of thousands of members—and have considerable general influence—but they frequently lack great expertise in the specific area of defense and foreign policy.

One organization that concentrates on a specific aspect of the foreign policy process is Amnesty International (AI). Although it considers itself more of a think tank because of the academic impartiality of its inquiry, AI is dedicated to the protection of human rights globally and investigates and publicizes instances of human rights abuses. It boasts 3 million supporters around the world—250,000 in the United States—and was awarded the Nobel Peace Prize in 1977 for its work. AI often comes into direct conflict with the State Department, which has the statutory mandate to produce a list of countries that are human rights abusers. The department's list, partially constructed with geopolitical considerations in mind (how important a country is to the United States regardless of its human rights record), is almost always shorter than the AI list.

Another way that groups differ is the extent to which interest groups have a continuous interest in foreign affairs. A continuity of interest helps create expertise, which makes the group's counsel more sought after than might otherwise be the case. In turn, the reputation for expertise makes the group's recruitment of experts easier. Examples of this kind of group are the Council on Foreign Relations (CFR) and the Foreign Policy Association (FPA). Groups with an occasional interest in foreign policy are selective in the foreign and defense issues they seek to influence. Normally having a primary focus in some other policy area, these groups intrude into the foreign policy area only when a specific issue directly affects them and only while their interests are engaged. Hundreds of companies and interest groups were involved in the last few years on lobbying for and against the Trans-Pacific Partnership.

Another way groups differ is that some groups represent "private" interests, such as the way the U.S. Chamber of Commerce represents large business interests, while other groups seek to represent the "public" at large, such as the Plowshares Fund, which seeks to reduce defense spending and arms sales.

One more way that groups differ is that not all the groups out there trying to influence the U.S. government are made up of American citizens. Indeed foreigners, notably foreign governments and foreign corporations, also share a lively interest in trying to affect U.S. government actions toward themselves and others, and they do so in a number of ways. Sometimes they use their own citizens, often their ambassador, as an informal lobbyist with the government. Prince Bandar bin Sultan, the Saudi ambassador to the United States from 1983 to 2005, was especially effective in fending off criticism of Saudi Arabia's alleged support of terrorist organizations such as Al Qaeda by allowing them to operate and raise money in its territory.

Foreign governments also have their interests advanced by hiring American lobbyists—often, former government officials—to represent them. People who represent foreign governments must register as foreign agents, and quite often, their value derives from their ability to gain access to officials for their foreign clients. Another way for foreign governments to influence U.S. policy is to nurture Americans whose origins are the same as the nation seeking the influence. "Hyphenated Americans" (so called because terms such as Italian Americans, Irish Americans, and so forth are often written with a hyphen) can be quite effective if these organizations can plausibly be argued to represent vital segments of the American public. Probably the largest and most successful of these is the Israel lobby and its action arm, notably AIPAC. One of the real explosions in the interest-group world of the last thirty years has been the emergence and proliferation of **"ethnic interest groups."** Their rise in activity level and prominence has not been without some controversy, so we discuss them as a distinct type of interest group.

Groups that are founded to promote the foreign policy interests of a particular subset of Americans who identify themselves (at least in part) along the lines of ethnicity and national origin are considered ethnic interest groups. Often these groups pressure the U.S. government to be friendlier toward their previous homeland, including offering more economic or perhaps military assistance for that country of origin. AIPAC is a classic example of this, promoting close ties between the United States and Israel and working to limit policies that AIPAC's leaders and members see as dangerous for Israel (such as arms sales to the Saudis). AIPAC is regularly cited as the most powerful ethnic interest group in America—and one of the most powerful interest groups in general, as well. Conversely, sometimes such groups lobby to limit aid toward, or to place sanctions on, the country of origin when the regime in that country is seen as harsh and dictatorial. The **Cuban American National Foundation (CANF)** is an example of this. CANF was founded in 1980 to promote the embargo of Cuba, the aim of which has been to try to force the end of the Castro regime on the island. (CANF evolved a fair amount in recent years, and its power, which was considerable in the 1980s and 1990s, has waned somewhat.) Today, ethnic interest groups—many of which also have PACs—are some of the most active foreign policy lobbies in America, seeking to represent the interests of "hyphenated Americans" across a broad range of ethnicities.

Political pressure from ethnic interest groups has evoked some controversy beyond the normal discomfort many have with lobbying. Some have raised the concern that these groups are really front operations for foreign governments. Others have argued that the presence of these groups serves to underscore our differences as a nation, rather than seeking common ground and assimilation—the American melting pot. Beyond that, skeptics claim that these groups promote a myopic view of America's "interests" in the world. There is really nothing special about these groups—all interest groups promote their self-interest over the interests of others, claiming that it is in "the national interest"; it's just that these groups come together based on ethnic heritage rather than some other interest. And as discussed at the start of this chapter, sometimes several groups emerge that have different views of what is in the interests of the former homeland, and they compete with each other (as with AIPAC and J Street) as well as against other interest groups. Nonetheless, the proliferation of these groups has raised the eyebrows of some observers.

Interest groups and the activities they engage in are a long-standing, integral part of the U.S. political system that is as American as apple pie. The tendency for people to equate their interests with the national interest is not something unique to the interest-group world. If there is a shortcoming to this system, it is the link between interests and money. Not all interests are equally well funded, so often it is not a "fair fight," and the presence of so much money in politics means that the political process can sometimes look unseemly, if not actually be corrupt.

Think Tanks

A sizable community of individuals with expertise on public policy matters has emerged and has increasingly sought to use its knowledge to affect foreign policy from not-for-profit, nonpartisan research institutes and organizations, including universities. Think tanks date to the years of the Kennedy administration, and before that name took root they were also called "brain banks," "think factories," and "egghead row" (because a number of the early organizations were located in a row on Massachusetts Avenue in Washington, D.C.). Today think tanks and interest groups both operate at the boundary between the government and the public, and like interest groups, think tanks have proliferated in recent years and become more partisan. They differ, however, in emphasis, membership, and the range of activities they undertake.

One of the basic purposes of both think tanks and interest groups is citizen education, although for different reasons. Interest groups tend to view education instrumentally, as a device to cause conversion to their interest. In contrast, think tanks have traditionally sought knowledge and its educational application more abstractly, as a way to improve government. In recent years, however, a new breed of think tanks—sometimes called advocacy tanks—began to develop knowledge for the purpose of persuasion.

The two entities differ in other significant ways. The emphasis of interest groups is overtly political: seeking to move policy in self-interested directions. Think tanks, though often ideologically identifiable, in theory at least adopt a more detached, scholarly view of policy. Similarly, most of those associated with think tanks are academics, in one sense or another, or people with experience-based expertise such as retired military officers or ex-government officials, whereas traditional politicians are more often associated with interest groups.

The movement that evolved into the modern think tanks began around the turn of the twentieth century. Its impetus came from a group of scholars, principally from the social sciences, who believed that public policy and process could be improved by applying social scientific means and research to them. The first identifiable think tank, the Russell Sage Foundation, was chartered in 1907 and was followed fairly quickly by others. These early organizations viewed themselves as citadels in which pure, disinterested research (research not associated with personal or institutional gain or partisan ends) could be pursued and the results could be dispassionately applied to societal problems. Think tanks that focus on foreign affairs began to emerge during the Cold War—the development of nuclear strategy became one of the activities of some think tanks—and in the political activism of the 1960s and the Vietnam War.

The people who work for them also define the nature of think tanks, and generally employees come from academia, military service, or prior civilian government service. The academics are usually individuals with doctoral degrees in political science, economics, history, or international relations, who are more interested in applied research (studying and influencing concrete public policy) than in abstract, theoretical, academic research or university-level teaching. As with interest groups, there is a bit of a revolving door between think tanks and the government. Before her appointment as UN ambassador and later secretary of state by President Clinton, Madeleine Albright was a college professor (Georgetown) and then served as president of the Center for National Policy. The deputy secretary of defense in the Bush administration, Paul Wolfowitz, was at the Johns Hopkins School of Advanced International Studies before joining the Bush campaign and administration. George W. Bush's national security advisor and later secretary of state, Condoleezza Rice, was provost at Stanford University and linked to the Hoover Institution at Stanford (an in-house, conservative think tank). The director of the Policy Planning Staff at the Department of State (sort of the State Department's own internal think tank) at the outset of the Obama administration, Anne-Marie Slaughter, had served as the dean of the Woodrow Wilson School at Princeton and now heads a think tank called New America.

As one might expect, retired military officers tend to be concentrated in think tanks primarily studying security issues rather than general foreign policy problems. Many who have retired below the rank of flag officer (general or admiral) are located in organizations that do contract work for the government or in institutes run in-house by the services. A number of the PhDs who work in think tanks also have military backgrounds, probably reflecting a greater action orientation than is normally associated with academic life. Retired flag officers can often be found in very prominent positions at think tanks. One prominent example (of many) of a retired military officer who headed a think tank is retired rear admiral Gene LaRoque, who was the president emeritus of the Center for Defense Information (CDI)—a leading think tank about military issues. The CDI merged with another group in 2012 called the Project on Government Oversight. The Center for Strategic and International Studies is another think tank that focuses its work on foreign and defense policy; it is led by Dr. John Hamre, a former deputy secretary of defense.

Think tanks are also defined by the sources of their funding. For most think tanks, funding comes from foundations, corporations, individual contributions and bequests (sometimes including contributions from foreign governments), sales of books and periodicals, and government-sponsored research and contracts.

Large foundations with considerable resources, such as the Ford, John D. and Catherine T. MacArthur, and Bill and Melinda Gates Foundations, and the Pew Charitable Trust, provide funds to support think-tank research. Corporations also provide funds for research institutes, and through bequests and large contributions some think tanks have substantial endowments that generate revenue to support their activities. The Brookings Institution, for instance, has an endowment of about $450 million, but most are not that well off and rely heavily on contributions from individuals, contracts, and to some extent the sales of books and journals (although those can easily lose money rather than raise funds). The RAND Corporation, which was created in 1948 largely to serve as a think tank for the newly independent U.S. Air Force and which still conducts much of its research for the military, generates substantial revenue from defense contracts.

One of the ways that think tanks differ from one another, besides their focus on specific policy areas, is by ideological or political persuasion. A number of institutes created in the 1970s were established out of the conservatives' belief that they needed a formal articulated agenda that could be used to appeal to the public or to help conservative candidates for office. The most prominent example of this is the **Heritage Foundation**. The American Enterprise Institute (AEI) is associated with the moderate, pro-market wing of the Republican Party. The Brookings Institution, on the other hand, has always been identified with positions that are more centrist-to-liberal. The Center for American Progress, directed by President Clinton's former chief of staff, John Podesta, was formed in 2003 in part as a counterweight for centrists and Democrats to balance against the weight of AEI and Heritage.

Some think tanks are actually government organizations. Each of the military services, for instance, maintains an in-house think tank usually associated with the war colleges. Thus, the army maintains its Strategic Studies Institute (SSI) at the U.S. Army War College; the navy, its Center for Naval Warfare Studies (CNWS) at the U.S. Naval War College; the air force has multiple research operations at the Air University; and the marine corps has the Center for Emerging Threats and Opportunities (CETO) in Quantico, Virginia.

Think tanks serve as talent banks (the term used by the Nixon administration) for the government. This process works in two directions. In one direction, when an administration leaves office and is replaced by another (especially when another political party wins the White House), some personnel dislocation occurs among the several thousand officials who hold political appointments and who find their services are no longer required by the new president. Many officials so removed do not want to leave the Washington scene altogether and even have aspirations of returning to senior government service in the future. For them, a position at a think tank can provide an attractive option. From the individual's viewpoint, a think tank appointment can serve as a safe haven, a sanctuary between periods of government service wherein the person can remain abreast of what is happening in Washington and available for recall. From the organizational vantage point, the association of important former governmental officials can enhance both the prestige and expertise of the organization. This movement is, of course, much the same as the revolving-door phenomenon already noted about interest groups. In the other direction, the staffs of the research institutes provide a ready talent pool for filling governmental positions. It has been argued, for instance, that the Brookings Institution, as well as the John F. Kennedy School of Government at Harvard University, provides a kind of "government in waiting" for any new Democratic president, just as the Heritage Foundation and AEI provide a source of policy inspiration and personnel for Republican administrations.

Think tanks are also a home for "electronic experts," helping fill the media's burgeoning need for information and expertise and at the same time providing opportunities for organizational and self-promotion. The media's needs date back to the Vietnam period, when events escalated beyond the expertise of the television networks and print media who, for instance, did not possess staff experts on Southeast Asian history and politics or the principles of guerrilla warfare. The media needed experts who exuded authority, and think tanks sought the exposure that having members of their staffs appearing on the evening news could provide. This demand has increased exponentially in the always-on media environment of today. CNN was the trendsetter, followed by other full-time news organizations such as CNBC, MSNBC, and Fox News, for example. By necessity, these channels engage in a great deal of news analysis in addition to reporting (there is, after all, lots of time to fill in twenty-four hours!). To analyze the news requires expert authorities, and the think tanks are more than happy to fill that need. This trend continues to expand due to the demand for news and analysis that spills into social networking sites and other means of constant contact.

As government funding for research became tougher to come by, think tanks were forced to compete with one another and with other institutions, such as universities, for dwindling resources. Think tanks came to rely more on individual donors for funding—as well as support from foreign governments—and the activities of many think tanks have come to mirror the political preferences of their donors, contributing to the politically polarized environment within which foreign policy is made today.

There is some concern about the purity of research efforts that emerges from think tanks as they become more activist and openly political, with the Heritage Foundation as the prototype of this type of advocacy tank. That organization admits openly that it engages in inquiry for promoting the conservative agenda, and it publicizes only those research findings that support its point of view. It also has a sister organization, **Heritage Action**, a 501(c)(4) group that raises money for political purposes. The Jewish Institute for National Security Affairs (JINSA) is another example; JINSA (founded in 1976) is perhaps best thought of as a hybrid organization: part interest group (it has members), part think tank (it does studies and tries to disseminate its expertise). Like an increasing number of such hybrid organizations, JINSA is anything but dispassionate in its analysis. The concern of many is that this partisan and political emphasis will undercut the reputation for scientific integrity that has been the foundation of think tank influence.

Complicating the terrain even further has been the proliferation of political consultants and public relations firms often hired by special interests to carry out "education" programs (for a hefty fee!). These types of actors do not represent think tanks per se and are not leaders of an interest group, but they are critical to the success of both and are steeped in political experience and connections. A fascinating foreign policy example of their activism can be found in the 2009 coup of the elected president of Honduras, Manuel Zelaya. After Zelaya was ousted by the Honduran military, a PR campaign was launched in the United States to convince the public and even government officials that Zelaya's removal was constitutional. An association of businesses in Honduras retained the services of several high-priced and well-connected consultants at PR firms in Washington, D.C., to help spin their side of the story. This lobbying "swamp" is discussed in intersection 7.2. The more partisan nature of think tanks, coupled with the emerging importance of consultants and PR firms, are both examples of how rapidly the ground is shifting under the foreign policy process today.

Intersection 7.2   Drain the Swamp?

One of the issues that Donald J. Trump was able to use effectively in the 2016 presidential election was public discontent with politics in America—and he did so particularly with his promise to "drain the swamp" when elected. The idea behind the slogan, and regular chant at rallies, was to root out politics as usual, corruption, and well-paid lobbyists. His campaign website said that part of draining the swamp was sweeping ethics reform that would limit the revolving door between government service and lobbying, congressional term limits, and campaign finance reform.

Talking about draining the swamp and actually draining the swamp are two different things. First, there might be differences of opinion about what the swamp is. Trump's appointments have included numerous high-profile Wall Street executives, former lobbyists, donors, and activists. The new secretary of state ran ExxonMobil, a global oil and gas company headquartered in Texas that is the eighth-largest company in the world. And his former campaign manager, Corey Lewandowski, started a lobbying firm after the election. Presumably these are not the alligators that Trump is concerned about, but it points to a second challenge of draining the swamp: what if only the alligators know how the swamp works? Trump comes to the White House as an outsider, but to effect change he will need people who understand the policy process and how to make it work. Just three months into his administration we have already seen staff turnover in the White House, continued high-profile vacancies in the bureaucracy, and policy failures on immigration and insurance reform—suggesting that those new to politics are having some challenges managing in this new environment. Do the "professionals" come back in now? Even if they are Republicans who said, "Never Trump"? This reminds us of a familiar quandary in politics: how does one reform what they think of as a corrupt process without using the corruptors to guide the venture?

Conclusion

Both think tanks and interest groups can be seen in the context of the system of checks and balances on which the political system operates. Nearly every interest has a group to represent it and to make sure its voice is heard, and think tanks span the range of intellectual points of view. In the overall context of the U.S. government, interest groups are perhaps a more important phenomenon than think tanks. The former are larger, more numerous, more visible, richer, and can bring electoral pressure to bear, and hence are more powerful. Think tanks, however, are probably more effective at influencing foreign and defense policy than are interest groups—although ethnic interest groups have become very active in recent years.

The two kinds of institutions share similarities and differences. Both, for instance, seek to influence policy rather than govern directly (although some think tank staffers and interest-group lobbyists move in and out of government), but they do so differently and for different reasons. Interest groups act self-interestedly: they attempt to move public policy so it will favor those they represent. The early think tanks in particular sought to improve government not from self-interest but out of an academically driven sense of improving the government. As discussed, however, this norm is becoming more ambiguous as advocacy tanks bring a political and often partisan agenda to their work.

The purposes of these organizations are reflected in the means they use. Although both seek to educate the public and government elites, their methods differ. The tools of interest groups are persuasion (lobbying), education, and pressure (including PACs and other campaign expenditure organizations). The use of pressure by PACs is the natural result of acting out of self-interest: specific outcomes are highly personalized. Because they presumably act disinterestedly, the think tanks use persuasion based in expertise and objective knowledge as their major tool—although some, such as the Heritage Foundation and its Heritage Action, take on elements very similar to interest groups and PACs.

Some of these distinctions are vanishing; some think tanks begin to operate increasingly like interest groups, and vice versa; hybrids seem to be on the rise, groups that are part think tank, part interest group, such as JINSA. The politically activist, and especially conservative, movement within the research institute community during the 1980s produced a hybrid think tank with a specific political agenda, and the Left followed suit. The tools may remain educational in the broad sense, but they result from directed, not disinterested, research—research aimed not at increasing the general pool of knowledge but at providing knowledge that reinforces political predilections.

Finally, the two institutions form a bridge between government and the broader society, which is the subject of the next chapter. In broad terms, interest groups aggregate, articulate, and seek to influence the public at large and the direction of foreign and defense policy. At the same time, the media are essential to the educational goals of both groups, and the growing phenomenon of the electronic expert provides a new link between the media, interest groups, and think tanks.

Study/Discussion Questions

1. What are the purposes of foreign policy interest groups? How do they serve a gatekeeping function between the government and the public?
2. How do interest groups go about trying to influence foreign policy?
3. What are ethnic interest groups, and why do some find their emergence to be controversial?
4. What is the iron triangle? How is Eisenhower's warning about the "military-industrial complex" a precursor of this political science concept?
5. What purpose have think tanks traditionally served? How is that changing?
6. In what ways is the distinction between an interest group and a think tank starting to break down?
7. What role do political action committees (PACs) play? What other kinds of groups such as PACs have emerged recently that might also try to influence foreign policy?
8. In terms of normative conceptions of democracy, is it fair that interest groups and think tanks have emerged as such important players in policy making? In what ways is it fair and reasonable? In what ways is it unfair and undemocratic?

Bibliography

Abelson, Donald E. *Do Think Tanks Matter? Assessing the Impact of Public Policy Institutes.* 2nd ed. Montreal: McGill-Queens University Press, 2009.

Ainsworth, Scott H. *Analyzing Interest Groups: Group Influence on People and Policies.* New York: Norton, 2002.

Arnsdorf, Isaac, Josh Dawsey, and Daniel Lippman. "Will 'Drain the Swamp' Be Trump's First Broken Promise?" *Politico*, December 23, 2016. Accessed January 2, 2017. http://www.politico.com/story/2016/12/trump-drain-swamp-promise-232938.

Berry, Jeffrey. *Lobbying for the People: The Political Behavior of Public Interest Groups.* Princeton, NJ: Princeton University Press, 2015.

Browne, William P. *Groups, Interests, and U.S. Public Policy.* Washington, DC: Georgetown University Press, 1998.

Cigler, Allan J., and Burdett Loomis, eds. *Interest Group Politics.* 9th ed. Washington, DC: CQ, 2016.

Delgado, Richard, Jean Stefancic, and Mark Tushnet. *No Mercy: How Conservative Think Tanks and Foundations Changed America's Social Agenda.* Philadelphia: Temple University Press, 1996.

Grossman, Gene M., and Elhanan Helpman. *Special Interest Groups.* Cambridge, MA: MIT Press, 2001.

Haney, Patrick J., and Walt Vanderbush. *Cuban Embargo: The Domestic Politics of an American Foreign Policy.* Pittsburgh: University of Pittsburgh Press, 2005.

Marrar, Khalil. *The Arab Lobby and U.S. Foreign Policy.* New York: Routledge, 2009.

McGann, James G. *2015 Global Go To Think Tank Index Report.* Philadelphia: University of Pennsylvania Scholarly Commons, 2016.

Mearsheimer, John J., and Stephen M. Walt. *The Israel Lobby and U.S. Foreign Policy.* New York: Farrar, Straus & Giroux, 2007.

Nownes, Anthony J. *Pressure and Power: Organized Interests in American Politics.* Boston: Houghton Mifflin, 2001.

Ricci, David M. *The Transformation of American Politics: The New Washington and the Rise of Think Tanks.* New Haven, CT: Yale University Press, 1994.

Rich, Andrew. *Think Tanks, Public Policy, and the Politics of Expertise.* New York: Cambridge University Press, 2004.

Smith, James Allen. *The Idea Brokers: Think Tanks and the Rise of the New Policy Elite.* New York: Free Press, 1993.

Smith, Tony. *Foreign Attachments.* Cambridge, MA: Harvard University Press, 2000.

Torres, Maria de los Angeles. *In the Land of Mirrors: Cuban Exile Politics in the United States.* Ann Arbor: University of Michigan, 2002.

Weiss, Carol H. *Organizations for Policy Analysis: Helping Government Think.* Newbury Park, CA: Sage, 1992.

Wiarda, Howard. *Think Tanks and Foreign Policy: The Foreign Policy Research Institute and Presidential Politics.* Lanham, MD: Lexington, 2010.

The Public and the Media 8

Social media has become a popular and powerful tool, and Twitter is a favorite of President Trump (@RealDonaldTrump).

Preview

The public and the media both play important roles in U.S. foreign policy. The public can push for certain foreign policies and serve as a restraint against unpopular initiatives. The public—or at least those who vote—picks winners in elections, and those winners go on to make foreign policy and, in the case of the president, to appoint others who help make foreign policy. The mass public pays little attention to foreign policy except during major crises (such as the attacks of 9/11), but some members of the public pay particularly close attention to foreign policy issues and try to play a more direct role in promoting their foreign policy preferences to government policy makers. Much of how the public, especially the mass public, "sees" foreign policy issues comes through the media. Print and electronic journalism and even social media try to inform the public and help hold government officials accountable to the public—and perhaps they also try to convince the public to see things a certain way. As this chapter discusses, the relationship between the people, the press, and the government is complex and symbiotic, not always in ways that are conducive to democratic accountability.

Key Concepts

Nightline
fourth estate
leaks
Operation Desert Storm
Almond-Lippmann consensus
mass public
rally effect
informed public
effective public
opinion leaders

halo effect
diversionary theory of war
pretty prudent public
no prior restraint
Pentagon Papers
watchdogging
media diplomacy
CNN effect
soft news

In June 2009 Iran's president Mahmoud Ahmadinejad easily won reelection over a number of candidates including "moderate" Mir Hossein Mousavi, and mass protests erupted. The "Green Revolution" followed—and its brutal crackdown. That revolution failed, but the use of social media by protesters as a way to both get information out and to communicate with each other was striking. As Clay Shirky discusses in *Foreign Affairs* magazine, the political power of social networking media is promising, perhaps, but not necessarily determinative. Follow-on studies have also focused on the limits of social media to force social and political change, as reported by Himelfarb and Aday in *Foreign Policy* magazine. Going a step further, Malcolm Gladwell highlights the dangers of "slacktivism," trading social networking for the hard work of effecting real political change.

The American public engages with news about global events and foreign policy in a way that is strikingly different from one generation ago. In the 1979 revolution in Iran, when Americans were held hostage inside the American embassy in Tehran for 444 days, a nightly show appeared on ABC to update viewers on the hostage crisis; over time that show became *Nightline*. In a sense, then, the media environment was driven by the flow of events. What about now—do events drive the media environment, or vice versa? Policy makers not only pay attention to these dynamics; they try to drive them. The White House has a web page (www.whitehouse.gov) and a Facebook page; it blogs, tweets, and is on Flickr, Google+, Instagram, and YouTube—and we just hired a new tweeter in chief whose late-night use of his Twitter account is legendary. For Trump and others, the use of these tools provides a way to establish a relationship directly with the public, without going through a news program or an interview or buying ads.

At a time when events around the world affect Americans more quickly and directly than ever before, and when news about these events is perhaps easier to get than ever before, the news may lead to even less understanding than in previous times. News via social media tends to be short and to the point; understanding international affairs requires more depth and focus. So at a time when it is more important than ever that Americans—and their leaders—understand global affairs so as to craft wise policies, it may be tougher than ever. Beyond that, the severely partisan nature of our politics has leaked into foreign policy, meaning that there is a lot of screaming about foreign policy, but less understanding.

Central to the philosophical underpinning of the American political system is the notion that sovereignty ultimately resides with individual citizens, who in turn delegate part of that sovereignty to government to carry out the duties of state. Governmental authority, including the authority to conduct foreign policy, flows from and is limited by the sovereignty that has been ceded by the people. Those who govern must also be accountable. The people reserve the right to inspect what their government does in carrying out the public trust and hence to decide whether the job is being done correctly. Elections are thus important accountability moments (see intersection 8.1 below for more on elections and foreign policy). This need for accountability ensures that leaders ignore public opinion at their peril. The First Amendment guarantees a free press, which assists the public in rendering its judgments by investigating and publicizing the performance of those who govern. Because a large part of the media's job is to act as watchdogs against incompetent or corrupt governmental action, a natural adversarial relationship exists between the **"fourth estate"** and those in government.

Intersection 8.1 — Foreign Policy Presidential Campaign Commercials

The classic statement about American presidential elections is that they are all about "pocketbook" issues; the famous sign in the campaign headquarters of the 1992 Clinton presidential campaign was—in case anyone was tempted to forget—"It's the economy, stupid." Nevertheless, there have been key times when foreign policy issues loomed large in presidential elections, which should come as no surprise since elections are classic intermestic events—about both foreign and domestic policy.

The website of the American Museum of the Moving Image has an ongoing display called "The Living Room Candidate" that catalogs the campaign commercials of the major party candidates for president in the television age (http://livingroomcandidate.org). While there are many great commercials worth watching, one in particular warrants attention here, from the 2004 election. Harking back to an image that Ronald Reagan used once, depicting the threat from the Soviet Union as a "bear in the woods," President George W. Bush ran a sequel of sorts, updated for the new "threat environment." If the danger of the Soviet Union during the height of the Cold War could be likened to a bear, George W. Bush's 2004 reelection campaign put forth that the danger from terrorism after 9/11 was more like the danger of being attacked by a pack of "wolves." With the camera focusing on wolves in the forest, the narrator accuses the Democratic challenger, Massachusetts senator John Kerry, of taking positions on defense that would have weakened America's defenses: "And weakness attracts those who are waiting to do America harm."

The 2004 election was very close, and was ultimately decided by fewer than two hundred thousand votes in Ohio. No one knew for sure how the terrorism issue would play in the election. Would voters want to stay with President Bush during this time of "war," or would they want to make a change, since the head of Al Qaeda—the organization that carried out the attacks of 9/11—Osama bin Laden, was still at large? The wolves ad was the Bush campaign's way of making its case that Bush was the more reliable choice.

Electronic information, social networking, and smart devices now permeate our lives. For many Americans, part of the content in those information flows is foreign policy news. But for better or worse, the evolution of the electronic information revolution has included the rise of niche media that cater to a particular audience and that promote seeing the "facts" in a certain way. Just as our politics has become increasingly partisan and divisive, the media environment within which politics takes place has also become more divisive—making it even more challenging to build consensus in foreign policy. This chapter considers the role of public opinion and the media together since it is almost impossible to talk about them separately.

Before turning to an examination of the effects of the public and the media on the foreign policy process and on individual foreign policies, it is useful to look at some examples of the practical impediments to notions of authority and accountability between the government and the people and between the media and the government that exist.

First, "secrecy" is a key component of foreign affairs. The ability to hide information from adversaries and to conceal what one knows about them and how one knows it can provide some advantage in dealing with other states. All this secrecy, though, can be a disadvantage for democratic accountability. If our leaders work in secret, how are we to judge their actions and hold them accountable? There are inherent trade-offs between accountability and security—a natural tension between secrecy and democracy. How much should we compromise our democratic ideals in order to be "safe," and for how long?

Sometimes secrecy is necessary, especially in the foreign affairs domain when it comes to protecting the details of an ongoing operation or to protect how leaders know what they know—called source sensitivity to protect "sources and methods." WikiLeaks, which started in November 2010 with a range of State Department cables detailing private conversations with foreign dignitaries, provides a glimpse into the world of (what was supposed to be) secret diplomacy. The scandal involving Hillary Clinton's e-mails that persisted throughout the 2016 presidential campaign, and the release of hacked e-mails (and maybe some fraudulent ones, too) from the Democratic National Committee as part of this campaign cycle, likely perpetrated by Russia and released by WikiLeaks, is a stark reminder of the challenging media environment we live in, of cyber-security concerns, and of the complex network of relationships that exists between the public, the media, leaders, allies, and enemies.

Second, the general public's "lack of foreign policy knowledge" is often cited for the public's historical ineffectiveness in influencing the foreign policy process.

A very small percentage of the population keeps abreast of foreign events, has traveled abroad, carries a passport, speaks a foreign language, or has taken formal courses at any level dealing with foreign cultures, history, or international relations. This lack of knowledge, combined with widespread perceptions that foreign affairs are so complicated as to be beyond the comprehension of the average citizen, reinforces the people's general ineffectiveness in influencing how government conducts foreign and national security affairs. One of the central roles of media is to try to educate citizens—but because of the public's general lack of foreign policy knowledge, are they susceptible to the media leading instead of educating them? And because of the power of "always on" news, do television and the Internet drive the policy process, demanding attention to certain issues and themselves being driven by the most provocative and extreme views—the loudest is best?

The relationship between the public and the media has been altered in recent years by (1) the emergence of a truly global electronic media, which changes both the public's access to and awareness of foreign policy events and issues, and by (2) the rise of media conglomeration (several electronic or print media— or their combination—owned by a single large corporation) that may adversely affect the breadth of reporting and opinion despite increases in media volume. Along with conglomeration has come an impressive cutting back on the foreign news bureaus of American newspapers and television networks. We may, in other words, be hearing the same slant on the news in multiple apparently independent but actually repetitive sources.

Finally, there is controversy about **leaks**. The only people legally bound to maintain the secrecy of classified information are those who have voluntarily done so as a condition of employment with the government. The media can try to get people who have access to classified information to "leak" it to the press, but readers need to exercise caution about leaks. Sometimes a leak is not really a leak at all, but more of a "trial balloon" where the government releases information as a test of sorts, to see how people will react to a piece of information or a potential policy change. When a release of information really is a "leak" from the inside, often the person leaking the information has an agenda behind the leak: perhaps to try to embarrass someone, or to try to shift the terms of a policy debate that the person is losing inside the government. And as we saw in the 2016 election, sometimes a leak is really a way for a hacking organization or a foreign government to try to influence the outcome of an election or a policy dispute! No matter the reason, while leaked information might be helpful and useful to the public, the public needs to be critical evaluators of leaks since there is usually a motive behind them. With these issues in mind, let's turn to a more straightforward examination of how both the public and the media are involved in the foreign policy process.

The Public

For most of U.S. history the public played a minor role in making and implementing the country's foreign policy. This was largely because the public was only rarely affected by foreign policy events, had little information about them, and, hence, had very little need or desire to be involved. World War II and, following it, the ascendance of the United States to the role of global superpower changed that. Whether it was waging Cold War against the Soviets or hot war against terrorists, the government needed to convince the public that what the United States did in the world was morally right and necessary. But how much participation of the public is necessary to meet our democratic ideals? Should the public's role be as limited as possible: to accept and ratify the wisdom of the professionals? Or because the public bears the burden of foreign policy decisions, should the public be more deeply involved? This debate is as old as the Republic.

Setting that unsolvable problem aside, what can we say about the role of the public in the foreign policy process? In one sense the public is a parameter setter. It does not possess detailed expertise in foreign affairs, it cannot set the agenda, nor is it likely to provide detailed guidance to policy makers on foreign policies. What the public can and does do, however, is set the broad outer boundaries, or parameters, of policy acceptability—boundaries within which policy makers have reasonable discretion to act. When government exceeds those limits, however, policy can be in trouble. The U.S. government learned this lesson the hard way in the Vietnam War, where government actions exceeded public tolerance and opposition ultimately forced the United States to abandon the effort.

Operation Desert Storm during the Persian Gulf War of 1990–1991 was in part an application of a new understanding about the relationship between the public and the government after Vietnam, one where the government would openly cultivate support for war ahead of time. When the public responded positively to the deployment of armed forces and reservists to the region, and after a blitz of attention to the way the media portrayed this "crisis," President George H. W. Bush then requested not a declaration of war but rather a congressional resolution supporting the troop commitment (a sequence repeated by George W. Bush in 2001 and 2002 before military operations in Afghanistan and Iraq, respectively). The administration also built a system for the media so that they could cover the war but not as freely as they did in Vietnam; they would not be censored per se, but they would certainly be led.

Confronting the Traditional View: Multiple "Publics"

Much of the literature on the public and foreign policy has stressed not what the public can and should do but the limitations on that role. The conventional view was that the public not only knew little about foreign policy, but what beliefs they did have were unorganized, unpredictable, wrong, and perhaps even irrational. This view came to be called the **Almond-Lippmann consensus**, after the work of prominent political scientist Gabriel Almond and writer and commentator Walter Lippmann.

The first step toward unpacking the limitations of the Almond-Lippmann consensus is to divide the electorate into a series of segments of increasing knowledge about foreign affairs, beginning with the **mass public**, the majority of people who have very little knowledge of or interest in foreign policy, and culminating with the small body of core decision makers who actually make and influence policy. This begins to give us a richer sense of the way the "public" engages with and is engaged by foreign policy.

The Mass Public At the outer limits of influence is the mass public, sometimes also called the inattentive public. It is by far the largest portion of the population, encompassing 75–80 percent of the total. The mass public tends to not seek out information about international affairs; they do not generally read stories about foreign affairs in newspapers or newsmagazines, do not read books on the subject, and perhaps even avoid those parts of news broadcasts dealing with foreign policy. As a result, the mass public not only tends to not know much about foreign affairs (which creates a democratic accountability problem), but they also tend to not have a well-developed foreign policy "belief system," or a coherent view of world events and of the role of the United States in the world. So their knowledge in the area is spotty, and their reactions to foreign policy (when they become aware of it) can be inconsistent.

Because of this, the mass public tends to become aware of or involved in foreign policy issues in three circumstances. The first occurs when a foreign policy event has a direct and personal bearing on people. Forty years ago, the draft for the Vietnam War was of this nature; more recently, attacks by ISIS are examples of the kinds of things that get the mass public's attention on foreign policy—at least temporarily.

A second circumstance occurs when broad publicity is given to international events. Images of death, destruction, and mass migration from the civil war in Syria, for example, can capture the mass public's attention when it receives consistent news coverage. And indeed there is a tendency for the mass public to "**rally** around the flag" at a time of national crisis or danger, whether it comes from natural (for instance, floods) or human (for example, terrorism) causes. One of the natural advantages of the presidency, as discussed in chapter 4, is the singularity of the office, and so when the public rallies around the flag, it usually means they rally around the president.

In the third circumstance, the president, others in the government, or outside groups (such as interest groups and think tanks) might make conscious efforts to mobilize public opinion. Think of President George W. Bush's effort to convince Americans of the need to remove Saddam Hussein from power in Iraq as an example of this dynamic. If the mass public had more knowledge of and experience in foreign affairs, they might have been more skeptical of the case for invasion that he made. The attention of the mass public to foreign policy tends to be sporadic, short-term, and somewhat malleable. Most members of the mass public tend to have no coherent existing opinions about most foreign policy issues.

The Informed Public The second segment of Americans is the **informed** (or attentive) **public**. This is the second-largest population segment, 10–20 percent of the population. The definition of the informed public is virtually the opposite of that of the mass public. Members of the informed public regularly seek out information on international affairs and foreign policy. They read foreign policy stories in newspapers and magazines (either online or in the old-fashioned print edition) and watch television coverage of international events. They also may seek out foreign news on satellite radio (such as the BBC), subscribe to podcasts about international events, and follow reporters and other thought leaders on Twitter.

Several groups of people typically fall into the ranks of the informed public. Local civic leaders, journalists, clergy, even college graduates who took a class on American foreign policy and who continue to track the issues, all help constitute the informed public. For most members of the informed public, their contact with foreign policy events is more indirect than direct. In general, they have relatively few direct contacts with the foreign policy process, although that is perhaps changing as more and more localities have direct relationships with foreign investors, establish "sister city" arrangements, or do business with defense installations or government contractors. With some exceptions, however, this means that informed public members achieve their understanding of foreign and defense policy issues secondhand rather than through direct personal experience.

The Effective Public The third group is the **effective public**, sometimes also called "**opinion leaders**" or foreign policy elites. Defined as that part of the public that actively seeks to influence the foreign and defense policy process, this group consists of a relatively small number, usually considered as less than 5 percent of the overall population. This group is composed of a mix of former policy makers, national opinion leaders, and foreign policy experts either at universities or at interest groups and think tanks. These opinion leaders can lead because they get attention from national media outlets and through social media, and they promote ideas that are consumed by the informed public regularly, and sometimes even by the mass public.

What distinguishes the effective public from the informed public is the former's depth of knowledge and the centrality of foreign and defense matters to their personal and professional lives. They do not just consume news; they are quoted in the news or are on news shows and websites as they advocate policy positions. Some of these elites will rotate into and out of government over time.

Core Decision Makers The final group consists of the core decision makers—the individuals responsible for actually formulating and executing foreign and defense policy. Those who make policy occupy key roles in both the executive and legislative branches. Within the executive branch, the most numerous are found at the levels of assistant secretary and above in the State and Defense departments, the international divisions of other cabinet-level agencies, and the NSC staff. Within the legislative branch, the most prominent examples are the chairs and ranking minority members of the most important congressional committees and their senior staffs.

This conventional analysis of the public's role is pessimistic and negative. It essentially argues that the vast majority of the population knows and cares little about foreign and defense policy issues to the point that their opinions can be largely ignored or easily molded to fit the policy maker's agenda. In this view, only those in the innermost circles—the elite public and the core decision makers—have the experience and expertise to make intelligent decisions on these issues. There is another way to look at the role of the public in foreign policy, however.

Toward a New View of the Public and Foreign Policy

A number of recent findings by U.S. foreign policy scholars have challenged the traditional view of the mass public, suggesting that even they may be more orderly and predictable in how they respond to foreign policy issues than the conventional view would suggest. Indeed, since the Vietnam era, a vast amount of research has focused on these issues and tends to find that the mass public's attitudes about foreign policy are less volatile and more structured than the old view suggests. Research also highlights the potential potency of public opinion about foreign policy endeavors, especially the extent to which presidents and members of Congress feel public pressure and fear public retaliation at the polls. Three such findings are worthy of some further discussion: the importance of the president's view of the public, the "rally" trend mentioned above, and public responses to different kinds of use of force.

One dynamic that conditions how and whether the public plays a role in American foreign policy is what the president thinks about this issue. As Foyle (1999) details, presidents who believe that the incorporation of the public's views into the foreign policy process is important will look for ways to do that; presidents who do not think it is important are less likely even to pay attention. The former view of leadership in a democracy is often called the "delegate" view (such as Bill Clinton), and the latter the "trustee" role (such as George W. Bush).

Foyle goes a step further to point out that presidents may not only differ in the extent to which they take public opinion into account when crafting foreign policy; they may also differ in whether they think public support is necessary to a policy's success. If a president thinks that the support of the public is important (regardless of whether the president wanted to take public opinion into account when crafting the policy), then the president will be far more active in trying to build public support for a policy than would a president who does not think public support matters to a policy's success. There is no one answer to the role of the public in the area of foreign policy, but rather, as Foyle points out, the answer is conditioned by the president's beliefs about what that role should be. Such an understanding helps provide a more nuanced view of the public and foreign policy than the conventional view might provide.

As discussed previously, there is a general tendency for the mass public to "rally" to the president in times of national crisis. Whether in the aftermath of a terrorist attack, such as the attacks of 9/11 or the 1995 bombing of the Alfred P. Murrah Federal Building in Oklahoma City, the mass public tends to rally to support the president in times of emergency. The flip side of the coin can be called a **halo effect**. The idea behind a halo is that the public tends to support the president at higher levels following a military strike that the public sees as quick and successful. Following the 2011 attack that killed Osama bin Laden, for example, public support for the president spiked temporarily. The dynamic here is different from a rally event, because in the rally someone else does something to you; in a halo effect, you initiate the action, but the public views it as quick and successful. Together these trends suggest an underlying order and predictability to the mass public that might not be accounted for in the conventional view.

It is worth pointing out that if political scientists can spot these trends, so too can presidents and their pollsters—and they have access to far more resources to poll the public than social scientists and polling operations do. Some have argued that a president might be tempted to try to take advantage of these trends, especially if their popularity is slipping, and execute some limited use of force, hoping to trigger the halo effect. The fancy name for this (admittedly cynical) view is the **"diversionary theory of war."** A couple of interesting movies are based on this premise: *Wag the Dog* (1997) and *Canadian Bacon* (1995).

There is a significant and complicated debate in the political science literature about the diversionary theory of war. The October 26, 1983, invasion of Grenada (Operation Urgent Fury), for example, happened so close in time to the October 23 bombing of the Marine barracks in Lebanon (which killed 241) that some suggested the Grenada operation was a diversion. Republican critics of President Bill Clinton assailed the cruise missile strikes on Afghanistan and Sudan that he ordered against Al Qaeda following two 1998 U.S. Embassy bombings in Africa because, they said, he was really trying to divert the public's attention from the Monica Lewinsky scandal that had just broken in the press.

Counterexamples also abound that emphasize how risk-averse American presidents are when it comes to risking casualties. They are, after all, politicians who have to stand for reelection; even if they are lame ducks, they care about whether their party holds the White House in future elections. In the summer of 1992, for instance, Saddam Hussein's challenges to the inspection regime agreed to at the end of the Persian Gulf War led many to suggest that President George H. W. Bush should order a bombing campaign against the Iraqi leader. Bush's standing in the polls leading into the 1992 election was so low, however, that some in the media suggested that Bush might use force to divert the public and trigger a halo. Bush did not order an attack, even though one might have been justified, at least in part because of a risk aversion to losing American lives (especially so close to an election). President Obama did not pursue military force against the Assad government in Syria in 2013 in part because of how soft public support was for such a war. Whether or not one subscribes to the diversionary perspective, these trends are so reliable and well documented that they suggest an underlying order to the mass public's view of foreign policy.

Another more recent scholarly development focuses on the way that the mass public may well know more about using force than the conventional view expects. There is a common saying about art: "I don't know much about art, but I know what I like." Well, it turns out that this saying might explain a lot about the mass public and the use of force in American foreign policy, at least since Vietnam. They may not know much about foreign policy, but they know what they like; and it turns out there is a surprising amount of order to their evaluations of foreign military interventions—far more than the Almond-Lippmann consensus would predict. Building on previous examinations of how the mass public responded to growing casualty figures in Vietnam (especially John Mueller's research), Bruce Jentleson's work has led the way.

It is possible to think about using force abroad as serving one of two political purposes: to overthrow the regime in place in a foreign country (regime change), or to force a change in the foreign policy behavior of a foreign country (likely to impose some restraint on their behavior). The mass public is generally wary of using force abroad, seeing it as the last option, but has supported the use of force both after the end of the Cold War and after 9/11 (see intersection 8.2). Its support for foreign military interventions appears to be tempered by the political objective of the operation.

Intersection 8.2   The Public and the War in Afghanistan

The Bill of Rights guarantees free speech, the right to petition the government, and to assemble. Here the people "take it to the streets."

Support for the war in Afghanistan by the mass public has evolved in interesting ways over the course of fifteen years of war. While the public was extremely positive about the war in the early months following the attacks of 9/11, support for the war started to become more complicated in 2005, and since 2009 it has become a very controversial subject with many crosscutting dynamics. In the early months of war, with the quick rout of the Taliban, large majorities of the U.S. public supported the war. When the war began to drag on as an extended counterinsurgency operation, however, an increasing number of Americans began questioning whether the effort and cost—in both lives and dollars—were worth it. By September 2009, for example, only about half of those polled thought troops should stay in Afghanistan. By 2011, a slim majority of Americans preferred that U.S. troops be removed from Afghanistan quickly. In 2015, the public was about evenly divided between those who agreed with President Obama's decision to have some troops remain in Afghanistan after he leaves office and those who disagreed.

At first this trend looks like what one might expect: high levels of support after 9/11 (a "rally" event), followed by declining support as the costs of war mount. Looking more deeply, however, two curious subplots emerge in the story, subplots that highlight the role of partisanship in foreign policy opinions. First, in 2016 the war's strongest supporters identified themselves as Republicans and conservatives—making the war in Afghanistan one of the rare policy areas where President Obama received high levels of support from the opposition party. Second, what one prefers to do with respect to troops in Afghanistan has become even more complicated in recent months because of concerns with the situation in Iraq and Syria and with ISIS. Most of the mass public has never had a class in counterterrorism policy, but they must draw conclusions about it regularly now and in the foreseeable future.

In general terms, there is more public support for the use of force when that use is aimed at forcing foreign policy restraint on an opponent rather than military operations aimed at regime change. Now, of course some military operations can have a dose of both objectives; the strike on Libya in 1986, for example, was both an effort to punish Libya for its support for international terrorism and an effort to kill or perhaps trigger the overthrow of Libya's leader, Muammar Gaddafi. Targets of the strike included, for example, military and intelligence sites thought to support and train terrorists (which sounds like trying to force foreign policy restraint on Libya) as well as on sites where Gaddafi was thought to be sleeping (regime change). In this case, as in others, it is possible to see the pattern of public support based on how different poll questions were asked of the mass public.

When people were asked if they supported the strike on Libya as a way to send a message about terrorism, the support scores were very high; when polls asked if they supported following up the strike with U.S. troops to overthrow Gaddafi, the support scores fell. In case after case, Jentleson's work shows that the mass public supported using force aimed at imposing restraint on an opponent at a generally higher level than they did efforts at overt regime change. That structure—which Jentleson argues is an underlying **"pretty prudent public"**—is far greater than the conventional view would suggest exists.

A couple of caveats are in order. One of the other objectives of U.S. military interventions since the end of the Cold War has been in the context of humanitarian crises. Here the public's reactions have been quite mixed; the early excitement about the possibility of using the American military to help relieve suffering has been tempered by the experiences in Somalia and the long haul in Bosnia. The tragic genocide in Rwanda, however, also reminds the American public of the necessity for some level of activity around these aims. Finally, the public's support for the invasion of Iraq in 2003 perhaps complicates this picture. A large majority of Americans supported that invasion and support held into 2004, although today, according to Gallup polls, most Americans think it was a mistake to send troops to Iraq.

The Changing Relationship between the Public and Foreign Policy

The changing nature of the national security environment caused and stimulated by the collapse of communism and reemphasized by the events of 9/11 and the recent terror attacks around the world connected with ISIS has more than an abstract importance to U.S. citizens. With the Cold War over and thus no apparent need for a huge standing military, during the 1990s the armed forces shrank by more than one-third. Responses to international terrorism, however, including large military actions in Afghanistan and Iraq and smaller ones elsewhere, have placed foreign affairs squarely and unavoidably before the public. This has led to an increase in attention to international affairs by the mass public, as they see foreign events as closer to home than they perhaps did in the past. Still, even this can be fleeting; attention skyrocketed immediately after 9/11, then settled down significantly, and now seems to percolate back up as events capture the public's attention, such as the 2013 Boston Marathon bombing and the ISIS attacks on Paris and Brussels in 2015 and 2016 and Istanbul in 2017.

In the past, national leaders made overt appeals for mass public support only when the most dramatic and personal events occurred, such as those involving peace and war. That situation has certainly changed. Not only are international events more directly relevant and more visible to Americans than before, but also the blurring of domestic and foreign policy—the emergence of intermestic politics—means that more support will have to be generated to back those policies that could affect domestic priorities. The domestic impact of international terrorism in terms of heightened security measures (have you flown on a commercial airliner recently?) and efforts to mobilize public support for those measures are a good example of this dynamic in action—and those efforts all run through some form of media. And it is possible that the very nature of the mass public is about to undergo a shift, in part because of generational change and in part because of the information revolution. Anne-Marie Slaughter, the State Department's policy planning staff director in the first two years of the Obama administration, has argued that today's college students can be thought of as our first truly "global" generation. Coming of age after the end of the Cold War, taking advantage of foreign travel and study abroad, and having access to technologies that allow people to stay in touch regularly and cheaply (by e-mail, text messaging, Facebook, Twitter, and Skype, for example), young people in America are uniquely positioned to see themselves as connected to people and events around the globe. So perhaps the mass public of the future will look more like the interested public of the past. In any event, it is nearly impossible to talk about the role of the public in foreign policy without also talking about the place from which the public gets its news (and often its opinions): the media.

The Media

Media is a shorthand term used to describe those individuals and organizations that collect and disseminate news, information, and interpretations about what is happening in the world. The media are divided historically into the print media, consisting of newspapers and newsmagazines, and the electronic or broadcast media, consisting of radio and television. This distinction, however, has become quite blurred in practice with the emergence of hybrids such as the electronic transmission of newspapers over the Internet and the expansion of Internet-based sources of information. With the emergence of blogs, independent websites, and Facebook pages, to name a few, it is increasingly difficult to draw easy textbook distinctions among the media. Moreover, cross-ownership of various media from different categories may blur the distinctiveness of content in the various forms.

Print Media

The print media are older than the purely electronic broadcast media. Their independence in observing and reporting on the operation of government is included in the First Amendment to the Constitution and was justified as a way to prevent the undue accumulation of power by individuals or governmental institutions. Their independence is assured because all the print media are independently owned by individuals outside government and are unregulated by governmental agencies. Although no one doubts the value of private ownership, it probably does influence the content of news. Privately owned media must make a profit to remain in business, after all (or have an owner with really deep pockets who is willing to take the economic losses), and are thus prone to report what readers and viewers will consume, which is usually late-breaking, spectacular events rather than more reflective matters.

The operative principle to ensure continued independence is the doctrine of "**no prior restraint**" on publication. This doctrine, first articulated in a 1931 Supreme Court case (*Near v. Minnesota*), states that there can be no prior censorship by government of reportage. (A practical exception is reportage of ongoing military campaigns that might provide information to the enemy.) This position was reinforced in the famous 1971 "**Pentagon Papers**" case, *New York Times v. United States*, when the Nixon administration tried to prevent the *Times* from publishing a secret history of American involvement in Vietnam that had been assembled by the government and leaked to the press. Some argue that the dynamics that surround the disclosures by WikiLeaks and the leaks by Edward Snowden bear some resemblance to this historic episode, although most disagree.

The print media cover foreign policy through the major newspapers, magazines, and wire services. Probably the most influential are the key national newspapers, such as the *New York Times* and the *Washington Post*, which have the time and resources to assign reporters and bureaus full-time to coverage of foreign and international events, and the national newspapers or publications that do not have a specific geographical locale (for example, *USA Today*, the *Wall Street Journal*, and the *Christian Science Monitor*). People in the policy process, the elite public, and members of the informed public read the flagship and national papers. The function of the major newsmagazines is to provide depth and interpretation to events initially reported on by the newspapers. Finally, wire services, such as the Associated Press, provide foreign and defense policy news to local newspapers that cannot report on foreign affairs on their own.

Electronic Media

The electronic broadcast media, unlike the print media, are subject to at least cursory regulation through the licensing process of the Federal Communications Commission (FCC). Basically, FCC regulations ensure that radio and television stations do not use transmission bands that interfere with one another's signals; less formally, FCC regulations mandate that in their reportage, the electronic media are expected to honor the principles of equal time to political candidates, the right of rebuttal, and the fairness doctrine in reporting.

The electronic media cover foreign policy issues through the major television and, to a lesser extent radio, networks and report the news to their affiliates. In addition, the emergence of international news–based outlets such as CNN, ITN, and others has created more or less the equivalent of the national newspapers in the form of a television station devoted solely to the news. Local television and radio stations rely on sources, such as the newspaper wire services and television feeds, to report foreign policy news, often covering a local "angle" on foreign policy and international affairs.

The Internet is a constantly evolving and growing source of information, including information about foreign policy and global affairs. It is impossible to count the number of sites covering foreign policy news—some solely, others at least in part—that have emerged in recent years. Some of these are web-based news sources not unlike traditional media; some are sites run by interest groups or think tanks; some are blogs that professional or amateur journalists maintain; some are merely websites that someone around the world has assembled about a certain topic. Unlike the more traditional media, there are few, if any, legal and certainly professional standards regarding the accuracy of what is transmitted over the web. As a result, the consumer of web "news" needs to be more critical about what he or she reads. As increasing numbers of Americans report that the web is their primary source of news, the issue of reliability is likely to become increasingly important.

As a source for news and education about politics and world affairs, the Internet has advantages and disadvantages. Positively, the Internet provides generally free access to an almost endless amount of information, limited only by the ability of the purveyor to link into the "Net" and the ingenuity of "surfers" in accessing those links. Negatively, universality of access means there is little or no filtering of Internet information for accuracy or general content. As a result, the Internet user has little basis for knowing if information obtained from nontraditional Internet sources is correct, and guidelines for assisting in assessing the cogency of Internet information are in their infancy. The explosion of Internet users worldwide, however, means access to those users is of increasing vitality to those with information to share; as long as that access remains unregulated, however, there will continue to be nefarious uses that only the discerning can distinguish.

One factor about the web as a source of information is that there is a huge range of types of sites out there, representing many different perspectives on global events and foreign policy. News through the web is decentralized and increasingly addresses "niche" audiences. Conversely, an additional factor is the partial merger between the Internet and television news and the corporate consolidation that is occurring in the media industry. It is not uncommon for television reporters to have their own websites, to which they direct viewers seeking more in-depth information or background on stories they report; nor is it uncommon for news to be reported by one entity about international affairs when it turns out the news source is materially connected to the news that is being reported. Finding neutral observers is increasingly difficult in the modern media age.

Traditional View of the Media

The media's function in the area of foreign policy, although evolving, has been controversial. To understand how the media stand between the people and the government, we first look at the traditional functions the media perform, noting how they are influenced by the nature of international affairs. The discussion then moves to how technological innovation is changing and expanding those functions.

The media's basic job is to observe and report the activities of government and the actions and thoughts of individual political figures. In this role, the media are sometimes actively sympathetic and cooperative with those about whom they report, and sometimes they are not. The media also serve as watchdogs of the public interest, particularly in areas where they perceive the possibility of breaches of the public trust. In this role, the government and the media are almost always adversaries.

Media activity in the foreign policy area can be thought of in terms of the following four functions. First, they collect and report the news, including what the government is doing. Collecting and reporting news is the most "objective" and least controversial activity in which the media engage, but the nature of foreign policy events complicates this process. Too many events happen around the world for the media to cover all of them simultaneously and with equal depth. Thus, the media are necessarily selective in what they cover and report. A common complaint about the American media in particular is that they only cover news from the developing world in times of wars, natural disasters, and other cataclysmic events. In this sense, the mainstream media might serve an "indexing" function, where news producers decide what stories from a multitude of possibilities are worthy of the public's attention.

The sheer scale and scope of events that occur worldwide also stretches the resources of news-gathering outlets. The downsizing of network news divisions (especially foreign news and the closures of foreign news bureaus) and the consolidation of many newspapers and other news outlets mean that fewer reporters are available to cover foreign news stories, leaving the American media increasingly reliant on foreign news organizations.

Another complicating element of reporting the news is that the media often tailors their coverage to what they see as the audience's interests. Finally, as Daniel Hallin argues, the media will "report" a story differently depending on the circumstances of the story. When a sphere of consensus exists among opinion leaders, the media are likely to reflect that consensus in their reporting (such as in the early years of the Vietnam War). When it becomes clear, however, that there is no consensus, the media are likely to report on this sphere as a "legitimate controversy." The fractured and increasingly partisan media environment might well even prey on such a circumstance—making it look as though controversies exist when there really is little controversy (but it makes for better television to put two people on the air yelling at each other).

A second basic function of the media goes beyond reporting to include investigating the news. Many reporters feel the need to determine the veracity of public pronouncements and to report instances in which they believe the public trust has not been well served (**watchdogging**). This function, which has increased dramatically in the past quarter-century, often places government officials and the media at loggerheads. Scandals around government lying to the public from

Vietnam to Watergate to Iran-Contra helped stoke the sense of importance of this mission of the press. While the public sometimes gets impatient with an "unpatriotic" press, perhaps it is worth remembering that a compliant media does no service to democracy.

A third function of the media is to interpret the news. Because of the public's lack of knowledge of international affairs, explaining the flow of events, and putting them in context and perspective, is a particularly important function. In the absence of media interpretation, the public would have only government officials, whose explanations are often motivated by self-interest and thus may be self-serving, to provide context.

One of the things that makes this controversial is that the national press, both print and electronic, is also alleged to have a liberal bias. Part of the basis for this claim is geographical: the national press is concentrated in New York City and Washington, D.C., which are generally more liberal than much of the rest of the country. It also partly results from the fact that more liberal, reform-minded young men and women tend to be drawn to journalism. Many members of the defense establishment believe this liberal bias is also anti-military, thereby adding to the strained relationship between the media and the military.

An alleged conservative bias in reporting after 9/11 has counterbalanced this perception. Rather than providing critical reportage of the conservative Bush administration's foreign and domestic policies, the counterargument is that the media were cowed into accepting and uncritically reporting the administration's "line" out of a fear of political retribution or criticism. And beyond that, media enterprises are businesses and are generally owned by bigger businesses that have profits in mind, and so there may be a level of corporate bias in how these organizations are run.

Another consideration is that foreign policy interpretation must occur largely in close proximity to events, when their full meaning cannot be known and when some or all of the parties involved may be directed to keep certain facts secret. The danger of the media's "instant analysis" is that when false interpretations of events are offered and accepted, they may continue to affect perceptions even after corrections have been made.

A fourth function might be called agenda setting. Do the media through their reporting essentially set the foreign policy agenda to which the government must respond, by driving attention to some issues and away from others? Those who worry about whether this dynamic occurs point to the television age and the power of images as part of the culprit for this. Foreign policy issues are normally complex and controversial, requiring considerable sharing of information with a public that is unequipped to make its own judgments. Television, however, is the medium of the short, pithy explanation; the thirty-second sound bite with a vivid optical imprint, the specialty of television, is quite unlike the leisurely analysis provided by some newspapers, magazines, and websites. Network news stories are rarely more than ninety seconds long, which may not be long enough to form other than cursory impressions—but the impressions that can be formed by even a brief image can be lasting and motivating, whether the image of a refugee child from Syria or the victim of violent extremism in Brussels.

Impact of the Digital Revolution

A series of technologies associated with the enormous growth in knowledge generation and dissemination is transforming the modern world of production, economics, politics, and communications. In ways that are hard for practitioners or scholars to fully understand, these advances are changing the conduct and patterns of international affairs, the way they are reported, and even the way policy is made.

Global television and social networking sites, such as Facebook and Twitter, are a prime factor in these changes. Digital advances have made the world increasingly transparent to media coverage and reporting. When we combine with this the ability to virtually reach out almost everywhere with technologies such as the smartphone, and to travel just about anywhere very quickly, there is very little that happens in the world that the media—and any regular person with a smartphone and a data connection—cannot observe and report if they choose to do so, which changes substantially how governments do their business.

One impact of this development on the policy process is sometimes called **"media diplomacy,"** whereby governments conduct some of their relationships with other governments by sending information about positions and the like back and forth through interviews with news outlets. China is well known for this, making news, for example, in the South China Sea as a way of altering the status quo of negotiations over the access to the high seas in the area. When the nuclear deal between key Western powers and Iran was being negotiated, those negotiations not only took place in private among the diplomats, but also in public in the form of press conferences where the sides would send signals to each other and to their own respective publics about the outlines of such a deal. Critics were also able to intrude on negotiations in this same way, whether those critics were in the U.S. Congress or the government of Israel—they all knew how to find a microphone and a video camera. President Trump has perhaps taken this to an all new level with his use of Twitter.

At one level, the way the media cover events influences public perceptions and thus helps structure the responses that the government can make. At the same time, media figures such as the major news anchors on cable television, and even talk show hosts on late-night television such as Stephen Colbert, can become important opinion leaders about world affairs. As a result of the global reach of the electronic media, the volume of material to which the public and policy makers are potentially exposed will continue to expand exponentially. Through their choices of what to publicize among a volume of events and issues beyond their ability to broadcast and the public's capacity to absorb, the media will help define the public agenda. This same increased volume and diversity of coverage means that the public will be exposed to more and more unfamiliar situations for which they will require interpretation. Media elites will fill at least part of that role. Electronic experts, as we discussed in the previous chapter—academics from the universities and think tanks, former government officials, and retired military officers who possess the knowledge of global issues—will also play such a role.

Has this new digital media age actually changed the way foreign policy is made in America, though? There has been much speculation about a **"CNN effect,"** or the idea that there is an impact of the twenty-four-hour news cycle and omnipresent Internet reality on the foreign policy process; however, there are few clear answers. The idea that the media can single-handedly set the foreign policy agenda by its decisions about what to show and what not to show, while tempting, misses the reliance of the mainstream media on the government itself for news about the world. With the closures of most foreign bureaus around the globe, the American press mostly collects its foreign news from briefings and leaks from the White House, the Defense Department, and the State Department. The influence road between the media and the government can run in both directions.

One effect that participants in the policy process seem to agree on is that the modern media age forces the policy process to speed up. The days when a president could sit on news for a week or more, as President Kennedy did in the 1962 Cuban Missile Crisis, are gone; private satellite companies, such as the ones that produce the images for Google Earth, would have found those missile launchers. The policy process probably has to go faster today than in the past and be more mindful of how events and policy can be susceptible to "spin" as well.

One obvious negative effect of this dynamic is that it is most likely the case that events are happening faster and are more interconnected than in the past; in a global village, we are all much more closely linked than in the past. And yet just at the time when things are more complicated and interconnected, policy makers have to make decisions faster and with more partial information; and they do so in a far more politically polarized public opinion environment. This is, in fact, one of the central challenges of making foreign policy in this new era.

One other relatively recent development in the media-public-government relationship is worth mentioning: the emergence of **"soft news"** about foreign policy, meaning news that takes more of a "human interest" angle. A "hard news" program about the war on terrorism, for example, would cover up-to-date statistics about casualties, troop deployments, and counterterrorism and counterinsurgency strategies. Soft news, on the other hand, might focus on the story of a wounded marine and his life before and after deployment to Afghanistan. Soft news is more focused on entertaining than fully informing the viewer (and is cheaper to produce with higher profit margins than either shows with many actors and elaborate scripts and sets, or hard news programs such as *60 Minutes* or *Frontline*).

While members of the informed public and elites may not find much value in soft news, it is interesting that in *Soft News Goes to War*, for example, Matthew Baum finds some evidence that being exposed to an issue through a soft news program can lead viewers at least some of the time to want to learn more about that issue, and they then turn to "harder" news. This might be a pathway to help move people from the ranks of the mass, disinterested public into the ranks of the interested public—or beyond.

One thing is certain: the pace of change in this area is so fast that it is hard to predict what the media environment will be like even in the near future. A few years ago if you had said that Turkish president Erdogan would use a FaceTime message to help fight back a coup attempt, as happened in July 2016, and that a site on the Internet was tracking his plane as it headed out of Turkey, circled, and then returned, you would have sounded crazy—but it happened. The media environment within which foreign policy is made and by which the public is educated and perhaps led will no doubt continue to evolve rapidly—posing a challenge to policy makers and citizens alike.

Conclusion

The roles of both the public and the media in the foreign policy–making process are changing. In the past, the traditional roles of both were relatively modest. The general public was basically compliant and reactive, allowing the elite to craft policy unless it went beyond public tolerance written in the most general terms. As for the media, they always focused more on the domestic agenda because they lacked the physical and technological ability to report extensively and in a timely fashion on all but a thin slice of international reality.

Both circumstances have changed. As the boundary between domestic and foreign policy has blurred and the direct, personal impact of foreign policy has increased, so has the public interest. In the days of the Cold War, the content of what the public was exposed to was more heavily oriented toward national security. With the Cold War over, international economic foreign policy factors became more important for a time, as were glaring abuses of the human condition. These issues are less abstract and more personal: they affect jobs and livelihoods and hence have greater salience than, say, the deterrent effect of a particular ballistic missile. The events of 9/11 swung public and media attention back to national security and patriotic fervor over how to deal with these newly identified enemies.

From this change may come greater public interest in foreign policy, gradually widening the population that forms the "interested public." However, access to reliable and unbiased information about these complicated events is increasingly hard to come by. Our extremely partisan politics have come to the foreign policy domain, and many are concerned that the modern media realities that surround the public and the policy-making process serve to pull us further apart.

The digital revolution has been more important in expanding the media's role in the foreign policy area than in domestic politics. All advances of this revolution are enhancing the media's ability to cover the domestic scene, although that ability was already present in abundance. The capacity to cover and interpret foreign policy events was always more circumspect, bounded by the speed with which oral descriptions and pictures could be transmitted from the far-flung corners of the globe. Technology has now made it as physically possible for news organizations based in New York City or Washington to air news about events in Africa as it is to cover occurrences in Ohio.

The public and the media share more than an individually enhanced role in the foreign policy–making process. Their roles are also intertwined. In the past, a basic limitation on the public's ability to receive and interpret information was timely access to information. Now, the availability of timely information has exploded. Can this help shrink the proportion of the public that is uninformed and uninterested in foreign affairs, and help make foreign policy more "democratic?" Or does it make foreign policy another set of issues that brews in the toxic stew that is our partisan and ideological divide? Only time will tell.

Study/Discussion Questions

1. In what ways does democracy depend on the public and the press for its health? Why does the foreign policy domain make that relationship more complicated?
2. What is the conventional view of the role of the American public in the foreign policy process? In what ways is that view at least incomplete?
3. What is a "rally?" What is a "halo?" How might leaders try to take advantage of these trends?
4. What kinds of media bias are relevant for our understanding of the role of the media in the foreign policy process?

5. What is "soft news," and how is it related to the uninformed public?
6. How has twenty-four-hour cable news and the increasing reach of the Internet altered the relationship between the U.S. government and the media?
7. What advantages over the media does the U.S. government still enjoy?
8. How has the modern media environment both made it easier and also harder for citizens to learn about foreign policy? How has it made it easier and harder for decision makers?

Bibliography

Alterman, Eric. *Who Speaks for America? Why Democracy Matters in Foreign Policy.* Ithaca, NY: Cornell University Press, 1998.
Baum, Matthew A. *Soft News Goes to War: Public Opinion and American Foreign Policy in the New Media Age.* Princeton, NJ: Princeton University Press, 2003.
Bishop, Bill, with Robert G. Cushing. *The Big Sort: Why the Clustering of Like-Minded America Is Tearing Us Apart.* New York: Houghton Mifflin, 2008.
Brace, Paul, and Barbara Hinckley. *Follow the Leader: Opinion Polls and the Modern Presidents.* New York: Basic, 1992.
Brody, Richard A. *Assessing the President: The Media, Elite Opinion, and Public Support.* Stanford, CA: Stanford University Press, 1991.
Cohen, Bernard C. *The Public's Impact on Foreign Policy.* Boston: Little, Brown, 1973.
Everts, Philip, and Pierangelo Isernia, eds. *Public Opinion and the International Uses of Force.* New York: Routledge, 2001.
Farnsworth, Stephen J., and S. Robert Lichter. *The Mediated Presidency: Television News and Presidential Governance.* Lanham, MD: Rowman & Littlefield, 2006.
Fiorina, Morris P., with Samuel J. Abrams and Jeremy C. Pope. *Culture War? The Myth of a Polarized America.* 3rd ed. New York: Longmans, 2010.
Foyle, Douglas C. *Counting the Public In: Presidents, Public Opinion, and Foreign Policy.* New York: Columbia University Press, 1999.
Fried, Amy. *Muffled Echoes: Oliver North and the Politics of Public Opinion.* New York: Columbia University Press, 1997.
Gladwell, Malcolm. "Small Change: Why the Revolution Will Not Be Tweeted." *New Yorker,* October 4, 2010.
Hallin, Daniel C. *The Uncensored War: The Media and Vietnam.* New York: Oxford University Press, 1986.
———. *We Keep America on Top of the World: Television Journalism and the Public Sphere.* New York: Routledge, 1994.

Himelfarb, Sheldon, and Sean Aday. "Media That Moves Millions." *Foreign Policy*, January 17, 2014.

Holsti, Ole R. *Public Opinion and American Foreign Policy.* Ann Arbor: University of Michigan Press, 1997.

Jacobs, Lawrence R., and Robert Y. Shapiro. *Politicians Don't Pander: Political Manipulation and the Loss of Democratic Responsiveness.* Chicago: University of Chicago Press, 2000.

Jentleson, Bruce W. "The Pretty Prudent Public: Post Post-Vietnam American Opinion on the Use of Military Force." *International Studies Quarterly* 36 (1992): 49–74.

Jentleson, Bruce, and Rebecca L. Britton. "Still Pretty Prudent: Post-Cold War American Public Opinion on the Use of Military Force." *Journal of Conflict Resolution* 42 (1998): 395–417.

Kull, Steven, and I. M. Destler. *Misreading the Public: The Myth of a New Isolationism.* Washington, DC: Brookings, 1999.

Mueller, John E. *Policy and Opinion in the Gulf War.* Chicago: University of Chicago Press, 1994.

———. *War, Presidents and Public Opinion.* New York: Wiley, 1973.

Nacos, Brigitte L., Robert Y. Shapiro, and Pierangelo Isernia, eds. *Decisionmaking in a Glass House: Mass Media, Public Opinion, and American and European Foreign Policy in the 21st Century.* Lanham, MD: Rowman & Littlefield, 2000.

Robinson, Piers. *The CNN Effect: The Myth of News Media, Foreign Policy and Intervention.* New York: Taylor & Francis, 2002.

Shirky, Clay. "The Political Power of Social Media." *Foreign Affairs*, January/February 2011.

Smith, Perry M. *How CNN Fought the* War: *A View from the Inside.* New York: Carol, 1991.

Sobel, Richard. *The Impact of Public Opinion on U.S. Foreign Policy since Vietnam.* New York: Oxford University Press, 2001.

Spragens, William C. *The Presidency and the Mass Media in the Age of Television.* Washington, DC: University Press of America, 1979.

Strobel, Warren P. *Late-Breaking Foreign Policy: The News Media's Influence on Peace Operations.* Washington, DC: U.S. Institute of Peace Press, 1997.

Sunstein, Cass R. *Republic.com 2.0.* Princeton, NJ: Princeton University Press, 2007.

Wittkopf, Eugene R. *Faces of Internationalism: Public Opinion and American Foreign Policy.* Durham, NC: Duke University Press, 1990.

9 National Security Policy and Problems

Retired Army Lt. General Michael Flynn was named the president's national security advisor, but later resigned. He is shown testifying to Congress before his retirement.

Preview

National security policy is the most prominent aspect of American foreign policy since World War II and the Cold War. Understanding the nature and importance of this area requires looking at it through the lens of national interests, threats, and risks, and how calculations about those important values apply to various ways of looking at national security problems and solutions. This analysis can then be applied to the most important national security concerns of the United States in the contemporary world. These include unstable states and their asymmetrical conflicts, described here as developing world internal conflicts (DWICs), terrorism, and the combination of these destabilizing influences in the Middle East, most notably the struggle in the Levant with the Islamic State.

Key Concepts

isolationism

liberal interventionism

realism

internationalism

survival interest

feasibility

interest-threat mismatch

conventional (symmetrical) warfare

unconventional (asymmetrical)
   warfare

threat-force mismatch

multinationalism

civil wars

developing world internal conflicts
   (DWICs)

cost-tolerance

lone wolf terrorists

terrorism suppression

anti-terrorism

counterterrorism

In its April 2016 edition, the *Atlantic* magazine featured an article titled "The Obama Doctrine." Written by Jeffrey Goldberg and based primarily on extensive interviews with the former president over a period of years, the article offers considerable insight into both how Obama viewed the world and how he organized and directed the country's national security efforts. The contours of that policy provide the context within which the new president must approach the same enduring issues, including those parts to be accepted, rejected, or amended. Understanding the Obama legacy provides the stepping-off point both for President Trump and for those who seek to understand the American national security stance in the world.

When he came to office in January 2009, Obama inherited a highly militarized national security situation that included, most prominently, American wars in both Iraq and Afghanistan, engagements initiated by his predecessor, George W. Bush. He had vowed during the 2008 campaign to end both conflicts—especially the war in Iraq. His reasoning, as recorded by Goldberg, included the belief that "rhetoric should be weaponized sparingly, if at all, in today's more ambiguous and complicated international arena." In its place, Obama developed a notion that force should be used much less often. He phrased this intention colorfully, arguing that the first task of his new presidency should be "Don't do stupid s——." This pungent observation applied particularly to what he viewed as an almost knee-jerk tendency to militarize situations as part of what he called the Washington "playbook." As he put it, "What I think is not smart is the idea that every time there is a problem, we send in our military to impose order. We just can't do that."

Because the use or threat of force is a major tool in the traditional kitbag of national security policy, the idea of a much more restrained view of when to use force—and especially major applications of force—is one on the most controversial elements of the Obama foreign policy legacy and one that his detractors tried to depict as being outside the foreign policy mainstream. Obama countered by depicting different approaches to thinking about foreign (including national security) policy in a four-cell scheme. One cell of that scheme was **isolationism**, the general attempt to withdraw from world events and leave their solution to others, an approach he dismissed as unworkable in a complex, interdependent environment. A second was **liberal interventionism**, the general proposition that the United States must be willing to use its military power to influence events widely in support of American values. He rejected this position, largely associated with neoconservatives, on the basis that its application tended to overuse and overextend American assets.

The two other positions come closer to the Obama view. He views himself as an adherent to **realism**, a philosophy described in chapter 1 that largely views the world in terms of the hierarchy of interests a country has and uses that hierarchy to order responses to challenges to interests, as discussed in the next section. The most important single tenet of realism in this view is to reserve the commitment of force to situations where vital interests are engaged. Finally, there is **internationalism**, the policy preference to engaging other states in foreign policy actions, a predilection Obama showed in areas such as the anti-IS coalition, negotiating an arms control agreement with Iran, and dealing with Libya, all to the exasperation of some of his detractors.

Trump gave early indications of liberal interventionism in areas such as policy toward Russia and Israel, and so the new administration may seek to tweak the Obama approach or try to reverse most of the framework it has inherited. Regardless of its preferences, it will have to act within a framework where it organizes questions of interests, threats, and risks and where it must develop approaches to dealing with the major and enduring problems the country faces.

National Security and Foreign Policy

National security and foreign policy are highly interrelated concepts. In principle, foreign policy is the fundamental, overriding concept, since it by definition deals with all aspects of the country's interactions with the outside world, including its intermestic elements. National security, on the other hand, deals with foreign and domestic threats to the United States: the officer's oath administered to commissioned officers of the armed forces includes the promise to "defend the Constitution of the United States against all enemies, foreign and domestic." In its most common expression, the national security segment is thought of as that part of foreign policy that deals with the threat or use of military force to achieve U.S. goals.

The relationship between the concepts is more complicated than that simple dichotomy, and has been since the end of World War II. As the relationship developed in the Cold War, national security concerns rose in importance to being the penultimate problem of foreign policy to the point that the two ideas seemed interchangeable. As noted earlier, the elevation of national security to equality with more general foreign policy was reflected in the National Security Act's elevation of the secretary of defense to coequal status with that of the secretary of state in the NSC. The relationship is further complicated by the emergence of other federal efforts such as the intelligence community and homeland security with a primarily national security component.

The emphasis on national security thus reflects the general militarization of foreign policy concerns in the past two-thirds of a century. The threat posed by the communist world had politico/diplomatic and economic elements, but it was primarily a militarily based danger that naturally elevated the custodians of the traditional instrument of national security—the military—to a heightened role. The communist threat has disappeared, but the influence remains in at least two ways. First, the tendency to view foreign policy through a national security mind-set remains a prominent part of the "playbook" that Obama describes and is a first option when crises arise within the foreign policy establishment. Second, the major threat of the twenty-first century has been international terrorism, which is certainly a national security problem with a strong military element.

The role of national security in foreign policy can be clarified by putting it into the framework of interests, threats, and risks introduced in chapter 2. Interests, it will be recalled, are conventionally divided into vital and less-than-vital (LTV) categories, with the tolerability of adverse outcomes the cleaving point between the two. The most extreme form of vital interest is the **survival interest**, referring to whether the country can physically survive a threat made to it. The quintessential example was the Cold War nuclear balance between the United States and the Soviet Union, where each possessed the physical capability to destroy one another as functioning societies. This threat was clearly military (if genocidal), and its solution was also military (the possession of adequate retaliatory forces to make an initial attack suicidal, or deterrence). Some would argue that environmental degradation, a nonmilitary problem, has the potential to threaten survival as well. Other interests fall progressively below this threshold, from still very important interests (e.g., the sanctity of allies) to LTV interests that inconvenience but do not intolerably affect the country. One of the sources of disagreement about the relative role of national security is when these less imperiling conditions warrant the recourse to the primary instrument of national security, military force.

Threats refer to policies, statements, and actions by foreign entities—states, or more recently nonstate actors—that promise to endanger or deny basic American rights. The most extreme, parallel to and deriving from survival interests, are existential threats, promises to take actions threatening the existence of the state and the lives of its members. Once again, Soviet nuclear forces posed the clearest existential threat in U.S. foreign policy history. That threat has largely dissipated since the breakup of the Soviet Union, and although, according to the *Bulletin of the Atomic Scientists*, Russia maintained about 1,600 nuclear warheads in 2014 capable of hitting U.S. targets, this threat is no longer considered imminent. Most observers, including prominently the former president, do not believe that terrorism poses a threat of this magnitude.

The policy tension between those who view foreign policy in more militarized terms and those who do not should be the question of when the United States should consider military, national security solutions to foreign policy problems. All other threats are, by definition, less severe than existential threats, and the question is when a particular threat should be met with American force and when it should not. The Bush administration took a more liberal interventionist position that included a greater willingness to use or threaten force, a position with roots in the Cold War paradigm. The Obama administration took a much more realist/internationalist position that suggested the military option as more of a last resort. As Obama himself put it in the *Atlantic* interview, "One of the reasons I am so focused on taking actions multilaterally where our vital interests are not at stake is that multilateralism regulates hubris." He added, "Real power means you get what you want without having to exert violence."

The relative importance of national security in overall foreign policy will be a major concern for the Trump administration. The Bush and Obama experiences offer post-9/11 bookends on the predilection to use force from which to choose: the Bush neoconservatives advocating a much more expansive view on the utility of force than the Obama foreign policy. How that debate plays out will have a major influence on whether a new foreign/national security paradigm emerges and what its content and direction may be. That debate will be influenced by at least three concerns as the country decides how it will deal with the risks that different approaches ameliorate or leave.

The first concern deals with the determination of those interests that do or do not require potential military responses. It is largely a debate between the realists, who argue that force should be reserved for truly vital interests, and the liberal interventionists, who argue that the criterion of vitality should be relaxed and that force should be considered to secure a broader range of interests. The two predilections help frame the relative emphasis on traditional foreign policy instruments such as diplomacy and military force as the primary instrument of policy implementation.

The other two concerns condition that debate. The second concern is with **feasibility**, the extent or likelihood that military force will actually be effective in securing whatever interests are at play in a given situation. It has been an integral part of conventional thinking rooted in the Cold War paradigm that military force can be useful, even decisive, in securing American interests in a broad variety of situations, and as a result, whenever a threatening situation emerges, a first reaction among the traditional national security elite is an advocacy of the resort to American force. The response to the Islamic State (discussed below) is a prime example, leavened by the inability of American arms to secure American interests in Iraq and Afghanistan during the 2000s. Defenders of military efficacy in a broad range of situations argue that failure tends to be the result of too restrictive applications of force. Realists maintain that an automatic recourse to military options tends to degrade the situations into which force is contemplated and leads to its insertion into situations where it is not relevant. Obama puts it pithily: "Dropping bombs on someone to prove you're willing to drop bombs on someone is just about the worst reason to use force." The feasibility of using national security tools to solve foreign policy problems will certainly be a hotly debated topic for the new administration.

The final consideration is the cost of military responses to foreign policy problems and raises a cost-risk consideration to national security concerns. Cost can have different elements. In national security discussions, the common dichotomy is conventionally described as "blood and treasure." The first element includes the degree to which American military lives are put at risk: how much American blood is justified by a military response in a given situation. In contemporary discussions, this dimension is often not highlighted, for reasons suggested in intersection 9.1. Treasure refers to actual expenditures on defense, and in the 2016 presidential campaign, candidate Trump vowed sizable increases while questioning the amount of military activity the United States could *afford* in the future.

Intersection 9.1	The AVF and the Cost of American Blood

The calculus of expending American blood and treasure has been different since 1972 than it was before then. Prior to the end of that year, all young Americans were subject to involuntary military service that potentially included being sent into combat and shedding their blood in support of American interests. Conscription (the draft) was suspended in 1972 at least partially because increasing numbers of Americans had come to believe that this potential sacrifice in the name of Vietnam was no longer acceptable. The All-Volunteer Force (AVF) has provided the vehicle for procuring the human power to carry out American use of military force since 1972. No American who has not volunteered for military service—and all its dangers and vulnerabilities—has faced involuntary service and the potential loss of their lives without their consent since.

The AVF has been extremely popular, and it is unlikely there will be any serious challenge to it in the near future. The only possible exception would be a major war of the size of World War II—or Vietnam—for which the AVF could not obtain enough volunteers to meet military needs. This reality is a great comfort to most Americans (including most of the people reading this book), but it may have consequences for the debate over the use of American force.

The fact of invulnerability to forced service means that most Americans—and their leaders who might choose to send forces into harm's way—have no personal stake in military decisions. Young people have "no skin in the game" in the sense that no military decision is likely to affect their personal lives unless they choose to become involved by volunteering, and decision makers do not have to include possible repercussions if their constituents or their families will be put at physical risk because of their decisions. The AVF makes average Americans and policy makers "bulletproof"—literally.

Does this make it easier for politicians to support the use of force rather than other foreign policy options? More to the point, does it make it *too* easy to advocate such courses of action? Would foreign policy decisions be more responsible if those who made those decisions knew they were putting unwilling Americans at risk of their lives? Does the AVF make the price of American blood too affordable?

The rush and trauma of events can assault a cool, rational process of policy calculation, and the contemporary environment clearly demonstrates that difficulty. The dual terrorist attacks in Paris on November 13, 2015, and in Brussels on March 22, 2016, created an entirely understandable sense of rage both in Europe and the United States that included calls for robust military retaliation against the territory occupied by the Islamic State. The stated purposes were both to punish those who had presumably authorized and orchestrated the attacks and to begin the bloody process of violently destroying IS. The goal was, in the minds of most Westerners, laudable, but did the emotion of the moment cloud rational calculation of interest levels (at least for the United States), feasibility, and cost?

The answers were not as crystalline as advocates on either side (realist or liberal interventionist) would portray them. Instead, they reflected the complex, often ambiguous and ambivalent, international environment in which national security policy now exists. The main elements in the confusing, changing, and often contradictory environment include major instability and the potential for violence in much of the developing world, the emergence of an enduring, dangerous outbreak of terrorism emanating mostly from the unstable regions, and a concentration of both those unsettling developments in the Middle East. The factors are clearly linked and even sequential. Understanding each and its dynamics is necessary to crafting and sustaining national security policy. These kinds of events will recur, and Trump will have to learn how to deal with them.

National Security Challenges

The contemporary world is a national security planner's nightmare. Unlike the Cold War, when the threat was very deadly (the existential threat of nuclear holocaust) and fixed (the enduring Soviet menace), the current environment for planning is much more fluid and indeterminate. This observation is particularly true when viewed through the interest-threat-risk lens.

It is sometimes said that interests do not change much, but that threats to them do. The most important American national interests have always begun with homeland protection and sanctity and extended to those parts of the world where the United States has an important stake—traditionally Europe and parts of Asia. Other parts of the world have been of lesser presence to the United States and thus of descending national security concern. During the Cold War, those interests and threats to them coincided, making it conceptually easy to align policy with dangers to be frustrated. Today, however, that has changed, and the situation is one of **interest-threat mismatch.** This means that the most important threats in the world are not toward the most important American interests. The terrorist threat to Western Europe is an exception. For the most part, the threats to stability and peace are concentrated in the developing world, where the United States has fewer interests. Hence, there is a mismatch: America's most important interests are hardly threatened, and the threats that do exist are in places hardly interesting to the United States. Parts of the Middle East have been an exception.

Physical threats and how to deal militarily with them are similarly misaligned. The U.S. armed forces have been designed to fight against similarly armed and organized national armed forces in the European tradition—what is known as **conventional or symmetrical warfare** (fighting conducted by similar forces fighting similarly under similar rules of engagement or ROEs). The violence that occurs now, however, is **unconventional or asymmetrical warfare** (fighting conducted by unlike combatants employing different means and ROEs). Much of the purpose of asymmetrical warfare is to frustrate the efforts of conventional forces. The result for the United States is difficult in two ways. First, these conflicts occur in places and over issues in which the United States has not traditionally had enough interest to justify military force under realist guidelines. Second is the **threat-force mismatch**, where the forces of the United States are clearly relevant and effective for fighting wars that no longer occur (e.g., symmetrical wars in Europe) but are not designed for or particularly effective against asymmetrical foes.

These dilemmas extend to the calculation of risk that, if not always expressed that way, is what much of the debate about national security is currently about. Historically, the calculation of national security has been to eliminate the most important, threatening problems first, and when resources are all committed, to leave other, presumably less important, priorities at risk. That calculation works when there is no interest-threat mismatch, but when there is, the hierarchy of concerns that must be serviced is far less clear, and the policy debate becomes over what problems must be countered and what can be left at risk. The current situation takes shape in these terms.

The Environment: Developing World Violence—the DWICs

Although it was largely ignored as a national security problem at the time, there were two major international trends with national security implications that emerged from World War II. The most obvious was the Cold War, and it appropriately received the most attention in national security policy development and implementation: had it not been successfully managed, the results would have been catastrophic. That concentration, however, diverted attention from the second trend, which has come to dominate national security concern in the post–Cold War world. That trend was decolonization of most of the developing world, especially in Africa and Asia. Decolonization was an outgrowth of the second world conflagration, because the traditional colonial powers were too weakened by the war effort to retain control of their far-flung empires. In 1945, most of mankind lived under colonial rule; by 1975, that bondage had largely disappeared. The resulting residue was the seedbed of contemporary instability and violence.

The basic problem was that the postcolonial map of the world was flawed. For the most part, the retreating colonialists granted independence to new states whose boundaries conformed to the borders of the colonial unit from which they sprang. In parts of Asia and almost all of Africa and the Middle East, those boundaries were unnatural, bringing together into artificial states aggregations of peoples with very different loyalties, traditions, religions, and histories whose only commonality had been that they were inhabitants of the same colony and were happy to see the European colonialists leave. In some cases, the citizens of these new states were able to overcome their differences enough to evolve into reasonably stable states. In others, they were not, and these states became the incubators of contemporary violence and instability.

The basic dilemma these artificial states shared was **multinationalism**, the condition where people of different national loyalties live within a common state. Nationality may be defined in various ways: ethnicity, language, physical appearance, common heritage, and perceived common experience are examples. In multinational states, the peoples are in close proximity to one another, and there is a good chance they have been rivals or even enemies who have been in conflict for a long time. In some new African states, for instance, some coastal tribes had moved inland, captured members of other tribes, and sold them into slavery, receiving in return weaponry to capture more members of groups that became postcolonial fellow citizens. In parts of the Middle East, clan-based blood feuds literally date back to Biblical times. The task before these newly independent citizens was to overcome their differences and to form new national political entities. Making the job more difficult was that in most cases, the new states were extremely poor and lacked an educated population capable of developing and leading these new entities.

The result was an instability that has boiled over into violence in many places. Usually, these wars are primarily internal or **civil wars**, contests between political opponents within existing states for the control of government. Because the borders within which these conflicts occur are both artificial and porous, fighting often spreads across borders in both directions: internal elements broadening their theaters of operation beyond state boundaries, or like-minded outsiders coming to the aid of one side or another. At heart, however, the basic dynamic of these conflicts is that they pit internal factions in violent conflict. They are, in other words, **developing world internal conflicts (DWICs)**.

Snow has developed the DWIC concept in several works (see *Thinking about National Security* and *The Case Against Military Intervention*) to emphasize two basic points about these kinds of violence that are the dominant form of extreme instability in the contemporary world. For now, at least, traditional, European-style interstate warfare between sovereign states has largely disappeared. Interstate wars became impractical during the Cold War, since countries that might otherwise have fought were generally on opposing sides in that conflict, and their engagement might raise the possibility of superpower engagement that could escalate to nuclear war. The last time the United States was involved in a traditional war was in Korea between 1950 and 1953.

Korea served as a harbinger of changes in the pattern of who fights. At one level, Korea was a traditional interstate war: the sovereign state of North Korea (the Democratic People's Republic of Korea or DPRK) invaded the sovereign state of South Korea (the Republic of Korea or ROK). These were, however, essentially artificial states formed from occupation zones in 1945, so the DPRK aggression was also a war of reunification, a civil war in its intent. Moreover, like wars to come, it featured outside intervention by sovereign states (the United States and the United Nations on the side of the ROK, China on the DPRK side), making the war both civil and international in terms of participants. This pattern would be reinforced in Vietnam, where North and South Vietnam (also artificial states) received material assistance on both sides in a war of unification (essentially a civil war).

This pattern evolved further since the end of the Cold War into the dominant pattern of DWICs. The end of the Cold War erased ideological competition for advantage in the developing world, where most of the violence resided, from the picture. At the same time, almost all of the countries of the developed world reached an informal accord that essentially said warfare between them was no longer thinkable. Since these were the places and countries that had engaged in traditional interstate warfare, there was nobody left with whom to fight such wars. A few isolated anomalies exist in the remnants of the old Soviet Union such as Ukraine, but these also have historic aspects: Russian interest in Ukraine has roots both in traditional Russian spheres of influence and paternalism regarding the fate of Ukrainians of Russian ethnicity.

What has evolved as the dominant form of conflict and violence is captured in the dual concepts in the DWIC term. The first part of the distinction is that most instability and violence occurs in the developing world, and especially in parts of Asia (notably the Middle East) and in Africa. These areas, unsurprisingly, are where the greatest imperfections in the postcolonial map have occurred, where the results have produced the highest instances of multinationalism as a stimulus to disorder and violence, and where generally unpromising economic situations provide the kindling for the fires of discontent. The problems differ somewhat from region to region: most of the violence in Africa, for instance, is tribal, with some overlay of religion due to conversion by Muslims and Christians. Some states have managed reasonably to accommodate their differences, but in the most diverse countries, including places where there is some basis for some material progress (e.g., Nigeria, Sudan), the penchant for violence is greatest. The Middle East, on the other hand, did not emerge from formal colonialism after World War II, but rather from mandated control after World War I. Deep and often cross-cutting bases for incompatibility leading to violence mark a number of the highly imperfect resulting states. Iraq and Syria, featured in a later section, are particularly vivid cases in point.

The other distinction is that these conflicts are almost all internal conflicts where the basic reasons for instability reside within national populations who cannot or will not reconcile those differences in a manner that will produce integrated national societies. Because of ethnic, religious, linguistic, cultural, or historical differences that often overlay one another, hatreds are great and seem resolvable only by one group or another seizing power and using that power at the expense of other groups. These societies are polarized in ways far deeper and more irresolvable than contemporary political divisions among Americans, which pale by comparison.

There are two major consequences for the outside world of the internal nature of these wars. First, internal wars are particularly desperate, personalized conflicts where the consequences of victory and defeat can be personal and group survival. As a result, they tend to be more emotional and absolute than conventional wars. Among other things, this means outside efforts to mediate them have limited success. DWICs hardly ever end with negotiated peaceful solutions. Sometimes there are interim interruptions in the fighting (e.g., the conflict between Sudan and its seceded area, South Sudan), but these are the exceptions, not the rule. Second, attempts to intervene and aid in or impose a settlement by outsiders hardly ever have positive outcomes.

From an American viewpoint, dealing with these situations is exacerbated by the level of American interests that are generally at stake. That the United States does not have long-standing interests in most of the developing world stems from two sources. First, most of the places where DWICs occur were colonies until the post–Cold War period; they were the colonial power's problem, and thus were not on the American radar. Second, before the end of World War II, the United States consciously eschewed a major global role and limited its international concerns to Europe and, to a lesser degree, other parts of the Western Hemisphere (the American empire wrested from Spain and dependencies such as Hawaii, Alaska, and the U.S. Virgin Islands were partial exceptions). With the exception of a growing interest in Middle Eastern oil, those interests never really grew much during the Cold War, except as a sideshow competition for influence with the Soviet Union or China.

The places DWICs occur are thus, by and large, parts of the interest-threat mismatch and thus not automatically relevant for national security concern or for the development of anything resembling a uniform policy toward the DWIC phenomenon. The calculation of how the United States should view these situations has thus been essentially ad hoc and idiosyncratic, a matter of deciding on an individual basis what, if any, level of American activism should be applied when different places explode.

The trio of concerns introduced earlier (interests, feasibility, and cost) can be applied to these situations. In most cases, the severity of American interests at play in DWICs is generally problematic and arguable. It is hardly ever unambiguously true that anything approaching vital American interests becomes engaged, meaning active involvement including military participation cannot be argued in realist terms. This problem underlay the Obama administration's reluctance to take a more activist role in Syria. This reticence is reinforced by the question of feasibility: can American military force be brought successfully to bear on the situation? The fact that these conflicts are primarily civil raises doubts about that effectiveness, as does the likelihood that the opponent will employ frustrating asymmetrical warfare techniques (discussed in the next section) against an American military intrusion, prolonging the intervention beyond American patience, causing growing American disillusion with it, and escalating the costs well beyond initial estimates. American intrusions into Iraq and Afghanistan exhibited all of these difficulties. The final concern is cost. Projections of likely costs in DWIC involvements not only routinely underestimate actual economic burdens by orders of magnitude, but since they also rarely succeed, raise the further criticism of waste: throwing money down the proverbial rat hole. The United States spent well over a trillion dollars in both Iraq and Afghanistan: what does it have to show for the investment?

The Military Problem: Countering Asymmetrical Warfare

The conceptual and physical deck is stacked against outside military intervention, and especially the recourse to U.S. and other Western force involvement, in the DWICs for two basic reasons. The first, as just described, is that they do not involve U.S. interests adequately to justify the employment of such force. They are not worth the cost, and because the conflicts are internal, the chances of outside success are slim under any circumstances. Added to that problem is the fact that the West, including the United States, has never devised an effective strategy for prevailing against the kind of military opposition it will almost certainly encounter if it does insert itself into the DWICs.

Western military forces are basically designed to fight European-style wars: conflicts involving traditional, symmetrical forces in the developed landscapes of reasonably flat terrain. This effectively translates into large standing armies reliant on mechanized means of transport and battle in places where instruments of war such as tanks and mobile artillery can be moved about and brought to bear. These instruments are difficult or impossible to employ where, for instance, a lack of roads and bridges cannot support tank armies. These large forces are supported by heavy air forces and, where appropriate, traditional naval assets.

The developing world is not a congenial place in which to wage such warfare. Physically, it does not resemble Europe (or North America) in terms of terrain, climate, or level of infrastructure development. The last three arguable DWICs in which the United States has been involved, for instance, have been fought in a mountainous, tropical environment (Vietnam), an arid, largely desert setting (Iraq), and rugged mountains with very little vegetation and harsh weather (Afghanistan). Most of the technology that distinguishes American military power from that of developing world fighters is largely obviated by these conditions. Airpower is the major exception, but despite the protestations of airpower enthusiasts, that weapons platform is rarely decisive in major conflicts against determined foes.

More to the point, however, indigenous opponents have adapted historical practices specifically to counteract the advantages of the Westerners. Many of these come from the Eastern, indirect style of warfare that emphasized maneuver and deception over the direct clash of armies. Sun Tzu's *The Art of War*, written more than 3,000 years ago, is a foundational presentation of this approach, which stands in stark contrast to the direct style of warfare that developed in the West and features the head-on clash of large, similarly armed forces in what are intended as climactic confrontations. What has evolved is a methodology for confronting more powerful forces than one possesses.

The contemporary name by which this approach is described is asymmetrical warfare. The term itself was first coined in a 1975 article by Andrew J. R. Mack in the journal *World Politics*. The title of the article, suggestively enough, was "Why Big Nations Lose Small Wars," and his answer was that smaller and weaker political entities, whether they represent states or groups within states, have devised ways to negate the advantages that large, powerful developed states' armed forces possess and to provide conditions where they will not only avoid defeat and destruction but even triumph against those "big" opponents. The heart of the approach is to change the rules so that one side fights one way and the other fights another way, and the result is that they fight differently, or asymmetrically.

The 2016 *Random House Dictionary* provides a representative definition of the asymmetrical phenomenon: "warfare in which opposing groups or nations have unequal military resources, and the weaker opponent uses unconventional methods and tactics . . . to exploit the vulnerabilities of the enemy." There is certainly nothing new or unique about this approach: it is the solution to the Biblical David and Goliath dilemma, where Goliath would like to battle toe-to-toe with the smaller and weaker David, and David finds an asymmetrical means to defeat the more powerful adversary. It has been known by a host of names, from partisan warfare to guerrilla warfare, and it is always an approach disdained by the stronger party, who believes it cowardly for the weaker opponent not to fight by the stronger opponent's rules, thereby guaranteeing the weaker side's defeat (and probable demise). When American patriots eschewed linear warfare (the symmetrical means of the day) and, borrowing from the Indians, hid behind rocks and trees and ambushed the Redcoats, one British general referred to their actions as the "dirty little war of terror and murder."

There is one good reason why groups adopt asymmetrical methods: they work. The contemporary problem of what an inferior military force can do when faced with a much stronger, usually invading force is as old as contacts between political groups, and the common thread behind such efforts is how to devise means to lessen or cancel the advantage the larger force has. In many cases, this resistance has taken the form of a "people's" effort to expel an unwanted outsider seeking to subjugate or destroy the victimized population. These efforts have not always succeeded: they did not work against the Mongol hordes until Genghis Khan and his armies overextended themselves, for instance. On the other hand, successful ways to organize resistance have built over time in the contemporary forms of people's wars, insurgency, and guerrilla warfare, to name a few of the names such efforts have taken. For the modern traditional military theorist, how to deal with asymmetrical opposition is the major military problem that must be confronted.

Part of the problem is that asymmetrical warfare is not a method or set of strategies and tactics; it is a methodology. This simple observation creates much of the problem of response to asymmetrical opposition. As an approach, asymmetry does not prescribe a set of rules or doctrines that says how one should fight a given enemy; instead, it suggests a more general way of thinking about the problem that suggests how to structure responses to particular situations. The experience of past asymmetrical warriors may suggest general rules—for instance, not to confront an opponent with superior firepower in such a way that the enemy can concentrate that advantage to destroy you—but these principles are adapted to the specific situation at hand, using experience as a guide to avoid what has failed in the past and to be adapted to the situation one faces.

As a methodology, asymmetrical warfare is very difficult to prepare for. The "game plan" of the asymmetrical warrior is not a clear set of actions for which one can plan, and when one sees it in action, take the proper steps to counter it—the classic doctrinal approach of the symmetrical warrior. There are no standard rules of engagement (ROEs) that dictate the actions of the asymmetrical warrior, rather a set of principles—surprise, isolation, and attack against isolated, inferior concentrations of the enemy, tactical retreat, ambush, to name a few—that guides adaptation to particular situations, locales, terrain, and the like. The doctrinal base of these actions is to adopt practices that have worked in similar situations (e.g., the use of improvised explosive devices [IEDs] in or alongside roads to attack and destroy enemy vehicles) and reject others that have failed.

The result is that no two asymmetrical wars are ever exactly the same. This is a matter of considerable frustration for an opponent, and especially one who is also an outsider. Unpredictability means that doctrinal solutions, the lifeblood of traditional Western armed forces, cannot be identified and serve as the basis for preparing forces for engagement. The whole purpose of much asymmetry is to catch the enemy off guard and to present him with situations and problems for which he is unprepared. When the symmetrical opponent is a foreigner, the problem is exacerbated by unfamiliarity with local physical and human conditions such as resentment of outsiders. These are the kinds of problems that a country like the United States faces if it proposes to involve itself in DWICs. The military does not like being thrown into these cauldrons, and they are, understandably enough, not the kind of fights at which they are best. Unfortunately for them and for us, they are the kinds of military "opportunities" that are available in the contemporary environment.

The Special Case of Terror

Terrorism, introduced in chapter 5, is a venerable, if not revered, form of violence. Like asymmetrical warfare, it is an approach to compelling compliance to a set of goals that a militarily and politically disadvantaged group may feel is the only way for achieving their goals. Like the asymmetrical warrior, terrorists cannot succeed by "playing" by the rules; only by ignoring those rules and acting in ways that force the enemy to take notice and comply do they have any chance. Their method is fright (the word terror comes from the Latin word for frighten). It is an asymmetrical technique that has been practiced since Biblical days; it has become a major part of the tapestry of national security concerns.

Definitions abound about what terrorism is. Almost all include some or all of four characteristics of terror: what acts constitute terror; what targets terrorists attack; what terrorist purposes are, and what kinds of political entities commit terrorism. Of the four, that latter is the most controversial. Some definitions explicitly exclude the governments of states as possible terrorists, limiting the practice to nonstate actors. Since the governments of countries commit acts that are generally considered terrorist for the purpose of frightening opponents (some of which are states and others that are not), this seems a questionable exclusion. Therefore, the definition here incorporates the other three traits: terrorism is the commission of atrocious acts against a target population normally to gain compliance with some demands on which the terrorists insist. The shape of terrorist gains meaning in terms of these three traits.

Terrorist acts are violent displays with several commonalities. First, the pose of terrorist acts is to frighten members of the target population. In ess the terrorist attacks, maims, and kills people, making the explicit or in threat that if members of the target group do not quit doing whatever the ist does not want them to do, they could be victims of the same kind of s or death. Sometimes these threats are direct and clearly specified; more often, they are not. The latter instances complicate coping with terrorist acts.

Second, terrorist acts are uniformly illegal. They involve the taking of life and the destruction of things, both of which are crimes and make terrorism at least partially a law enforcement problem. Terrorists argue that they are in a state of war against the target group, making themselves warriors or soldiers and making what they do political acts excluded from normal societal rules of behavior. The old saw "One man's terrorist is another man's freedom fighter" captures the terrorist position, which elevates what they do to acts of war. It is a position uniformly rejected by those who are the targets of terror and who see terrorists as deranged criminals rather than soldiers.

Third, there are other, more internal reasons for terrorist acts. Jenkins, writing in 2004, suggests six: gaining special concessions (gaining the release of members from jail, for instance), generating publicity, demoralizing the target population, egging the opponent into harmful overreaction, forcing compliance by the target population, or punishing disobedience. Stern (2003) adds improving internal group morale to the list.

Terrorist acts are intended to attack the **cost-tolerance** of those against whom they are directed. This term refers to how much suffering a target is willing to endure before deciding that he or she is unwilling to accept more pain and that it is less unacceptable to submit to terrorist demands than to continue resistance. If a target's morale and determination are high, the target has a high cost-tolerance and it is difficult for the terrorist to succeed. If resolve wavers or is overcome, so is cost-tolerance. In that case, the terrorist may succeed.

For the terrorist to prevail, he or she must choose targets that attack and overcome the victim's cost-tolerance. Broadly speaking, there are two kinds of targets. The first is people, who are ultimately what the terrorist seeks to influence. Killing people is an obvious way to affect members of the target group, and it is best accomplished in two circumstances. One is where an attack will cause maximum surprise. Detonating a bomb in a crowded airport or subway tunnel maximizes carnage, leaves people apprehensive about being so exposed in the future, and makes them wonder why authorities cannot protect them. The other category is attacking things of great physical or symbolic value to people. Blowing up a bridge is an example. The problem that attacks on places represent is that the list of potential targets is extremely large and expandable, and if terrorist suppressors figure out how to defend one category, terrorists simply move on to another category (a process known as target substitution). The 9/11 attacks encompassed both kinds of targets: killing nearly 3,000 people and bringing down New York's World Trade Center towers.

The final terrorism trait is terrorist purposes. Terrorism is, in a sense, an asymmetrical warfare method by which a materially inferior group tries to realize its goals, and terrorism ultimately gains whatever coherence it has in terms of its ability or inability to achieve its political ends. The problem is that these goals are often not well known, may not be articulated at all, or may be dismissed as unrealistic, even lunatic. Osama bin Laden wrote a number of manifestos during the 1990s (available online as "The Ladenese Epistles") that said the reason for

Al Qaeda terror was to force Westerners (notably the Americans) to withdraw military force from the "holy lands" (principally Saudi Arabia). Implicit in these demands was that terrorist attacks would cease upon compliance. Sometimes the purposes are either obscure or unarticulated. Timothy McVeigh, for instance, attacked the Murrah Federal Building in Oklahoma City in 1995, killing 159, allegedly in retaliation for a federal attack against militants near Waco, Texas (Branch Davidians). The salient point about terrorist purposes is that, except for limited, tactical objectives, they rarely if ever succeed in attaining their grand political objectives.

This leaves three questions that must be answered. The first is, how are terrorists organized? In essence, there are two broad answers. The most consequential terrorist movements are organized into defined groups. These groups vary in size (from some African groups that probably have a handful of active members to the Islamic State with thousands of adherents) and organization. One of the most interesting parts of the organization of terrorism has been its evolution in the face of the electronic revolution. At the time of 9/11, many organizations were traditionally configured (something called the commander-cadre model) where leaders issued orders and edicts to followers to carry out. Advances in surveillance techniques allowed monitoring and interruption of communications, and this model was replaced by a "virtual" model, where parts of organizations either do not communicate directly or do so through code. Terrorists have grown especially adept at utilizing the Internet for communicating and recruitment.

The second question is, who are the terrorists? Most research suggests that the people who join these organizations come from one of two backgrounds. Some are disaffected intellectuals, who adopt religious and other philosophies that impel them to violence. Followers—the "foot soldiers"—tend to be young men and women who find themselves in socioeconomic situations where they see very little future for themselves and are drawn to the extremism of terrorist activity because it provides glamour or meaning to an existence that seems to offer neither. This kind of profile was developed in watching the Middle East, where a "youth bulge" (a large peer group of citizens) in the teenage years living in ghetto conditions provided the recruitment base for groups such as Al Qaeda. The same profile has more recently been associated with young Muslims in both Europe and North America. Some of these disaffected people join formal organizations, and others become **lone wolf terrorists** individuals with no formal institutional affiliations who have personal grievances that they seek to redress through terrorist activities. The Unabomber, Kaczynski, although middle-aged, is a prime example.

The third question is, how do you deal with terrorists? It is a question that has evolved considerably and received increasing attention since the 9/11 attacks. A great deal of the focus of **terrorism** suppression, a generic term that covers all efforts, has been focused on the management of the U.S. government, including notably the creation of the Department of Homeland Security to marshal and coordinate solving the problem, a process discussed in chapter 5. Understanding the suppression requires looking at three asp the goals of terrorism policy, the forms of that activity, and approaches to implementing that policy.

The first aspect is what the goal of terrorism suppression should be. The obvious, emotional response is that it must be destroyed, since safety cannot be assured as long as the terrorists exist. A more measured response is that it should be contained at the lowest possible level, a position that reflects the long, two-millennia persistence of terror and the difficulty, and likely impossibility, of eradicating all reasons people become terrorists and thus all the people who become terrorists. The debate is a question of ideal versus practicable solutions. Although largely unspoken because popular sentiment clearly prefers, even requires, a verbal commitment to eradication, the less popular but possibly attainable goal may be to reduce the level of terrorism to "acceptable" levels, whatever that may mean to different people. Trump suggested eradication as a campaign goal.

The second concern is what kinds of activities can be undertaken to approach the goal, and the standard distinction is between **anti-terrorism** and **counterterrorism**. The terms are sometimes used interchangeably but actually are distinct. Anti-terrorism refers to defensive efforts to reduce the vulnerability of targets to attacks and to mitigate the effects of such attacks as do occur. Most anti-terrorist efforts are domestic, and are aimed at frustrating terrorist efforts on American soil. Anti-terrorism consists of two kinds of activities. One is reducing vulnerability by making it harder to gain access to places to attack; airport security is an example. The other involves mitigating the impact of attacks by reducing the damage that can be done (protecting the White House from terrorist bombers by blocking off vehicular access to Pennsylvania Avenue, for example) or by emergency reclamation of sites that have been attacked (a FEMA responsibility). Since 2001, the American anti-terrorist record has been exemplary. Counterterrorism consists of offensive, including military, measures to prevent, deter, or respond to potential or actual terrorist attacks. Counterterrorism seeks to preempt terrorist attacks or to punish perpetrators who do conduct attacks. These efforts often take place outside the United States and have a natural appeal because of their proactive nature.

The third problem is who should develop and implement terrorism suppression, and it has two aspects. One is the relative emphasis on military and nonmilitary actions. The other is on unilateral or multilateral approaches. Terrorism suppression involves both military and nonmilitary effort. Most military activity occurs in overseas counterterrorist actions but can include National Guard assistance in anti-terror cleanups. Nonmilitary actions are concentrated on law enforcement activities, including apprehension of terrorist plotters and curbing penetration of the borders by terrorists. Most nonmilitary efforts are domestic but also include investigation of foreign terrorist events by the FBI and other law enforcement agencies. Much of American terrorism suppression has been unilateral, but as attacks from multilateral organizations such as the Islamic State have spread geographically, multilateral cooperation among the terrorism suppressors in various countries has increased, especially between American and European efforts. The logistics of cooperation, however, are often difficult, as intersection 9.2 suggests.

Intersection 9.2 — Coordinating International Terrorism Efforts

The firebombing of a Paris magazine's headquarters in 2015 was a stark reminder of the physical reach of Islamic terrorists.

As terrorism efforts have become more international (terrorist organizations operating across state borders and in various countries), so too has the need for terrorism suppression efforts become international, and thus a foreign policy concern. To some extent, coordination has been ongoing for some time, but the spate of attacks by IS in places like Paris, Brussels, Berlin, and elsewhere has highlighted the need for better coordination among states.

The need is obvious, especially in the identification and monitoring of suspected terrorists. Attacks may be instigated and planned in one country for execution in another, making cooperation among states imperative to avoid the death and destruction attacks can inflict. As organizations like IS have become more aggressive in their terrorist activities, international cooperation has become more imperative. It is, however, not always easy, for one or both of two reasons.

First, ideal cooperation includes both the point of origin of terrorism plots and their destinations, and the governments at both ends of the pipeline are not always close working friends. Terrorists often are residents of Middle Eastern countries that may either lack intelligence apparatuses to provide critical information, or they may be reluctant to share such information for fear of domestic repercussions. In these countries, intelligence and com-local government and foreign intelligence agencies like the CIA often comprenenvironment. pete, thereby creating a competitive, even adversarial rather than coo in cooperating

Second, much of the effort involves clandestine efforts by of secrets by the countries. The nature of secret operations requires the maltraced back to clan- "spies," and there is reluctance to share information that value highly. This causes destine sources the anonymity of whom the nation m one another. friction at operational levels that may underc ies continues to rise as terrorist cooperation at the policy level. Even friendly ous activities, the internationaliza-

If the number of terrorist episodes is particularly true currently in regard to organizations internationalize their rear, regardless of the disposition of the IS tion of terrorism suppression e to contain this growing m the Islamic State, but i threat.

The Concrete Dilemma: The U.S. and the Islamic State

The Islamic State has been the primary national security menace of the mid-2010s. It goes by several names: it prefers IS, but it is also referred to as the Islamic State in Iraq and Syria (ISIS) and the Islamic State in the Levant (ISIL). Regardless of designation, it has emerged as the primary global terrorism threat, surpassing Al Qaeda (AQ) in the public mind since the 2011 assassination of AQ founder Osama bin Laden. IS and AQ are now global competitors; IS's apparent success and the resulting apparent threat it poses have become a major national security issue in the United States.

IS represents a different kind of terrorist threat than more "traditional" organizations. In addition to being a terrorist threat, it also uses methods and espouses goals that go well beyond the aspirations of most terrorist organizations. Most notably, IS aspires to create a new state, a global caliphate (successor) to the old Arab Empire, and this grandiose ambition requires that it be more than a terrorist organization. IS represents a hybrid threat that combines terrorism with traditional state activity such as territorial acquisition, governance, and defense, burdens terrorist organizations rarely aspire to or incur. IS represents a different threat; even if its most expansive ambitions are fantasies, the difference makes it no less menacing or dangerous.

What makes IS different? The following list, largely borrowed from *The Middle East, Oil, and the U.S. National Security Policy*, suggests some of the most salient differences and the implications of those differences both for IS and for those opposing them.

First, IS, despite its additional characteristics, remains a terrorist organization at heart. It was founded originally as Al Qaeda in Iraq (AQI) during the American occupation by a Jordanian immigrant, Abu Musab al-Zarqawi, as a Sunni resistance organization. When American air attacks killed the leader in 2006, AQI went underground but did not disband, returning to public view as pa... of the Sunni resistance to the rule of Syria's Bashar al-Assad in 2013. Abu Bakr a...aghdadi led this resurgence, and has since declared himself as the caliph of the I...ic State. IS added new techniques and purposes in the process, but terrorism...

Second...ns an important part of its organizational DNA.

gious terroris...lamic State is the largest and most affluent of the Islamic religious terrorists. Masters of electronics and the use of various aspects of the Internet, it...s. ...ited well, and it is still able to put a fighting force— including large n... ...f foreigners attracted by its electronic presence—of between 25,000 an... ...the field in the name of the caliphate. Moreover, through a combinati... ...business activities (e.g., appropriating and sell-ing Syrian oil), crimina... ...ing banks in towns it occupies), and private contributions (mostly fro... ...nnis in the oil-rich Gulf states and Saudi Arabia), it is affluent well... ...itor organizations. IS represents the largest contemporary terrorist... ...some orders of magnitude.

Third, IS has territorial an... ...rm of the caliphate that elevate it conceptually above other terr... ...but that also create vulnera-bilities for it. Historically, terrorist... ...had as their primary pur-poses getting other groups to do so... ...but could not achieve by more standard, conventional means, because whatever they demand lacked sufficient popular support for less stressful forms of pursuit. IS has gone a long step beyond the humility of influencing power to gaining and wielding it, and that is a responsibility that requires very different approaches and emphases than that of the terrorist. Terrorists seek to influence (including overthrowing) governments; territory-seeking organizations seek to create and actually govern territory. Because of their terrorist beginnings, their means of governing may be harsh and contain elements of terror, but they must also do the mundane jobs of government, such as providing public services and defending their territory from hostile outsiders. IS claims it wants to establish a "global" caliphate, which helps explain its expansion into other Muslim countries. Its ability to accomplish this goal is problematical.

The need to calculate beyond imperiling the security of others through terror may prove to be the Achilles' heel of IS. For one thing, it forces IS to devote resources that might be used for expansion to defending against outsiders. At the same time, having what they consider their own sovereign territory also makes them a target for the wrath of those against whom they have committed both acts of terror and other military acts. One of the great difficulties of terrorism suppression, and especially counterterrorism, is where to direct retaliatory fury. When terrorists reside in sovereign jurisdictions that are not their own (and maybe countries, such as Pakistan, that are partners of those seeking retaliation), the suppressors are in a bind of not wanting to kill inadvertently citizens of friendly countries or violating the sovereignty of friendly states. This tension has been a major thorn in American relations with Pakistan since the United States began the campaign against Al Qaeda in that country. When the terrorists are housed in and dispatched from sovereign states they claim to represent—as in terrorism sponsored and directed by the caliphate—this dilemma dissolves. Moreover, the forces defending the caliphate cannot simply cede territory and melt into the terrain like guerrilla fighters.

Fourth, internally contradictory goals and methods that arise from being both defenders of a sovereign state and terrorists could be the undoing of IS. They must play what might be called the "terror and territory game" to achieve the organization's diverse goals, and it may prove impossible to pursue both successfully and simultaneously. At the tactical level, the dual goals of terror and statehood may not seem contradictory. States have been known to employ terror against their populations (Argentina in the 1970s, for instance) and to cow reluctant population segments into docility toward the central government (the Sudanese government against rebellious Darfur province in the 2000s, as an example). Fundamentally, however, governments cannot exist entirely as terrorists. Governing a sovereign territory and population entails obligations that are common to all governments and will inevitably make the governors of the caliphate/terrorists more like their enemies than they now appear.

The Achilles' heel is particularly evident when it comes to the practical implications of being the rulers of the caliphate. Baghdadi and his followers have consistently maintained that the creation of the caliphate is the primary mission of IS and that it can only succeed in creating the Islamic purity leading to an apocalyptic confrontation with the West (which it prophesies) if it remains a territorial state. If the caliphate falls or is dismembered, IS fails. It may be able to fall back upon continued terrorism as a recruiting tool or to demonstrate its continuing presence, but apparently many of its converts are attracted to living in a sovereign "paradise" that the caliphate promises. If that place no longer exists, it is hard to see how IS can linger long as a major force. In 2016, there were indications that these contradictions were affecting IS recruitment.

The territorial and terrorist aspects also contradict one another. The Islamic State encounters resistance from its neighbors from whose own territory it is carved (the Syrians, Iraqis, and Kurds in particular), and if it continues to spread, it will create other sources of regional opposition. This outcome, of course, is exactly what the United States would like to see; it potentially obviates any temptation for U.S. direct involvement. When IS broadens its violence to include terrorism outside its region (the West), it invites military retaliation against its territory and membership.

At this point, the contradiction becomes a paradox. In some ways, reversal to terrorism is an alternative strategy for IS, at least as a recruiting tool: it demonstrates the continued vitality of the organization, and the aerial bombardment retaliation it endures creates martyrs to the cause. Both outcomes aid in the recruitment of new members, especially from the West. At the same time, that retaliation may weaken the ability of the regime to maintain control of the caliphate, its major goal. The dilemma is how to serve both the recruitment/morale value of terror with the ultimate goal of establishing and maintaining the caliphate. It is a dilemma the organization will progressively have to face and try to reconcile.

These difficulties became evident in spring 2016, as the terms of the territory and terror came into increasing conflict. Two trends emerged. First, attacks from various quarters in the region were retracting the effective size of the caliphate, with estimates ranging from 20 to 40 percent of the territory it had originally conquered falling into hostile hands. Some of this interchange was more symbolic than anything else: large parts of the territory that IS had originally annexed were barely populated wasteland, and that was also what they were losing. Regardless, a state government that cannot hold its own sovereign territory cannot be said to be succeeding, and this has been the primary marker of success IS has established.

The second trend was an increasing resort to terror, notably the spectacular attacks in Paris and Brussels. It may be that these were motivated by the fact that both France and Belgium joined the air war against the caliphate shortly before they were attacked, and it may be that the attacks were intended as demonstrations of the continued potency of IS as a terrorist organization. If it is true, as suggested, that terror is the placebo for territorial success in the territory/terror game, these attacks seem an act of weakness more than strength.

This leaves two questions to be asked about IS. As an American foreign policy concern, the disposition of IS relates closely to American support for the replacement of Syria's Assad. IS, of course, burst on the public scene as part of the resistance and gradually emerged both as the most powerful member of the anti-Assad coalition and as a separate menace. Because IS poses a terrorist men-ace to the United States and Syria does not, IS has pushed Syria from the U.S. policy spotlight. In this light, in which order to pursue these goals is the first policy question.

The ordering has consequences for U.S. policy and the region. On one hand, they cannot be pursued simultaneously without creating contradictions. Support for the overthrow of Assad inevitably benefits IS, which would be a prominent candidate to replace him—and this does not serve U.S. policy ends since it enlarges and consolidates the caliphate. Attacking IS first, in turn, strengthens Assad, because it removes the most powerful opponent the regime faces, thereby freeing it to pursue and destroy other, less potent, opponents. There is the additional concern with the religious "optics" of tilting one way or the other. Concentrating on destroying IS can be viewed, especially within the region, as anti-Sunni, because the Syrian government and the population in the caliphate-controlled parts of Iraq are largely Sunni. Attacking Syria first, on the other hand, appears to be anti-Shiite, since both the Syrian and Iraqi govern-ments are controlled by Shiites. The United States has no publicly articulated policy favoring one sect over the other and probably historically had a primary interest in staying out of the conflict between the two.

From an American viewpoint, this ordering and its importance depend on an interest-threat-risk analysis. What U.S. interests are involved in either conflict, particularly one side prevailing over the other? Beyond humanitarian concerns, the United States has no premier interests in who governs Syria. IS confined to its present and hopefully contracting boundaries creates a terrorist platform that may be important to destroy, but poses no existential threat.

Threats and risks flow from the assessment of interests. How much of a threat exists depends on what interests IS put at risk. In the present situation, IS poses a potential threat to the United States, but it poses much more of an actual threat to regional powers and American allies in Europe. Those countries that are most threatened face the greatest risk if IS continues but have, until recently, shown little inclination to neutralize the risk.

The assessment of what the United States should do resides in the psycho-logical realm of what makes us feel secure. The degree of threat is also subjec-tive: some Americans feel more threatened by IS than others. In 2016, Obama viewed the problem regionally and downplayed it. As Goldberg reports Obama's conclusions: "The first is that the Middle East is no longer terribly important to American interests. The second is . . . there (is) little the United States can do to make it a better place." He concludes that American military involvement "leads to warfare, to the deaths of U.S. soldiers, and to the eventual hemorrhaging of U.S. power and credibility." There are, of course, other possible conclusions, depending on threat assessment.

The other question is how to kill it, if that seems necessary. One possibility has always been a heavy American-led ground attack. If conducted largely uni-laterally (with token participation by European allies and regional actors), this would almost certainly lead to a prolonged U.S. occupation such as that in Iraq a decade ago—hardly an optimal outcome. The other is for regional actors to coalesce and lead the "liberation" of the caliphate. The attraction of this solution is that if the territorial caliphate disappears, IS has been decisively defeated and has no continuing reason to exist beyond a role as a terrorist organization (a not inconsiderable but different problem).

The problem is who will accomplish the task. The regional candidates are unpromising. The oil-rich states are Sunni, covertly sympathetic to the IS philosophy, and do not possess adequate ground forces for the task. The Kurds are only truly interested in defending Kurdistan. The Turks have the forces to do the job and are NATO allies, but they suffer most of the same Sunni misgivings as the Gulf states. Ironically, the only regional actor with both the forces and motivation would probably be Shiite Iran working in concert with Shiite Iraqis. This combination would certainly maximize Sunni resistance, and is a prospect no American president could possibly endorse. The result is a dilemma the Trump administration will have to try to solve.

Conclusion

National security is a paramount concern of American foreign policy so important that it is often discussed as if it were a separate area—national security policy. The reasons arise from its content: national security is about the safety, even the survival, of the American people. This fact also creates an emotional aura around national security matters that is not shared by other areas of policy where the interests and threats to them are not so severe.

One way to assess the nature of threat is through the dichotomy between the danger and the deadliness that different threats pose. Danger, in this context, refers to the likelihood that particular threats will be carried out. In the contemporary scene, the danger of terrorist attacks somewhere in the world is very high; how likely they are on American soil is more arguable. At the same time, the danger of an attack on the United States from most developing world countries, including those undergoing DWICs, is quite low.

Deadliness refers to the consequences of threats if they are carried out. The deadliest possible threat was an all-out nuclear strike against the United States by the Soviet Union during the Cold War. Other attacks are of lower levels of deadliness. In the contemporary environment, it is difficult, bordering on hysterical, to argue that American survival, the ultimate deadly threat, is particularly endangered.

This distinction frames the concerns in which the policy debate proceeds. As discussed, the primary sources of instability and violence in the world are in the form of DWICs. These conflicts are not inconsequential, but hardly any of them raise concerns about the danger of their spread to the United States or the deadliness such a spread might entail. Terrorism certainly poses a dangerous threat (sometimes connected to DWICs), but it is hardly deadly in the way a nuclear war would be. The deadliest possibilities probably attach to nuclear weapons in the hands of dangerous countries, and in these cases, prudent policy dictates that an approach that will lower or eliminate the danger such weapons pose is important.

There is little positive agreement on the parameters or content of American national security. The reason is largely environmental: the national security problem of the second half of the 2010s lacks the clarity of danger of a Cold War that was exceedingly deadly but that, largely thanks to that fact, became less dangerous as nuclear possessors came to appreciate the apocalyptic consequences of nuclear war. There is no shortage of threats in the current environment: it is clearly dangerous. The goal must thus be how to manage the deadliness of the competitions that exist and to reduce the dangers wherever possible. It is a delicate and difficult task, and one on which there is considerable disagreement.

Study/Discussion Questions

1. President Obama came to office seeking to demilitarize foreign policy. Has President Trump contributed to this emphasis or moved toward a more militarily "robust" national security policy? Discuss.
2. How do foreign and national security policy relate to one another? Discuss the basic distinctive elements of national security (interests, threats, and risks) and how they define this policy area.
3. Why has violence in the developing world come to define the major pattern of international violence and instability in the post–Cold War world? What is a DWIC? What kinds of problems do DWICs pose for national security problems in terms of interests, feasibility, and cost?
4. What is asymmetrical warfare? Discuss its genesis, the problem it seeks to overcome, its general purpose and approach, its prevalence in the DWICs, and how it poses a major difficulty for American national security policy. What does it mean to refer to it as a methodology rather than a method?
5. Why is terrorism a "special case" for national security policy? Define and describe terrorism as it has evolved in the contemporary world. What are the major problems of dealing with it?
6. Describe the nature and problem posed by IS to the Middle East and the United States. How does it exemplify other problems discussed in the chapter? Why is it so difficult physically and conceptually to deal with? What do *you* think the United States should do about this threat?

Bibliography

Bacevich, Andrew K. *Washington Rules: America's Path to Permanent War*. New York: Henry Holt, 2010.
Cockburn, Patrick. *The Rise of the Islamic State: ISIS and the New Sunni Revolution*. London: Verso, 2015.
Cronin, Audrey Kurth, and James Ludes, eds. *Modern Terrorism: Elements of a Grand Strategy*. Washington, DC: Georgetown University Press, 2003.
Dueck, Colin. *The Obama Doctrine: American Grand Strategy Today*. Oxford: Oxford University Press, 2015.

Goldberg, Jeffrey. "The Obama Doctrine." *Atlantic*, April 2016, 70–90.

Haass, Richard N. *Wars of Necessity, Wars of Choice: A Memoir of Two Iraq Wars*. New York: Simon & Schuster, 2009.

Hoffman, Bruce. *Inside Terrorism*. 2nd ed. New York: Columbia University Press, 2006.

Jenkins, Brian. "International Terrorism," in *The Use of Force: Military Power and International Relations*, 6th ed., edited by Robert J. Arts and Kenneth N. Waltz. Lanham, MD: Rowman & Littlefield, 2004.

Kristensen, Hans M., and Robert S. Norris. "Russian Nuclear Forces 2014." *Bulletin of the Atomic Scientists* 70, no. 2 (March/April 2014): 75–85.

Latham, Michael E. *The Right Kind of Revolution: Modernization, Development, and U.S. Foreign Policy from the Cold War to the Present*. Ithaca, NY: Cornell University Press, 2011.

Lowther, Adam B. *Americans and Asymmetrical Warfare: Lebanon, Somalia, and Afghanistan*. Westport, CT: Praeger Security International, 2007.

Mack, Andrew J. R. "Why Big Nations Lose Small Wars." *World Politics* 27, no. 2 (April 1975): 175–200.

McCants, William. *The ISIS Apocalypse: The History, Strategy, and Doomsday Vision of the Islamic State*. New York: St. Martin's, 2015.

Snow, Donald M. *The Case Against Military Intervention: Why We Do It and Why It Fails*. New York and London: Routledge, 2016.

———. *Distant Thunder: Third World Conflict and the New International Order*. New York: St. Martin's, 1993.

———. *The Middle East, Oil, and the U.S. National Security Policy*. Lanham, MD: Rowman & Littlefield, 2016.

———. *National Security*. 6th ed. New York and London: Routledge, 2017.

———. *Thinking about National Security: Strategy, Policy, and Issues*. New York and London: Routledge, 2016.

Snow, Donald M., and Dennis M. Drew. *From Lexington to Desert Storm and Beyond: War and Politics in the American Experience*. 3rd ed. Armonk, NY: Sharpe, 2010.

Stern, Jessica. *Terrorism in the Name of God: Why Religious Militants Kill*. New York: Ecco, 2003.

Stern, Jessica, and J. M. Berger. *ISIS: The State of Terror*. Reprint. New York: Ecco, 2016.

Sun Tzu. *The Art of War*. Translated by Samuel P. Griffith. Oxford: Oxford University Press, 1963.

Weiss, Michael, and Hassan Hassan. *ISIS: Inside the Army of Terror*. New York: Regan Arts, 2015.

Wiegley, Russell F. *The American Way of War*. New York: Macmillan, 1973.

Foreign Economic Policy

10

In March 2016 President Obama became the first U.S. President to visit Cuba since Calvin Coolidge in 1928.

Preview

The purpose of this chapter is to examine foreign economic policy as a policy space and to explore the economic instruments of statecraft that the U.S. government employs as tools of national power. We begin by examining the evolution and current challenges to the international economic order that began to take shape after World War II, the "Bretton Woods system," which emphasized increasingly free trade and multilateral agreement. The globalization that followed has been a key part of Republican and Democratic policies for decades, but came under intense fire in the 2016 presidential election, as the public has become mired in the downsides, or what economists call the negative externalities, of free trade. In order to understand how presidents pursue U.S. interests and values through economic policy, we then turn to a discussion of the tools of economic statecraft and the agencies that help the inhabitant of the White House make foreign economic policy. The discussion includes a focus on avenues for congressional involvement in this area as well, and for the political activity of trade groups and the public in lobbying about trade policy.

Key Concepts

North American Free Trade
  Agreement (NAFTA)

economic nationalism

protectionism

globalization

economic liberalism

tariffs

nontariff barriers

micro-level effects

macro-level effects

Bretton Woods

International Monetary Fund (IMF)

International Bank for
  Reconstruction and Development
  (IBRD)

General Agreement on Tariffs and
  Trade (GATT)

World Trade Organization (WTO)

Organization of Petroleum
  Exporting Countries (OPEC)

Washington consensus

European Union (EU)

Asia-Pacific Economic Cooperation
  (APEC)

Trans-Pacific Partnership (TPP)

multinational corporations (MNCs)

comparative advantage

fair trade

power

two-level game

U.S. Trade Representative (USTR)

Trade Promotion Authority ("Fast
  Track")

foreign aid

USAID

Millennium Challenge Corporation
  (MCC)

military assistance

sanctions

embargo

smart sanctions

The presidential election in 1992 may seem like a long time ago, but several things from that cycle will sound familiar to today's readers. The Republican president, George H. W. Bush, was quite unpopular—falling from a high of nearly 95 percent approval when the United States and its allies won the Persian Gulf War, ejecting Saddam Hussein's Iraqi forces from Kuwait in a massive military action. It was a "change" election. The question was, what kind of change? Two southern moderate Democrats suggested one way forward. Bill Clinton (who would of course win the White House) and his running mate, Al Gore, ran on an agenda that included, among other things, the **North American Free Trade Agreement (NAFTA)**, a sweeping trade treaty that would make the movement of people and goods very easy across the United States, Mexico, and Canada. The Clinton view was that free trade would help create cheaper products from imports, and better, higher paying jobs that would build exports. President Bush was also in favor of NAFTA but a third candidate, Texas billionaire Ross Perot, entered the race on an anti-NAFTA platform. Perot famously argued that NAFTA would create a "giant sucking sound" of jobs fleeing the relatively high-wage industrial Midwest to low-wage Mexico. Clinton won, NAFTA passed, and in a macro sense NAFTA has been a success (or at worst a draw) for all involved.

But in 2016 this anti–free trade position made a big comeback in the candidacy of another businessman-turned-politician, Donald Trump. Donald Trump ran as an economic nationalist, arguing that NAFTA was a "disaster" that he promised to tear up and renegotiate; his rhetoric harkened back to an election when another businessman ran against another Clinton and against NAFTA. We heard less about tearing up NAFTA after the election, so time will tell where Trump heads on this and other trade agreements. One thing is certain: the politics of free trade, an issue since the birth of the Republic, is as alive as ever.

✳   ✳   ✳

Since the end of World War II, international economics has increasingly emphasized capitalism, markets, and free trade. This economic position is steeped in the international application of the theory that trade liberalization—that is, the reduction or tariff and nontariff barriers to trade among countries—will lead to greater efficiencies and increases in wealth that will surpass any other form of international economic policy, including communism and **economic nationalism** or "**protectionism**." A widening circle of countries around the world has experienced impressive macroeconomic growth and innovation as global capitalism and free trade has taken root, but not without its critics. **Globalization**, the process of the integration of global economics and politics that has been facilitated and intensified by free trade and modern technology, has created great wealth, but it has also disrupted national economies and left many on the outside of its benefits. It was long a calling cry of liberal democrats and supporters of organized labor; Donald Trump brought much of the Republican Party to this position as well in the recent election, meaning that there is now growing bipartisan concern about the growth of free trade. As usual, our future depends in part on our past.

International Economics in the American Experience

An enduring part of the American foreign policy tradition has been to try to separate general foreign policy—those interactions with foreign governments that are primarily political or military in nature—from economic relations with other states. This tradition goes back to the founding days of the American republic. George Washington presented this view in his farewell address when he linked his general rule of "no permanent alliances" with other countries to the economic realm. By the twentieth century the United States was increasingly interested in commercial activity as if it could be held apart from other foreign policy activity. During the period between the World Wars, for example, "splendid isolationism," as its champions described it, applied in the political realm, but that did not mean the United States would not and should not engage in commercial relations with all countries; indeed, one of the purposes of non-alignment and noninvolvement in Europe's political affairs was to facilitate American commerce to all sides as war clouds gathered. The end of World War II and the rise of the Cold War led to two distinct economic and political spheres: the capitalist West and the communist East, which competed against each other around the globe.

The end of the Cold War seemed to bring an end to this economic competition, with markets as the new global standard, but the new era is not without its controversies.

The first of these is a disagreement in the United States over protectionism versus free trade. They are the extreme ends of the spectrum regarding the extent to which international commerce should be interfered with and regulated by governments. Free trade emerges from the overarching perspective of classic **economic liberalism**. The U.S. dedication to free trade, or laissez-faire economics, is as long-standing as the Republic. In short, this view holds that markets are the best mechanism for wealth creation and that government intervention in the economy harms the generation of wealth. This view derives from a belief in the mutual benefits of exchange and that economic relations can be a positive sum, or win-win game. This view holds that tools such as **tariffs** (a fancy word for "tax") and **nontariff barriers** (such as import quotas) only get in the way of wealth generation in the long run. The free trade position thus entails the removal of the barriers to trade so that commerce can flow "freely" across state boundaries. Free trade is at the heart of globalization. It is a position that argues that opening the international system to the greatest possible competition enhances overall global economic development and thus the greater good of everyone.

Protectionism, or economic nationalism, also has a long tradition in U.S. history and emerges from the realist perspective on politics that sees international economics not as separate from politics but indeed as a part of the struggle for states to get and maintain power and security. The idea here is that economic power is a key component of national power, that power resources are not distributed evenly around the globe, and that part of the responsibility of national leaders is to cultivate and protect the national economy from the influence attempts of others—that indeed, doing so is a key component of one's "security." The economic nationalist perspective, also sometimes called mercantilism or neomercantilism (to denote the modern versions of it) was laid out forcefully in 1791 by Alexander Hamilton in a *Report on the Subject of Manufactures*. "Not only wealth but the independence and security of a country appear to be materially connected with the prosperity of manufacturers. Every nation . . . ought to endeavor to possess within itself all the essentials of national supply."

Protectionism, as the name implies, is the practice of placing barriers on the entry of goods and services from abroad in the form of tariffs, quotas, or outright prohibitions on importation. The purpose of such barriers is to "protect" indigenous industries from outsiders who can produce similar goods and services at a lower cost and thus would sell at lower prices than indigenous products, thereby undercutting their sales. Tariffs, which are essentially taxes or levies on affected goods, raise the cost of otherwise cheaper foreign goods to higher prices than indigenous goods, thereby protecting them by making them cheaper to consumers. Protectionism is a practice historically associated with any country undergoing the development process whose "infant industries" (as less efficient, new internal concerns are often called) cannot compete freely against foreign intruders, but this economic nationalist impulse is also present in advanced industrial and postindustrial settings like the United States.

Another debate surrounds the differential impact that economic decisions have on individuals and societies, and can be expressed in terms of micro- versus macro-level effects. **Micro-level effects** are the direct consequences of economic actions on individual people; **macro-level effects**, on the other hand, refer to the overall systemic effects of particular economic actions on national economies or the international economic system. While in principle these two levels of effects are not necessarily incompatible and contradictory, in application they often are. Free trade agreements like NAFTA, for example, can lead to positive macro-level developments (like total job creation) but they also put some people out of work—a negative micro-level effect.

After World War II the United States—as the leading superpower in the West—led the development of a new international economic order that both promoted markets and capitalism and the movement toward free trade *and* served American economic and political interests. The creation of the **Bretton Woods** economic system (named after the resort town in New Hampshire where the agreements were reached) included the **International Monetary Fund (IMF)** to deal with currency stabilization and balance-of-payments difficulties; the **International Bank for Reconstruction and Development (IBRD)**, more popularly known as the World Bank, as a source of lending to countries; and the **General Agreement on Tariffs and Trade (GATT)** as a multilateral agreement to reduce tariff and nontariff barriers to trade over time among the member countries. The GATT was essentially replaced in 1995 by the new **World Trade Organization (WTO)**, which includes nearly all the world's most important countries among its 164 current members. Undergirding this entire system was U.S. leadership in two forms: these institutions were headquartered in Washington, D.C., and the currency for all countries was fixed to the value of the U.S. dollar—the "greenback"—which was fixed to the value of gold at $35 per ounce. The Nixon administration ended the "gold standard" in 1971, leading some to say the Bretton Woods system died then, but the other institutions live on in an era of "floating" currency rates.

While the Cold War period pitted the United States and its capitalist and democratic allies against the Soviet Union and its communist allies, the 1970s produced at least two more interesting twists on international economics (the first being the shift from the gold standard). First, it became apparent that not all communist states cohered under Soviet leadership, leading the United States and the People's Republic of China to move closer together and against the Soviets. Second, a new player on the world stage appeared in a way that rocked the global economy in significant ways in 1973 and 1977 when the **Organization of Petroleum Exporting Countries (OPEC)**, led by its Middle Eastern members, successfully cut oil production and greatly raised the cost of oil to consuming countries. Since most developed countries, including the United States, were highly dependent on oil as an energy source, this rise in prices shook economies around the world, slowed economic growth, and most visibly led to long lines for limited supplies of gas. It also led to renewed calls for energy conservation, to move from oil to renewable sources of energy, and to be less reliant on "foreign" oil. The oil shocks, in a sense, helped remind Americans of what Alexander

Hamilton warned in the 1700s, that you are not secure when you do not control resources that are vital to your well-being.

The Globalizing Economy

The guiding value of the international economic system since the early 1990s has been globalization, a blanket concept that encompasses the growing together of world economies into what is emerging as at least the outline of a truly global, overarching set of economic relations. The values that underlie this movement have been called the **Washington consensus** because of how the United States has sought to persuade or cajole other countries to pursue multilateral free trade agreements and a focus on markets, deregulation, and privatization in domestic economies. With downturns and embarrassments like the economic crashes of 1998 and 2008, some of the shine has worn off this model, but it nonetheless remains the basic building block for the international system, what Friedman calls the "system of globalization."

Part of the new system of globalization has been the emergence of regional trade blocks, including NAFTA in the Americas and the **European Union (EU)**. Born as the European Coal and Steel Community in 1951 with six member states, it has gradually evolved to include twenty-eight member states in Europe, the economies of which are virtually entirely integrated and among whom no economic barriers to trade exist. The vote in Great Britain to exit the EU ("Brexit") in 2016 calls into question the future of the EU. The **Asia-Pacific Economic Cooperation (APEC)** involved twenty-one member states including the United States and its fellow NAFTA members, China, Japan, South Korea, Russia, Indonesia, Australia, New Zealand, and Thailand, as well as Chile and a number of smaller states. APEC is not a free trade zone, but tries to promote this goal. The **Trans-Pacific Partnership (TPP)** was to be a broad trade agreement among Pacific powers, including the United States but not including China; the future of the TPP is now in question following Donald Trump's election. Beyond these multilayer efforts, the United States also has a long list of bilateral agreements with countries around the world.

Other important building blocks of this globalizing economy include the advances in communications technology that have aided the free flow of knowledge and also helped create global markets, and high technology that has led to incredible increases in productivity and innovation. Global companies, or **multinational corporations (MNCs)**, have also evolved over time. Before the computer age, international corporations generally referred to companies headquartered in one country but doing business in other countries. These companies were, however, primarily national companies (companies owned, managed by, and producing goods in one country) with multinational activities. By contrast, the high technology and information revolutions have allowed the emergence of truly multinational corporations. Companies can now be owned by nationals in many countries, be managed by international teams with headquarters in various countries, and produce products or services with contributions of parts or ideas from sources in several different countries.

Global financial markets have also been transformed. Before the telecommunications revolution, for instance, investors were largely limited to the stock exchanges in their own countries because of limits in information availability and market access. Opportunities for Americans, for instance, to invest in Asian ventures were limited by the speed at which those opportunities and supporting evidence could be obtained, and often it could not be in a timely manner. Moreover, access to markets in other places was restricted by time and technology. In 1990, the idea of being able to buy stock instantly in real time in Asian markets halfway around the world was inconceivable; today, it is a mouse click away.

At the heart of globalization and free trade is the principle of **comparative advantage** at the international level. The comparative advantage principle, as articulated by the economist David Ricardo in the late nineteenth century, is that within any economic unit, those who produce a good or service at the lowest possible cost with the greatest quality (or, in other words, those who have an advantage compared to others in producing the commodity) should be encouraged to produce enough of that good to meet the market demand, whereas those who produce that same commodity less efficiently should be discouraged from continuing to do so, and should pursue an area of production where they do possess or can develop comparative advantage. Theoretically, at least, the market's "unseen hand" will result in all producers making things and rendering services at the lowest possible cost with highest quality to consumers, who benefit as a result. Also theoretically, everyone can find an area in which they can achieve comparative advantage so that no one is punished by applying the principle. Market integrity is guaranteed because there will likely be more than one producer of any commodity who can achieve rough comparative advantage, thereby avoiding monopoly creation and the distortions that a monopoly capitalist can exercise in the marketplace.

The beneficial operation of the theory of comparative advantage is not universally accepted, and two objections that become prominent in objections to globalization are often cited. One of these is market distortions, where producers may seek to manipulate the marketplace to give advantage to their own goods and undercut competitors. At the international level, national trade barriers that artificially place added costs onto imported goods, thus removing their natural comparative advantage, are an example that free trade seeks to surmount. Another objection is the assumption that all entities within the economic unit can in fact find something at which they have or can develop comparative advantage. In the contemporary economic situation, for instance, the lack of ability to find new good jobs for workers displaced from the coal and steel industries calls the lofty principles into question.

Free Trade and Fair Trade

The promotion of multilateral free trade has been official U.S. international economic policy for over two decades, the economic preference of the last five U.S. presidents (Ronald Reagan, George H. W. Bush, Bill Clinton, George W. Bush, and Barack Obama). While they each had their moments of protectionism (e.g.,

Reagan to slow car imports from Japan or George W. Bush to protect steel workers in Ohio, Pennsylvania, and West Virginia from imports), they were all free traders. President Trump is a more complicated figure; he has benefited greatly from the global marketplace, and so in that sense must believe in free trade and markets, but he rode a wave of economic nationalism to the White House with a skepticism about the mutually beneficial nature of economic exchange that suggests the age of the multilateral free trade agreement may take a backseat to protectionism or mercantilism (discussed more fully below).

Within the United States (and elsewhere), the debate about the advocacy of free trade tends to center on the question of differential impacts of free trade/ globalization on different groups within society and the society as a whole. To examine this argument, it is useful to frame it in terms of a matrix that contains two different sets of concepts already introduced, with one added element. The macro level of analysis centers on the national or international level and thus the effects that globalization-spreading free trade has on those units of analysis. At the national level, this focuses on actions such as increases in measures of overall economic performance (e.g., gross domestic product, volume of trade), which have usually been positive whenever barrier-removing actions have been taken, and most advocacies of free trade have been based at this level. At the international level, the focus is on overall worldwide (or at least affected system-wide) growth economically, and at positive political spinoffs, such as greater cooperation and friendship between countries that participate in these schemes. Indeed, one of the important political arguments in favor of globalization is that it is likely to reduce the amount of international violence by reducing animosities and intertwining countries in webs of economic interdependence that make war between them difficult or even impossible (the first step in European economic integration was to combine the coal and steel capabilities of France and Germany in such a way as to make it impossible for either to independently produce the steel necessary to build war machines they could use against one another as they had in the past).

The micro level of analysis centers on the impacts that free trade has on individuals and groups within national economic units. Since the process emphasizes adjusting economies away from products and services in which they lack comparative advantage to areas where they have it, there is inevitably in practice adjustment that must occur that will have a negative impact on those displaced— at least temporarily—and thus this is the level at which most objections are registered. Indeed, the question and process of how to deal with and make temporary and minimally painful the micro-level suffering forms the most basic and difficult question of approaches to implementing globalization-generating change.

A free trade approach begins from the premise that removing barriers to trade is economically efficient and thus beneficial in promoting economic growth and profits. Within Western views of economics, the opposite view, protectionism, is also an answer to the question of maintaining national economic strength and thus profitability, but one that reaches an opposite conclusion about what nurtures that outcome, exposure of one's economy to competition with others or protection of the economy from that competition. The advocacy of one position or the other reflects, at least implicitly, an assessment of the comparative advantage that one perceives that the overall economy or selected parts of it possess.

Another way to think about this debate, though, is to think about "fair" trade as a position that sits between these two extremes of the free trade and the protectionist positions. Fair traders tend to focus on the equity of free trade arrangements, both for domestic interests and internationally. The **fair trade** argument with regard to the removal of barriers to foreign sources of goods and services seeks to ensure that foreign producers operate under the same basic rules as do American producers, thus producing fairness or equity in the competition. One example of this insistence surrounds environmental standards in different countries, a source of general concern among opponents of free trade. The problem is that some foreign producers gain or enhance their comparative advantage over American counterparts by adopting minimal environmental standards in their production practices, normally with the assent of their governments. In the United States, meeting environmental standards, notably cleaning up toxic waste byproducts of production, is borne by the producers and entails additional costs that add to the price of goods produced. By avoiding the imposition and costs of such cleanup, foreign producers can lower their production costs and thus the prices of their goods. An asymmetry of environmental requirements unbalances the terms of competition by making it cheaper for noncompliers to do business, in addition to creating ecological problems. The result is an advocacy for strict environmental requirements in free trade arrangements.

When it comes to dealing with the disruptions of free trade, free traders often seek fairer treatment of victims of free trade arrangements, especially industries whose lack of comparative advantage undermines them when free trade is institutionalized. Fair traders insist that provisions be included in free trade arrangements to anticipate and compensate those who will be losers in this process, through the provision of education and training programs for those whose jobs in uncompetitive industries are lost, the recruitment of alternative industries and jobs into affected areas, and the like. The impact of growing free trade on the labor-intensive textile industry in the Carolinas is often cited as a prime example of the devastating effects that free trade without assistance for those adversely affected can have.

The distinctions between these approaches gain additional meaning organized around the macro and micro levels of analysis of the economy. Macro analyses, as already noted, tend to concentrate on the overall systemic effects at the national level (or sometimes, sectors of the national economy), and it has become virtually a matter of economic dogma that free trade is the best way to promote overall economic growth (the tide that lifts all boats). Thus, macro-level analyses tend to be pro–free trade and tend to be associated with those political units most associated with a concern for the overall economy—in the federal structure, the executive branch of government. Micro-level analysis, on the other hand, focuses on the effects of free trade or protection on individual industries and ultimately on individual people who may be affected favorably or unfavorably by such impacts. This analysis thus contains an element of criticism of free trade largely missing from macro-level analyses and has, in the contemporary debate, been more associated with protectionism, although the criticisms are rarely put explicitly in those terms because they appear parochial.

The fair trade position offers a compromise of sorts on the macro-micro dimension. Fair traders tend not to be hostile to free trade in general, accepting the overall logic of the free trade argument. They are, however, more sensitive to the negative effects on sectors or industries, and seek inclusion in free trade arrangements to soften or eliminate negative impacts. While few American presidents have PhDs in international economics (none have!), it should also come as no surprise that politicians might from time to time set aside their economic or other beliefs to curry favor with voters. Politics is about picking winners in democracies, and foreign economic policy is most certainly political. American policy makers try to use foreign economic policy as a tool to promote state (and maybe even personal political) interests. For much of the last seventy years, those interests have mostly been pursued through the promotion of free trade and global integration. Perhaps a new calculation of those interests is under way.

The purpose of this chapter is not just to recount the debates about free trade, or to provide a brief overview of the development of the liberal economic order—in the classical economic "liberal" sense of the focus on markets and free trade rather than government intervention in the economy—although the chapter aims to serve as a quick primer on these issues. The real key for this chapter is to see how policy makers try to pursue what they see as American interests and values through economics and economic policy. Having covered these basic conceptual and historical issues, now we can turn to how things like trade agreements are in fact also tools of statecraft.

Power and Economic Statecraft

The Prussian general and military expert Carl von Clausewitz famously observed in his tome *On War* (published after his death in 1832) that war is a continuation of politics waged with different means. It is useful to think about foreign economic policy as a continuation of politics by economic means, rather than thinking of it as something inherently different from the other foreign policy contexts discussed in this text. For centuries, countries have tried to accrue power to increase their sense of "security." Economic power is a key part of any security equation; how one gets it, retains it, and grows it is a matter of statecraft as old as any other.

The United States has generally approached foreign economic statecraft with a predisposition toward capitalism, markets, and free trade—all hallmarks of the American political culture. These ideals may have set the United States apart from other states over time; other states pursued, for example, colonialism and imperialism as their approach to foreign economic policy (namely, the British Empire) or communism (such as the Soviet Union), but all have in common a link between ideals and interests. The U.S. preference for markets and free trade may be an ideal, but it also reflects a sense that these arrangements are in the interests of the United States and the U.S. economy. It is thus often better to think about how the United States uses economic and other nonmilitary levers to pursue what leaders see as in the country's interest rather than abstract principles when the two come into conflict.

The concept of **power** is one of the most often used yet ill-defined concepts in the study of politics. For some, power means having certain resources; for others, it means the ability to get the outcomes that you want; other times it means the ability to influence others. In the study of foreign policy and international relations, though, there have been some efforts to be clearer about what "power" means and how states try to get and use it.

Hard power refers to resources that exist and can be "counted." Military assets, for example, are hard power. The size and vitality of a nation's economy is a form of hard power. These are resources that can be offered to others in a positive or negative form. Military power can be used as a "carrot," or an inducement, in the form of military aid or assistance; it can also be used as a "stick," a punishment used to take away resources, or land, from others. Economic resources can also be used in carrot or stick form, to try to persuade others to help attain national objectives. This discussion continues in more detail, but it starts here with trying to build a framework for thinking about these tools.

In recent years the term soft power has been used frequently, especially in reference to the United States. As first described by Joseph S. Nye Jr., the term is meant to capture the importance of resources that are less tangible (or capable of being counted) than hard power. Soft power normally refers to such things as culture, beliefs, and attitudes—things that draw others to you. An important base of American power, it is argued, is American ideas such as freedom, democracy, and self-government, and also American music, culture, movies, and even fast-food restaurants. There used to be a Gatorade commercial campaign with the tagline "Be Like Mike," asserting that everyone wanted to be like basketball great Michael Jordan. A great base of American soft power, many argue, is the extent to which people around the world want to be like the United States. Power like this eludes attempts at counting, or quantification, but many argue that it is an essential component of American power in the global system, or an emerging weakness that must be strengthened through things such as better use of foreign aid and public diplomacy campaigns, as will be discussed shortly.

Another often used conception of power, especially with respect to the United States, is sticky power. Walter Russell Mead, for example, argues that part of America's power in the world is based on how others encounter the United States through things such as trade and travel, and then they are "stuck" to the United States, drawn into a web of relations that has benefits from which other states would not want to be extricated. Central to this conception of power is international economics and economic institutions, led by the United States. A key form of America's sticky power, then, is global capitalism and the institutions that keep it running, led by the United States. Some of these institutions—the Bretton Woods international organizations, for example—were discussed above.

With this in mind it is interesting to note that the top trading partners of the United States are (in descending order) China, Canada, Mexico, Japan, Germany, South Korea, the United Kingdom, France, Taiwan, and India. Many of these are obviously neighbors and longtime allies, but they constitute trade relationships embedded in webs of other areas as well—evidence of the "sticky" nature of trade.

A final way to think about power that bears on this discussion is smart power—the idea that an essential component of statecraft is the ability of the United States to successfully blend soft, hard, and sticky power in a coherent approach to foreign policy. The United States may have dominated the global economy in the past, for example, but it will not do so in the future without careful management and decision making. Proponents of smart power assert that U.S. leadership going forward will be based on the capacity of the U.S. government to blend hard- and soft-power resources, diplomacy, public diplomacy, foreign-aid programs, and the like, to promote a global system that favors the United States. The United States will not have the power to "command" the global system to behave in a certain way (certainly not like after World War II), but will have to use a range of economic and political tools to lead and coax in order to create a system conducive to the interests that leaders set forth.

The metaphor of a **"two-level game"** is a useful analytic device for helping understand the dynamics of international bargaining and negotiation that tries to capture the twin pressures U.S. leaders face when crafting foreign economic policy. The idea of a two-level game, as developed by Robert D. Putnam, is that national leaders must simultaneously "negotiate" at an international level (with leaders of other countries or organizations) and at a domestic level (finding a policy that is acceptable to other powerful actors in the political system). Indeed, as the text has discussed in previous chapters, at the domestic level the president must think about Congress, public opinion, and interest groups. Foreign-trade deals, for example, must not only be acceptable to U.S. leaders and the leader abroad with whom the United States is negotiating; they also must be acceptable at the domestic level. The TPP, for example, was negotiated over seven years, but ran aground during the 2016 U.S. presidential election when it became clear the agreement was not acceptable to Congress or the public. So when crafting foreign economic policy with the tools discussed below, the two-level-game concept helps remind us that U.S. leaders are constantly "playing" at both levels (see figure 10.1).

Level 1: Other state leaders

⇑⇓

State leaders must simultaneously negotiate with

⇓⇑

Level 2: Other domestic political actors

Figure 10.1 International Bargaining as a Two-Level Game

Foreign Economic Bureaucracy

As in security policy, presidents do not make decisions about foreign economic policy alone, but rather they draw on the help and expertise of different executive branch agencies than are consulted in other policy domains. While the State Department is a key player in crafting and implementing foreign economic policy, a range of other agencies play a central role here. The president draws on the advice of both the Council of Economic Advisers (CEA) and the National Economic Council (NEC).

The CEA, established in 1947 as an economic advisory body to the president, primarily advises the president about the domestic economy (such as the budget, taxes, and unemployment). The NEC, however, is far newer (established by President Clinton in 1993) and is meant to advise the president on global economic policy. The NEC was meant to be an economic version of the more long-standing National Security Council (NSC). Like the NSC, the NEC is meant to be the hub of an interagency process, with a director who tries to coordinate the range of agencies that play a role in international economics, such as Treasury, State, Energy, Commerce, Agriculture, Labor, and the U.S. Trade Representative.

Three other executive agencies warrant special mention. With the increased emphasis on trade agreements that has been a hallmark of U.S. foreign economic policy—particularly since the end of the Cold War—the Commerce Department has become a much more central figure in foreign policy than perhaps used to be the case. Commerce is a lead agency when it comes to promoting trade and especially with respect to promoting U.S. exports abroad. The "Commercial Services" function at Commerce in many ways mirrors the types of services that U.S. embassies and the State Department provide for U.S. citizens abroad, in this case trying to support U.S. businesses that seek access to foreign markets.

The Treasury Department is a key figure in foreign economic policy as well. The International Affairs Office has responsibility for promoting U.S. economic interests around the globe, and it works closely with the international economic institutions discussed earlier in the chapter, such as the World Bank, IMF, and WTO. Another wing of the Treasury Department, the Terrorism and Financial Intelligence Office, houses a number of units relevant to foreign policy, including serving as the point agency for pursuing the financial backers of terrorists and terrorist organizations. An additional part of the Treasury Department—and one particularly important for foreign economic policy—is the Office of Foreign Assets Control (OFAC). OFAC enforces economic and trade sanctions imposed by the United States on other countries and on terrorist organizations. While the United States has used trade sanctions since early in the Republic, today's OFAC dates to the Korean War era, when President Truman blocked access to all Chinese and North Korean assets that the U.S. government could control.

Finally, the office of the **U.S. Trade Representative (USTR)** takes the lead in negotiating trade agreements with other countries. Starting in the 1960s and following both congressional and presidential initiatives, today the USTR holds Cabinet-level rank and is responsible for coordinating U.S. trade policy, negotiating trade agreements, and advising the president on trade matters.

Congress and Foreign Economic Policy

It is important to note that Congress has important and constitutionally guaranteed powers with respect to foreign economic policy. Article 1, Section 8, of the Constitution specifically gives Congress the power to "regulate foreign commerce," thus designating Congress as a central player in this domain. Congress has helped structure the foreign economic policy components of the executive branch, such as ordering the creation of the USTR; and many trade agreements are treaties, which must be ratified by a two-thirds supermajority of the U.S. Senate. As the chapter on Congress discusses, the Legislature has also from time to time approved the use of a different mechanism for negotiating and ratifying trade agreements—the **Trade Promotion Authority** (so-called **Fast Track**), by which trade agreements come before both the House and the Senate for a simple majority vote, during which no amendments are allowed. The Trade Promotion Authority has been in force on and off since the 1970s, usually approved by Congress for a few years at a time when the national mood is conducive to free trade. Fast Track authority had lapsed in 2007, but in 2015 Congress conferred it again to the president for six years, primarily to move the TPP to the Hill. Interestingly, the opposition to TPP was from Democrats, not Republicans, with very few Democrats in the House or Senate voting for the measure. Now attention turns to Donald Trump, who urged against giving Fast Track to President Obama, and who now inherits the negotiating power for new trade deals.

Congress does not pass every piece of foreign economic policy, of course. Presidents regularly use their initiative to offer foreign economic rewards and levy punishments, and for example, via executive order direct OFAC to implement sanctions against a target state. This chapter discusses some examples of both policy forms. Before turning to that, however, and a discussion of the economic instruments used as part of foreign policy, some discussion of the strategies that drive the use of these tools is in order.

Tools of Influence

A wide range of tools beyond the use of force is available to U.S. policy makers to try to influence others and to address foreign policy problems. While military force can be used to punish an enemy or assist an ally, economic instruments can also be used as carrots and sticks in order to wield influence. Most often policy makers will use several of these tools at once to try to influence other actors and address foreign policy problems. Military assistance might be partnered with other forms of foreign assistance and increased trade flows, for example, to reward or try to induce behavior that U.S. leaders see as in American interests. Sanctions, an end to foreign assistance, and even the use of force might be packaged as a way to put pressure on a regime—steps taken by the United States against Libya in 2011, for example. As this chapter has discussed, selecting which tools to use, and how to use them, is a question of statecraft. The discussion now turns to the tools themselves, which are highlighted in table 10.1.

TABLE 10.1 Carrots and Sticks	
Punishment	**Reward**
Military	**Military**
Destroy targets	Protect an ally
Take away land	Defend an ally
Occupy	Assist militarily/withdraw forces
Economic	**Economic**
Impose sanctions	Supply aid
Boycott	Spur investment
Impose embargo	Make trade agreement
Freeze assets	Give credits

Foreign Aid

Foreign aid, or "foreign assistance," refers to a complex set of programs designed to promote U.S. interests around the world. The U.S. government currently spends funds abroad within seven specific categories: democracy, human rights, and governance; education and social services; economic development; environment (the smallest program); health; humanitarian assistance; and peace and security. For 2017, the Obama administration requested from Congress approximately $34 billion in foreign assistance spending; a little over $8 billion of that would go to peace and security programs, while about $1 billion would go to programs aimed at the environment.

Several budgetary points deserve notice. First, it is important to remember that these are extremely small amounts in the context of a multitrillion-dollar federal budget. Second, much of this funding has been targeted at the growing global HIV/AIDS epidemic, and more recently, combating terrorism and the Zika virus. Finally, while the United States is one of the world's largest foreign-assistance donors in terms of absolute dollars, when the size of a country's economy is considered, the United States lags behind all other advanced industrial democracies on foreign aid by the resulting ratio of assistance to total GDP.

The organizational centerpiece of U.S. foreign-assistance programs is the U.S. Agency for International Development (**USAID**). USAID had been an independent executive branch agency until the 1990s, when it was folded into the Department of State. Some foreign aid spending comes through other elements of the State Department, but USAID is the frontrunner in this area. The spending on foreign aid programs goes to foreign governments but also to contractors, nongovernmental actors, and international organizations.

Foreign assistance can take a variety of forms. Loans, debt forgiveness, equipment, training, and commodities (such as goods and medicine) are common types of assistance. While government agencies such as USAID oversee the use of particular assistance programs, most often the assistance is actually carried out by nongovernmental organizations (NGOs), charitable groups, and private contractors.

Foreign aid has its critics. Many argue that, especially in a time of economic hardship at home, even such a small part of the federal budget ought to be used to address domestic problems (or not spent at all). Some have also urged bureaucratic changes in the U.S. government to streamline the aid process; indeed, there have been many such reforms in recent years. Others point out that often the money that goes to foreign regimes ends up being wasted, or worse yet, funneled into the private bank accounts of corrupt officials. Aid might even spur more corruption, with some pointing to evidence that as aid levels increased, economic development decreased over the last several decades.

There are many reasons to support foreign assistance programs as well. One argument in favor of foreign aid hinges on the link between foreign aid and strategic U.S. interests. Foreign aid is not all about altruism, after all. A large portion of U.S. assistance goes to key allies such as Egypt and Israel, to support broader U.S. foreign policy goals such as promoting stability in the Middle East. Other assistance, such as spending on HIV/AIDS and on Zika, is in part motivated by self-interest in addition to altruism—to stop the spread of infectious disease that might eventually affect Americans if not controlled overseas. In other words, these programs are aimed at helping create the kind of world in which the United States can thrive.

The post–World War II Marshall Plan is a good example of this combination of motives. The 1947 European Recovery Program was an economic recovery act for Western Europe. It was altruistic in the sense that the United States invested some $13 billion in the economies of Europe to help them recover after the war. The Marshall Plan also pursued the strategic interests of the United States, however, by helping show the strength of capitalism, building up America's allies against the Soviet bloc, and helping spur the growth of markets that would become larger consumers in the American economy. The motives demonstrate clearly both altruism and self-interest.

Another point that highlights the dual nature of foreign aid, which is often not well appreciated by Americans, is that most of what goes "out" as foreign aid ends up finding its way back into the American economy. Large portions of U.S. food aid, and credits that can be used to buy products and services, are tied to spending on American goods and services (what is known as procurement tying). Thus food aid is good for broad U.S. goals (it can make the United States look good in the eyes of starving and malnourished people around the world), it is altruistic (feeding hungry people is a good thing to do), and it benefits American farmers, who get paid to produce the food. This same logic also applies to much military assistance. Military-aid programs often emphasize selling military equipment (such as aircraft) to foreign governments; the money never leaves the United States, but is instead used to pay American manufacturers of the equipment. Indeed, the U.S. government is quite open about the fact that it sees foreign-assistance programs as aimed not only at providing a helping hand to others but also at promoting American political, economic, and strategic interests.

Millennium Challenge

At the turn of the new millennium in 2000, the United Nations issued a declaration of "Millennium Development Goals," aimed at reducing poverty and increasing health, education, and development by 2015. As part of its effort to respond to these goals and to change how foreign aid works, the Bush administration began the Millennium Challenge by founding the **Millennium Challenge Corporation (MCC)** in 2004. This new agency would administer the Millennium Challenge Account, a new component of the U.S. foreign assistance portfolio. The MCC functions somewhat differently from the rest of the federal bureaucracy that deals with foreign assistance. It is a government corporation that has a chief executive officer and a board of directors (chaired by the secretary of state), with an annual budget of a little less than $1 billion.

The goal of the MCC is to promote economic development, good governance, and market solutions with low- and middle-income countries struggling with development. The kinds of programs that are funded, usually in the form of five-year "compacts" with the countries, include anticorruption programs, agricultural projects, clean water projects, programs to address HIV/AIDS, and irrigation and transportation construction. As an example of one of the MCC compacts, in February 2008, a five-year, $698 million compact was initiated with Tanzania. The funds are aimed at projects that will reduce poverty and stimulate economic growth through targeted investments in transportation (roads), energy (reliable electrical power), and clean potable water.

The MCC is a small part of the fabric of foreign assistance, but it is a new approach and one that many foreign-assistance advocates hope will grow over time. As is discussed in the following section, much of U.S. foreign assistance is actually in the form of military assistance and aid to address drugs and terrorism. The MCC could become a more primary vehicle for supporting programs aimed at the other foreign-assistance priorities, which are traditionally more the domain of USAID. Needless to say, there are some bureaucratic struggles over this issue, between both the agencies involved and their supporters in Congress.

Military Assistance

Providing **military assistance** in one form or another to friends and allies is a common form of "foreign aid," although it may not be what Americans commonly think of when they consider the nature of foreign-assistance programs. Military-assistance programs often take the form of providing equipment or training to other countries, often as a reward for their pursuit of foreign and security policy aims that the United States shares. Peacekeeping funds for non-UN operations also are a form of military assistance. Military-assistance programs are overseen by the State Department but implemented by the Department of Defense.

During the Cold War, military assistance was a key way to aid—and lure—allies. From the 1970s through 2016, for example, a large proportion of foreign military-assistance spending went to the Middle East as a way to promote a range of policy goals in the region; most of it has gone to Israel and Egypt, with far smaller amounts going to Jordan and others in the region. Since the 1970s Israel has been the largest single recipient of foreign aid, much of it in the form of military assistance. In recent years Iraq and Afghanistan have also received large portions of this budget.

The use of foreign assistance of all types—but especially military assistance—as a lever or "carrot" to induce and reward assistance with the war on terrorism has become a central theme since 2001. The other side of the coin, cutting or withdrawing aid as punishment for the lack of support, has also been utilized as a "stick." Aid to countries such as Yemen, Libya, Pakistan, and many of the states in Central Asia, for example, has been linked to counterterrorism, as well as aid to Colombia for assistance with "narcoterrorism." When all of the components of the foreign-assistance budget are combined, they make up approximately $54 billion, with military assistance composing roughly $15 billion of that total.

Sanctions

The use of economic **sanctions** is another instrument of statecraft that is often used against target states or groups in order to influence their behavior. It is important to remember that sanctions can be used in either positive (carrot) or negative (stick) form, because once imposed, the removal or easing of sanctions can be used to try to coax or reward changed behavior. Sanctions can be put in place either by legislation or by executive order. Sanctions are a common tool of U.S. foreign policy and one that many see as occupying a sort of middle ground between diplomatic communications on the one hand and the use of military force on the other. In practice, however, sanctions are rarely used on their own but as part of a package of initiatives (such as foreign assistance or the threat of force) aimed at target states or groups.

Intersection 10.1 — Obama and the End of the Cuban Embargo?

President Trump says he will build a wall entirely along the nearly two-thousand-mile-long border with Mexico.

The United States has had an embargo of Cuba, in one form or another, since the days when Dwight Eisenhower, who left the presidency in 1961, was in the White House. The purpose of the embargo, which was put in place by presidential order, was to hurt the Cuban economy so that perhaps the Cuban people would rise up to overthrow Fidel Castro; a secondary goal was to punish Cuba for its foreign policy behavior being aligned with the Soviets; a Soviet ally just ninety miles off the Florida coast deserved some kind of harsh American response, many thought, and sanctions against it as part of the broader policy of containment made sense. But what to do with the embargo policy once the Soviet Union ceased to exist and the Cold War collapsed? When the Cold War ended between 1989 and 1991, some argued that the embargo should be made even tighter, since now without Soviet assistance to prop it up the Cuban economy might finally collapse under the pressure. Others argued that the end of the Cold War should also mean the end of the embargo; it was now time to "normalize" relations between the United States and the island.

In the 1990s American policy toward Cuba—and in a classic case of intermestic policy, also a policy to placate Cuban American voters in South Florida—went back and forth, now driven not just by the White House, which sometimes wanted to ease the embargo, but also by embargo proponents in Congress who wanted to tighten it. Congress passed the Cuban Democracy Act in 1992, and the Helms-Burton Act in 1996, both aimed at tightening the embargo; but both left open some options for a president who was inclined to loosen parts of the embargo in order to reach out to the Cuban people. No matter the policy preferences of the president—Clinton and Obama wanted to loosen the embargo, while Bush wanted to tighten it—none of them liked Congress calling the shots on an important case of foreign policy.

For the last fifteen years, those who oppose part or all of the embargo policy include much of the political Left (which has been anti-embargo for a long time), but increasingly it includes traditional Republican audiences such as libertarians, and also trade groups, big business, big agriculture, the chamber of commerce, and many governors from states across the country who want to do business in Cuba. The embargo's supporters tend to consist of hardened Cold Warriors and Cuban Americans, and others who agree with them, who see the Castro regime as continuing to repress its people—even after Fidel's death in 2016.

Having won the White House without the help of the embargo hard-liners, with the Castro brothers on their way out, and with public opinion in the United States and in the Cuban American community moving toward engagement with Cuba, President Obama made sweeping changes to the embargo—easing most of its restrictions, and reopening diplomatic ties between the United States and Cuba with the U.S. Embassy in Havana reopened in 2016 for the first time in fifty-four years. Obama himself visited the island and even took in a baseball game. Signs were that Obama would try to get an ambassador appointment through the Senate in a lame duck session of Congress after the 2016 election—but the election of Donald Trump upset that plan!

On the campaign trail candidate Trump said at first that Obama's opening to Cuba was "fine," and that fifty years was enough—although he would have cut a better deal! But with the election approaching and sensing the chance to win Florida, and with it perhaps the White House, Trump made an appearance in Miami where he declared he'd reverse the openings with Cuba—much to the delight of embargo hard-liners. Since the openings President Obama pursued were all by executive order, President Trump can reverse them over time, technically. The question is whether things have moved so far down the field that there is now no turning back. Whether you agree with the embargo or not as a part of American foreign policy, it is hard to look at it and not recognize that the Cuban embargo is as much about U.S. domestic *politics* as it is about foreign security and *economic policy*.

The term *sanctions* actually represents an umbrella term meant to identify a range of economic levers that policy makers may use. One extreme form of sanctions is an **embargo**, or a total ban on trade, travel, and investment, with another country. This is a rare form of sanction; as discussed in intersection 10.1, even the famous "Cuban embargo" is not really a full embargo of Cuba, since it allows limited economic interactions such as Cuban Americans sending money to relatives in Cuba. A less extreme, though still severe, form of sanction is a boycott. A boycott is a restriction on the import of all or some particular goods or services from another country. The term tends to connote a total ban—such as the one in place against "conflict" or "blood" diamonds from Sierra Leone—but could also take the form of limits (or quotas) that are put in place on imports from another country (such as the restrictions on the number of cars per year that could be imported from Japan that were in place in the 1980s). It should be evident that there is a strong link between these instruments and both trade policy and efforts at coercive diplomacy, as discussed above.

Another form of sanctions is to freeze the financial assets of a country's leadership that are held in your country. For example, during the Iranian Revolution in 1979 when Americans at the U.S. Embassy were held hostage, President Carter froze billions of dollars' worth of Iranian assets held in the United States. (He also severed diplomatic relations with Iran and put a boycott in place on oil from Iran.) More recently, the U.S. government froze assets of the Libyan government with an estimated value of nearly $33 billion, and in July 2011 announced that it would make those assets available to the anti-Gaddafi rebel coalition, the Interim National Transitional Council, when it recognized that group as the legal government of the country. And in an interesting example of how these tools have evolved over time, in 2015 President Obama ordered the assets of seven Venezuelan officials to be frozen—officials the U.S. government believes helped stoke the national security threat from this South American country.

A final form of sanction is called *divestment*. If a positive form of foreign economic policy is to promote investment in a country, the opposite is also true in the case where the United States orders American individuals and commercial enterprises to divest their activities in another country. A form of divestment was part of the sanctions ordered against South Africa in the 1980s that many argue helped move the apartheid regime toward its end.

Two other points are worth noting about sanctions. First, they are a tempting tool for policy makers to use as a way to protest behavior with which the U.S. government disagrees. They became so common in the 1990s that some argued that there was a sanctions epidemic breaking out in American foreign policy. Note, too, that these sanctions are often bundled with other tools as part of an influence attempt. Second, they rarely work, at least to the degree or end for which they were imposed. To some extent this is because the global economy is such that pressure from the United States can often be compensated for by the economic activities of others, and cases of comprehensive, multilateral sanctions are very rare. Even when they do "work," as with the fall of apartheid in South Africa, it is hard to know for sure that the sanctions per se were the cause of the change.

"Smart" Sanctions

Another aspect or type of sanctions that has received increased attention in recent years is so-called **smart sanctions**. Smart sanctions are meant to be more targeted types of sanctions, aimed at a country's rulers rather than blanket sanctions that indiscriminately harm a country's population. If traditional sanctions are the economic equivalent of a military "carpet bombing" campaign, smart sanctions are designed to be more like a "surgical" air strike that targets the regime but tries not to punish the innocent. They can include mechanisms like freezing the personal assets of a foreign leader or reducing a leader's (and even that person's family's) ability to travel abroad by not allowing visas to be issued. Whatever the tool, the idea is to use targeted economic mechanisms to build pressure on the leadership of a country rather than make the population suffer.

The interest in developing more targeted sanctions, rather than using blanket sanctions against a country, emerged from at least two impulses. First, there was a growing sense that sanctions as they had been used rarely accomplished their goals. Comprehensive sanctions may have played an important part in bringing down the apartheid regime in South Africa, but that is perhaps an exception. In that case there was near-universal adoption of sanctions around the globe; rarely has a similar coordinated effort been possible against any other country. So if these kinds of sanctions policies do not work very well, perhaps it is time to try something else.

Second, there is a strong strain of concern in the United States and around the world about the ethical, humanitarian, and moral implications of broad sanctions policies. This dynamic rose to prominence in the 1970s and has certainly accelerated since the end of the Cold War. Sanctions may or may not work to change the behavior of a regime (or change the regime), but one thing about them is sure: They will harm the population, especially those who are weakest and most at risk, including children, women, the sick, and the elderly. When forcing change proves impossible, making the population sicker and weaker likely undermines U.S. policy goals rather than promoting them—thus the interest in crafting more targeted, "smart" sanctions that do not, as the old saying goes, "punish the innocent."

Unfortunately, "smart" sanctions also have difficulties in application. To date, they appear not to have been any more successful when employed than their broader cousins. The very public scandal that surrounded the UN's Oil-for-Food Program in Iraq also badly damaged its reputation. This program, which ran from 1993 until 2003, was the kind of initiative meant to allow a more targeted approach to sanctions. Under it, Iraqi oil would be sold on the global market and the money earned would be used to buy food for the Iraqi population. In a tragic case of good intentions gone awry, it turns out that the program led to billions of dollars in kickbacks from the oil industry to Iraqi and UN officials involved in administering the program, and to substantial oil smuggling. Rulers got rich, and many of the program's managers did too, but relatively little relief was brought to the Iraqi people. One of the program's directors quit in frustration, noting that sanctions (however well meaning) only harm innocent civilians. The scandal underscores the difficulty of using the sanctions lever to try to influence others.

According to the Treasury Department's Office of Foreign Assets Control, in 2017 the United States had some form of sanctions in place against twenty-one targets. Many of these are classic cases of sanctions levied against states, such as those against Cuba, Iran, Syria, Myanmar, and North Korea. Some others are more targeted. Sanctions with respect to Cote d'Ivoire, for example, are actually prohibitions against any individuals having transactions with a list of people identified as upsetting the peace in that West African country. There is also a variety of sanctions in place meant to block the economic activity of those involved in terrorism and the drug trade. As intersection 10.2 discusses, there are many countries on whom we do not currently have sanctions, but it would not be hard to imagine a move toward some form of sanction, because of either the country's economic policies or humanitarian and democratic status.

Intersection 10.2	**The United States, the Philippines, and Presidents Duterte and Trump**

One of the closest economic and security relations the United States has in the Pacific is with the Philippines. The United States administrated the Philippines from 1898 and the end of the Spanish-American War until the Philippines gained its independence after the end of World War II, except for a period of Japanese occupation during the war. Since that time, for seventy years, the two countries have had a treaty of alliance and are close trading and security partners. According to the State Department, there are about 4 million Americans of Philippine descent, more than 200,000 Americans live and work in the Philippines now, and more than 600,000 Americans visit there each year. The United States is the third-largest trading partner for the Philippines. For many years two of the largest U.S. military installations in the world were in the Philippines, Clark Air Force Base and Subic Bay Naval Base, though the United States left both installations when the Cold War ended. U.S. forces regularly train with Philippine forces as part of the global war on terror, primarily aimed at Abu Sayyaf—an Islamic terrorist organization—in the south of the country. Because of the highly educated citizenry, the Philippines has also become the global capital for call center companies—with more than a million people, of the roughly 100 million who live in the Philippines, employed in this business outsourcing industry, mostly for U.S.-based companies. It is hard to imagine the relationship between the United States and the Philippines turning bad— but that might be what is happening before our very eyes in a classic case of simultaneous two-level games and the intersection between domestic and foreign policy on security and economics.

Rodrigo Duterte, a flamboyant and plain-talking former governor, was elected president in 2016. No one thing could perhaps come between the United States and the Philippines, and indeed here there are many issues. First, stylistically, Duterte has spoken quite harshly of the United States and of President Obama, saying that the American president should "go to hell." (He has also spoken in harsh terms about the EU and the Pope—but spoken highly of Hitler!) More substantively, he has called for an end to joint military exercises between U.S. and Filipino forces, and that he will "break up" with America. He may be pursuing closer economic and military relations with China—which comes at a very dangerous time as China looks to expand its military presence in the South China Sea in ways that have dramatic implications for the United States, the

Philippines, Vietnam, Japan, South Korea, and others. He also seems to be leading an effort to address the drug addiction problem in the Philippines by "extra-judicial killings," that is, by rounding up, jailing, and often killing suspected drug sellers and drug users without any formal due process of law. According to Human Rights Watch, more than 5,000 people have been killed as part of this effort since Duterte took office at the end of June 2016.

Interestingly, Donald Trump has not renounced Duterte's use of violence, or his harsh statements, since Trump won the White House—so perhaps these two leaders will find a way to work together. Duterte claims that Trump endorsed his approach to the war on drugs, a statement that Trump has not contradicted. Still, at some point national interests and values could bring increased stress to the relationship.

Trump's talk about American companies that outsource jobs may be one way that the relationship between these two countries ends up in the crosshairs in the coming years. Moves to align with China and against American interests in the South China Sea would be another, as would be allowing an Al Qaeda–related group the ability to train. The human rights situation in the Philippines, if the extrajudicial killings continue or increase, could attract the attention of human rights groups and Congress. Since the relationship between the two countries is so fulsome, there are myriad carrots and sticks the United States could seek to manipulate to punish the Philippines, as shown in figure 10.2. The United States could put sanctions on the Philippines, or refuse to sell military equipment or aid with military training (although Duterte seems to be heading in that direction all on his own), for example. There will be many flashpoints in the coming years; while not highly likely, this could be one of them and bears watching.

Libya is an interesting example of U.S. sanctions policy. In the 1980s, the Reagan administration imposed a variety of sanctions on Libya for its support of international terrorism, including a travel ban and a boycott of Libyan oil. Those sanctions were widened following the 1986 terrorist bombing of a Berlin disco. Military action also was taken against the Gaddafi regime, and Libya was on the State Department's list of terrorism-supporting states. The UN joined in the sanctions regime against Libya following the terrorist bombing of Pan Am Flight 103, which exploded over Lockerbie, Scotland, in 1988. In 1996 the Libya sanctions were joined with others in a law passed by Congress called the Iran-Libya Sanctions Act (ILSA).

Starting in the late 1990s, the Gaddafi regime and Great Britain had some secret contacts about how Libya could become reintegrated into the global economy. These discussions started to come to fruition in 1999 when Libya surrendered the Lockerbie bombing suspects for trial. Further progress was made in 2003 when Libya agreed to pay compensation to the families of the bombing's victims. In 2004 President Bush ended the full range of U.S. sanctions on Libya following these steps and Libya's turning over its weapons of mass destruction program to the United States.

In 2011, however, the sanctions would return, as already noted. As the political protests of the Arab Spring spread to Libya, the Gaddafi regime turned the full force of its military on the protesters, and horrendous violence well chronicled by the electronic media followed. The United States, the EU, and the UN reemployed sanctions and imposed a no-fly zone on Libyan aircraft. NATO air power was also put to use against targets of the Gaddafi regime. This effort to use sanctions and limited military force to drive the Gaddafi regime from power is one of the most recent examples of these dynamics. Also visible in this case are the tragic unintended consequences of a violent and failed state left behind after Gaddafi's overthrow.

Conclusion

Foreign economic policy is inherently intermestic—it simultaneously is both foreign and domestic. Indeed, the domestic ramifications of foreign economic policy tend to be felt immediately by American workers. Policy in this domain is also very controversial, as the 2016 election cycle vividly portrayed. Do free trade agreements promote American jobs? There's an answer to this question in theory, in the textbooks, but politics is about the answer in practice, on the street, and on the election path. Presidents have used the levers of foreign economic policy to pursue American interests and ideas for the history of the Republic, and now we enter a new phase where skepticism about free trade deals runs high.

The acquisition and use of power and the tools of statecraft in order to promote foreign policy aims is perhaps more art than science. As this chapter has discussed, there is a broad range of instruments that U.S. policy makers have at their disposal short of using military power against a target in order to try to influence others. Trying to find the right mix of hard and soft power, the right levers to pull and buttons to push, the right mix of carrots and sticks, is the essence of statecraft.

The use of foreign assistance is a common tactic in efforts to reward allies and punish enemies. The American public may not understand "foreign aid" very well, with recent surveys showing that most Americans think the foreign-aid budget is far larger than it is, but policy makers realize that foreign assistance programs offer several avenues for promoting U.S. interests abroad and addressing common problems. An extremely small part of the federal budget, foreign assistance efforts have increased in recent years as terrorism and security concerns increased, but the efforts to address humanitarian problems, hunger, and disease are also important components of U.S. foreign assistance policies.

Economic sanctions are a widely used instrument of power, if not a widely effective one. Sanctions are attractive as a way to punish enemies that seems fairly low-risk to Americans and U.S. military forces. As discussed previously, they also exist in a variety of forms and so can be added to and tightened—or subtracted from or loosened—as part of an ongoing effort to influence the behavior of others. These are not "on" or "off" mechanisms, but normally complex combinations of particular components. The appeal, and perhaps the weakness of sanctions as policy instruments exist in this complexity.

Study/Discussion Questions

1. What is the theory of comparative advantage? How is it critical to thinking about an international economic system based in free trade and globalization?
2. What is/was the Bretton Woods system of global economics? Is it "dead"?
3. What have been the principal means by which the United States has attempted to promote free trade? Elaborate, using examples.
4. Summarize the continuing debate over free trade, including the notions of levels of analysis and approaches to the subject in your answer.
5. What is the difference between "hard" power and "soft" power?

How does foreign economic policy fit into these conceptions of power?
6. Describe the idea of trade policy as a "two-level game."
7. How are "free trade" and "protectionism" not so much opposing concepts as they are tools used by foreign economic policy makers?
8. What specific mechanisms are parts of the umbrella term "foreign assistance"?
9. What specific types of actions count as forms of "sanctions"? Why are they attractive as policy instruments?
10.

Bibliography

Alden, Edward. *Failure to Adjust: How Americans Got Left Behind in the Global Economy*. New York: Council on Foreign Relations, 2016.

Altman, Robert. "The Great Crash." *Foreign Affairs*, January/February 2009, 2–14.

Armitage, Richard, and Joseph S. Nye Jr. *CSIS Commission on Smart Power: A Smarter, More Secure America*. Washington, DC: Center for Strategic and International Studies, 2007.

Art, Robert J., and Patrick M. Cronin, eds. *The United States and Coercive Diplomacy*. Washington, DC: U.S. Institute of Peace Press, 2003.

Baldwin, David A. *Economic Statecraft*. Princeton, NJ: Princeton University Press, 1985.

Bauman, Zygmunt. *Globalization: The Human Consequences*. New York: Columbia University Press, 1998.

Bergsten, C. Fred. *The United States and the World Economy: Foreign Economic Policy for the Next Decade*. Washington, DC: Institute for International Economics, 2005.

Bolton, Alexander. "Transition Official: Trump Will Not Rip Up NAFTA." *The Hill*, December 4, 2016, http://thehill.com/business-a-lobbying/business-a-lobbying/308764-transition-official-trump-will-not-rip-up-nafta.

Bourguignon, François. "Inequality and Globalization: How the Rich Get Richer as the Poor Catch Up." *Foreign Affairs*, January/February 2016.

Brown, D. Clayton. *Globalization and America Since 1945*. Wilmington, DE: Scholarly Resources, 2003.

Brown, Sherrod. *Myths of Free Trade: Why America's Trade Policy Has Failed*. New York: The New Press, 2006.

Caputo, Mark. "In Miami, Trump Morphs Back into a Cuba Hardliner." *Politico*, September 16, 2016.

Cortright, David, George A. Lopez, and Joseph Stephanides, eds. *Smart Sanctions: Targeting Economic Statecraft*. Lanham, MD: Rowman & Littlefield, 2002.

Davis, Susan. "Congress Renews 'Fast Track' Trade Authority." *USA Today*, June 24, 2015, http://www.usatoday.com/story/news/politics/2015/06/24/congress-renews-fast-track/29226629.

Destler, I. M. *American Trade Politics*. 4th ed. Washington, DC: Institute for International Economics, 2005.

Dierks, Rosa Gomez. *Introduction to Globalization: Political and Economic Perspectives for a New Era*. Chicago: Burnham, 2001.

Dregner, Daniel W. *U.S. Trade Policy: Free versus Fair*. New York: Council on Foreign Relations Press, 2006.

Drury, A. Cooper. *Economic Sanctions and Presidential Decisions*. New York: Palgrave Macmillan, 2005.

Eichengreen, Barry J. *Globalizing Capital: A History of the International Monetary System*. 2nd ed. Princeton, NJ: Princeton University Press, 2008.

———. *Hall of Mirrors: The Great Depression, the Great Recession, and the Uses—and Misuses—of History*. New York: Oxford University Press, 2016.

Erikson, Daniel P. *The Cuba Wars: Fidel Castro, the United States, and the Next Revolution*. New York: Bloomsbury, 2008.

Evans, Peter B., Harold K. Jacobson, and Robert D. Putnam, eds. *Double-Edged Diplomacy: International Bargaining and Domestic Politics*. Berkeley: University of California Press, 1993.

Friedman, Thomas L. *The Lexus and the Olive Tree: Understanding Globalization*. 2nd ed. New York: Picador, 2012.

———. *The World Is Flat: A Brief History of the Twenty-First Century*. New York: Farrar, Straus & Giroux, 2005.

Friedman, Thomas L., and Michael Mandelbaum. *That Used to Be Us: How America Fell Behind in the World It Invented and How We Can Come Back*. New York: Gale, 2012.

George, Alexander L. *Forceful Persuasion: Coercive Diplomacy as an Alternative to War*. Washington, DC: U.S. Institute of Peace Press, 1991.

George, Alexander L., and William E. Simons, eds. *The Limits of Coercive Diplomacy*. 2nd ed. Boulder, CO: Westview, 1994.

Haass, Richard N., and Meghan L. O'Sullivan. *Honey and Vinegar: Incentives, Sanctions and Foreign Policy*. Washington, DC: Brookings, 2000.

Haney, Patrick J., and Walt Vanderbush. *The Cuban Embargo: The Domestic Politics of an American Foreign Policy*. Pittsburgh: University of Pittsburgh Press, 2005.

Hogan, Michael J. *The Marshall Plan: America, Britain, and the Reconstruction of Western Europe, 1947–1952*. New York: Cambridge University Press, 1987.

Hufbauer, Gary. "Ross Perot Was Wrong About NAFTA." *New York Times*, November 25, 2013.

Irwin, Douglas A. *Free Trade Under Fire*. 4th ed. Princeton, NJ: Princeton University Press, 2015.

Katel, Peter. "Reviving Manufacturing: Can the U.S. Regain its Global Lead—and Factory Jobs?" *CQ Researcher* 21, no. 26 (July 22, 2011).

Kennedy, Paul G. *The Rise and Fall of the Great Powers*. New York: Random House, 1987.

Kirshner, Orin, Edward M. Bernstein, and Institute for Agriculture and Trade Policy. *The Bretton Woods-GATT System: Retrospect and Prospect after Fifty Years*. Armonk, NY: Sharpe, 1995.

Lauren, Paul, Gordon A. Craig, and Alexander L. George. *Force and Statecraft: Diplomatic Challenges of Our Time.* 5th ed. New York: Oxford University Press, 2013.

Lee, Don. "The Philippines Has Become the Call Center Capital of the World." *Los Angeles Times,* February 1, 2015, http://www.latimes.com/business/la-fi-philippines-econo my-20150202-story.html.

Lundsgaarde, Erik. *The Domestic Politics of Foreign Aid.* New York: Routledge, 2013.

McBride, Stephen, and John Wiseman, eds. *Globalization and Its Discontents.* New York: St. Martin's, 2000.

Mead, Walter Russell. "America's Sticky Power." *Foreign Policy,* March 2004.

Morley, Morris H., and Christopher McGillion. *Unfinished Business: America and Cuba After the Cold War, 1989–2001.* New York: Cambridge University Press, 2002.

Morrison, Wayne M., James K. Jackson, Vivian C. Jones, M. Angeles Villarreal, Rachel F. Fefer, and Ashley Feng. "U.S. Trade Concepts, Performance, and Policy: Frequently Asked Questions." Congressional Research Service Report RL33944, March 25, 2016.

Naim, Moises. "Think Again: Globalization." *Foreign Policy,* March/April 2009, 28–34.

Nye, Joseph S., Jr. *The Future of Power.* New York: Public Affairs Press, 2011.

———. *Soft Power: The Means to Success in World Politics.* New York: Public Affairs Press, 2005.

Panagariya, Arvind. "Think Again: International Trade." *Foreign Policy,* November/ December 2003, 20–29.

Picard, Louis, and Terry Buss. *A Fragile Balance: Re-examining the History of Foreign Aid, Security, and Diplomacy.* Sterling, VA: Kumarian, 2009.

Piketty, Thomas. Translated by Arthur Goldhammer. *The Economics of Inequality.* Cambridge, MA: Harvard University Press, 2015.

Schaeffer, Robert K. *Understanding Globalization: The Social Consequences of Political, Economic, and Environmental Change.* 5th ed. Lanham, MD: Rowman & Littlefield, 2016.

Spero, Joan Edelman, and Jeffrey A. Hart. *The Politics of International Economics.* 7th ed. Boston: Cengage, 2010.

Steger, Manfred B. *Globalization: A Very Short Introduction.* Updated. New York: Oxford University Press, 2013.

Stiglitz, Joseph E. *Free Fall: America, Free Markets, and the Winking World Economy.* New York: Norton, 2009.

———. *Globalization and Its Discontents.* New York: Norton, 2003.

———. *The Great Divide: Unequal Societies and What We Can Do About Them.* New York: Norton, 2015.

Tarnoff, Curt, and Marian L. Lawson. "Foreign Aid: An Introduction to U.S. Programs and Policy." Congressional Research Service Report R40213, June 17, 2016.

U.S. Department of State, Bureau of East Asian and Pacific Affairs. "Fact Sheet: U.S. Relations with the Philippines." December 15, 2016. Accessed December 27, 2016. https://www.state.gov/r/pa/ei/bgn/2794.htm.

11   Trans-State Issues and American Foreign Policy

Immigration was a major issue in the 2016 election, and has continued to be controversial in President Trump's first year in office.

Preview

Trans-state issues are problems that transcend international boundaries and cannot be solved by the actions of any single state. They are truly international in nature, and as such, require the actions of multiple states, preferably acting in concert, to redress. Addressing these problems requires foreign policy interactions between those states that contribute to and are affected by the particular trans-state issue. What makes these issues particularly difficult is that the states that have some interest in particular issues may have differing and conflicting views both on the nature of the problem (including whether it *is* a problem) and on the solution to it, including the degree to which a particular outcome requires their sacrifice. These issues can have enormous impacts on the human condition and the situations of different groups of people.

There is a large and growing number of these trans-state issues. For present purposes, we have selected two clusters of issues that fairly represent both the nature and range of these problems and especially current interest and disagreement within the American foreign policy community. The first is human rights, democracy, and migration; the other is the environment and global climate change. Both were prominent issues in the 2016 presidential election campaign, although both have much broader international ramifications, and implications for the United States, including important economic consequences.

Key Concepts

climate change

fossil fuels

intergovernmental organizations (IGOs)

nongovernmental organizations (NGOs)

chlorofluorocarbons (CFCs)

sovereignty

International Criminal Court (ICC)

interdependence

negative human rights

positive human rights

third wave of democratization

Beijing summits (1995)

Universal Declaration on Human Rights

genocide

greenhouse effect

Kyoto Protocol

Paris Agreement

The 2016 election was fiercely contested on many levels, with stark differences between the Republican and Democratic candidates that extended across the domestic and foreign policy spectrums. These disagreements certainly extended to a complex set of trans-state policy issues: problems that transcend international boundaries and that cannot be solved by the actions of individual states acting in isolation. The debates during the campaign were generally not depicted as trans-state issues per se, but that is exactly what many of these issues are. The stances the candidates and their followers took aimed at international efforts to address these issues—undercutting these efforts in some cases—and also affected the views of the United States and its foreign policy that many around the world hold.

Two issues stood out in the campaign and will be a continuing part of the unfolding of foreign policy during the Trump administration. One of these relates to the basic nature of human rights. Part of the debate is over attempts to more widely spread democracy, and in the last decade it has extended to the more specific problem of immigrants and refugees. It is a complex debate: immigration has historically been one of the bedrock credos of the United States, which is quite literally a nation of immigrants and much of whose prosperity has been the partial result of an inflow of new blood into the country. In 2016, this principle was called into question over the matter of unauthorized immigrants from Mexico and Central America to the United States. Violent upheavals associated with the Islamic State extended the debate to refugees fleeing the Middle East (and particularly Syria) into both the United States and the EU because of the danger that terrorists would penetrate countries while hidden among the refugees.

The other issue is the environment, and more specifically the question of **climate change** and global warming. This is also a very controversial political question in the United States, with ramifications for the extent and quality of American efforts to address this problem. Within the United States, concern about climate change and energy are often connected. One side of the debate argues that climate change is unproven and possibly bogus, and that treating it as real impedes American efforts to maximize energy production and thus economic prosperity. The oil and gas industry is a leading advocate of this position. The other side, supported by almost the entire scientific community, argues that the effect of burning **fossil fuels** is real and deleterious and must be controlled and reduced. This position calls for sharp reductions in using fossil fuels for energy production to reduce the amount of greenhouse gases in the environment that are heating up the planet. With Trump having won the election while making no secret of his views that climate change is a "hoax," that the United States will build a wall across the southern border and deport millions of undocumented workers, and that we should not allow Muslim immigrants from certain regions into the country, only time will tell how far he is able to move on these issues, how fast, and with what results.

*   *   *

Trans-state issues are also particularly difficult to address—let alone solve— because, among other reasons, they require multilateral action and are inherently intermestic in nature; often what one needs to achieve at the international level does not correspond to achievability at the domestic level. This is especially true in the United States, which is a consistent leader in promoting international responses to trans-state issues, but then ends up opposing them once the global response is crafted because of the hurdles of domestic politics. This means that getting the kind of broad bipartisan agreement that is necessary for the United States to try to lead on these issues is harder than ever.

These problems are often referred to as trans-state issues, defined as problems caused by the actions of states or other actors that transcend state boundaries in ways over which states have little control and that cannot be solved by the actions of individual states or other actors within states alone. The term, however, is far from a perfect name for this class of issues. One of the sets of issues discussed below is human rights and democracy, but this set of problems only meets part of the criteria in the definition. Violations of human rights can be solved by the actions of individual states; the problem is that not all states, for different reasons, enforce the same standards. There is a viewpoint, discussed later, that argues that when human rights are curtailed anywhere, they are curtailed everywhere: that the fabric of human rights and freedom is a seamless cloth and so our rights are all interconnected.

Moreover, not all trans-state problems or their solutions result from state action; nongovernmental organizations such as crime cartels and terrorist groups may cause global problems, whereas **intergovernmental organizations (IGOs),** groups that have states as members (such as the UN), and **nongovernmental organizations (NGOs),** groups that transcend state boundaries and have individuals as members, such as Doctors Without Borders/Médecins Sans Frontières, may contribute to solutions. As a result, this chapter concentrates on examples of major emerging trans-state issues that have achieved and are likely to retain prominence on the foreign policy agenda for some time.

The roster of these global problems covers a broad array of both physical and social conditions on the globe and is depressingly long. There are multiple causes of this emerging set of problems. In some cases such as environmental degradation, the problems are the result of direct human actions in some countries that affect others, such as the use of **chlorofluorocarbons (CFCs)** that attack the ozone layer and expose increasing parts of the world to the harmful effects of ultraviolet radiation. Drug smuggling is an instance where the actions of individuals and groups within countries create a problem that individual states alone cannot control. This points to yet another source: the rise of organized private groups within and among states that contribute both to the growth of problems and to their solutions. Indeed, NGOs are especially prominent in identifying problems and the need for solutions, especially in the human rights area.

In many ways, the trans-state and other emerging issues represent the downside, or at least the challenge, to what are otherwise thought of as positive international trends: the rise of democracies, markets, and freer trade, the expansion of the freedom of travel and movement of people and products and ideas. Those are the good sides of the end of the Cold War: the deepening of globalization, the increasingly interconnected world in which we now live. The dark side of these trends has also risen; they disrupted many previously established patterns without obvious replacement (such as the decline in manufacturing jobs in the Midwest), and even the fruits of these positive advances are not universally or evenly enjoyed.

These issues are also intensely political in several ways. First, many are classically intermestic, with domestic and international dimensions and repercussions; the debate about multilateral free trade deals that we saw in the 2016 elections, especially about the benefits and costs of NAFTA, highlights this dynamic all too well.

Second, the structure of a number of many of these trans-state issues can end up pitting the developed and the developing world against each other. In areas such as environmental pollution, economically developing states such as China and India are asked to ease off the burning of relatively cheap fossil fuels while their economies are still developing, while advanced industrial states remain major pollution producers but are also better suited to transition away from coal and oil. The promotion of human rights initiatives, as another example, often emanates from the West and can be seen by some in the developing world as a new form of Western cultural imperialism.

The third way that these issues can be intensely political has to do with the nexus between global efforts to address these problems and the principle of **sovereignty**, the idea that all states are equal and there is no higher authority that can compel the behavior of states. While it is technically true that all states are sovereign and thus encounter no higher authority in the global system, in practice some states are more sovereign (that is, more powerful) than others, and no state can really stand apart from the rest of the system. The presence of so many IGOs (such as NATO or the EU) and NGOs—both of which are in some sense competitors to the nation-state as a form of organization in world politics—also underscores that sovereignty is far from absolute. Many countries are very sensitive to this point, but the United States has been particularly so. The George W. Bush administration, for example, took a particularly hard line against international efforts that might infringe on American sovereignty or security, whether it was an effort to address the environment (Kyoto Accords), crimes against humanity (the **International Criminal Court or ICC**), or (perhaps as surprisingly) a stronger treaty against biological weapons. The idea that international agreements might force the United States to engage in actions it would not otherwise undertake was anathema to the Bush administration and often put the United States at odds with much of the rest of the international community. While the Obama administration was less strident about U.S. involvement in these efforts, the new Trump administration with its "America First" slogan is likely to take a very dim view of any agreement that limits American sovereignty and freedom of action.

The United States is central to the evolution of these problems and their solutions. The human rights movement is in many important ways an extension of the dialogue within the United States on civil and women's rights. At the same time, problems plaguing the United States, such as the flood of illegal narcotics entering the country and the destabilizing effects of the drug trade on neighboring countries, especially Mexico, are trans-state issues at their core. Controversy on these issues seems to follow the United States because shifts in control of the White House often lead to important policy changes. The Clinton administration, for example, was in favor of vigorous American participation in a range of global efforts at collective problem solving; the Bush administration reversed much of that effort; the Obama administration returned to the table; but now the Trump team may back away again.

What is central and common to these issues is that they defy solutions by single states. In the case of a trans-state issue such as stopping the flow of drugs, the United States is only in partial control of its fate. Despite efforts to educate the citizenry about the deleterious effects of drug use and attempts to intercept incoming supplies of illicit materials, the campaign only stands a chance of being successful if there is widespread international cooperation to shut down the sources of drugs, to make their transshipment more difficult, and to reduce demand. In the meantime, drugs—like TVs—are cheaper, more plentiful, and of higher quality than ever before. Stopping international terrorism faces similar challenges. At least some degree of coordinated effort is required to make progress on these issues.

Many of these issues seem abstract and thus ignorable because their effects are neither obvious nor immediate. How am I adversely affected today by driving a gas guzzler? Or how does the CIA's waterboarding a terrorist hurt me personally? Most are issues on which Americans generally agree in principle, but often not in practice—especially when they are adversely affected by the "solution." No one, for instance, is for pollution—there is no "Pollute the Planet PAC"— but Donald Trump won the White House in part by promising to bring back the coal industry and roll back strict EPA regulations on power plant emissions. The immediate prospect of jobs and cheaper power (neither of which is likely to happen anyway) won out over the longer-term concerns about CO_2 emissions and climate change.

The rest of the chapter focuses on two clusters of emerging trans-state issues, clusters selected because of their visibility and importance in the American political dialogue and because they are nice examples of this broader class of issues. Each issue has received a great deal of exposure and discussion both within the United States and in international forums and will continue to do so. Each discussion begins by describing the problem and explaining why it is an important issue. It then looks at the status of the problem, including progress and barriers to progress. Each discussion concludes with an assessment of U.S. interests and the position—or positions—that the United States has adopted in recent years.

Human Rights, Democracy, and Immigration

The central proposition dominating the human rights movement is the idea that all humans have certain basic, inalienable rights and there is a universal obligation to enforce and protect those rights; prominent among those human rights is political freedom and self-determination: democracy. The concern is not strictly a trans-state issue because individual states could enforce a uniform code through their own individual actions. All states, of course, do not do this; there are widespread differences in the quality of the human condition and even disagreement—sometimes honest and heartfelt, sometimes cynically political—about what composes the conditions to which humans are entitled. Moreover, the expressions and concerns are often gender based, since women in many societies have historically enjoyed far fewer rights than men. The treatment of children, and the use of child soldiers, has also become a prominent part of the dialogue.

The searing images of families fleeing war-torn Syria and Iraq raise another element of the debate about human rights—what about the rights of these migrants to be able to live and work freely in another country? More than 20 million people currently live outside their home country, often living and working in the shadows or in camps for migrants. They often take enormous risks to flee their homes, and die in the process. What are our collective responsibilities to these people, born with the same inalienable rights as the rest of us, according to at least one school of thought on this issue? So while in some ways these issues are separable, that is, we could think about individual issues of human rights, the spread of democracy, and the migrant crisis, in truth these issues all stem from a common debate about the proper treatment of human beings.

Describing the Problems

The growth of the global economy and the rise of **interdependence** have created greater economic prosperity, but they have also created a world where we are in a sense less in control of our destiny because of the interrelated nature of world affairs. As the process of globalization has intensified, so too have calls for increased human rights and political freedom—even while these forces may weaken sovereignty. Economic and political democracy represents the economic and political expressions of freedom, and their connection helps produce what Singer and Wildavsky call a "quality economy," where free people are highly motivated and thus more productive and innovative than those who are not free. The preference of the United States has been, by and large, to promote this when possible.

Demands for uniform human rights tend to come in two varieties: one discussed here, the other touched on later. In the first category are basic civil and political rights (such as the freedoms of speech, assembly, and religion contained in the U.S. Bill of Rights), including rights fought for in the civil rights and anti-discrimination movements in the United States, such as freedom from discrimination in hiring or in public places. These are sometimes referred to as **negative human rights** because they state actions that cannot be taken against people.

In the second category are basic human economic and social rights—the right, for example, to an adequate diet or a certain level of education. These are sometimes referred to as **positive human rights**, or minimum quality-of-life standards, because they entail positive conditions to which their advocates maintain people are entitled.

The assertion of a set of human rights is a relatively recent phenomenon in the history of the global system. Historically, the superiority of the sovereign authority of the state has meant that rulers routinely have been able to do to their citizens whatever they were physically capable of doing. The classic, absolute assertion of sovereignty maintains that within the sovereign domain of the state, the ruler has the right to do whatever he or she wants, and no right allows others to challenge such action, even when it entails the suppression or killing of parts of the population.

The philosophical birthplace of the human rights and democracy movement arguably is in the seventeenth-century work of John Locke, the British philosopher from whom many of the ideas that underlay the American republic were derived. Among his contributions, which can be seen in contemporary discussions, are notions of popular sovereignty (the idea that individuals, not the state, are the primary repository of sovereignty) implicit in advocacies of intrusions against governments engaged in human rights violations (see intersection 11.1 on torture).

Intersection 11.1   Torture

After the shocking terrorist attacks of 9/11 many were concerned that a second wave of attacks would follow. Were there more "sleeper cells" out there, waiting? Vice President Richard Cheney famously commented that, given this threat environment, the United States would have to operate on "the dark side," taking steps we would not normally take in peacetime. As the insurgency in Iraq intensified in 2003, the need for immediate intelligence on impending attacks on U.S. troops in Iraq and on U.S. interests around the world also intensified, leading the Bush administration to approve a variety of "enhanced interrogation" techniques for use on prisoners, including some steps such as "waterboarding" that are generally recognized as forms of "torture." In 2004, a cache of pictures from the Abu Ghraib prison in Iraq stunned Americans and the world, depicting in graphic terms the way prisoners were being treated by U.S. troops. When Barack Obama came to office in January 2009, be banned waterboarding and other forms of torture, which put U.S. policy back on ground that was codified in U.S. law and in a variety of treaties to which the U.S. is a party, including the Geneva Conventions.

This seemed to settle the issues, but in his run for the White House Donald Trump promised to return to waterboarding; he said that he believes "torture works," and that the United States needs to get a whole lot tougher on fighting terrorism. Many Republicans disagree with Trump's position, including Arizona senator John McCain (himself a POW in Vietnam who was tortured for years), South Carolina senator Lindsey Graham, and Trump's secretary of defense, Marine general James "Mad Dog" Mattis. The ban on the use of torture has been seen as a position that favors basic human rights, and provides a political high ground from which to criticize regimes that violate the basic rights of their people for decades. Is the United States about the head back to the "dark side?"

Contemporary advocates of human rights and democracy (for example, NGOs such as Amnesty International and Freedom House) can be thought of as grounded in two related foci. Where human rights, including the political freedom that defines democracy, are not present in particular countries, advocates aim to provide democratization for all citizens. Since the end of the Cold War, the late political scientist Samuel P. Huntington argued, we have entered a **"third wave" of democratization** (the first two waves came immediately after the world wars) that is spreading democracy to regions where it was previously not present or certainly not universal (the former Soviet Union and Central and South America, in particular).

The other focus is less universal, involving the forceful advocacy of human rights for categories of citizens within countries who have been denied rights. The most visible and forceful advocacies have been for women's rights, the extension of political and economic rights to women in societies that have treated women as inferiors. The two **Beijing summits** in 1995 focused on women's rights and led to the Beijing Declaration with a "Bill of Rights for Women" that contains provisions calling for equal inheritance rights, equal access to education and medical services, and the right of all women to decide freely concerning matters of sexuality (namely, childbearing), to cite a few of the more prominent rights.

Another emphasis has been on the rights of political and economic migrants. The UN High Commissioner on Human Rights, among others, tries to promote a view that sees migration in the broader context of the human rights movement, and "works for the promotion, protection and fulfillment of the human rights of all migrants, regardless of their status or circumstance, with a particular focus on those women, men and children who are most marginalized and at risk of human rights violations."

Status of Human Rights and Democracy Issues

Now that the Cold War competition no longer dominates the foreign policy agenda, the issue of human rights has emerged as a major foreign policy concern for many governments, including that of the United States. Indeed, the promotion of democracy—even in the form of military action to force regime change—was a key component of the Bush Doctrine that emerged after 9/11. In the absence of a major ideological opponent to Western-style democracy, it is not surprising that the issue has largely been framed in Western terms.

The human rights movement has clearly benefited from the end of the Cold War and the emergence of the Western system of political democracy and market-based economics as the nearly universally accepted form of political and economic organization. Modern electronic and social media, the influence of prominent individuals who promote and draw attention to these issues, and the activities of NGOs have aided this wave of democratization.

State brutality has long been reported by the traditional print media, but the advent of the electronic global village, to borrow Marshall McLuhan's famous term, has made such reporting much more accessible and vivid. Global news organizations, accelerated by social media, transmit information from any point on the globe to another in real time as events are happening. The nature of visual reporting creates an evocative atmosphere not possible with the written word: we can see atrocities, for instance, with a shock value the printed word could hardly evoke.

The result is coverage and publicity of events that more than likely would have been neglected only a few years ago. Practically no place on the globe is too remote or physically inaccessible anymore. It is becoming increasingly difficult to hide inhumanity even in authoritarian states. Images of North Korea, one of the most closed societies on earth, appear with some regularity. The stories and scenes from Aleppo—devastated since 2012 by the Syrian civil war made worse by Russian military force—are now well known. The pictures of the lifeless body of three-year-old Syrian boy Alam Kurdi, who drowned in the Mediterranean while trying to escape to Europe and washed ashore in Turkey in September 2015, help make the dire nature of the Syrian refugee crisis clear to even the most hard-hearted observers.

Individual leaders have also done much to spur the world's awareness of human rights violations. Former American president Jimmy Carter, for one, won the admiration of oppressed people throughout the world for his elevation of human rights to the top of the foreign policy agenda during his single term. Another example is the Dalai Lama, who regularly promotes the importance of a universal concept of human rights. Actor Emma Watson, best known for her role as Hermione Granger in the *Harry Potter* films, is a UN Women Global Goodwill Ambassador, promoting the rights of women and gender equality in powerful ways around the world.

Nongovernmental organizations are also prominent human rights advocates. Some serve as monitors of the human rights records of states. Amnesty International (AI), for example, annually produces a list of countries where it alleges human rights abuses occur. Another is Human Rights Watch, which burst into the public spotlight when it accused the Chinese government of massive neglect in the orphanage scandal in 1995. Refugees International advocates on behalf of displaced persons around the world. NGOs work both to alleviate suffering and to draw public attention to human rights abuses and suffering around the world.

The modern human rights movement was first raised in the twentieth century by President Woodrow Wilson in his Fourteen Points at the end of World War I, and the issue resurfaced in World War II, where the victorious Allies were not only fighting for their physical survival, but also "in the name of freedom." Revelations about Hitler's Holocaust further stimulated a postwar emphasis on human rights and intensified the broad desire to create a more humane world and to end genocide. The United Nations was formed in part "to observe and to respect human rights."

The United Nations has been the focal point for the global human rights movement since the organization's inception and has helped lead to the creation of many international human rights treaties. The UN General Assembly adopted the Convention on the Prevention and Punishment of the Crime of Genocide in 1948 as the direct result of international revulsion toward Germany's systematic extermination of the European Jewish population in the Holocaust. The convention provided the legal precedent for establishing war crimes tribunals for both Bosnia and Rwanda and is embedded in definitions of crimes against humanity adjudicated by the International Criminal Court (ICC). The United States did not ratify the convention until 1988, a clear sign of American ambivalence about the issue, and the United States has not ratified the treaty that would make it a part of the ICC—even though the United States was central to its creation.

The UN General Assembly also adopted the **Universal Declaration on Human Rights** in 1948. This document provided the most sweeping set of international norms protecting the rights of individuals from their governments (the negative, or political, rights noted earlier) and creating standards of living to which people are entitled (the positive, or social, rights).

The Geneva Conventions provide rights and protections for civilians, soldiers, and prisoners in times of war. The United States is a signatory to the conventions, which outlaw murder, torture, and cruel and humiliating treatment.

The United States and Human Rights

The United States has been a major player in drafting almost all the human rights accords, many of which closely parallel the American Bill of Rights and U.S. law. The United States is a party to most of the major human rights accords that exist, but at the same time, there has been considerable opposition to adopting these treaties in the United States, and the United States is not a party to several of them even today, including the 1948 Convention Concerning Freedom of Association and Protection of the Right to Organize, and the 1950 Convention for the Suppression of the Traffic in Persons and of the Exploitation of the Prostitution of Others. From what sources does American ambivalence about these treaties arise?

There are philosophical and political objections. One is the dilution of sovereignty; if the United States signs an international treaty, that document's provisions become part of U.S. law enforceable in U.S. courts. If a treaty's provisions contradict U.S. law, the treaty's dictates supersede the existing statute and take precedent over it. It is because of this feature that the opposition to these treaties based on diluting sovereignty is often argued; it is also why treaties require Senate action.

This leads to a more practical, political concern, particularly as these treaties assert the positive or social rights of people. The debate over the status of women, minorities, or children, and especially to what conditions they are entitled, has both a domestic and an international aspect. The international assertion of a right to an adequate standard of living for all people, for example, has an obvious parallel in the domestic debate over welfare, health care, and a whole host of other entitlements. If one is politically opposed to the provision of certain entitlements to groups of American citizens, then one will be wary of promoting the same rights internationally, especially if international agreements might pose standards that would have to be enforced within the United States, to which some Americans are opposed. And yet, without American support, solutions to these problems are likely to be fleeting.

The United States is still sometimes caught in a tension between promoting human rights and democracy on the one hand, and promoting stability and security on the other. Many were critical when President Obama deepened relations with Vietnam, Myanmar, and China, because of the bad human rights records in these places. And no doubt the continuing war on terrorism has led the U.S. government to forge friendly relations with some authoritarian leaders, such as in Saudi Arabia, Kazakhstan, and others. Donald Trump is not the only critic, though perhaps the most significant one, who argues that the stability of Saddam Hussein's regime in Iraq was more in U.S. interests than has been the chaos that has followed its fall.

Still, the United States pushes for more democracy and human rights when possible for a variety of reasons. First, there is a widely shared belief that the spread of democracy enhances U.S. national security. Democratic states historically have not gone to war with one another except where democracy is not well established and disputes predate democratization. The U.S. invasion of Iraq should show that democracies are not necessarily inherently peaceful, but the argument is that they tend not go to war with each other. Second, democratic states are the most reliable bulwark for protecting human rights. Although violations of individual rights occur from time to time even in democratic societies, systematic violations of basic political rights are less likely because they are antithetical to the very concept of democratic self-government. Democratic governance and human rights are two sides of the same coin.

Third, for the most part, democratic regimes are more responsible and law-abiding members of the international community than are dictatorships.

After all, political democracies are grounded in the rule of law and political accountability. However, democracies are also subject to changes in public opinion that may make today's policy untenable tomorrow. Finally, the growth of the global economy is closely related to the combined effects of political democratization and free and open market-based economies. Many argue that the two are related because they represent the political and economic manifestations of the same basic principles of freedom and liberty.

The problem that hampers the spread of universal human rights is the lack of a reliable enforcement mechanism. In a sovereign system, no force is superior to that of the state. In the human rights field, this becomes a problem when governments abuse their citizens—especially to the extremity of the systematic slaughter of population segments (**genocide**). In this case, there may be (and are) appeals to a higher authority in order to right wrongs. However, even some nonoffending states, including the United States, sometimes resist such demands, fearing the precedent they set: if someone else's sovereignty can be violated, then who is to say mine might not be sometime in the future? This point became highly emotional in the United States concerning the ICC.

The absence of legitimate supranational (above the state) mechanisms means that international efforts must be more indirect. For example, when faced with evidence of human rights violations, states or combinations of states may threaten to cut off foreign aid until the abuses cease, which may be effective if the target relies on such assistance. If the violator does not depend on foreign aid, of course, such a threat is ineffective. Economic sanctions offer another possibility, but the result may be that the population target one seeks to help will bear the burden of the suffering (North Korea is an example). The problem of universality compounds the difficulty. The simple fact is that there is substantial disagreement among different parts of the world on what constitutes human rights. Many of the most serious differences are gender related; in much of the world, the rights of women (including female children) are considerably more circumscribed than they are for men. In most cases, these differences are encased in long-held practices and traditions creating advantages for men that they do not want to forfeit, and can be rooted in long-standing cultural and religious differences. For example, the hijab is seen as protecting women from what their culture believes to be pervasive corruptive influences—and so it is not seen locally as a form of repression, as most Americans believe, but as a way to create a protective privacy. As one can imagine, many from the developing world thus see statements such as the Universal Declaration on Human Rights as an expression of Western values.

These issues have gained even more prominence following the 2011 revolutions and uprisings in the Middle East and North Africa. Calls for political change and openness spread through Iran, Tunisia, Egypt, Yemen, Bahrain, Jordan, Syria, Libya, and elsewhere. The United States has once again been in the odd position of sometimes promoting change and sometimes backing strong-arm governments against the protesters. The certainty and stability of the policies of an authoritarian government can be tough to give up when faced with the unpredictability of what might follow, especially given some degree of anti-American sentiment in the region.

The dynamics of migration, for either economic or survival purposes, is a complex subject beyond present purposes (see intersection 11.2). Nevins, in a study of the U.S.-Mexican relationship, points out that the controversy centers on the border. Borders, he argues, historically serve one or both of two purposes: as a line of control to monitor and choose who does and does not enter or leave the country. Donald Trump emphasized this view during his presidential campaign, suggesting dramatically that a country that cannot control its border has its sovereignty compromised to the point that its statehood is questionable. The other function of borders is as a gateway that welcomes people and goods and services into the country. This interpretation is emphasized by those who view immigration as a form of worker recruitment and replenishment. As a contemporary foreign policy problem for the United States, the question is the degree to which a restrictive policy will tarnish both the American ideal as a democratic haven (the Statue of Liberty's promise) and as a place to which young people will want to come. With the talk of banning Muslims from certain regions from immigrating to the United States, of building a wall on our southern border, of waging a war against "radical Islam," as some have suggested, of getting a lot tougher on terrorism, a reorientation of American foreign policy would seem to be under way. It remains to be seen whether President Trump is able to consolidate these shifts, and if he does whether they hurt the American "brand."

| Intersection 11.2 | **The Immigration Economic "Time Bomb"** |

One of the major problems facing modern industrial states is demographic in nature. It is a simple and indisputable fact that populations in the most developed countries (the United States, the countries of the EU, China, and Japan most prominently) are aging. What this means is that growing numbers of citizens are living to ages where they are no longer part of the active workforce. At the same time, all of these countries have relatively low birth rates, meaning that younger workers cannot replace those retiring. In turn, the potential consequences of this trend (fewer workers, more retirees) are that welfare benefits rise (more people claim benefits, fewer people are earning the incomes to pay them) and decreases in productivity because there are fewer people producing work. This strain has already afflicted Japan, causing an economic slowdown and the effective end of the Japanese economic "miracle," it afflicts the EU, and it is becoming a problem in China, in large part because of the "one child" policy (couples allowed only a single offspring) of the latter twentieth century.

There are only two solutions to this problem. One of these is to import young workers from other countries to do the work that the indigenous population cannot do. The other is to make do with the shortage. Replenishing the workforce with immigrants (including refugees) has been the American solution, and it has historically worked well, as the promise of America has attracted successive immigrant waves to the country. It has also been the European solution, but it has become controversial, since many of the new immigrants and refugees come from the Middle East, do not assimilate easily, and may have some potential terrorists among them. Immigration policy was one of the reasons for the Brexit movement in the United Kingdom. Because of traditions of racial purity, neither Japan nor China opts for immigration, a choice that has cost Japan some prosperity and will have the same effect on China.

The 2016 campaign indirectly highlighted this problem for the United States. Much of the immigration of young workers has historically come from the Western Hemisphere and from parts of Asia. Both are affected by proposed restrictions on immigration and harsh limits on refugees. What price will the United States pay if it continues to act as if a demographic time bomb does not exist for this country as well?

Source: Donald M. Snow, *Regional Cases in Foreign Policy* (Lanham, MD: Rowman & Littlefield, 2017), chapters 3 and 5 for China and Brexit.

Climate Change and the Environment

Since human civilization began to develop, part of its effect has been to manipulate, change, and in some cases degrade the physical environment. As the numbers of human communities, population size, and sophistication have increased, so has manipulation of the natural setting of the planet. For most of the human experience, the major purpose of this manipulation was to improve the human condition for some or all people. Concerns about the deleterious effects that "fooling with Mother Nature" might have are fairly recent, mostly emanating from the scientific community.

Environmental degradation has become a broad-based scientific problem with wide-ranging effects. General environmental degradation, resource usages and their environmental impacts, and climate change are among the most obvious general manifestations of the complex of concerns surrounding the environment. Water pollution, nuclear waste, desertification, energy policy, and degradation of the ecosystem are related concerns—but there will doubtless be others as human "development" and population grows.

Environmental issues are classic trans-state problems: almost all of them occur in more than one state and cannot be satisfactorily addressed or solved by the actions of individual states. The major problems surrounding all of them arise from two basic sources: recognition and acceptance of the problem as a problem, and agreement on both the necessity and nature of multilateral solutions in which all offenders take part. These dynamics generally have both international and domestic political manifestations. In the American debate, for instance, there are political factions that deny the mounting science about problems and the need to address them, a debate often tinged with political self-interest. At the same time, the dynamics of the "tragedy of the commons" (the idea that because the environment is so great that problems of its degradation can be passed along to other members of the commons) act against agreeing on and enforcing solutions against offenders.

These issues are also generally complex and highly technical, with both their definitions and solutions based on complicated, even arcane scientific bases the general public does not fully comprehend and which partisans can and do manipulate to their own ends. For present purposes, we have chosen one environmental problem to exemplify the trans-state nature of environmental problems: climate change. The problem (assuming one accepts there is a problem) is global, with many states contributing to it, and it clearly can only be addressed and "solved" by the concerted efforts of all those countries that are part of the problem (essentially everyone). Whether global warming exists or exactly what it is remains a matter of controversy, especially in the American debate. The problem thus has both domestic and foreign policy content in the United States: there is a domestic debate about the existence of global warming and a consequent disagreement about the extent to which this country should lead or be bound by international efforts to alleviate it (whether to participate in overcoming the tragedy of the commons).

Nature of the Climate Change Problem

The heart of the climate change dynamic is the question of energy production. For most of human history, the chief source of energy for human use came from the burning of wood, which provided heat for comfort and cooking and eventually extended to things such as manufacturing and transportation. As long as human populations were relatively small and demands reasonably low, wood was an adequate source that met dual criteria of availability and renewability: people burned less wood than was produced in nature. Moreover, it was not burned in such large quantities that the carbon dioxide released by its ignition could not be absorbed by the ecosystem. The Industrial Revolution and growing global population upset that balance by demanding more energy and resulted in the exploitation of other fossil fuels, notably from petroleum and coal. This conversion increased energy production dramatically, but the use of new sources of fossil fuel energy also overwhelmed the ability of nature to negate its negative effects. The ultimate result has been growing accumulations of carbon dioxide that threaten the ecosystem due to global warming. The current challenge is to find alternative energy sources from non-fossil-fuel sources that do not emit carbon dioxide.

The problem of climate change hinges on rising global temperatures and the impact of this rise. These changes are, in almost all physical descriptions, the result of excess burning of fossil fuels for a variety of purposes. One of the byproducts of incinerating these carbon-based energy sources is the release of carbon dioxide (CO_2) into the atmosphere. When the ecosystem is at equipoise, the excesses are absorbed by the ecosystem, principally by photosynthesis in carbon "sinks" that chemically break apart the CO_2 molecules and allow the resulting particles to be released harmlessly into the atmosphere. The historic source of this conversion has been tropical rain forests, which accomplish the photosynthesis that creates the conversion. CO_2 that is not photosynthesized remains trapped in the atmosphere, where it blocks the escape of heat from the sun and creates an effective "**greenhouse effect**" that holds the heat in the atmosphere and results in a gradual increase in global temperatures.

Global warming, and its solution, thus has two related basic components. One side of the problem is the release of quantities of CO_2 into the atmosphere beyond the ability of the environment to eliminate its excesses—a question of the supply of CO_2. The obvious solution is to reduce the volume of that discharge, and that is the basis of most efforts aimed at reducing global warming. The other side of a solution is to increase the ability of the ecosystem to process CO_2 emissions. Rain forest conversion is the heart of this solution, but it faces challenges. The major difficulty is that deforestation is occurring in many rain forests, as trees are cut to facilitate economic development. The result is that the natural capacity to reduce CO_2 content in the atmosphere is decreasing, placing even greater emphasis on reducing the amount of carbon dioxide entering the atmosphere. Since the burning of excessive amounts of fossil fuels is the chief source of increased accumulation, it becomes the target of climate controllers.

There is general but not universal agreement on the existence and dimensions of the problem. Since 1900 the amount of CO_2 in the atmosphere has increased significantly, with a consequent average global temperature rise of 2–3 degrees Fahrenheit. Projections at current rates could result in a rise of 2–9 degrees by the middle of this century. As developing countries such as India industrialize and use more energy for transportation (private cars), carbon dioxide levels will expand unless something is done to arrest or reverse them.

As the enormous discrepancy in projected temperature rises over the next third of a century suggests, there is a good bit of disagreement about the dynamics and consequences of carbon dioxide pollution. A rise of two degrees would be serious and a rise of 9 degrees apocalyptic, but which estimate is more realistic? The answer is that it depends on who one listens to on the subject. Most climate scientists argue that the problem is very serious and agree with a 2010 assessment by Thompson, whose studies of ice cores concluded, "There is now a very clear pattern in the scientific community documenting that the earth is warming, that warming is due largely to human activity, that warming is causing important changes in climate, and that rapid and perhaps catastrophic changes in the near future are very possible." If these assertions are correct, then climate control efforts are clearly mandated.

Not everyone agrees, and disagreement is based on scientific, political, or economic grounds. Among America's scientists, a small minority (generally less than five percent of the total) argues that human-made climate change is a fiction. They tend to point to historical periods of climate fluctuation (e.g., the ice age) and to maintain that there is little evidence that the changes currently being experienced are anything but historically normal fluctuations (assertions for which they generally offer only anecdotal evidence). Economically, the argument is that carbon dioxide reduction can currently only be achieved at great economic cost to those who attempt it. The single best indicator of economic vitality is energy use, and the only methods for reducing emissions currently available are to reduce or eliminate burning fossil fuels. If one country does so while others do not abstain, that country (or countries) will suffer economically compared to those who do not reduce their consumption, a variation of the tragedy of the commons. Politically, much of the American opposition comes from the fossil fuel industries themselves, notably outlets of the coal and oil and gas industries (such as the American Petroleum Institute), who spend large amounts of money seeking to influence citizens and toward electing sympathetic political candidates.

The controversies that surround the debate over climate change affect the viability of proposals to deal with it in international forums. If one eliminates large increases in the size and carrying capacity of rain forests (it takes trees too long to grow to be helpful in the short to medium futures), then one is left with three possible approaches. At one extreme is simply denying the problem and doing nothing about it, an approach that has become impossible to sustain given the evidence. At the other extreme is a total cessation of fossil fuel production and use to remove their contributions to environmental degradation. That option is impractical because too much of global energy is produced in this way, thus making it economically catastrophic and politically impossible. Moreover, there are not yet alternative, non–carbon dioxide methods of energy production available to fill the resulting energy gap.

That leaves a third option, which is gradually to reduce carbon dioxide emissions through a combination of conservation and conversion to alternative energy sources currently being developed worldwide. There is ongoing development of some energy forms such as solar, wind, and even atomic energy that cannot yet produce enough energy fully to substitute for fossil fuels, and "silver bullet" technologies such as harnessing fusion energy from seawater remain horizon possibilities. In the United States, the exploitation of oil and natural gas from hydraulic fracturing of shale formations (so-called fracking—see intersection 11.3) has opened another possible source of less polluting, if still fossil-based energy.

Intersection 11.3 Shale Oil and Gas—A Fracking Good Alternative?

Fracking, or hydraulic fracturing, is a controversial and increasingly widespread method of obtaining oil and natural gas.

The revolution in oil and gas production from shale formations has become one of the most exciting but controversial aspects of the American, and potentially worldwide, energy and climate change equation. The excitement comes from two sources. First, the United States and Canada are preeminent in the technology for extracting shale oil and gas from the earth's crust, and their efforts have changed the global petroleum balance, moving the United States to a position of near independence from foreign sources of oil and especially natural gas. Second, natural gas produces less than one-half the carbon dioxide as coal, and the conversion of American power plants from coal to natural gas has allowed the country to move close to targeted emission levels. The possibility of reductions in the conversion process is especially intriguing for China, which produces over 90 percent of its power from coal and is also the world's leading polluter (see table 11.1 in the next section).

The extraction of shale oil comes with caveats. One is ecological and has two aspects. Fracking involves injecting massive amounts of chemically treated water into shale seams to create pressure that frees shale oil and gas from the seams for recovery. The shale "cocktail," as it is sometimes known, contains toxic chemicals that must either be removed from the spent water (which is very expensive and resisted by oil companies) and consumes great amounts of water, which lowers water tables (a particular problem in China). At the same time, it is becoming more scientifically evident that this extraction process may also affect the geological structure of areas where fracking occurs, resulting in increased frequency of serious earthquakes in those locations. This latter concern has caused some communities to ban fracking operations. President Trump is said to be a strong supporter of fracking.

Source: Donald M. Snow, *The Middle East, Oil, and the American National Security* (Lanham, MD: Rowman & Littlefield, 2016).

The energy/pollution problem thus comes into focus. Shale oil is thus not really a solution to the problem. Shale oil and gas extraction may be less carbon dioxide producing than some other fossil fuels, but it still pollutes. The most that can be said for it is that it pollutes at lower levels than the worst fossil fuels. Only a movement toward energy production from other than fossil fuels can respond to that goal. The problem, as noted at the outset of the discussion, is that there is no obvious alternative to fossil fuel burning for the present, unless one is willing to accept draconian reduction in global energy production and its negative consequences for the human condition. The answer lies in finding an alternate source of energy that is abundant (ideally self-replacing), economically feasible to produce, and not polluting in new ways. While the search for such a source continues, the best that can be done is to try to slow the deleterious effects of fossil fuel burning until a new source comes on line.

The Climate Control Dynamic

Although many people associate the scientific and political efforts to understand and curb global warming as a relatively recent phenomenon, it really has had a much longer history than that. Scientists began to observe climatic patterns that pointed to a rise in global temperatures in the middle of the twentieth century, and international collaboration at both the scientific and political levels, largely sponsored by arms of the United Nations, is now about forty years old. The climate problem first surfaced in the public eye with the highly publicized but ultimately failed Earth Summit of 1992 and came to a climax with the **Kyoto Protocol** of 1997. Kyoto became the touchstone of the climate movement, but its general acceptance was limited by the highly technical nature of the restrictions and changes it sought to institute, combined with the fact that the ecological disaster it predicted was not immediate, but a projection that would occur very gradually and thus did not appear imminently compelling. As a result, the movement has always had a slightly "wonky" feel with which average citizens cannot personally relate with any ease.

Two countries have been especially important in this process, for different reasons. The first is the United States. Its prominence arose because, as the most industrially developed country in the world, it was at the top of emissions lists until recently, meaning that American participation has always been necessary if international efforts to control global warming were to have any reasonable chance of meaningful reductions. China has also been a major factor, because the rise of China as a major former developing country now industrializing—and thus polluting—has provided the symbol of the problem of the future. China is now the largest source of pollution, and how it handles that status will be important for future developing countries, of which India is the great example.

The role of the United States has been enigmatic, notably because of the politically derived ambivalence toward the process. The United States has been the greatest champion of the climate control process and the greatest barrier to achieving progress. Historically, this ambivalence has been political along partisan lines. Democrats have traditionally supported the international process, whereas Republicans (who tend to be aligned with the oil and gas industry) have opposed these efforts, with the U.S. government both championing and then leading the opposition to specific measures. In 1992, for instance, the George H. W. Bush administration was an early champion of the Earth Summit, with the U.S. representative leading the movement toward producing a comprehensive agreement until Bush was convinced that the oil industry, whose financial support was necessary in his 1992 reelection campaign, opposed it. Before the agreement was adopted, Bush condemned it, leaving the U.S. delegation embarrassed and the agreement in tatters. In 1997, the Democratic Clinton administration was a leader in negotiating the Kyoto Protocol and signed it. The Senate did not affirm it, and in 2001 George W. Bush renounced it and withdrew American participation. Will this pattern hold for Republican President Trump? The fate of American participation in the **Paris Agreement** of 2015 will be the test.

The Climate Change Process

The international effort to curb global warming began formally in 1979, when the first World Climate Conference (WCC) was held in Geneva, Switzerland, sponsored by the World Meteorological Organization (WMO). That conference helped lead to the creation of the Intergovernmental Panel on Climate Change (IPCC) in 1988, which has become a major component of UN-sponsored climate control initiatives. Subsequent Geneva conferences took place in 1990 and 2009, the latter helping to set the agenda for the largely failed Copenhagen conference in 2009. In 1990, the second WCC issued a call for a global climate initiative, and in 1991 the UN created the UN Framework Convention on Climate Change (UNFCCC). One of its provisions was an annual Conference of the Parties (COP), which has become the acronym and yardstick for international efforts.

The early crown jewel of the international effort was the Kyoto Protocol of 1997. The overarching purpose of the protocol was reduction in the production and emission of greenhouse gases and the arrest and reversal of effects caused by them. It is a complicated set of guidelines and requirements understandable only by the scientists who created it, but it set a baseline goal of reducing worldwide carbon dioxide emissions by 5 percent below the baseline by the period 2008–2012, the latter the year the protocol expired.

While its goal was not opposed (although some climate control opponents deny the need for it), its implementation was. People simply did not understand the goals it set or the measures for determining whether they were met. More important, implementation fell very heavily on some countries and hardly at all on others. Eighty-six percent of the targeted reductions (reflecting their contribution to global emissions) fell on four regions: 36 percent for the United States, 24 percent by the European Union, 17.4 percent by the Russian Federation, and 8.5 percent by Japan. The next largest quota was for Australia, responsible for a reduction of 2.1 percent. Most developing world countries, notably China and India, were excluded from reductions, because at the time their contribution to pollution was minimal—a situation that would subsequently change.

These quotas were of more than academic interest. To reach these goals, the most heavily targeted countries would have to cut back considerably on their consumption of fossil fuels with no available substitutes. In turn, this would lower energy production and imperil economic activity given the heavy dependence of economies on fossil fuel energy for manufacturing and transportation. Estimates at the time suggested that the United States would have to reduce energy production by as much as 7 percent to meet its emission targets. At the same time, the regulations exempted rising powers such as China and India, providing them with an apparent free pass to industrialize without having to worry about environmental impact. The result was an anomaly pointed out by Helm in 2012: "The focus was on emissions in those countries where emissions were not growing very much—rather than countries where they were growing very rapidly."

These provisions were especially politically toxic in the United States. The Clinton administration signed the accord but did not submit it to a Senate that almost certainly would have rejected it. When he came to office in 2001, George W. Bush renounced the protocol as discriminatory and creating an unfair burden, and he withdrew it from Senate consideration. As a result, the United States was not a participating party to Kyoto.

The protocol had a fifteen-year period in force, meaning it would expire in 2012. Writing in 2004, Browne explained why it was of limited duration and why it had to be replaced by a follow-on agreement. "Kyoto was only the starting point of a very long endeavor," he wrote, that would need to be updated as new knowledge accumulated about climate change. Further, he argued that the ability to change without upsetting the economy was already occurring, science and its applications were advancing, and the public was becoming increasingly supportive of the climate movement.

The path to a replacement for Kyoto has been difficult. In December 2007, on the tenth anniversary of the accord, the UNCCC met in Bali, Indonesia, to advance the cause, which entailed setting new deep emissions goals and targets for the participants and attempting to alter the status of countries such as China and India. Both—but especially China—had become major and growing contributors to the problem since 1967. The meeting did not produce a concrete proposal or, as Fuller and Rivkin pointed out at the time, "any binding agreements." China was a reluctant participant, and the document produced at the meeting, the so-called Bali Road Map, was only a set of guidelines for the serious negotiation of a new agreement at Copenhagen in 2009. Because it did not bind any country to specific actions, it was endorsed by the Bush administration.

Turning the road map into a concrete agreement proved to be the hard part—the devil in the details—for the Obama administration that entered the White House in 2009. With the expiration date for Kyoto impending, a meeting was convened in Copenhagen in December. As mandated in the Bali road map, the participants were supposed to agree on a framework to succeed the Kyoto document—and the meeting failed almost entirely.

A major reason for failure at Copenhagen was not American obstruction, since new president Obama was and remained throughout his tenure in office a committed supporter of international global warming reductions. After meeting for more than a week of wrangling over goals and measures of progress, the conference essentially deadlocked without proposing or enacting any binding standards, nor did it draft a framework document for a treaty to be enacted by 2012. As the meeting wound down, what the UNFCCC website called an Informal High Level Event took place on December 18, the day before the conference was scheduled to adjourn. The United States, China, India, Brazil, and South Africa met, resulting in a call for a goal of no more than a 2 degree Fahrenheit global temperature increase. At the time, this was considered a modest accomplishment, and it did not stimulate much progress in 2011, when another meeting was held in Durban, South Africa, that Helm labeled "a disaster," or at Doha in 2012. At the end of 2012, the Kyoto Protocol expired without fanfare.

The lasting impact of Copenhagen may have been that it brought the United States into discussions and agreement with the major developing world countries that felt threatened by the climate control regime. Most notably, it involved China, which was rapidly moving to the unenviable position of the world's greatest polluter, and the United States, whose preeminence China was eclipsing, into common cause. A direct link between the "informal high level event" and Chinese-American cooperation in Paris may be impossible to draw, but they are linked by chronology. The importance of Chinese-American accord was that it publicly brought China, an exempt polluter under Kyoto, under the umbrella of the international movement (creating a precedent for other industrializing countries) and it overcame many American objections of China as a free rider that could profit industrially because it could pollute while other states such as the United States could not (a prime argument used against Kyoto).

The 2015 Paris Agreement (PA) was negotiated with two major parameters. The first was that the global warming problem was predicted to be getting much worse, with identified polluters leading the way. Table 11.1 summarizes the contribution of the major carbon producers in 2016, limited to the sixteen countries that each produced 1 percent or more of global carbon dioxide.

The table illustrates several points regarding the global distribution of pollution. There are more than 190 parties to the agreement, but the first sixteen create more than two-thirds of carbon emissions. Most other, smaller contributors are part of the agreement, but their sacrifice is individually quite small. Second, if the contribution of the twenty-eight EU members (including the UK) is aggregated, their total is almost as great as the United States at slightly over 17 percent; this means the three largest contributors are pouring about 55 percent of the pollutants into the atmosphere. Noncompliance by one or more of these three essentially means that international efforts will fall short of projections and that, as a result, Chinese and American mutual support is the sine qua non for carbon pollution reduction. Third, the agreement's outliers are a kind of rogues' gallery, currently led by Russia and Turkey, although the Russian Federation has indicated that it would join in 2017.

It is within these parameters that the Paris meeting (COP 21) was held between November 30 and December 15, 2015. The Kyoto Protocol had not been in effect for about three years, and compliance with its guidelines (as augmented by suggestions at intervening conferences like Copenhagen) was voluntary. According to most climate scientists, conditions were worsening with dire

TABLE 11.1   **Worst Global Carbon Offenders**

Rank	Country	Contribution (%)	Field Accession to Treaty
1	China	20.09	Yes
2	United States	17.89	Yes
3	Russia	7.53	No
4	Japan	3.79	Yes
5	Germany	2.56	Yes
6	Brazil	1.9	Yes
7	South Korea (ROK)	1.85	Yes
8 (tie)	Iran	1.70	No
8 (tie)	Mexico	1.70	Yes
10	United Kingdom	1.55	Yes (filed 11/17/16)
11 (tie)	India	1.49	Yes
11 (tie)	Indonesia	1.49	Yes
13	Republic of S. Africa	1.46	Yes
14	France	1.31	Yes
15	Turkey	1.24	No
16	Poland	1.06	Yes
Total		68.61	

Note: As of November 2016.

consequences unless something drastic was done. At the same time, the United States and China attended as essential "allies" on the agenda and its requirements. The key event in this alliance was an agreement on November 12, 2014, between President Obama and General Secretary Xi Jinping to limit greenhouse gas emissions. As Obama put it, "we showed that it was possible to bridge the old divide between developed and developing nations. . . . That was the foundation of success at Paris." To symbolize this newfound accord on the problem, the two countries simultaneously submitted their letters of accession to the PA on September 3, 2016.

The heart of the sixteen-page Paris Agreement is a pledge on the part of the signatories to work to limit global temperature increase between its entry into force and 2050 to no more than 2 degrees Celsius. Given current levels of pollution growth, it is estimated that sometime between 2030 and 2050, emissions would have to be reduced to zero. On Earth Day 2016 (April 22), 174 countries signed the agreement in New York. Signing the document was preliminary to formal accession to its provisions, which is an ongoing process; it has been assumed (particularly after U.S. and Chinese accession) that the 55 percent of pollution emission for it to take effect would be reached by the end of 2016. The goals of the agreement were reiterated by the COP 22 meeting in November–December 2016 in Marrakech, Morocco.

Will the Paris Agreement work? There are two criteria by which to judge its likelihood of success or failure. One is whether states, and especially the leading powers, seriously attempt the goals to which they committed themselves. These goals are essentially voluntary, and there are no punitive consequences of failing to do so; in essence, the Paris Agreement entreats member states to cooperate and to move toward reductions. Substantively, as suggested in its Article 3, it suggests, "The efforts of all Parties will represent a progression over time, while recognizing the need to support developing country Parties for the effective implementation of this Agreement." Penalties for noncompliance for members are procedural. This means that should parties, for instance, fail to reach stated emission goals, they can be called into account through a process that Leggett and Lattanzio describe in a Congressional Research Service report as "name and shame." It does not specify legal penalties for failure to reach goals.

This distinction is politically important: the reason that requirements are voluntary and not punitive is that mandatory penalties for noncompliance (such as those suggested in the Kyoto Protocol) would enliven opponents to the whole climate control international movement as an infringement on national sovereignty. The countries that are historically the most sensitive to this possibility are, ironically, China and the United States. It is likely that trying to make violations punishable by an international body would have precluded its acceptance by the United States. The Obama administration tacitly admitted the degree of partisan opposition it would face by deciding to treat the Paris Agreement as an executive agreement rather than a treaty that the Senate would have to ratify. This decision, however, could be rescinded by subsequent action by the successor Trump administration. After his electoral victory, Trump said that the United States would pull out of the climate agreement, but as of May 2017 Trump's team of advisors were still split on whether the United States would actually withdraw.

The voluntary nature of requirements clearly weakens the enforceability of the agreement and probably compromises the likelihood that it will reach its goals. That weakness, however, may prove the necessary price to restrain the Trump administration from denouncing the Paris Agreement and withdrawing from it. The fact that Trump's politically active daughter Ivanka is an outspoken advocate of climate control who has suggested that global warming may be her signature issue may also be a positive harbinger.

The issue of climate control is, as already noted, both complex and controversial. It is complex because the direst consequences are in the future that, by definition, no one can empirically prove. The science suggests that global warming is real and potentially catastrophic, but its exact nature is not scientifically certain; how to measure it and mitigate it are not perfectly predictable. Moreover, it is so technical that the average person cannot independently judge all the evidence. It is controversial because it is politically divisive. Complying with the measures necessary to reduce carbon emissions is expensive and will require major adjustments, including reductions, in conventional energy use. The adjustments will be expensive and their impacts on the global energy equation uncertain enough to frighten those in the energy "business" to enliven their spirited political opposition. The problem and its solution will be with us for a long time.

Conclusion

This chapter examines the dynamics of trans-state issues by discussing two critical ones: the interrelated concerns of human rights, democracy, and migration, and environmental change. There is no shortage of additional issues that we could have explored: population growth, food security and sustainable fisheries, disease and pandemics, human trafficking—the list goes on. As different as they are, what these problems share is that they all pose serious political challenges that require the actions of states working in concert to solve or at least to contain them, and the politics within states often make that policy coordination difficult or even impossible.

Most of these issues share the further political commonality of having both an international and a domestic side where the two aspects further complicate the formation and implementation of effective policy. At the international level, trans-state issues are by definition international: they transcend boundaries in ways over which states have little control and that they cannot solve unilaterally. At the domestic level, their solutions often conflict with national prerogatives. Climate change in the United States is an obvious example.

The final note to make about trans-state issues is that they are not going to go away. As the world's population continues to grow, the pressures behind both of the sets of issues discussed here will, if anything, increase in intensity. Moreover, the worldwide reach of the global media makes their impact all the more visible and the potential effects on Americans of problems generated elsewhere more easily recognizable. Disease does not honor lines on a map, and stemming the global ravages of a disease in a small African village—the outbreak of the deadly Ebola virus in West Africa in 2015, for example—require highly coordinated international efforts involving a network of states, IGOs, and NGOs. Trans-state issues, like foreign policy more generally, are not easily addressed and do not end at the water's edge.

Study/Discussion Questions

1. Why are trans-state issues so difficult to solve? Why are they so politicized and partisan in the United States?
2. What might some of the trade-offs be between trying to solve these issues and trying to retain the concept of sovereignty?
3. What kinds of rights fall into the rubric of human rights? Is democracy a human right?
4. What is the difference between positive and negative human rights? Is one more controversial than the other?

5. Why has the United States not always been on the forefront of the human rights and democracy promotion movement?
6. What is global climate change, and why is it so controversial?
7. What does the Paris Agreement try to do? Explain the path from Kyoto through Copenhagen to Paris.
8. How does making policy with respect to trans-state issues such as those covered here differ from, for example, policy making with respect to more classic security issues?

Bibliography

Adams, Jill U. "Air Pollution and Climate Change." *CQ Researcher* 25, no. 14 (November 13, 2015): 961–84.

Anderson, Terry, and Harry I. Miller, eds. *The Greening of U.S. Foreign Policy.* Palo Alto, CA: Hoover Institution Press, 2000.

Apodaca, Claire. *The Paradoxes of U.S. Human Rights Policy.* New York: Taylor & Francis, 2006.

Betsill, Michele M., and Elisabeth Corell, eds. *NGO Diplomacy: The Influence of Nongovernmental Organizations in International Environmental Negotiations.* Cambridge, MA: MIT Press, 2007.

Beyond Kyoto: Advancing the International Effort against Climate Change. Arlington, VA: Pew Center on Global Climate Change, 2003.

Browne, John. "Beyond Kyoto." *Foreign Affairs,* July/August 2004, 20–32.

Brysk, Allison, ed. *Globalization and Human Rights.* Berkeley: University of California Press, 2002.

Choucri, Nazli, and Dinsha Mintree. "Globalization, Migration, and New Challenges to Governance." *Current History* 108, no. 717 (April 2009): 173–79.

COP 21. *COP 21—Final Agreement—Paris 2015: 2015 Paris United Nations Climate Change Conference.* New York: CreateSpace Independent Publishing Platform, 2015.

Deihl, Paul F., and Nils Petter Gleditsch, eds. *Environmental Conflict.* Boulder, CO: Westview, 2001.

Diamond, Larry. *In Search of Democracy.* London: Routledge, 2011.

Donnelly, Jack. *International Human Rights.* Boulder, CO: Westview, 2006.

Feinstein, Lee, and Todd Lindberg. *Means to an End: U.S. Interest in the International Criminal Court.* Washington, DC: Brookings, 2009.

Fuller, Thomas, and Andrew C. Rivkin. "China Plan Looks Beyond Bush's Tenure." *New York Times* online, December 16, 2007.

Goldstone, Jack A. "The New Population Bomb: The Four Megatrends That Will Change the World." *Foreign Affairs,* January/February 2010, 31–43.

Gore, Al. *Earth in the Balance*. Emmaus, PA: Rodale, 2007.

Harris, Paul G., ed. *Climate Change and American Foreign Policy*. New York: Palgrave Macmillan, 2000.

Helm, Dieter. *The Carbon Crunch: How We're Getting Climate Change Wrong—and How to Fix It*. New Haven, CT: Yale University Press, 2012.

Hersh, Seymour M. *Chain of Command: The Road from 9.11 to Abu Ghraib*. New York: HarperCollins, 2005.

Huntington, Samuel P. *The Third Wave: Democratization in the Late Twentieth Century*. Norman: University of Oklahoma Press, 1991.

Korey, William. *The Promises We Keep: Human Rights, the Helsinki Process and American Foreign Policy*. New York: St. Martin's, 1993.

Koser, Khalid. "Why Immigration Matters." *Current History* 198, no. 717 (April 2009): 147–53.

Kouchakji, Katie. *From Kyoto to Paris*. San Francisco: Blurb, 2016.

Leggett, Jane A. "Paris Agreement: United States, China Move to Become Parties to Climate Change Treaty." *CRS Insight*, September 12, 2016.

Leggett, Jane A., and Richard K. Lattanzio. *Climate Change: Frequently Asked Questions about the 2015 Paris Agreement*. Washington, DC: Congressional Research Service, September 1, 2016.

Lizza, Ryan. "As the World Burns: How the Senate and the White House Missed Their Best Chance to Deal with Climate Change." *New Yorker*, October 11, 2010. http://www.newyorker.com/reporting/2010/10/11/101011fa_fact_lizza.

Luedtke, Adam. "'Crisis' and Reality in European Immigration Policy." *Current History* 114, no. 770 (March 2015): 89–94.

Mann, Charles C. "What If We Never Run Out of Oil?" *Atlantic*, May 2013, 48–63.

McLuhan, Marshall. *The Gutenberg Galaxy*. Toronto: University of Toronto Press, 1962.

Mertus, Julie. *Bait and Switch: Human Rights and U.S. Foreign Policy*, 2nd ed. New York: Taylor & Francis, 2008.

———. *Human Rights and Conflict: Exploring the Links between Rights, Law, and Peacebuilding*. Washington, DC: U.S. Institute of Peace Press, 2013.

Miller, Shirley, ed. *The 2015 Paris Agreement on Climate Change: Elements and Related Matters*. Hauppauge, NY: Nova Science Publishing, 2017.

Nevins, Joseph. *Gatekeepers and Beyond: The War on "Illegals" and the Remaking of the U.S.-Mexico Boundary*. New York: Routledge, 2010.

Pearson, Charles S. *Economics and the Challenge of Global Warming*. New York: Cambridge University Press, 2011.

Pfiffner, James P. *Torture as Public Policy: Restoring U.S. Credibility on the World Stage*. New York: Routledge, 2010.

Pollack, Henry. *A World Without Ice*. New York: Penguin, 2009.

Power, Samantha. *Chasing the Flame: Sergio Vieira de Mello and the Fight to Save the World*. New York: Penguin, 2008.

———. *A Problem from Hell: America in the Age of Genocide*. New York: HarperCollins, 2002.

Romm, Joseph. *Climate Change: What Everyone Needs to Know*. New York: Oxford University Press, 2015.

Sikkink, Kathryn, Stephen C. Ropp, and Thomas Risse. *The Power of Human Rights: International Norms and Domestic Change*. New York: Cambridge University Press, 2010.

Singer, Max, and Aaron Wildavsky. *The Real World Order: Zones of Peace/Zones of Turmoil*. Rev. ed. Washington, DC: CQ, 1996.

Stern, Seth. "Torture Debate." *CQ Global Researcher* 1, no. 9 (September 2007): 211–36.

Sweet, William. *Climate Diplomacy from Rio to Paris: The Effort to Contain Global Warming.* New Haven, CT: Yale University Press, 2016.

Thompson, Lonnie. "Climate Change: The Evidence and Our Options." *Behavior Analyst* 33 (Fall 2010): 153–70.

United Nations, Office of the High Commissioner for Human Rights. "Migration and Human Rights," accessed December 4, 2016, http://www.ohchr.org/EN/Issues/Migration/Pages/MigrationAndHumanRightsIndex.aspx.

Van Heat, Nicholas. "The Rise of Refugee Diasporas." *Current History* 108, no. 717 (April 2009): 180–85.

PART IV THE FUTURE

12 Conclusions: Back to the Water's Edge

The skyline of New York behind the Statue of Liberty symbolizes the water's edge that is supposed to be the boundary for partisan discussions of foreign policy.

Preview

The new Trump administration inherits a complex and contentious foreign policy agenda. One of the new president's major challenges is to craft a stance toward world problems, an area in which he has had less than extensive prior exposure. Part of the challenge will be domestic in terms of things such as funding and achieving bipartisan support for his initiatives, but he will have to develop policies toward the three major foreign policy areas addressed in this volume: national security, international economics, and trans-state issues. His views on each area are evolving.

Key Concepts

sequestration

Super Committee

"destruction of the Islamic State"

North Atlantic Treaty Organization (NATO)

NAFTA

immigration

refugees

O n November 8, 2016, Americans elected a new president, a new House of Representatives, and one-third of a new Senate. The election was deeply, even darkly contested, revealing many of the less decorous characteristics discussed in this volume, such as the extreme hyperpartisanship in the electorate and elected bodies and the highly emotional tone of campaign rhetoric illustrating deep ideological divisions. Much of the malicious cacophony was domestic in its content, reflecting themes and policy areas on which Americans are deeply divided. In the end, President Donald J. Trump won an electoral college majority that made him the chief executive, following a historical trend in which the party in office for two consecutive terms is turned out in its third try, and Republican majorities were returned in both houses of Congress, although slightly smaller than after the 2014 election. Having the same party in the White House and in the majority in both houses repeated the situation in 2008, when Barack Obama became president.

The contest for the presidency was a unique political event on several levels. First, it featured the second and third oldest candidates in American history nominated by the major parties running against one another in Donald J. Trump (seventy) and Hillary Clinton (sixty-eight). The only older candidate was Ronald Reagan in 1980. Second, the candidates were the two most disliked contenders in political history since opinion research began monitoring elections; many Americans went to the polls not to vote for one but to vote against the other, and many others simply did not vote. Third, this disdain was fed upon by the rhetoric of the contenders. "The Donald," as Trump was known, was vilified as a temperamentally unsuited, narcissistic boor by the Clinton campaign, whereas the GOP nominee referred to his opponent simply as "Crooked Hillary." In their final televised debate, the candidates refused to shake hands with one another both at the beginning or the end of the event.

The greatest contrast in the campaign, and the one most relevant to foreign policy, may have been over the comparative political experience of the two candidates. Donald J. Trump was the quintessential political outsider, a billionaire businessman who made his fortune in real estate development and much of his fame as a reality television celebrity. He had never been elected to a political office at any level, a point of pride in his campaign because it gave him the unique ability to rise above the abyss of contemporary politics. Hillary Clinton, by contrast, was the quintessential veteran political insider. She proudly boasted of her thirty years of experience assailing the country's political ills from a variety of perspectives and platforms, from extra-governmental activism after graduating from law school to being first lady of Arkansas and the United States, a U.S. Senator from New York, and secretary of state of the United States.

This experience gap was nowhere more evident than in American foreign policy, which itself was a major point of contention between the two candidates. They disagreed on nearly every foreign policy concern. Clinton, of course, had a far more detailed resume on foreign policy issues, having voted on many as a senator from 2001 to 2009, and then presided over their formulation and execution during the first Obama term from 2009 to 2013. Trump, by contrast, had no direct participation in the foreign policy process before becoming a candidate, and his relative inexperience was clearly manifested in the generality, occasional contradiction, and even adequacy of some of the policies he advocated. Trump's message of change included an attack on foreign policy conventional wisdom, from the desirability of free trade agreements to how to deal with IS.

The Trump victory represented one of the biggest upsets in presidential election history. Because the White House was "captured" by someone with no real experience in foreign policy, it sent shock waves around the world, as governments attempted to assess what the new administration's election would mean for their relations with the United States and for international affairs. Some uncertainties were addressed as Trump assembled the new foreign policy "team," but how it will evolve will probably be uncertain for some time to come.

For present purposes, a major concern is whether the new atmosphere allows foreign policy to move back toward the "water's edge," the analogy raised in the first two chapters, or whether the extreme partisanship of the twenty-first century will continue. From a foreign and national security perspective, how will the new administration guide the country through the turbulent waters of foreign policy?

The campaign rhetoric of 2016 offered stark contrasts about policy direction in and across all three of the basic policy arenas raised in part III. In the most general terms, new president Trump suggested that he would adopt very different policy priorities and emphases. Many of Trump's ideas were not developed in detail, but reflected the kind of disgust with the status quo that underlay his more general orientation to policy and that had formed the basis of much of his appeal to the voting public. His stance on multilateral trade agreements and their argued negative impact on American jobs was a particular point of emphasis. The Clinton campaign also attempted to paint Trump as unfit by experience and temperament to deal with the intricacies and dangers of the commander in chief role, but these arguments did not prove conclusive in the November voting.

It is at least arguable (and political scientists will almost certainly argue about this) that foreign policy concerns were more prominently debated than is typically the case, but that, as usual, voters were more interested in domestic concerns. Certainly that seems to have been the case with Trump voters, who were drawn to their candidate's emphasis on "bread and butter" issues. It is a virtual axiom that foreign policy issues are pivotal in elections only when there is a traumatic foreign crisis that seems to demand great continuity (FDR's third and fourth terms, for instance) or enrages the public to "throw out the bums" (Vietnam and the 1968 election). Some of the positions candidate Trump took on a variety of issues—from the use of nuclear weapons to free trade agreements to climate change—and his apparent enamor for Russian leader Vladimir Putin created some concern among Democrats, but these worries did not result in a strong enough turnout for Clinton in the election. Election week had hardly ended before the president-elect moderated his position on some issues such as NATO (where, at one point, he had threatened an American withdrawal because European allies did not pay their full dues); how his positions evolve will determine Trump's foreign policy and global reactions to it.

It is, of course, too early to make strong, definitive predictions about foreign policy directions and specific policies. One of the purposes of this volume, however, has been to try to bring foreign policy closer to the reader, and it would subvert our own intent not to attempt to address concerns raised earlier in the volume. To that end, we will examine, sequentially, the domestic political impacts of the election on foreign policy and how that policy is likely to evolve in the critical areas of national security, international economics, and trans-state issues.

Domestic Political Factors

The election did not end hyperpartisanship or the prospect of continuing legislative gridlock from American national politics. Because the Republican Party won the White House and maintained control of both houses of Congress, it may be able to enact more of its agenda than if it had not. The 2016 election replicated the case for the Democrats from 2009 to 2011. The balance between the major parties in the two houses of Congress changed at the margins in 2016, but it is not clear what kind of mandate the new president has to enact his agenda, at least partially because of significant disagreements between the Trump White House and the congressional GOP leadership. The need for sixty votes in the Senate on major legislation provides the Democrats with the ability to obstruct parts of the Trump agenda, thus increasing the likelihood of a continuation of the tradition of a spirited "invitation to struggle" between the two branches.

The foreign policy area, as argued earlier, is affected differently by gridlock and hyperpartisanship than the domestic policy arena. The major artifact of gridlock for international affairs has been the stagnation of resources available. The inability of the two branches to reach agreement on a federal budget means that the federal government will be forced to keep funding itself through the status quo–loaded method of continuing resolutions that perpetuates ongoing budgetary priorities. If part of the inertia in the budgetary process includes continuation of **sequestration** (see intersection 12.1), the national security area, which bears half the cost of reductions mandated by that process, will be adversely affected.

Intersection 12.1	**What Is Sequestration? And Why?**

What is known as "sequester" was a result of congressional hyperpartisanship and gridlock in 2011. During the debate over the overall federal budget, a compromise was reached with a condition that a new budget would include provisions to lower the projected federal debt accumulation by $1.2 trillion. Unable to agree on how to reach that end, the two houses agreed to form a Joint Select Committee on Budget Reduction (quickly dubbed the **Super Committee**) to reach a deal acceptable to both. The committee was bipartisan (equal numbers from each party) and bicameral (both houses represented) and was given the charge to reach a compromise agreement by Thanksgiving 2011. Composed of six members from each party, at least one person would have to cross party lines to create a majority for any plan. No one did, and the Super Committee failed.

There was, however, a hidden cost. The two houses agreed that if no agreement could be reached, the funds for the $1.2 trillion would automatically be taken in equal amounts from the defense and nondefense budgets for the balance of the decade. This prospect was considered so odious by both sides that they assumed it would force a compromise. It did not, and sequestration went into effect on March 1, 2013. It is the single largest portion of the budgetary shortfall against which the new president campaigned. Revoking it would be the most obvious way to restore defense budgets. A divided presidency and Congress could not do so. Whether control of both by the GOP will allow its revocation could be a bellwether for the administration.

Sequestration is likely to be in the spotlight early in the Trump term, for at least two reasons. First, sequestration mandates cuts in government spending with their biggest impact in defense spending, rescinding of which was an election priority. Sequestered funds come from discretionary spending (expenditures that must be appropriated annually), and the defense budget bears half of those reductions. The sequester stands directly in the way of Trump fulfilling his pledge to increase defense spending. Second, the cost of ending sequestration would require a reexamination of the federal budget. The reason for the legislation that spawned sequestration, after all, was to stimulate a bipartisan review of spending, and removing sequestration would reopen that debate. No one likes sequestration, which is a positive motivation to review and rescind it. Thus, it provides a possible lever to stimulate bipartisan discussions that could reduce the poisonous atmosphere in Washington. It could, of course, also make matters worse if cooperation proves impossible.

Overall, foreign policy is less directly affected by continuing political gridlock than is domestic policy. The network of relations between the United States and foreign governments is largely regulated by international law and convention, and the executive branch routinely enters into many obligations with other governments in the form of executive agreements that, unless they require the expenditure of public monies, require no congressional assent but can be revoked. Similarly, the president as commander in chief has reasonably broad latitude in the deployment of armed forces, although there are practical political limits on that discretion. Similarly, the president is not constitutionally prohibited from reversing many international obligations. If President Trump proposes to implement some of the more extensive modifications of foreign policy he suggested in his election campaign, these sources of discretion could also be dragged into the toxic muck of U.S. politics.

Policy Arenas

How much will foreign policy change under the new administration? During the presidential campaign, the new president raised concerns over all three areas identified in part III. He suggested a more militant view on national security policy, including both the "revitalization" of American military forces he argued had been depleted under his predecessor, and a new approach to "destroy" IS. In the economic area, he offered a scathing repudiation of American free trade policies, including a promise to radically modify or revoke U.S. commitment to NAFTA. He was also disdainful of climate change policies, especially in the area of limits on the exploitation and use of fossil fuels. His promise to build an impenetrable border fence, of course, was a signature part of his campaign. In each case, the policies he promoted have met with considerable foreign opposition. Some issues crossed categories. Immigration and refugee policy is an example. Trump opposed Muslim immigration on security grounds, but importing foreign workers is also how the United States has solved the problem of workforce aging that troubles the economies of many countries. The problem is also a significant human rights concern, since refugees typically are fleeing suffering, deprivation, and the threat of death.

His choice of foreign and national security advisors partially indicates the degree to which President Trump will pursue change in each of these areas. Like virtually everything surrounding the Trump ascendancy to the White House, his choices for his closest foreign policy aides have been controversial, generally along one or both of two lines. One is experience: nominees for Cabinet posts have, in some cases, virtually no experience in the conduct of foreign policy. Former South Carolina governor Nikki Haley, Trump's choice for ambassador to the UN, has no diplomatic experience at all, and Secretary of State Rex Tillerson's foreign experience basically has been confined to negotiating oil deals for Exxon-Mobil, for whom he has worked for his whole career. Tillerson's appointment also raises potential conflict of interest problems, as suggested in intersection 12.2. In the national security area, Trump has chosen retired generals for key posts: former marine general James Mattis for secretary of defense, Marine General John Kelly as secretary of homeland security, and Army Lt. General H. R. McMaster as national security advisor. All except McMaster are recently retired, and some critics wonder if they will bring a healthy diversity on national security matters.

Intersection 12.2 — Tillerson, Russian Oil, and the Prospect of Conflicts of Interest

Secretary of State Rex Tillerson greets Russian president Vladimir Putin during a meeting in Moscow when he was CEO of ExxonMobil, a company with extensive oil exploration and drilling operations in Russia.

Secretary of State Rex Tillerson's major foreign experience has been negotiating and implementing agreements with the Russian government to develop oil reserves in places (Siberia and the Arctic) where Russia lacks the technology to mine those reserves without help. Were the government of Vladimir Putin and the United States on friendlier terms, this would not be a problem, and Putin has promoted closer relations with the new administration.

Why may this be a problem? The answer is the dependence

of the Russian economy on oil revenues, which agreements between ExxonMobil and the Russians increase. Without increased oil, the Russian economy becomes perilously shaky, making the withdrawing of aid to Russian oil development a potential weapon for the United States to extract concessions from Putin. Does Tillerson's connection here (which he has formally severed) create a conflict of interest? Since he and the company he worked for have an interest in their share of Russian oil profits, are they predisposed not to impose sanctions that might otherwise be imposed? Will his and his former employer's ties to Putin influence the way they deal with a historical adversary? These are interesting questions.

The president's ability to change foreign as opposed to domestic policy is broader. Other than presidential orders imposed with congressional concurrence, most domestic policies are the result of legislation and can only be reversed by countermanding congressional actions. Rescinding the Affordable Care Act is an example. In foreign affairs, however, more of the barriers are international than domestic. Although the constitutional bases are ambiguous, presidents have acted to reverse not only executive agreements but even treaties (the 1979 *Goldwater v. Carter* ruling by the Supreme Court is a precedent of sorts). Treaties and executive agreements create an international legal obligation for the parties enacting them, and generally can only be broken by consent of both (or all) parties. In particular, the United States can remove itself from some of these agreements, but if they are multilateral (the Iran nuclear agreement, for instance), the obligations remain for those other powers that do not withdraw. These matters are complex, but they represent real limits on the unilateral abilities of the president to alter established policy.

Knowing who will be advising Trump on foreign policy matters does not allow one to predict the detailed trajectory of the Trump administration's dealings with the world. It is impossible to predict the variety of challenges the Trump team will face, and their perspectives will undoubtedly be reshaped by an as yet indeterminate set of experiences. The 2016 campaign, however, offered some hints about Trump's likely orientations toward the three areas discussed here, and looking at these from the perspective of the early Trump White House may offer some glimpse into how the Trump foreign policy will evolve.

National Security Policy

The new president's handling of national security matters is one of the most crucial elements of his presidency. As indicated in chapter 9, the United States is confronted with multiple difficult challenges in the contemporary world, in addition to ongoing matters of literal life and death in areas such as the handling of relations with Russia, disposition of the nuclear arsenal, continued American levels of participation in NATO, and appropriate levels of funding for defense within the budget process. These issues produced strong, arguably bellicose statements during the 2016 election campaign, and other issues will emerge as Trump's presidency unfolds. A major criterion by which his performance in office will be evaluated is the extent to which he modifies or continues the kind of confrontational rhetoric he displayed during the campaign. Early indications suggested a movement away from the harsher assertions of the campaign.

Some of his strongest language and promises were directed at the problem of IS and terrorism more broadly. In some of his most virulent rhetoric, he promised the "**destruction of the Islamic State**" by military force, presumably including the expanded use of American military forces. At several points, he suggested that he knew more than the military about the IS threat and how to confront it (including keeping secret operational plans for liberating Mosul, a city of two million sitting on a plain) rather than letting the enemy know a liberation attempt was imminent. Some of his proposed actions included restrictions on Muslims entering the country from a Middle East many of them sought to flee as refugees on the grounds that terrorist infiltrators would be among those trying to get into the country. At their most extreme, these proposals even included a "registry" of Muslims (who constitute about 1 percent of the U.S. population) in this country. He further vowed to pursue other international terrorists and to reduce or eliminate the global terrorism problem. All of these promises were responses to long-standing, intractable problems, and it has not been initially clear whether the new administration's national security team can be more successful than those they replaced.

The destruction of IS brought relations with Russia to the fore. Since IS remains active in both Iraq and Syria, any attempt to isolate and destroy it must include action in Syria, which continues to be engaged in the bloody civil war that has been raging there since 2011. Russia, of course, is Syria's single major power ally in the area, and Russia has brought major military force to bear (almost exclusively air power) against Assad's opponents, presumably including IS. Russian air action has been characteristically brutal (the 1995 campaign that leveled the Chechen capital of Grozny is a model of sorts) and, according to outsiders, directed more at Assad's opponents other than IS than at IS itself. During the presidential campaign, Trump expressed praise for Vladimir Putin (who presumably has provided direction for the air campaign) and for closer U.S.-Russian relations. How this policy emphasis and the simultaneous effort to destroy IS can be reconciled (if it can be) is an open question.

Because the most deadly aspect of U.S. relations with the then Soviet Union was over possible nuclear conflict, Russian possession of the substantial remnants of the Soviet arsenal also remains a question. During one of his off-the-cuff remarks during the campaign, Trump indicated less inhibition on the actual use of nuclear weapons than his Cold War predecessors had. The policy emphasis on nuclear deterrence has faded since the Soviet Union imploded, and the idea of actually using nuclear weapons has remained verboten, with the occasional exception of threats by North Korea's Kim Jong-un.

The bulwark of American national security policy since World War II has been the American commitment to the **North Atlantic Treaty Organization (NATO)**, America's first peacetime and long-standing military alliance. The NATO pledge to defend Western Europe goes back to 1949, and has been the bedrock of Atlantic relations. The end of the Cold War removed the major military threat to the alliance, but NATO has since spread to almost all of Europe and is considered of the highest importance by Europeans to their security. When presidential candidate Trump accused the European members of being essentially "free riders" and suggested the United States might rethink its commitment, the result was great fear in European capitals. After the election, Trump backed away from these comments and reiterated his commitment to the alliance.

A highlight of Trump's campaign was to increase military spending to compensate for the depletion in resources he alleged had occurred under his predecessor. This promise is likely to run afoul of conflicting economic priorities and problems. One is sequestration, the rescinding of which would be the most direct way to increase defense dollars. Doing so would also re-create the deficit problems that were the reason the provision was initiated in the first place and would open Pandora's box in other budgetary areas, including Trump's own proposals for tax cuts and increased spending in areas such as infrastructure. It is not clear how these issues will be resolved, but doing so will not be easy.

International Economic Policy

At the heart of the domestic appeal of Trump's campaign was his concerted appeal to the white blue-collar class, and in particularly, workers in manufacturing industries who have seen their jobs evaporate and not be replaced. Trump claimed the job losses were largely the result of flawed free trade economic agreements into which the United States had entered that had the effect of shipping manufacturing jobs overseas to countries that, by virtue of lower labor costs, could produce goods more cheaply than American workers. The provisions of these arrangements, he further asserted, are so favorable to foreign countries that these goods were then allowed to return to the United States with very low duties, thereby completing the nonvirtuous circle undercutting the American economy and the livelihood of Americans.

In the candidate's rendering, the villains in this arrangement were inept American trade negotiators and much smarter foreign negotiators who saddled the United States with systematically unfavorable international trade arrangements that benefited foreign countries at American expense. Trump singled out two countries, China and Mexico, for particular criticism, since both carry on considerable economic interchanges with the United States. Particularly in the case of China, the result is a huge balance of trade deficit that is the result of American ineptitude at negotiation and Chinese cheating on agreements. These shortcomings, he maintained, could only be remedied by two basic actions that he suggested he was far better prepared to carry out than his opponent.

The first, and most controversial, element of his solution was to revoke trade agreements that adversely affect the United States. **NAFTA** was, during the campaign, the arrangement that was most frequently cited as basically flawed and, in Trump's rendering, the source of the greatest loss of manufacturing jobs, millions of which he maintained had moved south since the agreement was implemented in 1994. (Ironically, of course, at the same time American jobs were flowing south to Mexico, Mexicans in large numbers were fleeing north into the United States illegally—mostly looking for jobs.) The confluence of the adverse effects of NAFTA and the illegal immigrant problem puts Mexico doubly in the sights of the Trump administration.

Second, the cure for this problem, in terms of the campaign rhetoric, was more skilled negotiation of trade agreements, which requires the conscription of the best American negotiators into the effort. His contention was that the most skilled and smartest negotiators were to be found in the private sector, and that he was uniquely positioned, by virtue of his background as a highly successful businessman, to enlist these skilled individuals and lead more successful negotiations to return American manufacturing jobs to the United States, and especially to the "rust belt" states of the upper Midwest that have experienced the greatest decline in recent years.

As might be expected in an area as complicated, contentious, and arcane as economic policy, these issues were the sources of disagreement during the campaign. The problems they raised and the campaign claims of the new administration are likely to be matters of disagreement, particularly since they raise the prospect of considerable expenditure of taxpayer dollars that is also a matter of disagreement.

This contentiousness is suggested by the question of what has actually caused American manufacturing jobs to disappear. Clearly, some loss is the result of trade arrangements that allowed some forms of manufacture to move to foreign countries. This is clearly a major part of the trade balance problem with China, which specializes in the production of technologically unsophisticated goods that do not require a highly sophisticated workforce or indigenous technological base. Both Americans and Europeans have historically encouraged the movement of many of those jobs to places such as China on the grounds, mentioned in chapter 11, that they also mean moving the pollution associated with the energy to power these enterprises away from North America and Europe. It is not at all clear, for instance, whether revised trade arrangements regulating textiles would provide a net economic and ecological benefit to Americans. As is the case with free trade generally, the macro effects of trade and its micro impact on workers are at some odds in this regard.

Another, and in many ways more fundamental, problem is the changing nature of manufacturing and how the United States wants to deal with it. Although a large number of manufacturing jobs have been lost in the American economy, one reason is the automation of so much of the process. It no longer takes as much human labor to produce many manufactured goods because robots and similar devices do much of the work, a problem that forcing the repatriation of low-technology jobs will not alleviate. Gearing American manufacturing to high-technology, lower-manpower-intensity manufactures is one way to increase American manufacturing share, but it requires a different kind of worker than those currently in the rust belt region.

Trans-State Issues

The two most prominent issues crossing state boundaries but that individual states cannot solve (trans-state issues) are climate change and refugee/immigration policy. Both are difficult, controversial problems and matters where the

Trump campaign positions are at odds with both domestic and international forces. The climate change issue centers on the provisions of the 2015 UN Climate Change Conference (Paris Agreement) and the extent to which a Trump administration that has had the support of climate change deniers will pursue implementation of American obligations agreed to by more than 200 countries in addition to the United States. On immigration, controversy has surrounded Trump's proposed negatively oriented policies toward Muslim immigrants (including refugees) and whether such attitudes will negatively affect the flow of young immigrants into the country to replace aging workers—a process through which the vitality of the American economy has historically had an advantage over other industrialized countries.

Climate change is both a domestic and international issue. As noted in chapter 11, the United States is the world's second-largest emitter of carbon gases into the atmosphere, only slightly behind China. As a result, gaining American support for the Paris Agreement was seen globally as a necessary part of the attempt to slow or reduce the rise in global temperatures associated with carbon emissions. The reasoning for this, supported strongly by the previous administration, was that the United States must serve as a model for other countries, and especially existing (e.g., China and the European Union) and potential (e.g., India) large emitters. It is hard to imagine much global progress without the United States taking a lead.

Elements with the ear of President Trump sound a negative chorus. The oil and gas industry, which favors much greater exploitation of shale oil and natural gas, heavily supported Trump. In addition, there is a small but very vocal minority in the scientific community that denies the existence of human-induced climate change and that argues, along with the energy lobby, that restricting emissions will reduce American energy availability with negative consequences on available power to fuel economic growth. Trump did not come down totally on either side of the climate change issue, but has supported increased energy production personally and in terms of some of the appointments he has made in areas such as the Department of the Interior, which controls the use of federal lands, and the Environmental Protection Agency (EPA).

The other issue of note will be **immigration** policy. This concern has both humanitarian and economic consequences, as previously noted. A large part of the pool of potential immigrants is **refugees** fleeing the ravages of war in the Middle East, and their plights are often dire and heart wrenching. The problem is that some of these refugees may be terrorists, whose exclusion from American soil is clearly a vital national security priority. Internationally, the refugee problem was one of the reasons for the success of Brexit, because EU actions restricted the ability of its members, including Great Britain, to limit migration into the UK (see Snow, *Regional Cases in Foreign Policy*, chapter 5, for an explanation). Trump has expressed considerable concern over the adequacy of background checks (vetting) of potential Middle East immigrants into the United States.

The problem, of course, has economic consequences. Populations in virtually all industrialized countries are aging, meaning available new members of the workforce are fewer. This affects social benefits policies, but it can lead to economic stagnation and potential decline if alternative sources of workers cannot be identified and brought in to do the work of retiring workers. The United States has historically overcome this problem through the immigration of eager young people to come to this country for economic reasons. It is not clear what the consequences of an immigration policy that makes the United States less of a beacon for immigrants could be on the replenishment of the American workforce, a problem already vexing countries such as Japan, China, and much of the EU.

Conclusion

These foreign policy difficulties represent some of the most pressing and consequential problems facing the new Trump administration, but there will undoubtedly be others that arise as events unfold. President Trump made only general (if often sweeping) comments on these problems in a campaign more clearly focused on the domestic agenda. For candidate Trump, foreign policy was a central concern mostly when it had a direct impact on domestic matters, such as the alleged negative impact of free trade arrangements on American manufacturing jobs. As president, he will discover that foreign affairs place a larger demand on his time and energies than he initially thought they might, a lesson all presidents learn.

How the Trump administration deals with foreign challenges will depend a great deal on how well the new commander in chief masters the steep learning curve and vagaries of foreign affairs. He will discover that some problems are not subject to the easy manipulation he suggested in the campaign. To cite one example, he may find that he really does not "know more than the generals" about the fight against the Islamic State and that "destroying" IS may be easier said than done. As is the case when a new party occupies the White House, there are many lessons to learn and relearn. The next four years are likely to be no different. Will President Trump lead us closer or farther away from the water's edge?

Study/Discussion Questions

1. How are the foreign and domestic problems facing the new administration similar and dissimilar? What is sequestration? How does it show the complications and interconnections between foreign and domestic priorities?

2. What national security concerns are likely to be important in the early Trump administration? Discuss each, including Trump's campaign stance on each and how or whether it has changed.

3. Why did President Trump identify international trade agreements as the most important international economic priority? What has he proposed to do about them? Will it work?

4. What are the two major transstate issues identified in the text? Discuss each. What is the heart of disagreement about each? Where does the president stand on each, and has his position changed since the election?

Bibliography

Adams, Gordon, and Cindy Williams. *Buying National Security: How America Plans and Pays for Its Global Role and Safety at Home.* New York: Routledge, 2009.

Berjas, George J. *Heaven's Door: Immigration Policy and the American Economy.* Princeton, NJ: Princeton University Press, 2001.

Boskin, Michael. *NAFTA at 20: The North American Free Trade Agreement Achievements and Challenges.* Palo Alto, CA: Hoover Institution Press, 2014.

Chu, Vivian, and Todd Garvey. *Executive Orders: Issuance, Modification, and Revocation.* Washington, DC: Congressional Research Service, April 16, 2014.

COP 21: Final Agreement—Paris 2015—Paris United Nations Climate Change Conference. New York: CreateSpace Independent Publishing Platform, 2015.

Fletcher, Ian. *Free Trade Doesn't Work: What Should Replace It and Why.* Washington, DC: Coalition for a Prosperous America, 2011.

Flynn, Michael T., and Michael Ledeen. *The Field of Fight: How We Can Win the War against Radical Islam and Its Allies.* New York: St. Martin's, 2016.

Folsom, Ralph. *NAFTA and Free Trade in the Americas in a Nutshell.* 5th ed. New York: West Academic, 2014.

Gest, Justin. *The New Minority: White Working Class Politics in an Age of Immigration and Inequality.* New York: Oxford University Press, 2016.

Haynes, Chris, Jennifer Morella, and S. Karthick Ramakrishnan. *Framing Immigrants: News Coverage, Public Opinion, and Policy.* Washington, DC: Russell Sage Foundation, 2016.

Higham, Andrew, and David Klein. *The Paris Climate Agreement: Analysis and Commentary.* Oxford: Oxford University Press, 2017.

Leggett, Jane A., and Richard Lattanzio. *Climate Change: Frequently Asked Questions about the 2015 Paris Agreement.* Washington, DC: Congressional Research Service, September 11, 2016.

Mann, Michael, and Lee R. Kump. *Dire Predictions: Understanding Climate Change.* 2nd ed. New York: DK, 2015.

Mattis, Jim, and Kari N. Schake, eds. *Warriors and Citizens: American Views of Our Military.* Palo Alto, CA: Hoover Institution Press, 2016.

"Paris Agreement." *United Nations Treaty Collection.* New York: United Nations, July 8, 2016.

Romm, Joseph. *Climate Change: What Everyone Needs to Know.* New York: Oxford University Press, 2015.

Rubin, Irene S. *The Politics of Public Budgeting: Getting and Spending, Borrowing and Balancing.* 7th ed. Washington, DC: CQ, 2013.

Snow, Donald M. *The Middle East, Oil, and American National Security.* Lanham, MD: Rowman & Littlefield, 2016.

———. *National Security.* 6th ed. New York: Routledge, 2017.

———. *Regional Cases in Foreign Policy.* 2nd ed. Lanham, MD: Rowman & Littlefield, 2017.

Sweet, William. *Climate Diplomacy from Rio to Paris: The Effort to Contain Global Warming.* New Haven, CT: Yale University Press, 2016.

Trump, Donald J. *Great Again: How to Fix Our Crippled America.* New York: Threshold, 2016.

Photo Credits

2 Underwood Archives/Contributor; **8** REUTERS/Alamy Stock Photo; **28** danhowl/iStock Photo; **46** US Marines Photo/Alamy Stock Photo; **55** ASSOCIATED PRESS; **62** REUTERS/Alamy Stock Photo; **78** dpa picture alliance/Alamy Stock Photo; **83** REUTERS/Alamy Stock Photo; **109** Stock Connection Blue/Alamy Stock Photo; **121** MediaPunch Inc/Alamy Stock Photo; **139** rypson/iStock Photo; **158** Everett Collection Historical/Alamy Stock Photo; **170** **506** collection/Alamy Stock Photo; **173** Bettmann/Contributor; **193** Urbanmyth/Alamy Stock Photo; **203** tunart/iStock Photo; **216** ZUMA Press, Inc./Alamy Stock Photo; **233** conejota/iStock photo; **241** Rex_Wholster/iStock Photo; **258** Sven Creutzmann/Mambo Photo/Contributor; **268** JordeAngjelovik/iStock Photo; **284** MajaPhoto/iStock Photo; **296** Andrew Parker/iStock Photo; **301** ITAR-TASS Photo Agency/Alamy Stock Photo

Index

Page numbers followed by *t* indicate tables.